Chaucerian Dream Visions and Complaints

Middle English Texts

General Editor

Russell A. Peck
University of Rochester

Associate Editor

Alan Lupack
University of Rochester

Assistant Editor

Dana M. Symons
University of Rochester

Advisory Board

Rita Copeland
University of Pennsylvania

Thomas G. Hahn
University of Rochester

Lisa Kiser
Ohio State University

R. A. Shoaf
University of Florida

Bonnie Wheeler
Southern Methodist University

The Middle English Texts Series is designed for classroom use. Its goal is to make available to teachers and students texts that occupy an important place in the literary and cultural canon but have not been readily available in student editions. The series does not include those authors, such as Chaucer, Langland, or Malory, whose English works are normally in print in good student editions. The focus is, instead, upon Middle English literature adjacent to those authors that teachers need in compiling the syllabuses they wish to teach. The editions maintain the linguistic integrity of the original work but within the parameters of modern reading conventions. The texts are printed in the modern alphabet and follow the practices of modern capitalization, word formation, and punctuation. Manuscript abbreviations are silently expanded, and *u/v* and *j/i* spellings are regularized according to modern orthography. Yogh is transcribed as *g*, *gh*, *y*, or *s*, according to the letter in modern English spelling to which it corresponds. Distinction between the second person pronoun and the definite article is made by spelling the one *thee* and the other *the*, and final *-e* that receives full syllabic value is accented (e.g., *charité*). Hard words, difficult phrases, and unusual idioms are glossed on the page, either in the right margin or at the foot of the page. Explanatory and textual notes appear at the end of the text, along with a glossary. The editions include short introductions on the history of the work, its merits and points of topical interest, and also contain briefly annotated bibliographies.

Chaucerian Dream Visions and Complaints

Edited by
Dana M. Symons

Published for TEAMS
(The Consortium for the Teaching of the Middle Ages)
in Association with the University of Rochester

by

MEDIEVAL INSTITUTE PUBLICATIONS
College of Arts & Sciences
Western Michigan University
Kalamazoo, Michigan
2004

Library of Congress Cataloging-in-Publication Data

Chaucerian dream visions and complaints / edited by Dana M. Symons.
    p. cm. -- (Middle English texts series)
 "Published for TEAMS (The Consortium for the Teaching of the Middle Ages) in
association with the University of Rochester."
 Includes bibliographical references.
 ISBN 1-58044-087-8 (pbk. : alk. paper)
 1. English poetry--Middle English, 1100-1500. 2. Complaint poetry, English
(Middle) 3. Fantasy poetry, English. 4. Visions--Poetry. 5. Dreams--Poetry. I.
Symons, Dana M., 1967- II. Western Michigan University. Medieval Institute
Publications. III. Consortium for the Teaching of the Middle Ages. IV. Middle
English texts (Kalamazoo, Mich.)
 PR1203.C64 2004
 821'.108--dc22

                                                           2004016827

ISBN 1-58044-087-8

Cover design by Linda K. Judy

Contents

Acknowledgments

My grateful thanks go most particularly to Russell A. Peck, the General Editor of the series, for his unflagging support of my work and his generous contributions to the volume at all phases. He made a number of suggestions regarding explanatory notes, and his additions to and comments on the introductions were invaluable. Without his support and expertise, this volume could never have been completed. Special thanks are also due to Andrew Galloway for his very careful reading of the entire volume in its near-final phase and for his generous correspondence with me on various questions that arose along the way. He caught many errors and made useful comments on the explanatory notes and introductions, as well as innumerable suggestions on the glossing of the texts. I am grateful to Michael Livingston for carefully reading the poems against the manuscripts and painstakingly checking the textual notes. I am also grateful to Thomas Hahn for his encouragement and for his commentary on the introductions at various stages, and to A. S. G. Edwards, who read an early draft of the whole volume as well as a later version of the General Introduction, and who patiently answered all my editorial questions. Thanks to Nancy Heckel for her proofreading at a near-final stage, and to Patricia Hollahan at Medieval Institute Publications, who gave the volume a thorough final review.

Thanks go to the National Endowment for the Humanities for its generous support of the Middle English Texts Series. I am grateful to the Bodleian Library, University of Oxford for permission to reproduce texts from Bodleian Library MSS Fairfax 16 and Arch. Selden. B. 24. I am also grateful to the libraries that provided microfilms of some of the manuscripts I consulted: the British Library, London; the Bodleian Library, Oxford; and the Library of the Marquess of Bath, Longleat House, Wiltshire.

Chaucerian Dream Visions and Complaints

General Introduction

With the exception of the Scottish *Quare of Jelusy*, the poems in this volume were all attributed to Chaucer by early compilers or editors of his work in the late fifteenth and early sixteenth centuries and were not removed from the Chaucer canon until the late eighteenth or nineteenth centuries, when they became identified simply as Chaucerian.[1] Yet despite the use of "Chaucerian" in the title, this volume seeks to reassess the appropriateness of examining late-medieval poetry mainly in terms of its debt to Chaucer. Chaucer's works were certainly influential in the period when these poems were likely written (the late fourteenth and early fifteenth centuries), but it is important to consider the history and consequences of using the term "Chaucerian" as a major scheme of categorization. Comparisons of Chaucer to other medieval poets who use, continue, or respond to his works have typically ended by emphasizing the superior value of Chaucer's poetry, yet this is problematic from several perspectives. Focusing on resemblances to Chaucer often demotes works to the status of imitation and directs attention away from invention, variation, or other aspects of late-medieval

---

[1] *La Belle Dame sans Mercy* was the first to be excluded. Eleanor Prescott Hammond observes in *Chaucer: A Bibliographical Manual* that Thomas Tyrwhitt rejected it for his 1775–78 edition of *The Canterbury Tales of Chaucer* (p. 432), and that it was left out of John Leland's list of Chaucer's works (p. 65), which appeared in his Life of Chaucer in *Commentarii de scriptoribus Britannicis*, published in 1709, though it must have been written much earlier since Leland died in 1552 (pp. 1, 7). Hammond reprints Leland's Life of Chaucer (pp. 1–7) and includes a table (pp. 61–62) comparing the lists of Thynne (1542), Leland (1557–59), and John Bale (1548). The other two poems once attributed to Chaucer remained in the Chaucer canon until Walter W. Skeat's edition of *Chaucerian and Other Pieces* in the late nineteenth century (Forni, p. 150), though Hammond notes that it was actually Henry Bradshaw who first rejected *A Complaynte of a Lovers Lyfe* from the canon and who "seems to have been the first to doubt [the] genuineness" of *The Boke of Cupide* (pp. 414, 421). According to Hammond, Bradshaw's "Skeleton of Chaucer's Canterbury Tales" (1867) was published posthumously as part of his *Collected Papers* in 1889 (p. 166). Hammond gives the full list of works Bradshaw rejected (p. 67). Although a number of spurious works were attributed to Chaucer in both manuscripts and early printed editions, *A Complaynte of a Lovers Lyfe* is the only poem in this volume to have a manuscript attribution to Chaucer (in Oxford, Bodleian Library MS Arch. Selden. B. 24; see the facsimile volume, intro. Julia Boffey and A. S. G. Edwards, 1997, p. 1 and fol. 129v).

generic and formal developments. Furthermore, the traits of late-medieval poetry that have caused it to be perceived as second-rate next to Chaucer might be better understood as the consequence of particular poetic concerns and interests. The Chaucer canon has not been stable historically and various tensions have been active in the establishment of the category "Chaucerian."[2] Even were the canon completely stable, it is not always possible to distinguish between genuine references to Chaucer and other types of influences.[3] Ultimately, the practice of using "Chaucerian" as the predominant method of categorization obscures other qualities of the poems that may have appealed to medieval audiences. It is therefore important to consider carefully the implications of our continued practice of anthologizing poetry not by Chaucer under the rubric "Chaucerian."

The focus here on dream vision and complaint means that most of the resemblances between Chaucer's works and the poems in this volume center on Chaucer's courtly love poetry: *Troilus and Criseyde*, *The Legend of Good Women*, *The Parliament of Fowls*, *The Book of the Duchess*, *The House of Fame*, *The Complaint of Mars* and other lyrics, and the translation of *The Romaunt of the Rose*, portions of which are thought to be Chaucer's. Echoes of *The Canterbury Tales* are restricted mainly to The Knight's Tale. Although *The Boke of Cupide* is the only poem here that might be considered a dream vision in the sense that the narrator reports the story of what happened when he was dreaming,[4] the other three poems, *A Complaynte of a Lovers Lyfe*, *The Quare of Jelusy*, and *La Belle Dame sans Mercy*, all rely heavily on dream vision conventions to frame a complaint or debate. But the fifteenth-century

---

[2] See, for example, Stephanie Trigg, *Congenial Souls: Reading Chaucer from Medieval to Postmodern* (Minneapolis: University of Minnesota Press, 2002). Trigg discusses Chaucer's reception by writers, editors, and critics beginning in the late Middle Ages and looks at how readers' desires to identify with Chaucer or symbolically to join "a company of Chaucerians" (p. xxi) operate in their responses to Chaucer. See also *Refiguring Chaucer in the Renaissance*, ed. Theresa M. Krier (Gainesville: University Press of Florida, 1998), a collection of essays that examines the reception of Chaucer's works from the early sixteenth to the early seventeenth centuries; and Kathleen Forni, who discusses canon-formation, arguing "the definition of 'Chaucerian' was and is made within a foundation of assumptions that are historically produced" (p. 164).

[3] See, for example, Boffey's comments that "[a]ttempts to spot echoes of Chaucer's lyrics in the poems of his successors are fraught with complications"; this is not only because presumed resonances with Chaucer "may depend rather upon a common source" but also because lingering doubts about the authorship of the lyrics mean that a supposed allusion "may be no more than a second-hand echo of Chaucer if the assumed model was itself in fact the work of a disciple" (1993, p. 24).

[4] It would be more accurate to describe it as a dream-like state, since he tells us, "I fel in such a slombre and a swowe — / Not al on slepe, ne fully wakyng" (lines 87–88), but the swoon was not an uncommon variant of the dream state, as James Wimsatt's discussion of the various models that surface in the French dream visions shows (see pp. 125–26).

English love visions presented here differ from their fourteenth-century models in the use of the ideal landscape setting (the *locus amoenus* of dream visions) in a context that contains a complaint or conversation overheard from a hidden vantage point instead of witnessed through a dream.[5] These poems draw on both *The Romance of the Rose* and Chaucerian dream visions, but probably also took inspiration from the fourteenth-century French *dits amoureux* tradition, which in some cases shows a similar use of the dream vision setting.[6] This suggests that fifteenth-century English poets were combining both French and English models of various genres to create their own version of a vernacular poetic that included a more prominent use of dream vision conventions in non-dream contexts than seen in earlier English poetry.

The action of these dreamless but voyeuristic[7] poems is for the most part predictable. The poem usually begins with a narrator who, after complaining for a few stanzas about his own troubles, stumbles upon a lone figure grieving or a couple engaged in private conversation and conceals himself in order to hear the complaint or debate that follows. The narrator, who never steps outside his role as passive listener, then explains how he recorded what was said and wraps up the story with his own conclusion, generally in the form of an envoy to lovers and/or his own beloved. There are a number of partial models in fourteenth-century English poetry

---

[5] Although *La Belle Dame sans Mercy* is a translation of Alain Chartier's French poem, Richard Roos added his own narrative frame that shows the influence of earlier English poetry by drawing in some ways on Chaucer's *Legend of Good Women*. The translation also to some extent echoes English poetry in word choice, imagery, and phraseology. I therefore consider Roos' translation as part of a native English tradition, which long included translation as one of its staple forms of poetic production.

[6] Another possible influence is the earlier French *chanson d'aventure* and its English successors. Helen Estabrook Sandison describes the *chanson dramatique* variety of the French *chanson d'aventure* as one where "the poet's rôle has not been so far extended that it is essential; it is that of silent witness, casual questioner, or officious counsellor, but never that of chief actor" (p. 10). The narrator of the English *chanson d'aventure* "observes the tradition of secrecy even when the adventure he is to relate lays no such necessity upon him" (p. 29). But, although the English poems, like the French, were usually set in a pleasant springtime landscape (pp. 26–27), Sandison explains that "the English poets do not dwell, as one might expect, on the freshness and beauty of reviving Nature" (p. 27), and prefer the "wylde wode" to its more gentle "shaded border" (p. 33). Moreover, in the English poems, the narrator frequently fails to maintain his status as watcher, being instead "quick to abandon the pretense that he himself watches or overhears the little drama which he presents; he easily forgets that he has claimed as his own the soliloquy which he quotes, and has even pointed out the definite day, hour, and place of its utterance. As a rule he refrains from mentioning himself and his hiding place or from recording his departure" (pp. 41–42).

[7] The notion of these narrators as engaged in a voyeuristic activity owes much to A. C. Spearing's *The Medieval Poet as Voyeur*, which discusses the phenomenon of looking/watching in English poetry in depth.

for framing a complaint similarly. Chaucer's *Complaint of Mars*, for example, sets up its complaint with a brief proem in which a bird explains that he will sing "the compleynt . . . / That woful Mars made atte departyng / From fresshe Venus in a morwenynge" (lines 24–26) in honor of Valentine's Day. The bird then tells the story of Mars and Venus, which incorporates Mars' complaint, after which the poem ends. Another prototype is John Gower's *Confessio Amantis*, where it is not completely clear that the narrator is dreaming, although he falls into a sort of swoon near the beginning and again near the end. There are also complaint models in the fourteenth-century French poetry that was itself influenced by *The Romance of the Rose*, such as Guillaume de Machaut's *Dit de la fonteinne amoureuse*, in which the sleepy narrator becomes a kind of *auditeur*, imagining a scene he does not actually see, when he hears a complaint through the bedroom window and spends the night writing it down. In the morning the narrator finds the speaker, a great lord suffering from love sickness, who asks the narrator to write a complaint recording his sorrow. After the narrator explains how he came to do this already, the poem ends with the two falling asleep and sharing a comforting dream.

The debate version of this dreamless structure has a close model in Machaut's *Jugement dou Roy de Behaingne* (*Judgment of the King of Bohemia*), which features a narrator who walks out into the woods on a spring morning and, seeing a lady and knight approach, hides himself in order to listen to their ensuing debate about love. In his introduction to Machaut's poem, R. Barton Palmer points out that, instead of "falling asleep and providing the arena for psychological allegory, the narrator becomes a witness to a drama that unfolds nearby."[8] Although there were pre-*Romance of the Rose* debates in Latin that included an eyewitness narrator,[9] the poems in this volume must be considered in a post-*Romance of the Rose* context. Palmer sees Machaut's *Jugement dou Roy de Behaingne* as a "modification of love-vision narrative" that "affected later writers," rather than as a poem influenced in significant ways by earlier debate models.[10] Palmer points out that Machaut's borrowings from *The Romance of the Rose* in the beginning of the poem create "the expectation that a dream vision will follow," an expectation that is then defeated when Machaut turns instead to "a genre, the love debate, which was subsumed within (and superseded by) the *Romance of the Rose*."[11] He goes on to point out that the poems in the love debate genre that preceded *The Romance of the Rose* "never achieved the same popularity and belonged largely to a much earlier age"; consequently, "these works are much less important for an understanding of the meaning of

---

[8] Palmer, p. xxiv.

[9] See, for example, John W. Conlee's general introduction to *Middle English Debate Poetry*, p. xiv–xv.

[10] Palmer, p. xxxii.

[11] Palmer, p. xxix.

Machaut's poem."[12] The implication here is that for fourteenth- and fifteenth-century poetry, the love debate is a genre seen largely through the lens of *The Romance of the Rose*. The framed complaints and debates in this volume must also be examined in this context, as well as against the ground of the fourteenth-century poetry, both English and French, that immediately preceded them.

One crucial difference between Machaut's dreamless poem and those in this volume is the fact that in *Jugement dou Roy de Behaingne* the narrator is ultimately discovered by the lady's dog, after which he acts to help reconcile the knight and lady, whose debate has come to an impasse, by leading them to the king of Bohemia for a resolution of their disagreement. Palmer describes the shifting role of Machaut's narrator, who begins as "the subject of the narrative," then becomes "the guarantor of its authenticity," and finally ends up as "its prime mover."[13] A second difference is that, while it appears that the setting for Machaut's poem is the generalized *locus amoenus* of dream visions, "the apparent universality of the orchard where the debate begins proves illusory," for "we learn that the drama is unfolding near Durbuy Castle" one of the king's residences.[14] Thus, despite a number of correspondences, precursors such as the *Jugement dou Roy de Behaingne* do not completely account for the form of the dreamless dream poems here, where the narrator never does more than watch and comment on the action that takes place in his idealized setting, suggesting that this is an innovation of writers who at once followed the lead of Chaucer and other fourteenth-century poets and revitalized these earlier treatments of generic conventions to suit their own interests.[15] As courtly "conventions" shift from rhetorical formulae to social gatherings, a literate society unfolds that enjoys listening to itself in sophisticated play, now made possible by their ownership of traditions of their own.

The redeployment of the conventions of dream vision, complaint, and debate suggests a self-conscious interest in formal experimentation that enthusiastically anticipates the multiplication of poetic forms that follow in the sixteenth and seventeenth centuries.[16] Kathryn L. Lynch sees

---

[12] Palmer, p. xxxi.

[13] Palmer, pp. xxv–xxvi.

[14] Palmer, p. xxxii.

[15] Wimsatt argues that "[d]espite the common assumption of critics, dream poems did not constitute a separate category of love narratives," claiming that a number of French *dits amoureux* "do not have a dream frame comparable to that of the *Roman de la Rose*" (p. 125). But Spearing, while acknowledging that "it is unlikely . . . to be possible to establish the dream-poem as a *completely* 'distinct literary kind,'" notes that "authors of medieval dream-poems themselves seem to have been conscious of writing within a distinct literary tradition of dreams and visions" (1976, p. 3).

[16] Lee Patterson argues that Chaucer participates in a movement begun in fourteenth-century French poetry to place complaints "within a narrative context" as a way of "seeking to contain the regressive

the dream vision in particular as a subgenre that for later poets "would embody the authority and conservatism for which [they] yearned as much as they did for change."[17] The competing desires for convention and innovation suggest that later poets' reception of the genre would be inclined both to conservatism and transformation. Thus, as A. C. Spearing observes, in *A Complaynte of a Lovers Lyfe* "Lydgate's awareness of the dream-poem as model may be indicated by his playful reversal of its framework: instead of beginning with sleep and ending with waking, the *Complaynte* begins with Lydgate waking and ends with him going to sleep."[18] Here, Lydgate's use of conventions normally associated with dream visions in a way that preserves the protocols even as it seems deliberately to subvert them signals the tension in the poem between traditional and transformative treatments of the genre. But this inversion of the dream vision does more than simply play with generic expectations; Spearing points to very real changes in the effects of such poetry when the dream context is missing. In the case of Chaucer's *Book of the Duchess*, one of the chief models for *Complaynte*, the use of the dream enables "the face-to-face encounter" between the narrator and the grieving knight, in effect "creat[ing] an imaginative space in which they can converse on relatively equal terms, as perhaps they could not properly have been represented as doing in waking life" due to their differing social stations.[19] In Lydgate's poem, there can be no tête-à-tête between the two because these differences in rank are no longer mediated by the context of a dream. Unlike Machaut's poems, no other context is provided for such an encounter. On the other hand, there is much delight to be had in spying, as this "new" genre encourages the thrills of voyeurism without the added responsibility for the "reconciliatory" role of Machaut's narrator in *Jugement dou Roy de Behaingne*.

But when the face-to-face experience presented in *The Book of the Duchess* is no longer offered, as in the anonymous *Quare of Jelusy*, Richard Roos' translation of *La Belle Dame sans Mercy*, and Lydgate's *Complaynte of a Lovers Lyfe*, the narrator is not simply reduced to the figure of eavesdropper or spy. In Spearing's reading, the narrator's spying on lovers in such poems functions as "the means by which private experience is brought into the public sphere," with the audience placed in the vicarious position of onlooker to the onlooker.[20] The interest in making private love public perhaps looks towards later preoccupations with private feeling

---

irony implicit within lyricism" (1992b, p. 66). The fifteenth-century practice of embedding complaints in a context normally associated with dream visions, however, might be seen more as a modification of the dream vision form than a particular desire to give the complaint a context.

[17] See *The High Medieval Dream Vision: Poetry, Philosophy, and Literary Form* (Stanford: Stanford University Press, 1988), p. 15

[18] Spearing (1993), p. 219.

[19] Spearing (1993), p. 220.

[20] Spearing (1993), p. 1.

that become prominent in Elizabethan lyrics.[21] The lyric voice attempts to tell of intensely personal passions. But in these medieval narratives passions become dislocated, as the narrator's voice at once acts to authenticate the narrative of complaint or debate at the same time as it inevitably mediates the experiences reported. Ultimately, the narrator, unable to talk about his own concerns, appropriates another's voice and story and in some cases uses it as a way to gain ground with his own beloved. Thus, one effect of placing dream vision conventions in the context of a complaint or debate without the mediation of a dream is to suggest the revelation of a real private experience while, at the same time, the distance provided by the dream is to some extent maintained. The shift in the use of these conventions helps the reader to look both ways: voyeuristically at another's situation and internally at her/his own heart, just as the narrator does at the same time as he enjoys the illusion of a shared (thus reified) experience — "me and my testament."

Another, perhaps more important, outcome of this appropriation of dream vision conventions is a reconfiguration of the connections between guide, narrator, dreamer, and reader. The dream vision proper frequently features a guide of some type who comes to take the narrator/dreamer through the landscape of the dream and explain or comment on what the dreamer sees. This counselor can be a character separated from the action entirely, as, for example, in Chaucer's *Parliament of Fowls*, or one more closely connected, as in *Pearl*, where the guide is the subject of the poem, Pearl, the narrator's dead daughter. In *Pearl*, the narrator learns to deal with his grief at the loss of the Pearl-maiden through the conversation he has with her. In Chaucer's *Book of the Duchess*, this pattern is inverted, for the narrator/dreamer himself functions as comforter to the knight he encounters, asking the knight a series of questions that invite him to tell his tale, thereby overcoming his grief.[22] When the complaint is no longer framed in a dream, the narrator then becomes the reader's guide in the land of the poem. Spearing suggests something like this when he argues that "as readers or listeners to such narratives, we too can be made to feel that we are secret observers."[23] But it seems that

---

[21] Compare J. Stephen Russell's remark that "[t]he most compelling reason for the dramatic disappearance of the dream vision was not political or philosophical or psychological: it was a literary reason. Put simply, the Renaissance rediscovered lyricism, the immediate depiction of powerful emotions in verse, a discovery which made the fragile, complex, allusive structure of the old dreams useless" (pp. 201–02). Russell does not see poems like Lydgate's *Complaynte* as part of a transitional moment between medieval love visions and early modern lyrics, but rather as examples of poems that are "arguably inspired by a dream vision but only in the most superficial ways" (p. 199).

[22] Wimsatt shows that *The Book of the Duchess* borrows "the pattern of complaint and consolation" from Machaut, who uses it in both *Remede de Fortune* (where the first-person narrator is the lover who complains and receives consolation) and *Dit de la fonteinne amoureuse* (p. 115).

[23] Spearing (1993), p. 1.

in becoming the reader's window into these secret observations, the dreamless poem shifts the reader's relationship to the functions of dreamer, guide, and narrator. The reader in this new arrangement comes to occupy the position once held by the dreamer, while the narrator becomes the reader's guide in the probing of personal consciousness.

This positioning would seem to give the narrator some authority over the meaning of the tale he tells, but in fact, as becomes clear in the poems here, it acts instead to undermine the authority of the narrative. Not only is the action no longer interpreted by a dream guide but it is also presented by a narrator who continually emphasizes his own incompetence as a poet and his status as merely a scribe or "skryvener" (*CLL*, line 194), who records but does not interfere or interpret. But the narrator's implicit claim that he therefore communicates the accurate, unmediated story does not hold true. The lack of a dream frame exposes the formal workings of the poem, for the narrator's separation from the action reveals the subjectivity inevitable with any kind of written mediation, and his self-deprecation emphasizes the possibility that such intervention amusingly distorts the events and/or voices the poem supposedly "transcribes." These poems thus achieve a kind of self-conscious separation between narrator and poet by presenting a narrator who is not dreaming but still does not form part of the main action. He is an outsider even as he insists on being in the know.

This emphasis on the trickiness of mediation raises the perennial anxiety of medieval English poetry about the status of literary language. Concern over the duplicity of language is in fact quite common. For example, in the debate poem *Wynnere and Wastoure*, the narrator begins by expressing concerns about the way in which speech enables people to deceive one another, because "nowe alle es witt and wyles that we with delyn, / Wyse wordes and slee, and icheon wryeth othere" ("now all is cleverness and cunning that we deal with, / Wise words and sly [i.e., deceptive language], and one hides the next [or, obscures another intention]," lines 5–6).[24] The narrator compares this unfavorably to an older, idyllic time when language was transparent, linking this with the characteristic idiom of romances, which he perceives as straightforward (lines 20 ff.). The nostalgic reference to the language of romances, often formulaic and repetitive, is in contrast to more elite literary forms, marked by ambiguity and difficulty of interpretation. This implies that for the narrator of *Wynnere and Wastoure* language in this idyllic romance-time is direct and artless, hiding nothing. But the very formulaic nature of romance language calls attention to the fact that it cannot truly be transparent, since the formulae themselves, instead of having inherent meanings, reproduce conventional interpretations and effects that arise out of the habitual use of them in characteristic contexts. The notion that language can transfer meaning directly from narrator to reader is likewise rejected

---

[24] See Warren Ginsberg's edition of the poem.

by the poems in this volume, which seek to raise questions about the effectiveness of representing private emotion in a poetic form.[25]

These changes in the dream vision raise important issues for late-medieval English audiences but go unremarked by critics perhaps because of the dominance of the Chaucerian model, in terms of both the relation of these later poems to the works of Chaucer and the importance of the Chaucerian aesthetic. Whether trying to ascertain the authorship of a work or the influences that informed it, establishing a link to Chaucer was a common preoccupation of much of the early scholarship on the apocryphal poems.[26] In Derek Pearsall's view, for example, Lydgate's poem is "a mosaic of Chaucerian themes and phrases," with passages that consist of "a tissue of borrowings,"[27] and "it is rarely necessary to go beyond Chaucer for Lydgate's specific borrowings" from French or classical models.[28] The fact that *Complaynte* "remained popular until its expulsion from the [Chaucer] canon in the nineteenth [century], after being acclaimed as one of the best of Chaucer's shorter poems" illustrates the power of Chaucer's name.[29] *La Belle Dame sans Mercy* has suffered similarly in the critical gaze of more recent readers, in contrast to its popularity in the fifteenth and sixteenth centuries when it was still thought to be Chaucer's work. C. S. Lewis, for example, viewed the poem as "an essentially second-rate theme redeemed by sheer good writing,"[30] while Walter W. Skeat dismissed it as "somewhat dull, owing to its needless prolixity."[31] No new editions of Roos' version of the poem have come out since the three late-nineteenth-century ones (two by Frederick J. Furnivall and one by Skeat), nor has the English translation received much scholarly attention, illustrating the persistence of these assessments.[32]

---

[25] Patterson points out that the complaint form "not only presupposes the perpetual intransigence of the lady — were she to respond to the lover's request she would not be worthy of it — but is invalidated by its very articulation: the more eloquent the lover, the less truthful his plea" ("Writing," p. 56).

[26] See Russell A. Peck, *Chaucer's Romaunt of the Rose and Boece, Treatise on the Astrolabe, Equatorie of the Planetis, Lost Works, and Chaucerian Apocrypha: An Annotated Bibliography, 1900–1985* (Toronto: University of Toronto Press, 1988), pp. 245 ff.; see especially pp. 309–12, and 327–37 for scholarship on the apocryphal poems included in this volume.

[27] Pearsall (1970), p. 85. Similarly, Spearing presents Lydgate's poem as one that borrows — images, conventions, settings — principally from Chaucer's work (this includes Chaucer's translation of *The Romaunt of the Rose*); see Spearing (1993), pp. 222–28.

[28] Pearsall (1970), p. 84.

[29] Pearsall (1970), p. 85.

[30] Lewis, p. 246.

[31] See Skeat's introductory remarks to his edition of the poem (1897), pp. lii and liii.

[32] See the Introduction to *La Belle Dame sans Mercy* in this volume.

Similarly, critics have both condemned and redeemed *The Boke of Cupide* through its relation to Chaucer. For example, employing a statistical comparison of various stylistic components of *The Boke of Cupide* with five of Chaucer's poems, William McColly suggests that the former "should be judged as nothing more than a primitive imitation" of Chaucer.[33] David Chamberlain's article "Clanvowe's Cuckoo," on the other hand, seeks to reinstate the poem as subtle and witty, rife with "literary jokes involving Chaucer."[34] J. Norton-Smith and I. Pravda, the most recent editors of *The Quare of Jelusy*, similarly assess that poem as a "Scottish imitation of Chaucerian and Lydgatian poetic form and ethical concerns composed just prior to the later, more accomplished, fifteenth- and sixteenth-century literary development beyond the Tweed which has come to be called 'Chaucerian.'"[35] The implication here seems to be that the later poets are "more accomplished" because they are more "Chaucerian." Because the poem is arguably more Lydgatian than Chaucerian, the insult is to both *The Quare of Jelusy* and Lydgate's place in literary history, suggesting that he is of negligible importance (and therefore so are his "imitators"), even though it is well known that many Scots poets, instead of focusing solely on Chaucer, saw Chaucer, Gower, and Lydgate as the triumvirate of "models to whom later poets declare their allegiance."[36] In all these instances, the poem's relationship to Chaucer becomes the measure of its success, but the fact that early readers see Chaucer as one among a group of English writers they emulated suggests the need to reevaluate our own assessments of Chaucer's value or importance. Thus, while the critical reputation of all these poems has often relied on their proximity, real or imagined, to Chaucer, it would be more accurate to see Chaucer as a literary presence — part of the playground — than as a source, and this is a playground in which fifteenth-century literature enjoyed sophisticated *plaisance*.

What makes the appeal of these poems to their earliest readers so unintelligible is that the bias towards Chaucer has frequently led critics to dismiss fifteenth-century poetry out of hand. Such a judgment operates on the basis of an a priori assumption that no matter how carefully Chaucerian works follow Chaucer, they never do what he did quite so well and are inevitably found lacking. In fact, according to Helen Cooney, poetry of this period has attracted more "sustained and emphatic distaste" than that of any other due to its perceived lack of originality and its supposed delight in form and ornamentation over intellectual engagement.[37] Instead of looking at fifteenth-century writers for what they had to offer their audiences, many critics were content to tell the story of late-medieval poetry as one of decline into "a literary wilder-

---

[33] McColly, p. 248. McColly compares *The Book of the Duchess*, Book 1 of *Troilus and Criseyde*, the Prologue to *The Legend of Good Women*, and *The Parliament of Fowls*.

[34] Chamberlain, p. 59.

[35] Norton-Smith and Pravda, p. 9.

[36] Spearing (1985), p. 61.

[37] See the introduction to *Nation, Court and Culture*, p. 9.

ness."[38] Cooney shows how Johan Huizinga's *Waning of the Middle Ages* and C. S. Lewis' *English Literature in the Sixteenth Century Excluding Drama* presented fifteenth-century poetry in ways that caused it to be "either ignored or reviled"[39] until the mid-1980s, when several revisionist projects "opened the way to new critical appreciations" of fifteenth-century literary efforts.[40]

Arguably, it is the very proximity of these texts to Chaucer that has resulted in their being persistently valued against what might be called a "Chaucerian aesthetic." But the pleasures of Chaucer's texts are no more universal or self-evident than those of, say, Lydgate. Rather, the appeal of a given text arises from the development of a specific set of expectations about what constitutes literary art. In the case of Chaucer, these expectations satisfy an acquired taste that cannot be applied indiscriminately to all Middle English poetry without having the rest of it suffer by comparison.[41] We probably cannot get away from our admiration of Chaucer, given how well he fits our own literary taste. We can, however, be more conscious of how this preference for his work colors our perceptions of and expectations about other medieval English writing. Through the examination of manuscript contexts and the practices of early printers and editors, it may be possible to discern something of the pleasures early audiences experienced in these poems.

As the contents of the manuscripts in which the poems in this volume appear indicate, many of the compilers of manuscript anthologies from the fifteenth and early sixteenth centuries enjoyed Chaucer primarily as a courtly love poet, with his dream visions, *The Legend of Good Women*, and shorter poems among the most popular selections.[42] This preference was sustained

---

[38] Cooney, p. 9.

[39] Cooney, p. 9. Compare H. S. Bennett's remarks in *Chaucer and the Fifteenth Century*: "The death of Chaucer in 1400 deprived England at a blow of her one outstanding author. His successors are to be found in a host of imitators" (p. 96). Though Bennett admits that "[t]he fifteenth century is by no means as barren of poetry as it used to be fashionable for critics to believe," he maintains that "the glory had departed, and the story of fifteenth-century poetry in England is largely the story of 'the shade of that which once was great', though momentary flashes reveal the fires underneath" (p. 96).

[40] Cooney, p. 10.

[41] This is by no means a new observation. Pearsall, for example, notes that "it is all Chaucer's fault" in accounting for the stark differences between the medieval and modern reception of Lydgate's work (1990, p. 39).

[42] See the detailed discussions of manuscript contexts in the introductions to the individual poems. Prominent among such collections are the manuscripts Hammond identified as the "Oxford group," which included, among others, three closely related manuscripts, Fairfax 16, Tanner 346, and Bodley 638, all fifteenth-century collections housed in the Bodleian Library, Oxford (1908, p. 339; Hammond describes the manuscripts and their relationship to one another on pp. 333–39). Other important antho-

in the early sixteenth century by William Thynne, who was the first to print *The Legend of Good Women* and Chaucer's translation of *The Romaunt of the Rose*.[43] According to R. F. Yeager, "Thynne's Chaucer . . . is a love poet, not a moralist."[44] On the other hand, at least one manuscript, London, British Library MS Cotton Vitellius E. xi, did appear to present Chaucer "as a relentlessly if succinctly moralizing figure, cited as a fount of proverbial wisdom rather than as the source of eloquence, the more familiar portrayal," a representation that "is reflected elsewhere in the attribution to Chaucer of proverbs and *sententiae* of different sorts."[45] These representations of Chaucer, and others that operated alongside them, suggest that in each case the selection of texts and the attribution of them to Chaucer reflected contemporary tastes, concerns, and interests. A closer look at manuscript anthologies and early printed editions thus helps illustrate the preferences of fifteenth- and sixteenth-century readers.

The high value of Chaucerian as a category begins to develop early, as evident from the way in which more and more works were included under the rubric "Chaucer" beginning even in the early to mid-fifteenth century, when the poetry of Clanvowe and Hoccleve, and later Lydgate, became part of the Chaucerian scheme. This points to the importance of Chaucerian poems, such as those in this volume, both in helping to promote and sustain interest in Chaucer and in forming this Chaucerian aesthetic. As Julia Boffey and John J. Thompson point out, "[a] growing taste for such anthologies made itself felt in the second half of the fifteenth century," and "[t]he nucleus of such manuscripts was generally formed by an assortment of Chaucer's minor poems, around which were fitted attempts to re-distil the influential 'aureat licour' — Lydgate's *Complaint of the Black Knight*, Clanvowe's *Cuckoo and Nightingale*, Hoccleve's *Letter of Cupid*."[46] But the view that the grouping of a selection of Chaucer's works with similar poems in manuscript anthologies necessarily stemmed from a desire for larger collections of Chaucer's works (as opposed to simply Chaucerian ones) does not accurately reflect the influences at work behind the compilation of all such late-medieval codices. Neither were such addenda simply an aspect of marketing; this type of collection reflects first of all the

---

logies include Cambridge University Library MS Ff.1.6, an amateur production spanning the period between the mid-fifteenth and early sixteenth centuries (see the facsimile of *The Findern Manuscript*, intro. Richard Beadle and A. E. B. Owen, pp. viii–xii) and a Scottish anthology, Bodleian Library MS Arch. Selden. B. 24, produced in the late fifteenth or early sixteenth century (see the facsimile volume, intro. Boffey and Edwards, 1997, pp. 3–4).

[43] Yeager, pp. 162–63.

[44] Yeager, p. 163.

[45] Boffey (1996), pp. 44–45, and 45n38. Boffey and Edwards (1998) also discuss Chaucer in the context of proverbial materials, pp. 212–13.

[46] Boffey and Thompson, p. 280.

audience's desires for lively vernacular literature, one of the pleasures offered by collections of Chaucerian verse.

The development of a market for Chaucer's poetry in particular may have had its inception in late-medieval anthologies such as Oxford, Bodleian Library MS Arch. Selden. B. 24, which attributes a number of spurious poems to Chaucer,[47] or in some measure through John Shirley's collections,[48] but the interest early editors had in producing a complete body of Chaucer's *Works* extended this practice over time in a way that seems to have influenced later perceptions of Chaucer's importance.[49] Here it is critical to recognize a distinction between *Chaucer* and *Chaucerian*. Because Thynne and his successors did not include works of a similar flavor without claiming Chaucer's authorship, as in some of the earlier manuscript anthologies, such a distinction was elided: all "Chaucerian" works became Chaucer's. The implications of this practice of identifying Chaucer as the author of every work in an anthology are twofold: first, that whatever has value is included as Chaucer's work, and second, that everything that is not by Chaucer in turn loses its value.[50]

An equally misleading side-effect of the long habit of viewing Chaucer as the only measure of Chaucerian is the tendency to discuss all late-medieval poets as if they were (or, if not, should have been) predominantly interested in producing imitations of Chaucer. Seeing allusions to Chaucer as a tired recycling of lines, or as mere borrowings, derivative and unoriginal, does not acknowledge the contributions of the "sons of Chaucer"[51] — writers like

---

[47] Edwards points out that this manuscript's "tendency to adjust and expand the Chaucerian canon" separates it "from the earlier Chaucerian compilations with their more conservative disposition to under-ascribe works to Chaucer" (1996, p. 59).

[48] For a discussion of Shirley's anthologies, see Boffey and Edwards, who point out that only certain of Shirley's attributions have been accepted, while others have been summarily rejected (1998, p. 203).

[49] See Hammond (1908), especially pp. 51–69, for a discussion of the various stages of the canon. Rossell Hope Robbins gives a list of the apocryphal works (1973, pp. 1061–62). See also F. W. Bonner, "The Genesis of the Chaucer Apocrypha," *Studies in Philology* 48 (1951), 461–81; Paul G. Ruggiers, ed., *Editing Chaucer: The Great Tradition* (Norman, OK: Pilgrim Books, 1984); Boffey and Edwards (1998); and Forni.

[50] These early editors were perhaps motivated by the desire to sell more books by making rival editions seem either less than complete or lacking in authority, but their interest in such a project was doubtless also due to the burgeoning antiquarian interests of the sixteenth century. Robert Costomiris sees Thynne's 1532 edition developing in a climate of "considerable antiquarian interest" (see "The Influence of Printed Editions and Manuscripts on the Canon of William Thynne's Canterbury Tales," in *Rewriting Chaucer: Culture, Authority, and the Idea of the Authentic Text, 1400–1602*, ed. Thomas A. Prendergast and Barbara Kline [Columbus: Ohio State University Press, 1999], pp. 237–57, at p. 239).

[51] Compare the Renaissance "Sons of Ben." (See the Introduction to *The Boke of Cupide*, p. 21n13.)

Clanvowe and Lydgate — to a vernacular English poetic tradition.[52] It does not, in fact, properly acknowledge Chaucer's own contribution as a poet alongside other poets, who inspired but also took inspiration, whose name identifies a variety of different types of creative output, an output that is not homogeneous or static but that involves, rather, a dynamic use of language and constantly shifting literary currents. Even those writers like Clanvowe, who were working deliberately and self-consciously with the models Chaucer provided, were engaging in a sophisticated literary game as a full participant with Chaucer, who may have set the tone and defined much of the territory, but who is not therefore the limit and definition of all originality.

In fact, the interplay between Chaucer's works and those of his "followers" is nuanced and complicated. "Chaucerian" poets looked not only to other English writers for inspiration[53] but also to the French writers whose work influenced Chaucer. Boffey points out that while many late-medieval English *dits amoureux* allude to Chaucer's dream poetry, Chaucer was not the sole influence, for "a range of French analogues, both venerable and right up-to-date, lie behind the later English poems."[54] Although in using French models, Clanvowe, Lydgate, Roos, and other "Chaucerian" poets were arguably following Chaucer's lead, this form of imitation in turn makes it difficult to disentangle specific echoes of Chaucer from other resonances — either those of his French influences or of an intervening English model in the form of an earlier "Chaucerian" poet. Nevertheless, Chaucer's importance has influenced critics to view all Chaucerian resonances as having their source in Chaucer without seriously examining other possibilities. This does not mean that Chaucer's impact should not be identified or even valued; it does, however, mean that inclusion in or exclusion from the category "Chaucer" should not be the primary basis for evaluating a Chaucerian work.

These Chaucerian poets formed a crucial part of the development of English vernacular traditions not only in their following of Chaucer but also in their own innovations. They, like Chaucer, looked to both continental and domestic models for inspiration. Other models of writing clearly influenced even those poets, such as Lydgate, who have a reputation in the later nineteenth century for turning out uninspired imitations of Chaucer. In truth, the quality of verse in such instances is less a matter of skill than it is of literary taste. We are the "primitives," inasmuch as, locked into formulae of the New Criticism, we appreciate so little of what constituted literary value in the fifteenth century, when the very foundations of English literary traditions were being excavated. A well-produced, relatively early collection, Oxford,

---

[52] Seth Lerer's book, *Chaucer and His Readers*, takes up this issue in depth.

[53] For example, Pearsall notes that "[t]he history of English poetry, and of much Scottish poetry too, in the fifteenth century is as much the record of Lydgate's influence as of Chaucer's" (1970, p. 1).

[54] Boffey (2001), pp. 114–15.

Bodleian Library MS Fairfax 16,[55] which includes versions of three of the four poems presented here, is a case in point. This mid-fifteenth-century collection exemplifies superbly how these influences operated in the late-medieval period. Looking at this collection, Boffey sees both those assembling the manuscript and the authors of the included works as consciously engaged in a process "of textual dialogue in which certain themes are debated and certain forms subjected to experimentation in ways which move easily in and out of a whole range of French and English models."[56] In such a case, regarding the selection of works in these anthologies as predominantly influenced by Chaucer erases both French and non-Chaucerian English models from consideration. It further skews any understanding of the nature of these collections — or their desirability — as repositories of English writing reflecting an active literary marketplace that valued Chaucer's productions alongside others now no longer perceived as representative of English poetry.

Although Fairfax 16 is among the earliest of these anthologies,[57] this is not an isolated instance; Boffey observes that a number of collections followed similar patterns of compilation, "accumulating material around Chaucer's dream poems" in ways that indicate the compilers' familiarity "with a range of both French and English texts," as well as their "lively awareness of current subjects of literary debate."[58] By assembling related works and "invit[ing] readers outside the primary audiences to enter into and perhaps extend the debates which were presumably of moment at first only for limited coteries," Boffey argues, manuscript anthologies highlighted both "the discussions conducted within the texts" and "the patterns of provocation and response played out between them."[59] This more inclusive account of literary practice allows for a dialectical model of interaction between French and English literary traditions in the composition and compilation of late-medieval English courtly love poetry and paints a picture of a sophisticated culture of literary play made possible by a rich tradition of poetic enterprise arising from vigorous vernacular traditions on both sides of the Channel.

As some of these manuscript anthologies indicate, the literary culture to whom the courtly poetry in this volume appealed was not solely London-based, but might be understood as "courtly" in the sense of falling under the sponsorship of "gentle houses" rather than that of

---

[55] John Norton-Smith puts the date at c. 1450 in his introduction to the facsimile volume (1979, p. vii); Edwards dates it in the 1440s (1996, p. 56); Boffey in the late 1430s or 1440s (1994, p. 114); Robbins gives it a date range of 1425–50 (see the MS listings for *La Belle Dame sans Mercy*, 1973, p. 1301).

[56] Boffey (1994), p. 115.

[57] Boffey (1994), p. 115.

[58] Boffey (1994), p. 121. Boffey sketches a pattern of textual movement between England and France that suggests one reason for these texts' engagement with both French and English models; see especially pp. 116–18.

[59] Boffey (1994), p. 121.

the royal household itself. Evidence for such a domestication of literature comes in part from the "private" compilation of anthologies such as the Findern manuscript (Cambridge University Library MS Ff.1.6), and the Thornton manuscript (Lincoln Cathedral MS 91),[60] both of which were produced provincially and unprofessionally.[61] The Findern manuscript in particular represents a collaborative effort on an unusual scale, containing entries by at least thirty different hands, and lacks the usual signs of professional production, indicating that this is likely the work of amateur scribes, perhaps members of the Findern family itself and their close associates.[62] A large portion of the manuscript contains very commonly copied works by Chaucer, Lydgate, Gower, and Hoccleve, along with pieces that were frequently associated with the works of these authors, such as *A Boke of Cupide* and *La Belle Dame sans Mercy*.[63] Rossell Hope Robbins calls Findern "a polite anthology," noting that it contains works that "are illustrative of what people concerned with the reading of English poetry thought valuable for preservation."[64] But, as some have pointed out, intermingled with the prominent and frequently copied courtly poetry that makes up the bulk of the manuscript are a number of shorter pieces, mostly lyrics and carols, that appear here in unique copies, suggesting that perhaps "some of these represented original contributions by the compilers,"[65] a view that is taken up at length by Sarah McNamer, who makes a case for considering fifteen of the lyrics as original works, specifically written by women.[66] If at least some of these short poems may

---

[60] Previously catalogued as MS A.5.2.

[61] For Findern, see the introduction to the facsimile volume of *The Findern Manuscript*, Beadle and Owen, pp. vii–viii and xi; for Thornton, see the introduction to the facsimile volume of *The Thornton Manuscript*, by D. S. Brewer and A. E. B. Owen, p. vii. Robert Thornton, who produced Lincoln Cathedral MS 91, also wrote out London, British Library Additional MS 31042 (Brewer and Owen, p. vii). From a prominent Yorkshire family, Thornton appears to have assembled these two books for his personal use (Brewer and Owen, pp. viii–ix). See also Boffey and Thompson, pp. 298–300.

[62] Beadle and Owen, pp. xi–xii and xiv. Robbins (1954) points to "professional hands" having copied many of the known works (pp. 629–30), concluding that "[t]he MS. thus suggests two sets of writers, local women amateurs and professional scribes" who were itinerant (p. 630); Sarah McNamer also sees this as the work of a mixture of "professional and amateur scribes" (p. 281).

[63] Robbins (1954), p. 611.

[64] Robbins (1954), pp. 611 and 612.

[65] Beadle and Owen, p. xii.

[66] McNamer argues that these Findern lyrics are not only written by women, but are also examples of poems that have "'missed the meaning' of the courtly tradition by taking its playful terms and using them in the service of sincere self-expression," adding that they should be considered "earnest and personal expressions" that "reveal a . . . sense of emotional depth, of real feeling" that resonates with "recognized documents of sincere female expression — the letters of the Paston, Stonor, and Cely women" (p. 289).

indeed be considered new pieces, we can see the operations of composition and copying in close proximity to one another, a pattern that illustrates the ways in which new voices might enter the old debates or invent new ones in a provincial setting, where London-based, royal courtly life must have seemed distant and immaterial.

That this volume itself participates in a pattern of "anthologizing" love complaints, debates, and visions with a Chaucerian flavor is no accident, following as it does on a long tradition of such groupings. On the other hand, such a collection that excludes Chaucer's work from its canon, if not from its title, can serve to highlight similarities between these Chaucerian poems that acknowledge and then go beyond their usual common denominator, Chaucer, perhaps stirring those of us who use this small collection to new dialogues, debates, and conversations of our own with and about these poems.

Editorial practices

Each of these editions offers a reading text based on a single manuscript copy, with emendations undertaken when needed for sense (where possible on the basis of readings from other manuscripts). In cases where several good copies in closely related manuscripts have survived, I have selected the earliest text from this group. These editions follow the standard editorial practices of the Middle English Texts Series; thus, modern capitalization, word formation, and punctuation practices are observed, and I silently expand manuscript abbreviations, regularize *u*/*v* and *j*/*i* spellings, and modernize the alphabet (this includes representing *y* as *g* in words where modern English has *g*, such as *gaf* for *yaf* or *agen* for *ayen*). Final -*e* that receives full syllabic value is accented (e.g., *charité*), and differentiation between *the* as the second person pronoun and *the* as the definite article is made by spelling the first *thee* and the second *the*. In addition to these alterations, initial *ff*- is transcribed as *F* in cases where it represents a capital letter, and *off* is reduced to *of* in cases where it means "of" in order to avoid confusion with "off." I have glossed the texts according to the difficulty of language and syntax. These marginal glosses are not intended as definitive interpretations, but rather as an aid to the reader in making sense of language that is difficult or unfamiliar. Since these are primarily student editions, I have not included a complete collation of all manuscripts. Variants

---

In so doing, McNamer implies that women's poetic expression limits itself to the arena of private, personal experience and refuses or misunderstands the "touches of irony and levity of tone" (p. 288) associated with literary courtly games. One argument against this is the compilation of the Findern Manuscript itself, whose lyrics would have had a public circulation, however limited, amongst the milieu in which it was produced. Elizabeth Hanson-Smith also argues that a number of the poems may have been written by women (see "A Woman's View of Courtly Love: The Findern Anthology Cambridge University Library MS. Ff.1.6," *Journal of Women's Studies in Literature* 1 [1979], 179–94).

for each poem are recorded in textual notes only in cases of emendation or significant textual variation; minor differences (e.g., in spelling or word division) are not noted.

Commonly Used Abbreviations

Anel.	*Anelida and Arcite*
BC	*The Boke of Cupide, God of Love*
BD	*The Book of the Duchess*
BDSM	*La Belle Dame sans Mercy*
CA	*Confessio Amantis* (Gower)
CLL	*A Complaynte of a Lovers Lyfe*
CT	*The Canterbury Tales*
Gen. deo.	*Genealogie deorum gentilium libri* (Boccaccio)
Gest Hyst.	*The "Gest Hystoriale" of the Destruction of Troy*
HF	*The House of Fame*
Hyg. Fab.	*Hygini Fabulae* (Hyginus)
IMEV	*Index of Middle English Verse* (Brown and Robbins)
LGW	*The Legend of Good Women*
MED	*Middle English Dictionary*
Metam.	*Metamorphoses* (Ovid)
OED	*Oxford English Dictionary*
PF	*The Parliament of Fowls*
QJ	*The Quare of Jelusy*
Romaunt	*The Romaunt of the Rose*
RR	*The Romance of the Rose* (Guillaume de Lorris and Jean de Meun)
TC	*Troilus and Criseyde*
Trevisa	*On the Properties of Things* (translation of *Bartholomaeus Anglicus De proprietatibus rerum*)
Vat. Myth.	*Vatican Mythographers* (ed. Kulcsár)

The Boke of Cupide, God of Love, or *The Cuckoo and the Nightingale*

Introduction

With *The Boke of Cupide, God of Love* John Clanvowe begins a modern English literary tradition.[1] Although he does not laud Chaucer by name, he is the first to write "Chaucerian" poetry, for himself and his friends, and also for Chaucer. Fifteenth-century poets would call Chaucer "floure of rethoryk / In Englissh tong and excellent poete,"[2] "worthie Chaucer glorious,"[3] "noble Chaucer, of makaris flour,"[4] "gronde of wel-seying . . . / My maister Chaucer,"[5] and "the honour of Englissh tonge," "maistir deere and fadir reverent, / My maistir Chaucer, flour of eloquence, / Mirour of fructuous entendement," "firste fyndere of our fair langage."[6] Although Chaucer would not be called "father" again until John Dryden termed him the "Father of English poetry" in his preface to *Fables Ancient and Modern* centuries later,[7] Edmund Spenser in the English Renaissance referred to him as "Dan Chaucer, well of English undefyled."[8]

Whatever merits there may be in such accolades, the identification of Chaucer as "ground," "father," "first finder [originator]," and "well" of English poetry would seem to present him

---

[1] Although other possibilities have been put forward, Sir John Clanvowe is the most likely author of the poem. See V. J. Scattergood, "The Authorship of *The Boke of Cupide*." Scattergood also includes a brief discussion in his introduction to *The Works of Sir John Clanvowe*, pp. 22–25.

[2] John Walton, trans., *Boethius: De consolatione philosophiae*, ed. Mark Science, EETS o.s. 170 (London: Oxford University Press, 1927), "Translator's Preface," st. 5 (p. 2).

[3] Robert Henryson, *The Testament of Cresseid*, line 41.

[4] William Dunbar, *Lament for the Makars*, line 50 (poem 21).

[5] John Lydgate, *Troy Book* 5.3519–21. Lydgate's verse contains many such examples.

[6] Thomas Hoccleve, *The Regiment of Princes*, ed. Charles Blythe (Kalamazoo, MI: Medieval Institute Publications, 1999), lines 1959, 1961–63, 4978.

[7] Frost, p. 397. Dryden's *Fables Ancient and Modern; Translated into Verse, from Homer, Ovid, Boccace, & Chaucer: With Original Poems* was first published in 1700.

[8] *The Faerie Queene* 4.2.32 (*The Complete Poetical Works of Spenser*, ed. R. E. Neil Dodge [Boston: Houghton Mifflin,1936]).

as foundation and inventor, father and source of poetic inspiration in English,[9] as if poets no longer need rely on the fountain Hippocrene, sacred to the muses. Praises of Chaucer that present him as a "father" or "source" of English poetry or poetic inspiration in such a way imply that his qualities as a poet are transhistorical, but, in fact, it is writers like Clanvowe, Spenser, and a host of others in between who created an enduring Chaucerian tradition by responding in vigorous and innovative ways to Chaucer's work. It is their efforts, as much as those of Chaucer, that generated an active vernacular literature in medieval England. Though one might expect that such praises of Chaucer would elevate in turn a writer like Clanvowe to the status of "father" or "first founder" of English literary tradition (since he is the first to write a Chaucerian poem that survives), they have instead diminished his importance and occluded his work. Similarly, while fifteenth-century writers looked to John Gower and John Lydgate as examples of poetic excellence alongside Chaucer,[10] Chaucer's work later overshadows the two almost entirely.[11] Although many of these poets achieved an entree to the tradition through their Chaucerian allusions and imitations, ironically, the literary canon they helped create disregarded them as derivative and extraneous. Ultimately, the high value placed on Chaucer has meant that the efforts of poets like Clanvowe, who helped fashion the Chaucerian aesthetic, lost their value as "original" works and came to seem instead pale imitations to be ejected from the Chaucer canon.

But Clanvowe was more than just an imitator. His *Boke of Cupide* draws significantly on earlier English writing, such as *The Owl and the Nightingale*, alongside Chaucer and the French poetry Chaucer embraced. In keeping with the dynamic of a literary tradition, Clanvowe is a "poet's poet," writing for a specific audience keenly attuned to the refinements of poetry making. Clanvowe shares this readership's interest in elevating vernacular poetry to

---

[9] See Christopher Cannon, *The Making of Chaucer's English: A Study of Words* (Cambridge, UK: Cambridge University Press, 1998). See also Seth Lerer, *Chaucer and His Readers*, especially the introduction, "The Subject of Chaucer Reception," pp. 3–21.

[10] Although all of Gower's English poetry came after Chaucer was well established as an "English" vernacular poet, Gower, in fact, was not a "Chaucerian" the way Lydgate was. But even by the mid-fifteenth century the two were linked with Chaucer.

[11] This points to a more complex and troubled relation between Chaucer and those who venerate him as "father," the possibility of an Oedipal relationship between Chaucer and those poets who wrote "Chaucerian" verse after him. One implication of such a charged acknowledgment of Chaucer's importance, in other words, is that poets who followed him were not simply celebrating his genius but attempting to distinguish themselves through their own appropriation of and redeployment of the elements of his style.

a high station in the fields of intellectual discourse and entertainment,[12] what Chaucer speaks of as the "best of sentence and moost solaas" (*CT* I[A]798). Clanvowe is one of those self-generated "sons of Chaucer,"[13] writing for a sophisticated audience that shares his delight in the artifice of poetry, with its conventions and its variety. In his interest in and anxiety about producing poetry in English, as opposed to Latin or French, he likewise espouses a tradition of vernacular writing that Chaucer followed but did not invent. Both these strains illustrate Clanvowe's participation in a lively vernacular literature that relies on a variety of traditions, both native and continental, that continue in later English poetry. Clanvowe is a tradition maker who writes as part of a cohort of imagination and wit — a cultural imagination and a cultural wit — that culminates in the English Renaissance among other devotees of language and wit.

At the beginning of Book 6 of *The Faerie Queene* Spenser, just such a devotee, invokes the delights of poetry as a therapeutic pleasure terrain for sophisticated audiences well versed in literary scenery:

The waies, through which my weary steps I guyde,
In this delightfull land of Faery,
Are so exceeding spacious and wyde,
And sprinckled with such sweet variety,
Of all that pleasant is to eare or eye,
That I, nigh ravisht with rare thoughts delight,
My tedious travell doe forget thereby;
And when I gin to feele decay of might,
It strength to me supplies, and chears my dulled spright. (6.Proem.1)

---

[12] Fiction's tendency to create meaning through analogy rather than logic gives it great potency in dealing with the inexplicability of higher truths. This correlates with Anselm's notion that "often we speak of things which we do not express with precision as they are; but by another expression we indicate what we are unwilling or unable to express with precision, as when we speak in riddles. And often we see a thing, not precisely as it is in itself, but through a likeness or image, as when we look upon a face in a mirror. And in this way, we often express and yet do not express, see and yet do not see, one and the same object; we express and see it through another; we do not express it, and do not see it by virtue of its own proper nature" (*Monologium*, ch. 65, in Anselm, *Basic Writings*, intro. Charles Hartshorne, trans. S. N. Deane [La Salle, IL: Open Court Classics, 1962], p. 129).

[13] The phrase "sons of Chaucer" is modeled on the self-styled "Sons of Ben," those seventeenth-century cavalier poets, such as Richard Lovelace, Robert Herrick, Thomas Carew, John Suckling, and Andrew Marvel, who saw Ben Jonson as their literary model. Clanvowe differs from Chaucer in his access to vernacular traditions that Chaucer had a hand in creating; Chaucer's own models were of necessity mainly continental, but Clanvowe was able to allude freely to those of Chaucer's works that predated his own efforts.

The restorative pathways through which Spenser would guide himself and his audience nearly two centuries after Chaucer are both old and new — perpetually fresh: a kind of literary playground with the power to "ravish" ardent tourists who peruse its lines. Some think of the English Renaissance as that time when classical literature was rediscovered, but Spenser is not thinking of rebirth in that way. He is celebrating vernacular poetry, as his praises of Chaucer show, and the riches of this English literary tradition are occupied by a burgeoning "Chaucerian family," of which Clanvowe was, perhaps, the eldest (if largely forgotten) son. To be sure, Spenser is much attuned to continental literature, both French and Italian, just as Chaucer and his circle were, but it is the vernacular language — his language and the language of his people — that he celebrates. At the same time, with his archaisms and borrowings from French and Latin, Spenser perhaps seeks to gain his own place in English poetry even as he pays tribute to Chaucer; his deliberately artificial language, akin in its polyglot resonances to the "quaint" verse of Chaucer, in effect suggests a "new" past for English poetry that includes his own efforts alongside those of his beloved "Dan Chaucer."[14] Indeed, Dryden remarked in his Preface to *Fables Ancient and Modern* that "Spenser more than once insinuates that the soul of Chaucer was transfused into his body; and that he was begotten by him two hundred years after his decease."[15]

As poets participating in a vibrant field of literary effort, Clanvowe and Spenser have much in common: they write poetry for and amidst poets. But the "Dan Chaucer" Spenser follows is comprised of Chaucer, Clanvowe, Hoccleve, Scogan, Lydgate, and a whole host of anonymous writers enjoying a Chaucerian fashion in poetry. In his *Boke of Cupide* Clanvowe is one of the first to respond to and borrow from the playing field of Chaucer's poetry. Writing even as Chaucer was beginning work on *The Canterbury Tales*,[16] he walks the well-sanded paths[17] of *The Tale of Palamon and Arcite* (which would become The Knight's Tale), *The Parliament of Fowls*, *The Legend of Good Women*, and *The Romance of the Rose*, and he does so with the audacity and delight of a proto-Spenser, an acolyte in the court of love poetry and

---

[14] See Nathan A. Gans, "Archaism and Neologism in Spenser's Diction," *Modern Philology* 76 (1979), 377–79. Gans points out the difficulties in identifying archaisms in Spenser: "The Elizabethan glossaries indicate that the question of Spenser's archaism is too complex to be resolved by counting *OED* citations. In the Elizabethan period, for example, neologism could itself be a form of archaism. One way of imitating the old poets — Chaucer, Lydgate, Occleve, and Hawes — was to neologize, since the sixteenth-century reputation of these writers depended, in part, on their enriching the language with new words" (p. 379).

[15] Frost, p. 388.

[16] Scattergood dates the poem 1386–91 on the basis of literary resonances with Chaucer (1975, p. 14).

[17] Compare Chaucer's *TC*, where Criseyde walks arm in arm with her companions along "sonded . . . weyes" (2.822), as she enters the realm of courtly behavior.

its servants, who slyly reinvents his master's work even as he celebrates it through impersonation. The self-stimulated paths of this adventurer, whose reading causes him to lie awake at night yearning for bird-talk, lead his eyes and ears into groves where nightingales might speak to him. His is a knowing voyeurism realized in the waking world of language and poetry.

From its inception, *The Boke of Cupide* inhabits a Chaucerian landscape, accompanied by the rhetoric of French dream visions. Clanvowe's poem is written for an audience that has a well-defined set of expectations and a highly developed taste for Chaucerian style, an audience that included Chaucer himself. Chaucer provided much of the background for the Clanvowes, Hoccleves, and Scogans (and, later, the Lydgates) who extended and reinvented his work. This explains why these poets begin to appear alongside their "original" (Chaucer) in Chaucerian anthologies; this begins even as early as Oxford, Bodleian Library manuscripts Fairfax 16 (c. 1430–50) and Tanner 346 (third quarter of the fifteenth century), and continues in William Thynne's 1532 edition of "Chaucer" and all subsequent printed editions for the next several hundred years. These Chaucerian writers, like the later poets of *The Flower and the Leaf* and *The Assembly of Ladies*, are all folded into "Chaucer" and adorn the paths of Spenser's "delightfull land of Faery," with its "sweet variety / Of al that pleasant is to eare or eye."

In its first two lines, *The Boke of Cupide, God of Love*, decked out in spring in its most colorful (rhetorical) dress, broadcasts its affiliation with the subject of love and, more specifically, with Chaucer's love poetry. As soon as we read them, we know this is the world Chaucer enjoyed — the love world of *The Parliament of Fowls*, of Cupid — "'God save swich a lord!' — I can na moore" (*PF*, line 14); the world of The Knight's Tale:

The God of Love, a benedicité!	*ah bless you*
How myghty and how grete a lorde is he! (lines 1–2)[18]	

But these borrowed lines are more than straightforward reproductions. The wit and humor of Clanvowe's poem depends on playing with and redeploying materials Chaucer provided; its deft retuning of phrases that have been used in other contexts shows that *The Boke of Cupide* is a full participant in a literary game requiring a good sense of fun, written for a vernacular, literate audience. Though for Clanvowe it was new, from our perspective this is a long-standing tradition, and the Chaucerian reverberations of Clanvowe's poem mark him as the first to shape this tradition by turning Chaucer into a reciprocating audience.

Clanvowe's plot is deliberately perplexed, given to self-agitation, as the narrator attempts to imagine himself into Chaucer's love world, desirous of a May experience with "feveres

---

[18] The opening two lines of Clanvowe's poem quoted here are borrowed from The Knight's Tale, indicating both the poem's interest in love and its close association with Chaucer's works. For a thorough reading of the poem's many resonances with The Knight's Tale and other works by Chaucer, see David Chamberlain and Charles Rutherford, respectively.

white," where one would sleep "but a lyte" (lines 41–42). Even though he feels "olde and unlusty," he works himself into a "hote and colde" state (lines 37, 39) that leaves him tossing and turning with love-longing on the "thirde nyght of May" (line 55).[19] Although he recognizes the arbitrary nature of Love, who makes some laugh and others sigh, some glad and others sad (lines 18–19), the narrator still yearns to hear the song of the nightingale, Love's messenger. Pondering a lovers' saying that "hit wer good to her the nyghtyngale / Rather then the leude cukkow syng" (lines 49–50), he decides to go out in search of the nightingale's song.

Outside, the meadows are "poudred with dayse" (line 63),[20] and the birds are preening, dancing, and leaping "on the spray . . . evermore two and two in fere [together]" (lines 77–78), having chosen their mates back in March. The birdsong is of such a soothing harmony that the narrator quickly falls into a swoon between sleeping and waking. But as soon as he succumbs to this half-sleeping state, instead of the thrilling trill of the nightingale, he hears the cuckoo's cry — for lovers an inauspicious sign indeed.[21] Angry that his lover's swoon yields only the song of "[t]hat sory bridde, the lewde cukkowe" (line 90), he grumbles, "who was then evel apayed but I!" (line 92). As if in answer, he hears a nightingale reply to the cuckoo and finds that in his self-induced state he is able to understand the two birds. The cuckoo and the nightingale at once begin an argument about the nature of their respective cries. The narrator, perhaps hoping to be lucky in love, favors the nightingale and prays that the cuckoo might suffer: "I prey to God that evel fire him brenne" (line 105).

The cuckoo argues that his own cry is "trewe and pleyn" (line 118), easily understood by all, and accuses the nightingale of speaking obscurely. The nightingale responds by suggesting in her cry — "Ocy! Ocy!" — that she very much wishes "[t]hat al tho wer shamefully slayne, / That menen oght agen Love amys" (lines 129–30), adding:

---

[19] May 3, the third day of the third month (the most potent of love days), often proves overwhelming to medieval lovers (the medieval calendar year began on March 25). In Ovid's *Fasti*, it marks the feast of the Floralia, when men and women abandon themselves to love and the woods. In Chaucer's *Troilus and Criseyde* it is the day on which Pandarus, awakened by the birds rehearsing the laments of Procne (the swallow) and Philomela (the nightingale), sets out to woo Criseyde on behalf of Troilus (*TC* 2.50–56 ff.); in The Knight's Tale, it is the day when Palamoun breaks out of prison in hope of winning Emelye, who goes strolling on May mornings such as the one on which Palamoun first beheld her (see *CT* I[A]1462–63 and 1034 ff.).

[20] Compare Chaucer's Prologue to *The Legend of Good Women*, where nothing can restrain the narrator as he throws aside his books (F.36–39) to set out in May to hear the birds and watch the daisies spring and spread against the sun as they declare lays of love, singing "Blessed be Seynt Valentyn" (F.145).

[21] This is because the cuckoo is often associated with a fear of cuckoldry (see explanatory notes to lines 90, 185, and 270).

"And also I wold al tho were dede,   *wish all those; dead*
That thenk not her lyve in love to lede,   *plan not their lives; lead*
For who that wol the God of Love not serve,   *will*
I dar wel say he is worthy for to sterve,   *die*
And for that skille 'Ocy! Ocy!' I crede."   *reason; cry*
   (lines 131–35)

The cuckoo rejects the nightingale's "queynt lawe, / That eyther shal I love or elles be slawe" and announces his refusal either to die or, while he lives, to put himself under "Loves yoke" (lines 136–37, 140). These responses, together with the cuckoo's dismissal of lovers as diseased and weak, rouse the incensed nightingale to a vociferous defense of love. She catalogues the virtues of the God of Love's service, arguing that it produces all goodness, honor, nobility, pleasure, heart's desire, perfect joy, trust, happiness, delight, cheerfulness, humility, faithful companionship, graciousness, generosity, courtesy, and fear of shame or doing wrong. Finally her list culminates in the claim that "he that truly Loves servaunt ys, / Wer lother to be schamed then to dye" (lines 159–60).

The cuckoo, on the other hand, argues that love is the cause of misfortune, sorrow, care, sickness, resentment, debate, anger, envy, reproof, shame, distrust, jealousy, pride, mischief, poverty, and madness. "Lovyng is an office of dispaire," he warns (line 176) that only leads to abandonment as soon as one turns one's back. The cuckoo's sniping against love finally provokes the nightingale to a personal attack — "Fye . . . on thi name and on thee!" (line 186) — but her defense reveals the liabilities of Love's service. Although she argues that lovers gain something from surrendering to Love, "[f]or Love his servant evermore amendeth [improves], / And fro al tachches [blemishes] him defendeth" (lines 191–92), it is equally clear that Love is the source of a lover's pain, since that is what "maketh him to brenne as eny fire" (line 193). Further, when she says that the God of Love "whom him likes, joy ynogh him sendeth" ("sends plenty of joy to whomever he likes," line 195), the nightingale echoes the narrator's observations at the beginning of the poem that Love is an arbitrary and willful master.

Willfulness is, in fact, the charge that the cuckoo levels next against Love, and it is one the nightingale cannot answer. After first contending that "Love hath no reson but his wille" (line 197) the cuckoo proceeds to expose the consequences of such willfulness. According to the cuckoo, Love is not worthy to be followed because "ofte sithe [frequently] untrew folke he esith, / And trew folke so bittirly displesith, / That for defaute of grace hee let hem spille [die]" (lines 198–200). This is because, like Fortune, Love "is blynde and may not se" (line 202) and in the court of Love truth seldom does any good, "[s]o dyverse and so wilful ys he [Love]" (line 205). After this attack the nightingale bursts into tears, through which, despite her assertion that she "can for tene [sorrow] sey not oon worde more" (line 209), she pleads with the God of Love for help in avenging herself on the cuckoo. Not one to hesitate when Love's duty calls, the narrator catches up a stone that he casts "hertly" (line 218) at the cuckoo, who flies away calling out, "Farewel, farewel, papyngay" (line 222) as he soars out of sight.

At the end of the poem the nightingale thanks the narrator for chasing away the cuckoo and promises to try to be the first singer he hears the next May (if she is still alive and not afraid). In the meantime, she hopes that the narrator will not believe anything the lying cuckoo said and suggests that looking at the daisy will ease the pain of lovesickness. The nightingale then sings a song to the narrator, "I shrewe hem al that be to Love untrewe" (line 250), before flying away to complain to the other birds about the cuckoo. The poem ends with the promise of a parliament to judge the cuckoo on the next Valentine's Day, after which the nightingale's song, "Terme of lyve, Love hath withholde me" (line 289), awakens the narrator abruptly.

Clanvowe's poem, conceived and performed in the rarified environs of the Chaucer circle, immediately takes residence in manuscripts that serve as anthologies — bouquets of like-minded verse for a poetry-hungry audience.[22] The three earliest collections that include the poem, Oxford, Bodleian Library MSS Fairfax 16, Tanner 346, and Bodley 638, are closely related in their selection of contents. In Fairfax 16, the largest and earliest of these, *The Boke of Cupide* lives in the company of Chaucer's *Legend of Good Women*, as well as his dream visions, complaints, and most of the shorter poems.[23] The manuscript also contains poems by Lydgate (including *A Complaynte of a Lovers Lyfe* and *The Temple of Glass*), Hoccleve (including *The Epistle of Cupid*), Richard Roos (*La Belle Dame sans Mercy*), and a few anonymous pieces.[24] Tanner 346 contains a smaller but very similar lineup, with Chaucer's *Legend of Good Women*, *Book of the Duchess*, *Parliament of Fowls*, *Anelida and Arcite*, *Complaint of Mars*, *Complaint of Venus*, and *Complaint unto Pity*; Hoccleve's *Epistle of Cupid*; Lydgate's *Complaynte of a Lovers Lyfe* and *Temple of Glass*; and some anonymous

---

[22] Julia Boffey and John J. Thompson discuss the relationships of many of the following manuscripts, pp. 280–83.

[23] *The Complaint of Mars*, *The Complaint of Venus*, *Anelida and Arcite*, *Truth*, *The Legend of Good Women*, *The Parliament of Fowls*, *The Book of the Duchess*, *The House of Fame*, *The Complaint unto Pity*, *An ABC*, *Fortune*, *Lenvoy de Chaucer a Scogan*, *The Complaint of Chaucer to His Purse*, *Lenvoy de Chaucer a Bukton*, *Lak of Stedfastnesse*, *Against Women Unconstant* (which some editors are doubtful about ascribing to Chaucer; see *The Riverside Chaucer*, pp. 636–37).

[24] Including the *Envoy to Alison* (*IMEV* 2479), *The Complaint against Hope* (*IMEV* 370), and *Complaynt D'Amours* (*IMEV* 1388; ascribed to Chaucer by some editors; see *The Riverside Chaucer*, p. 637). After the first two booklets, the manuscript ends with several smaller, tacked-on booklets containing Lydgate's *Reason and Sensuality* and anonymous pieces, including *How a Lover Praiseth His Lady* (*IMEV* 4043), *Venus Mass* (*IMEV* 4186), and so on. See the list of contents for the manuscript in the facsimile volume, intro. John Norton-Smith (1979), pp. xxiii–xxix.

pieces.[25] Bodley 638 reproduces many of these same works, including Chaucer's *Legend of Good Women*, *Parliament of Fowls*, *Book of the Duchess*, *House of Fame*, *Anelida and Arcite*, *Complaint unto Pity*, *An ABC*, and *Fortune*; Lydgate's *Complaynte of a Lovers Lyfe*[26] and *Temple of Glass*; Hoccleve's *Letter of Cupid*; and some anonymous pieces.[27] In their focus on dream visions, complaints, and the shorter lyrics, these three anthologies seem primarily interested in Chaucer as a courtly love poet.[28]

Oxford, Bodleian Library MS Arch. Selden. B. 24, a Scottish anthology, begins with Chaucer's *Troilus and Criseyde*, followed by a number of short proverb-style poems;[29] and also includes Chaucer's *Legend of Good Women*, *Parliament of Fowls*, *Complaint of Mars*, and *Complaint of Venus*; Lydgate's *Complaynte of a Lovers Lyfe*; Hoccleve's *Mother of God* and *Letter of Cupid*; two short religious lyrics;[30] *The Kingis Quair*; and a number of pieces unique to this manuscript, including *The Quare of Jelusy* (included in the present volume), several only a few stanzas in length.[31] Although the contents seem not quite as cohesive as in the other three manuscripts, this may reflect in part a different scheme of unification, that of Chaucer as author. In fact, Arch. Selden. B. 24 seems concerned with producing an anthology not just of courtly love poetry, but more specifically of Chaucer's works; thus, of the first fourteen items, which contain the Middle English selections, six are by Chaucer, and another five are inaccurately identified as his, while only three, including *The Boke of Cupide*, remain unattributed.[32] This is in contrast to manuscripts Fairfax 16, Tanner 346, and Bodley 638, discussed above, which note the authorship of Chaucer's shorter pieces, such as *Fortune*, *Truth*, or *The Complaint to His Purse*, but leave the dream visions and longer complaints

---

[25] The *Envoy to Alison* (see note 24), *A Lover's Plaint* (*IMEV* 402), and *A Complaint for Lack of Sight* (*IMEV* 828). See the table of contents to the facsimile volume, intro. Pamela Robinson, p. vii.

[26] This is missing the first 467 lines due to the manuscript's acephalous state.

[27] Including the *Complaint against Hope* and *Complaynt D'Amours* (see note 24). The contents of the manuscript are listed in Robinson's introduction to the facsimile volume, pp. xvii–xxii.

[28] Eleanor Prescott Hammond designated these manuscripts as part of the "Oxford group," noting their close relationship and suggesting they derived from a common exemplar (1908, pp. 333–39).

[29] "Greneacres" stanza (*IMEV* 524), Chaucer's *Truth*, Walton's extract on Boethius (*IMEV* 2820 and 1597), "Deuise proues and eke humylitee" (*IMEV* 679).

[30] "O hie emperice and quene celestiall" (*IMEV* 2461) and "This warldly Ioy is onuly fantasy" (*IMEV* 3660).

[31] These include "The Lay of Sorrow" (*IMEV* 482) and "The Lufaris Complaynt" (*IMEV* 564), and other religious and secular lyrics. For further details, see the contents listed in the facsimile volume, intro. Julia Boffey and A. S. G. Edwards (1997), pp. 1–3.

[32] See the contents in the facsimile volume, intro. Boffey and Edwards (1997), pp. 1–3.

without attribution. By the same token, the poems by Lydgate, Hoccleve, and others are just as likely to be presented anonymously in these collections.

In the Findern manuscript (Cambridge University Library MS Ff.1.6), discussed in the General Introduction to this volume,[33] the major Chaucerian poems (Chaucer's *Complaint unto Pity*, *The Parliament of Fowls*, extracts and some of his shorter poems; Hoccleve's *Letter of Cupid*; and Richard Roos' *La Belle Dame sans Mercy*) are interspersed with a number of selections from Gower's *Confessio Amantis*, various works by Lydgate (e.g., "The Wicked Tongue"), and many anonymous short lyric poems and carols, a significant number of which appear as unique copies in Findern. What is notable is that Findern's collection does not group the usual set of Chaucerian poems as closely to one another as the other manuscripts discussed here. Each of the "major" contributions is surrounded by smaller anonymous pieces that form a significant portion of the manuscript.[34] In Findern an interest in lyric and complaint forms seems to drive most of the selections, giving *The Boke of Cupide* a less unified and less Chaucerian context. While certainly having a stake in the "game of love," the collection seems to display less of an interest in Chaucer's work than the others, with only six of the 62 items by Chaucer, a number equaled by selections from Gower's *Confessio Amantis*, while there are four items by Lydgate. By far the largest selection of works (more than half the items) comes in the form of short lyrics, carols, and complaints, most of which are anonymous.[35] Findern, like the other anthologies, reflects the interests and needs of its audience, and *The Boke of Cupide* and other Chaucerian pieces seem to have occupied a different space in their literary imagination — that, perhaps, of inspiration, if the arguments for some of the anonymous lyrics "represent[ing] original contributions by the compilers" are to be believed.[36]

---

[33] See pp. 16–17.

[34] For example, the first three items are extracts from Gower's *Confessio Amantis* (a section from the Tale of Tereus and Philomela from Book 5 [missing the first 370 lines], a section from Book 4 where Amans and Genius discuss Idleness in the prologue to the Tale of Rosiphelee, which is the third item), the fourth is Chaucer's *Complaint unto Pity*, followed by five short complaints, after which comes a missing folio, and then *The Boke of Cupide*. A short lyric follows Clanvowe's poem, then Chaucer's *Parliament of Fowls*, The Tale of Three Questions from Gower's *Confessio Amantis*, and another five anonymous pieces. These are followed in turn by four short items by Chaucer: *Complaint to His Purse*, Anelida's complaint from *Anelida and Arcite*, the tale of Thisbe from *The Legend of Good Women*, and *The Complaint of Venus*, and the manuscript continues in this vein. See the contents of the facsimile volume, intro. Richard Beadle and A. E. B. Owen, pp. xix–xxx.

[35] See the contents in Beadle and Owen's introduction to the facsimile volume (pp. xix–xxx).

[36] Beadle and Owen, p. xii. See also the discussion in the General Introduction, pp. 16–17, and p. 16n66.

That *The Boke of Cupide* is Chaucerian there can be no doubt, and that it was written by Clanvowe is virtually certain. In the Findern manuscript the poem ends with the attribution "explicit Clanvowe,"[37] and most scholars agree on this basis that the poem was written by Sir John Clanvowe, one of Chaucer's contemporaries who died in 1391.[38] Lee Patterson is doubtless right in his assertion that Clanvowe was a friend and "literary colleague"of Chaucer.[39] Retained first by Edward III and then by Richard II, Clanvowe was one of a group of knights who were, if not outright Lollards, at least Lollard sympathizers.[40] Not yet condemned as heretics in the late 1380s, the Lollards were a group of religious dissidents whose arguments reflected the thought of John Wyclif, an Oxford theologian. Concerned with the increasing signs of Church decadence, the lack of education amongst the clergy, and the dependence of the laity upon clerical authority, Wyclif and his followers argued for a direct relationship between each individual and God, without the need for mediation by a priest. Wyclif began translating the Bible into English as a part of an attempt to make the interpretation of God's word available to everyone.[41] That Clanvowe had such interests is suggested

---

[37] See fol. 28r.

[38] Some have suggested that Thomas Clanvowe (probably John Clanvowe's son) may have been the author in the early fifteenth century, but, according to Scattergood, the consistent use of final *-e* in the poem is parallel with Chaucer's use and therefore points to a fourteenth-century date (1964, p. 143). This view is seconded by K. B. McFarlane, who argues that, while it is possible that Thomas Clanvowe wrote the poem, "the friend of Chaucer has a rather better claim and this is reinforced by the slightly old-fashioned metrical character: it is Chaucerian rather than post-Chaucerian" (p. 184). The fact that Sir John Clanvowe was the author of a tract entitled *The Two Ways* also shows that he had literary interests. Although some scholars have proposed that the reference to Clanvowe could refer to a scribe, no scribe by that name has been found. For more on the debates over authorship, see Scattergood (1975), pp. 22 ff., and (1964), pp. 137–49.

[39] Patterson, 1992a, p. 9.

[40] See McFarlane for details about Clanvowe's relationship to these knights and to the king's household. Patterson points out that "Walsingham [in his *Chronicon*] included Clanvowe as one of the so-called Lollard knights in the royal household, and it seems clear that he and the men with whom he associated shared the purist, biblicist piety that was widespread in the late fourteenth century and that the Lollards developed into a full-blown, theologically sophisticated heresy" (1992a, pp. 12–13).

[41] For a more detailed discussion of the Lollard movement, see Stephen Justice, pp. 662–89. James H. Morey, *Book and Verse: A Guide to Middle English Biblical Literature* (Urbana: University of Illinois Press, 2000), points out that the laity would have had access to a variety of biblical stories through the tradition of vernacular biblical paraphrase. The contrast, according to Morey, was that "[t]he Lollards produced a straight prose translation, devoid of commentary, while biblical paraphrasers freely adapted selected passages with frequent glosses, moralizations, and apocryphal digressions" to help readers interpret and make sense of the biblical passages addressed (p. 11).

by his composition of a prose tract *The Two Ways*, "a treatise which shows some sympathy with Lollard positions."[42]

Of the four poems included in this volume, Clanvowe's is not only closest in time to Chaucer, but also arguably has the most "Chaucerian" flavor. The poem is heavily indebted to *The Parliament of Fowls* as well as The Knight's Tale, and the reference to the meadow of daisies in the beginning of the poem hints at the possibility that he wrote it after Chaucer had composed the Prologue to *The Legend of Good Women* (c. late 1386). The poem's resonances with Chaucer's poetry point to its intertextual richness, displaying a deep pattern of allusion to Chaucer and, to a lesser extent, to the French marguerite poetry on which Chaucer himself drew, as well as earlier English bird debates.[43] In fact, *The Boke of Cupide* was not excluded from the Chaucer canon until the late nineteenth century, a fact that John Conlee notes "is not at all surprising" because of its overt use of Chaucerian components and "its wryly comic treatment of love and lovers," which gives it a particularly Chaucerian tone.[44] Though William McColly argues on the basis of a statistical comparison between *The Boke of Cupide* and some of Chaucer's best known poetry that Clanvowe's poem is "nothing more than a primitive imitation" of Chaucer,[45] David Chamberlain's view of the poem as a witty font of "literary jokes involving Chaucer"[46] is the more common perception amongst scholars.

The Boke of Cupide follows established traditions in combining dream vision with debate, two genres that not infrequently took love as their subject, but also, in their self-consciousness,

---

[42] Scattergood (1975), p. 19. Scattergood goes on to point out that at one point Clanvowe uses "the word *loller* ([line] 512), a word meaning 'loafer' or 'idler', a term often deliberately and scornfully misapplied to Lollards" (p. 20). Justice argues that Clanvowe's use of the term "loller" in *The Two Ways* does not so much show that he is a Wycliffite as illustrate "that Clanvowe embraces such insults, and feels himself and those like him scorned by the court world, by those who frankly pursue their 'eeses and . . . lustes,'" concluding ultimately that "[t]here is little in Clanvowe's work to suggest what he believed" (p. 671).

[43] In fact, as the poem's most recent editor, Scattergood (1975), points out, in its opposition of the two birds the poem owes something to French poetry, since no other Middle English debate poem uses the cuckoo and the nightingale as opponents (see his discussion of Jean de Condé's *La messe des oiseaus* and Eustache Deschamps' balade "En ce douls temps" ["Plaintes d'amoureux," no. 476], pp. 10–12). Scattergood maintains, nevertheless, that the "main literary inspiration . . . is Chaucer" and notes the influence of *The Parliament of Fowls* (p. 12).

[44] Conlee, p. 249.

[45] McColly, p. 248. McColly compares *The Book of the Duchess*, *Troilus and Criseyde* (Book 1), the Prologue to *The Legend of Good Women*, and *The Parliament of Fowls*.

[46] See especially p. 59.

examined the rigors of debate itself.[47] More specifically *The Boke of Cupide* is in a tradition of bird debates, such as the early Middle English poem *The Owl and the Nightingale*, the thirteenth-century *Thrush and the Nightingale*, or the later, fragmentary *Clerk and the Nightingale*.[48] It ostensibly shares with many of these a preoccupation with the nature of love or fidelity; it also partakes to some degree of the debate poet's impulse to use legal discourse and become embroiled in contemporary religious or political issues. In *The Owl and the Nightingale*, for example, the birds both "at times adopt a homiletic style" as they argue about the relationship of their respective songs — and habits of living — to their love of and service to the Church,[49] and the two birds' arguments further convey a "legalistic flavor" because of the use of "legal tags and terms,"[50] as well as exempla and proverbs.[51] These tendencies, together with the debate structure, give the impression of "the pleas and counter-pleas of advocates."[52] In fact, though some critics have tried to downplay the use of legal terminology, the critical wrangling over the poem's connection or lack thereof to the law, court procedure, legal discourse, and so on points to its centrality.[53] Clanvowe's poem is to some extent looking

---

[47] For more on Middle English debate poetry, see Conlee's general introduction to *Middle English Debate Poetry*; for more on the dream vision, see Spearing's *Medieval Dream-Poetry*.

[48] See Conlee's discussion of Middle English bird debates, pp. xxii–xxiv. Chaucer's *Parliament of Fowls* or French works like Jean de Condé's *La messe des oiseaus* are more properly bird parliaments than one-on-one debates.

[49] See Eric Gerald Stanley's introduction to *The Owl and the Nightingale*, p. 30.

[50] Stanley, p. 28.

[51] Stanley, pp. 33–34.

[52] Stanley, p. 28. Though earlier critics argued that the two birds follow legal procedure closely, use legal terminology consistently, and even reproduce a law case, Stanley contends that in fact there is not much technical detail, and that the terms used are ones that "must have been familiar to the layman" (p. 28). He argues instead that the use of legal discourse can be accounted for by the influence of "the style of the Latin debate poems that are the products of [legal] schools" (p. 28). Michael A. Witt argues even more insistently that "the focus is on the birds, not upon a careful following of a law-court procedure," and "it is important to emphasize that such terms are general and concentrated in only one passage of fifteen lines in a poem nearly 1800 lines long" (p. 290). Monica Brzezinski Potkay argues that "the legal system which grounds the arguments of the Owl and the Nightingale is a theoretical one, that of natural law — the law which the Middle Ages thought to be, as it were, the law of a higher court, Gods' own law that furnishes the basis of all other legal systems which rule human beings" (p. 368).

[53] Bruce Holsinger points to "[t]he sheer number of convincing yet diverging legal arguments" about the poem, arguing that "these many . . . studies suggest that the poem's overriding concern may be with any one of the following: canon law, secular law, natural law, marriage law, theoretical law, or procedural law; or rather, it may be with all of them at the same time; or rather, it may be with the conflicts, gaps, overlaps, and elisions *between* these systems and practices of law. The central legal

beyond Chaucer towards this earlier English tradition of bird debates, though there is certainly plenty of political subject matter in Chaucer's *Parliament of Fowls*.[54]

Where *The Thrush and the Nightingale* and *The Clerk and the Nightingale* both center on the nature of women, *The Boke of Cupide* resembles *The Owl and the Nightingale* in that the focus of the debate is the birds' respective cries. The uses of legal language in Clanvowe's poem occur mostly on the cuckoo's side, as when he queries the nightingale's cry and calls it a "queynt lawe" (line 136) and claims he will not follow her "counseyl" (line 165), or when he calls loving "an office of dispaire" (line 176), and argues that, although the lover may "beget" a little pleasure from love, as soon as he lets his attention lapse he gets what he deserves ("He may ful sone of age have his eire," line 180), and finally concludes that in Love's "court ful selde trouthe avayleth" (line 204). But ultimately, these gestures towards legal argument seem no more than token, and *The Boke of Cupide* does not appear as invested in the trappings of legal language as the earlier poem is. For example, where the narrator of *The Owl and the Nightingale* is called to adjudicate between the two birds, in *The Boke of Cupide* the narrator is never asked to play the role of judge and in any case clearly takes the nightingale's side before the debate even begins. Where the owl and the nightingale make constant overt recourse to proverbs and hurl legal language at one another, turning their thickets into a courtroom setting, most of the emphasis in the argument between Clanvowe's birds centers on the qualities of love and the duty/fate of its servants, with little interest in legalities. Nevertheless, Clanvowe's poem clearly invokes the pleasures of the debate genre it shares with *The Owl and the Nightingale* — pleasures that consist of listening to the antagonists and taking sides: it succeeds, in other words, in making readers into contestants themselves.

And critical readings of Clanvowe's poem have been just as heated, investigating both its treatment of courtly love and its more political or religious concerns. Thus, some critics have taken the poem's initial declaration at face value and read it as a poem about love. In this vein, the debate has been interpreted as a contest between concupiscence and marriage[55] or cynicism

---

concern of *The Owl and the Nightingale* is, in a word, jurisdiction" (p. 165; italics in original). Holsinger's view is that "the poem deploys an array of legal terminologies and procedures as a means of exploring what its writer saw as a liturgical problem, namely, what sorts of music belong where and when and with what results" (p. 156).

[54] See Russell A. Peck's discussions of possible political readings of *The Parliament of Fowls* in "Love, Politics, and Plot in the *Parlement of Foules*," *Chaucer Review* 24 (1990), 290–305.

[55] David Lampe argues that the poem's central theme is that of adulterous love; the debate is a reflection of the birds' traditional natures, with the cuckoo representing the cuckolded husband, and the nightingale both adulterous love and devout piety. He sees the poem as a "subtly humorous demonstration of the effects of concupiscence upon the narrator and of the proper remedy, marriage" (p. 61).

and maudlin sentimentality.[56] But despite the poem's declared focus on love, the alignment of the nightingale and the cuckoo with language use and gender has suggested to other critics that the love debate masks religious or political resonances. Accordingly, some scholars have focused on the historical circumstances surrounding the poem's production, interpreting the debate as a controversy over erotic and divine love,[57] polyphonic and monophonic music,[58] courtly language and "truth-telling,"[59] or the Church and Lollardy.[60] This variety of responses gives the poem a layered effect, where surface and depth play against each other, and the difficulty of sorting through the possible readings clearly becomes another part of the poem's appeal.

Most interpretations focus on the differences between the speech of the cuckoo and the nightingale (in effect, their respective cries), and this is in fact what the two birds themselves focus on. As the cuckoo's "trewe and pleyn" singing (line 118) squares off against the nightingale's "nyse, queynt crie" (line 123), the cuckoo establishes the terms of the debate by claiming that his own language is unambiguous, while the nightingale's words are incomprehensible. In his complaint the cuckoo specifically targets the nightingale's cry "Ocy! Ocy!" (line 124), for which he demands an explanation. The nightingale says that the cry means that whoever is against love will be killed, revealing that the word "ocy" is the imperative form of the Old French verb *occier*, "to kill." This set of exchanges lies at the heart of the debate between the two birds and marks the heat of the tension.[61]

---

[56] Rutherford suggests that it is not the birds' traditional associations that give the poem meaning but "the rhetoric of the contestants and the debate structure" (p. 357). He reads the cuckoo as "rational" and "cynical," and the nightingale as "emotionally committed," suggesting that the tension between reason and the irrationality of love is the central, driving force behind their argument (p. 358). Interestingly, Rutherford does not draw an explicit connection between gender and these qualities (i.e., masculine reason and feminine emotionality).

[57] Chamberlain argues that the cuckoo is a figure of Christ while the nightingale is Cupid's corrupt, willful messenger.

[58] For discussion of the cuckoo's "pleyn" singing (i.e., plain-song or monophonic music [line 118]) and the nightingale's ability to "breke" the song in her "throte" (i.e., polyphonic music [lines 119–20]), see Walter W. Skeat (1897), p. 527n118; Scattergood (1975), p. 83n118–20; and Conlee, p. 257n113–20.

[59] See Patterson, 1992a.

[60] See Kirsten Johnson Otey.

[61] The suggestion that "ocy" is the imperative of *occier* has been noted by a number of critics; see, e.g., Scattergood (1975), p. 84. Arguing that Clanvowe associates the God of Love with the Church in the poem, Otey suggests the nightingale may in fact be speaking Latin rather than French on the grounds that the word might be interpreted as "the medieval Latin prefix 'occi' . . . related to the French and likewise meaning to strike down or kill" (p. 143). Patterson reads the cuckoo's response in part as an interroga-

The opposition between transparent and ornate speech suggests a concern over the clarity of language common to medieval poetry. But more than the traditional medieval preoccupation with ambiguity, the poem's concerns would seem to reveal a specific interest in the status or potential of English as a literary language. That is, the poem engages in a debate over the validity of the vernacular that ultimately will help expand the playing field of poetic delight that Spenser so generously imagines. The French root of the nightingale's cry turns the confrontation into one beween "queynt" French and "pleyn" English, where the cuckoo's "trewe and pleyn" song that may be understood by "every wight" (lines 118, 121) suggests its affiliation with the vernacular. English (accessible to everyone), opposes the nightingale's elusive song (courtly/aristocratic French), which the cuckoo implicitly condemns with his references to ornate embellishment: "my songe is bothe trewe and pleyn, / Althogh I cannot breke hit so in veyne / As thou dost in thy throte, I wote ner how" (lines 118–20). Here, the cuckoo lauds his own song as the unvarnished truth, claiming that he lacks the skill to give his melody the kind of pointless frills that the nightingale generates "in veyne."

Although typically the vernacular is gendered female (the "mother tongue"), the fact that the nightingale is female and the cuckoo male (as is clear from the pronouns used for each) suggests a new alignment of English as masculine and French as feminine. The cuckoo's characterization of the nightingale's cry as a "queynt lawe" that invokes the dire conundrum "eyther shal I love or elles be slawe" (lines 136–37) emphasizes both the ornate qualities of the cry and the hidden violence inherent in the God of Love's code. At worst, you die; at best, if you *do* listen to the nightingale's "queynt crie," the cuckoo seems to suggest, you may end up seduced by her "queynt lawe," a "papyngay" (line 222) like the narrator, good only for rote entertainment at court.[62] The cuckoo refuses both these possibilities, saying, "For myn entent is neyther for to dye, / Ne while I lyve in Loves yoke to drawe" (lines 139–40). The nightingale's answer equates the naturally "gentil" ("noble," line 150) with those who want to enter Love's service, while she condemns the cuckoo for having a "cherles hert" (line 147). Here the nightingale uses the word "churl" as a term of contempt, dismissing the cuckoo not merely as commoner without rank, but more specifically as a scoundrelly fellow who lacks the requisite "gentility" to serve Love. The poem thus sets up an opposition between English, coded as

---

tion of "the social practices of the court," which included the misleading use of language and singing in French (1992a, p. 23). He argues that the cuckoo's complaint about the nightingale's cry is one that "reflects contemporary discussion about the politics of language," pointing to "the elitist dialect of the nightingale, a discourse that requires an armature of special knowledge and specific ideological commitments to be understood: 'ocy' is not only the traditional literary representation of the nightingale's song, and is not only in French, but encapsulates in a single word the absolutist ideology that is at the center of courtliness" (p. 23).

[62] For a fuller discussion of the possible implications of this insult, see explanatory note to line 222.

unadorned, true, reasonable, accessible to everyone, even "manly," and French, which is aristocratic, feminized, ornate, excessively emotional, violent, and veiled or secretive.

This encounter between English and French, as embodied in the cuckoo and the nightingale, perhaps expresses a concern about what it means to be writing in the common (non-aristocratic) language of the people. At this moment, just as English was emerging as a full-blown literary language, many practitioners — Chaucer among them — expressed discomfort with writing in English, since it was primarily a spoken language. Latin and French were the languages of privilege — of ecclesiastical, literary, legal, and courtly discourse. Preoccupied with the lack of writing conventions in English, scribes and/or authors of early texts, such as Orm's *Ormulum* and the texts in the AB dialect (the *Ancrene Wisse* and the Katherine Group texts), had made concerted efforts to create consistent dialect and spelling conventions of their own.[63] Although Chaucer, Clanvowe, and their immediate contemporaries formed part of a literary movement that was self-conscious and ambitious in unprecedented ways, nonetheless they shared these concerns about the propriety of using English instead of Latin or French in the absence of an English literary tradition, and this formed a central theme of their writing.

At the same time as it raises issues such as the appropriate use of the vernacular, the poem can also be read as a participant in a rich tradition of similar poetry preoccupied with courtly love. More particularly, I want to suggest that *The Boke of Cupide* may be a response, not just to Chaucer's *Parliament of Fowls* and The Knight's Tale, but also to his *Legend of Good Women*.[64] Although V. J. Scattergood argues that it is unclear whether or not Chaucer's *Legend*

---

[63] See Thomas Hahn's discussion of Orm's *Ormulum* ("Early Middle English," pp. 85–87). Hahn explains that Orm "developed a quasi-phonetic system of spelling conventions that, in their attempt to enable literacy to reproduce spoken English, demonstrate an ethnographic accuracy that modern linguists have frequently admired," adding that his "desperation in concocting this orthographical extravaganza suggests how keenly he felt the absence of writing traditions in English" (pp. 86, 87). The phrase "AB language" comes from J. R. R. Tolkien's attempt to characterize the linguistic and orthographic uniformity of a group of texts from two different manuscripts copied by different scribes (see "*Ancrene Wisse* and *Hali Meidhad*," *Essays and Studies* 14 [1928], 104–26). In the introduction to his edition of the *Ancrene Wisse*, Robert Hasenfratz notes that "[w]hat is remarkable about the AB language is not so much that it represents a distinctive regional dialect, but the fact that it is really a kind of standard *written* language . . . and such a standard implies a common literate community" (p. 21; italics in original).

[64] Certainly the date is right. Peck's discussions of the daisy poetic and spring's relationship to imagination in Chaucer's poetry could equally apply to Clanvowe's poem. See Russell A. Peck, "Chaucer and the Imagination," *Studies in the Age of Chaucer* Proceedings 2 (1986), 33–48 (keynote address to the New Chaucer Society), and "Chaucerian Poetics and the Prologue to the *Legend of Good Women*," in *Chaucer in the Eighties*, ed. Julian N. Wasserman and Robert J. Blanch (Syracuse: Syracuse University Press, 1986), pp. 39–55.

provided inspiration for *The Boke of Cupide*,[65] nevertheless, the nightingale's declaration that "he that truly Loves servaunt ys, / Wer lother to be schamed then to dye" (lines 159–60) seems to take up the theme of Chaucer's poem, which suggests the irrationality of such a claim through its dark stories of women who do actually die for their fidelity in love. *The Boke of Cupide*'s dream-setting in the field of daisies, similar to that of the Prologue to the *Legend*, would seem to affirm such a reading, but, since the daisy cult was also popular among French writers who may also have influenced Clanvowe, it is not easy to make such an explicit connection. More suggestive is the accusation the God of Love makes to the narrator in the Prologue to the *Legend*. The God of Love calls the narrator his "foo" (F.322) and explains that this is because

> . . . of myn olde servauntes thow mysseyest,
> And hynderest hem with thy translacioun,
> And lettest folk from hire devocioun
> To serve me, and holdest it folye
> To serve Love. Thou maist yt nat denye,
> For in pleyn text, withouten nede of glose,
> Thou hast translated the Romaunce of the Rose,
> That is an heresye ayeins my lawe,
> And makest wise folk fro me withdrawe. (F.323–31)

Although ostensibly the "heresye ayeins my lawe" refers to the poem *The Romance of the Rose* itself, another possible reading of the line suggests that the "heresye" here is really the translation of what should be hidden into "pleyn text, withouten nede of glose" (in other words exposing the truth about Love by writing about it in English rather than French). This is further suggested by the fact that it is explicitly the narrator's "translacioun" that "hynderest" Love's "olde servauntes," rather than the French poem. If the truth about Love is that "he can make of wise folke ful nyse," as the narrator of *The Boke of Cupide* puts it (line 13), then knowing that may indeed have the effect of "mak[ing] wise folk fro [Love] withdrawe." And if Love's "lawe" is anything like the nightingale's explanation of the meaning of her cry — "That eyther shal I love or elles be slawe," in the cuckoo's "plain" paraphrase (line 137) — telling such an unvarnished truth might indeed drive Love's servants away. These resonances between the particular details of the Prologue to the *Legend* and the concerns of Clanvowe's poem suggest that *The Boke of Cupide* may have taken its inspiration from the issues raised in Chaucer's Prologue.[66]

---

[65] Scattergood (1975), p. 12.

[66] The title given to the *Legend* in the Introduction to The Man of Law's Tale, "The Seintes Legende of Cupide" (*CT* II[B¹]61) is also suggestive, especially given the likelihood that the Introduction to The

Introduction to The Boke of Cupide, God of Love

As in *The Owl and the Nightingale*, the various readings of Clanvowe's poem hinge on a particular interpretation of the birds and their perceived affiliation with a certain type of speech or language. In the case of *The Boke of Cupide*, the lighthearted presentation, brisk pace, lively dialogue, and sly humor would seem geared to deflect serious readings of the poem, but the way in which critical responses persist in attempting to decipher the "meaning" of the two figures illustrates one of the primary pleasures of Clanvowe's poem, that of dense and layered analysis. Like Chaucer's Wife of Bath, the two figures of the cuckoo and the nightingale give the impression of "real" speakers producing "natural" dialogue in their spirited repartee[67] but turn out upon closer examination to invoke a host of literary allusions and invite a variety of complicated, often conflicting readings. The poem itself resembles the debate between its two principals in that its brevity and seeming simplicity mask a complicated array of ambiguous possibilities that lends itself to perpetual interpretation. Kirsten Johnson Otey argues that *The Boke of Cupide* "poses as a courtly love poem" but is really "ask[ing] provocative questions about dissident theological and ecclesiastical opinions."[68] Certainly these antitheses do not have to be mutually exclusive. In some ways what makes Clanvowe's poem resonate so well with Chaucer's works is its capacity to uphold a number of readings simultaneously, which is clearly one of the pleasures of such highly literary writing. Of course, this ambiguity is not limited to Chaucer's work, as debate poems such as the aforementioned *Owl and the Nightingale*, or courtly poetry like *Sir Gawain and the Green Knight*, equally able to sustain a variety of possible readings, illustrate.[69] In Clanvowe's case, it is the combination of allusion and the

---

Man of Law's Tale reflects an early stage in the planning of *The Canterbury Tales*, when the Man of Law was to tell a tale "in prose" (possibly *Melibee*), *CT* II(B¹)96. That is, it is quite possible that Chaucer's *Legend* was known under this title c. 1386–87 when Clanvowe was writing.

[67] This is in contrast to, for example, the somewhat stilted and formulaic presentation of the lady and lover in *La Belle Dame sans Mercy* (see the Introduction to that poem, below).

[68] Otey, p. 108. Otey argues that the poem expresses concerns similar to those of the Lollards with whom Clanvowe sympathized, suggesting that the God of Love is aligned with the Church, while the cuckoo "is associated with Christ . . . creating an opposition between Christ and Church which is counterintuitive but which is at the heart of Lollard doctrine" (p. 111). She concludes that the poem uses "the genre of courtly love poetry to raise controversial religious and linguistic issues" and "subverts the genre to produce an underlying text that addresses the religious culture of the day" (p. 149; for her full argument, see pp. 104–49). Justice argues that "there is nothing obviously religious" about *The Boke of Cupide*, and sees its ties to Lollardy as "more a cultural than a theological matter," with the nightingale enjoying the comfortable ease condemned by the plain-speaking cuckoo, who is in turn scorned for being a churl (p. 671).

[69] One is reminded of Duns Scotus' practice in suppositional logic of laying out a proposition, then providing three or four contrary proofs. For example, in "Concerning Human Knowledge" (V), Scotus asks whether it is possible to know truth in this life without the help of God. He then lays out four points

dual-voicing of the narrative — at once lighthearted and slyly critical — that makes the model of Chaucer resonate so well.[70]

What the poem finally achieves is the very Chaucerian effect of tensions held in suspended animation. Clanvowe, after the manner of Chaucer, invites us to side with the cuckoo's advocation of "trewe and pleyn" against the "queynt" and perhaps deadly cry of the nightingale and her "papyngay," only to trick us in the end, as the cuckoo in his "plain" way continually "glosses" the nightingale, offering interpretations of her claims and supposedly telling the truth about the God of Love; all the while the literary contest invites us as readers to strive in turn to change the "trewe and pleyn" poem into a "queynt crie" of our own, obsessively spinning more and more complicated readings out of what seems superficially a straightforward debate. Literary writing in English, it seems, is no less "queynt" than the French it claims to best. The multiplicity of possible readings and the way in which the characters and their debate encourage speculation about meaning without ever offering a satisfactory resolution suggest that Clanvowe's joke is on his readers, who insist on taking him seriously despite his invitation to play. It is a "sentence-and-solaas" joke truly worthy of Chaucer himself, one an audience that has developed a taste for such literary play would be sure to appreciate. The allusions to Chaucer's work and the recycling of Chaucerian themes and phrases make *The Boke of Cupide* even more wittily delightful for initiated readers of Chaucer. Nevertheless, the clear connections to earlier Middle English bird debates, in particular *The Owl and the Nightingale*, as well as to French poetry, show Clanvowe not simply as an imitator but also as a maker who stamps his own mark on the Chaucerian verse he creates.

---

in favor and one against before going into a protracted discussion of all the possibilities. In "The Spirituality and Immortality of the Human Soul" (VI), Scotus poses the question "Can it be known by natural reason that there will be a general resurrection of mankind" (p. 143) and offers three arguments for and three against the proposition, followed by detailed dissection of all the possible readings of each point. See John Duns Scotus, *Philosophical Writings: A Selection*, ed. and trans. Allan Wolter, O. F. M. (Edinburgh: Thomas Nelson and Sons, 1962; rpt. Indianapolis: Bobbs-Merrill Co., 1964).

[70] Patterson, who sees the opposition as one not between French and English per se, but rather between courtly language and "truth-telling" (1992a, pp. 19 ff.), argues that "the court cannot be spoken to in any language but its own, a language able to accommodate and neutralize all criticism," which means that "[t]o speak 'trewe and pleyne' is finally impossible: within the court all discourse becomes nuanced, multivalent, facile," and thus *The Boke of Cupide* cannot help but be a courtier's frippery" (p. 26). Patterson's view is that the exclusion of the cuckoo from the courtly discourse shared by the nightingale and the narrator at the end of the poem is less significant "than the way in which [the cuckoo] is gradually absorbed into court discourse," so that he "no longer poses a threat to courtly social practices" (pp. 24, 25).

Note on the text

The Boke of Cupide appears in the five manuscripts discussed above and listed in detail below.[71] The poem is also incorporated in several early printed editions of Chaucer, those by William Thynne, John Stow, and Thomas Speght. Skeat classifies the extant texts into two groups: *A*, comprising the Findern manuscript, Tanner 346, and Thynne; and *B*, made up of Fairfax 16 and Bodley 638, with Arch. Selden. B. 24 apparently as a third group, "which has readings of its own."[72] Skeat regarded *A* as the superior set of manuscripts, adding that "MS. Ff. is, in some respects, the most important," giving no explanation for either assumption.[73] Scattergood groups the manuscripts similarly, but includes Arch. Selden. B. 24 with the others in Skeat's group *A*, noting that, though "they have in common 17 errors," the high number of unique errors in each text shows that correspondences between the four versions in this group are not as close as those between the Fairfax 16 and Bodley 638 copies, "which share more than 30 common errors" but have relatively few unique errors.[74] According to Scattergood's calculations, the Fairfax 16 and Bodley 638 versions are closely related, and "[i]t may be that they derive from a common exemplar; but neither can have been copied from the other."[75]

This edition of the poem is based on the text in Fairfax 16,[76] with emendations and some alternate readings from the other manuscripts recorded in the textual notes, according to the practices laid out in the General Introduction. I have taken the horizontal stroke above words such as *brēne* (line 105) to be an abbreviation for a nasal consonant (*n*/*m*) and have expanded accordingly. Other strokes and flourishes are disregarded as otiose. Fairfax 16 is probably the earliest of the manuscripts, though Tanner 346 may be contemporary or only slightly later; the Tanner 346 copy, however, contains a number of errors, including missing and transposed lines, a problem that Thynne's edition shares.[77] Bodley 638 is somewhat later (third quarter of

---

[71] For a more thorough description of the manuscripts and a discussion of their relationships to one another, see Scattergood (1975), pp. 14–16.

[72] Skeat (1897), p. lvii.

[73] Skeat (1897), p. lvii.

[74] Scattergood (1975), p. 16.

[75] Scattergood (1975), p. 16.

[76] Norton-Smith (1979) gives a detailed description of the manuscript in the facsimile volume.

[77] Robert Costomiris argues that Thynne probably based his edition on Tanner 346. See also Scattergood's descriptions of the two (1975), pp. 15, 16. Despite these problems, Conlee based his text on Tanner 346, as did Frederick Startridge Ellis. Scattergood used Fairfax 16, as did Erich Vollmer, while Skeat (1897) used Thynne's 1532 text as the basis for his edition. Thomas J. Garbáty does not specify which manuscript he uses, but his text is probably also based on Thynne (see Francis Lee Utley, who notes that "Thynne's 1532 edition forms the base for most editions subsequent to Skeat" [p. 883]).

the fifteenth century),[78] and would also be a good choice. Arch. Selden. B. 24 is from the late fifteenth or early sixteenth century and contains an incomplete copy.[79] The Findern manuscript, a largely amateur production, is also among the latest of the extant witnesses.[80]

Indexed in

IMEV 3361.

Manuscripts

Oxford, Bodleian Library MS Fairfax 16 (*SC* 3896), fols. 35v–39v (c. 1430–50). [Base text for this edition.]

Oxford, Bodleian Library MS Tanner 346 (*SC* 10173), fols. 97r–101r (mid- to late fifteenth century). [Adds four stanzas (balade with envoy).]

Oxford, Bodleian Library MS Bodley 638 (*SC* 2078), fols. 11v–16r (late fifteenth century).

Cambridge University Library MS Ff.1.6. (Findern MS), fols. 22r–28r (c. 1500). [Adds two seven-line stanzas after the *Explicit*.]

Oxford, Bodleian Library MS Arch. Selden. B. 24 (*SC* 3354), fols. 138v–141v (late fifteenth or early sixteenth century). [Lines 1–246 only.]

Early printed editions

Thynne, William, ed. *The Workes of Geffray Chaucer Newly Printed: With Dyuers Workes Whiche Were Neuer in Print Before*. London: T. Godfray, 1532. [STC 5068. Rpt. 1542, STC 5069; ?1550, STC 5071. Adds balade with envoy. Based on Tanner 346.][81]

---

[78] The date is Utley's estimate (see the manuscript descriptions in his bibliography section, p. 883).

[79] For discussion of the date, see the facsimile volume, intro. Boffey and Edwards (1997), pp. 3–4.

[80] See the introduction to the facsimile volume, Beadle and Owen, p. xi.

[81] Costomiris makes a convincing case for Thynne's use of Tanner 346.

Stow, John, ed. *The Workes of Geffrey Chaucer: Newly Printed, With Diuers Addicions, Whiche were Neuer in Printe Before: With the Siege and Destruccion of the Worthy Citee of Thebes, Compiled by Jhon Lidgate.* London: J. Wight, 1561. [STC 5075. Based on Thynne.]

Speght, Thomas, ed. *The Workes of our Antient and Lerned English Poet, Geffrey Chavcer, newly Printed.* London: G. Bishop, 1598. [STC 5077. Rpt. 1602, STC 5080; 1687. Based on Thynne.]

The Boke of Cupide, God of Love, or
The Cuckoo and the Nightingale

	The God of Love, a benedicité!	*ah bless you*
	How myghty and how grete a lorde is he!	
	For he can make of low hertys hie,	*hearts high [ones]*
	And high hertis low and like for to die,	
5	And herde hertis he can make fre.	*stingy; generous*
	And he can make, within a lytel stounde,	
	Of seke folke ful fresh, hool, and sounde,[1]	
	And of hoole he can make seke;	*healthy [people]; sick (i.e., lovesick)*
	He can bynde and unbynde eke,	*bind; unbind also*
10	What he wole have bounde and unbounde.	*will*
	To telle his myght my wit may not suffice,	
	For he may do al that he can devyse;	*conceive*
	For he can make of wise folke ful nyse,	*people very foolish [ones]*
	And in lyther folke dystroye vise,	*wicked people destroy vice*
15	And proude hertys he can make agryse.	*frightened*
	Shortely, al that evere he wol he may:	*In short; will (wishes); can*
	Agenst him ther dar no wight sey nay,	*Against; no person dares to say no (i.e., refuse)*
	For he can glade and greve whom him lyketh,	
	And who that he wol, don him laugh or siketh,[2]	
20	And most his myght he sheweth ever in May.	*shows always*
	For every trew, gentil hert fre	*true (faithful), courteous, noble heart*
	That with him is, or thinketh to be,	*plans to be [with him]*

---

[1] Lines 6–7: *And he can make, within a short while, / Of sick (i.e., lovesick) people completely vigorous, whole, and sound [ones] (i.e., he can assuage the sorrow of lovesick people)*

[2] Lines 18–19: *For he can gladden and grieve (make sorrowful) whomever it pleases him to, / And whomever he wishes, [he can] make laugh or sigh [with lovesickness]*

	Agens May now shal have somme steryng,	*Toward; inclination*
	Other to joy, or elles to morenynge,	*Either; else to mourning*
25	In no seson so grette, as thynkes me.	*it seems to me*
	For when they mow her the briddes sing,	*may hear the birds*
	And see the floures and the leves spring,	*flowers; leaves spring [forth]*
	That bringes into hertis remembraunce	*hearts' store of memories*
	A maner ease, medled with grevaunce	*kind [of] comfort; tempered with misery*
30	And lusty thoghtes ful of grete longynge.	*joyful*
	And of that longynge cometh hevynesse,	*sorrow*
	And therof groues oft grete seknesse,	*from that results; sickness (i.e., lovesickness)*
	And for lak of that that they desyre;	*lack; desire*
	And thus in May ben hertys set on fire,	*are hearts*
35	And so they brenne forthe in grete distresse.	*are continuously inflamed*
	I speke this of felyng, truly,	*say; [because] of feeling*
	For althogh I be olde and unlusty,	*feeble*
	Yet have I felt of that sekenes in May,	
	Bothe hote and colde, an accesse every day,	*a fever (lovesickness)*
40	How sore, ywis, ther wot no wight but I.	*painful, certainly, no one knows*
	I am so slayn with the feveres white,	*stricken; pallid fevers (a stage of lovesickness)*
	Of al this May yet slept I but a lyte;	*little*
	And also hit is unlyke for to be	*it; unlikely to be [the case]*
	That eny hert shulde slepy be,	*any heart should be lethargic*
45	In whom that Love his firy dart wol smyte.	*which; wishes to thrust*
	But as I lay this other nyght wakyng,	*awake*
	I thoght how lovers had a tokenyng,	*saying*
	And among hem hit was a comune tale,	*them; common saying*
	That hit wer good to her the nyghtyngale	*would be; hear*
50	Rather then the leude cukkow syng.	*than the ill-mannered (crude)*
	And then I thoght anon as hit was day,	*as soon as*
	I wolde goo somme whedir for to assay	*would go somewhere to try*
	Yf that I myght a nyghtyngale here;	*If; hear*
	For yet I non had herd of al this yere,	*so far this year I had heard none*
55	And hit was the thirde nyght of May.	

	And anon as I the day espied,	
	No lenger wolde I in my bed abyde;	*longer did I want; stay (abide)*
	But into a wode that was fast by,	*wood; close at hand*
	I went forthe allone prively,	*alone secretly*
60	And helde my way don on a broke syde.	*traveled down along the bank of a brook*

	Til I come into a launde of white and grene,	*came; clearing*
	So feire oon had I nevere in bene.	*I had never been in so fair [a] one*
	The grounde was grene, poudred with dayse,	*sprinkled; daisies*
	The floures and the gras al ilike hie,	*flowers; grass; equally high*
65	Al grene and white — was nothing elles sene.	*else seen*

	Ther sat I doune amonge the feire floures	*flowers*
	And sawe the briddes crepe out of her boures,	*birds creep; their bowers*
	Ther as they had rested hem al nyght.	*Where; themselves*
	They were so joyful of the dayes lyght,	*day's*
70	That they began of May to don ther houres.	*sing their [canonical] hours (i.e., prime)*

	They coude that servise alle bye rote.	*knew; Divine Office; by*
	Ther was mony a lovely note:	*many; bird song*
	Somme songe loude, as they had pleyned,[1]	
	And somme in other maner voys yfeyned,	*another kind [of] voice sang softly*
75	And somme al out, with a lowde throte.	*loud voice*

	They pruned hem, and made hem ryght gay,	*preened themselves; merry*
	And daunseden, and lepten on the spray,	*pranced; skipped; branch*
	And evermore two and two in fere,	*together*
	Ryght so as they had chosen hem to yere	*Exactly as; this year*
80	In Marche, upoun Seynt Valentynes day.	

	And the ryver that I sat upon,	*river [bank]*
	Hit made suche a noyse as hit ronne,	*noise; ran*
	Acordaunt to the foules ermonye.	*In accordance with; birds' harmonious singing*
	Me thoght hit was the best melodye	*It seemed to me it*
85	That myght be herd of eny man.	

---

[1] *Some sang loudly, as if they were complaining*

	And for delyte — I note ner how —	*delight; do not at all know how*
	I fel in such a slombre and a swowe —	*fell; doze; state of sleep*
	Not al on slepe, ne fully wakyng —	*completely asleep, nor fully awake*
	And in that swowe me thoght I herde singe	
90	That sory bridde, the lewde cukkowe,	*sorry bird; ill-mannered (crude)*

	And that was on a tre right fast bye;	*tree*
	But who was then evel apayed but I!	*displeased/dissatisfied*
	"Now God," quod I, "that died upoun the Croise,	*Cross*
	Give sorowe on thee, and on thy foule voyse,	*Heap trouble; foul voice*
95	For lytel joy have I now of thy crie."	*little*

	And as I with the cukkow gan chide,	*began [to] rail against the cuckoo*
	I herde, in the next busshe me beside,	
	A nyghtyngale so lustely singe,	*joyfully (vigorously)*
	That with her clere voys she made rynge	*magnificent (pure) song; reverberate*
100	Thro-out al the grene wode wide.	*From one side to the other; leafy wood*

	"A, good nyghtyngale," quod I then,	*said*
	"A lytell hast thou be to longe hen,	*You have been away a little too long*
	For her hath be the lewde cukkow,	*here has been*
	And songen songes rather then thou.	*sung songs instead of you*
105	I prey to God that evel fire him brenne."	*pray; deadly; burn*

	But now I wil yow tel a wonder thinge:	*will tell you an amazing thing*
	As longe as I lay in that swonynge,	*swoon*
	Me thoght I wist al that the briddes ment,	*I understood (knew); birds*
	And what they seyde, and what was her entent,	*their meaning (intent)*
110	And of her speche I had good knouynge.	*their speech; understanding*

	And then herd I the nyghtyngale sey,	
	"Now, good cukkow, go sommewhere thy wey,	*some place*
	And let us that can syng duel here;	*[those of] us who; stay*
	For every wight escheweth thee to here;	*person avoids hearing you*
115	Thy songes be so elynge, in gode fey."	*songs are so tedious (ailing), truly*

	"What?" quoth he, "What may thee eyle now?	*said; ail*
	Hit thynkes me I syng as wel as thow;	*It seems to me; you (thou)*
	For my songe is bothe trewe and pleyn,	*honest (true); unembellished (plainsong)*

The Boke of Cupide, God of Love

| | Althogh I cannot breke hit so in veyne | *trill (modulate) it (i.e., the song); frivolously* |
| 120 | As thou dost in thy throte, I wote ner how. | *I do not at all know how* |

	"And every wight may understond me,	*person can*
	But, nyghtyngale, so may they not thee,	
	For thou hast mony a nyse, queynt crie.	*strange (foolish), peculiar (deceptive)*
	I have herd thee seye 'Ocy! Ocy!'	*Ocy! Ocy! (i.e., the song of the nightingale)*
125	Who myght wete what that shuld be?"	*know*

	"O fole," quoth she, "wost thou not what that is?	*fool; know*
	When that I sey 'Ocy! Ocy!' iwisse,	*indeed*
	Then mene I that I wolde wonder fayne	*I mean; I very eagerly wish*
	That al tho wer shamefully slayne,	*all [of] them were ignominiously slain*
130	That menen oght agen Love amys.	*Who intend anything wicked against Love*

	"And also I wold al tho were dede,	*wish all those; dead*
	That thenk not her lyve in love to lede,	*plan not their lives; lead*
	For who that wol the God of Love not serve,	*will*
	I dar wel say he is worthy for to sterve;	*die*
135	And for that skille 'Ocy! Ocy!' I crede."	*reason; cry*

	"Ey!" quoth the cukkow, "ywis, this is a queynt lawe,	*certainly; peculiar*
	That eyther shal I love or elles be slawe.	*either; else be killed*
	But I forsake al suche companye,	
	For myn entent is neyther for to dye,	*neither to die*
140	Ne while I lyve in Loves yoke to drawe.	*Nor; Love's*

	"For lovers be the folke that lyven on lyve,	
	That most disese han, and most unthrive,[1]	
	And most enduren sorowe, wo, and care,	
	And, at the last, failen of her welfaire.	*finally, fail to secure their success*
145	What nedith hit agens trweth to strive?"[2]	

---

[1] Lines 141–42: *For lovers are the people [of all] who are alive, / Who suffer most (have most suffering), and are most unfortunate (unsuccessful)*

[2] *What is the point of striving against truth (i.e., of not acknowledging the truth)*

"What?" quoth she, "Thou art out of thy mynde!   *mind*
How maist thou in thy cherles hert fynde *can; find [it] in your churl's (mean) heart*
To speke of Loves servauntes in this wyse?   *Love's servants; way*
For in this worlde is noon so good servise   *[there] is no service so good*
150 To every wight that gentil ys of kynde.   *is noble by nature*

"For therof truly cometh al goodnesse,
Al honour, and al gentilnesse,   *nobility*
Worship, ese, and al hertys lust, *Worthiness; comfort (gratification); heart's desire*
Perfyt joy and ful ensured trust,   *Perfect; fully assured*
155 Jolité, plesaunce, and freshenesse,   *Gaiety; delight; cheerfulness*

"Louelyhed and trew companye,   *Humility; faithful companionship*
Semelyhed, largenesse, and curtesie,   *Graciousness, generosity; courtesy*
Drede of shame and for to don amys;   *Fear; of doing wrong (amiss)*
For he that truly Loves servaunt ys,   *Love's; is*
160 Wer lother to be schamed then to dye. *Were more reluctant (loath); disgraced than*

"And that ys sothe, al that I sey;   *is [the] truth; say*
In that beleve I wil bothe lyve and dye,   *belief*
And, cukkow, so rede I thee, that thou do, iwis." *I advise you; certainly*
"Ye then," quoth he, "God let me never have blis, *Yea; bliss*
165 If evere I to thy counseyl obey.

"Nyghtyngale, thou spekest wonder faire,   *very eloquently*
But, for al that, the sothe is the contreyre.   *truth; contrary*
For loving in yong folke is but rage,   *young people; rashness*
And in olde hit is a grete dotage;   *[the] old; folly (madness)*
170 Who most hit useth, most he shal apeyre. *engage in it; be injured*

"For therof cometh disese and hevynesse,   *misfortune (sorrow)*
Sorow and care and mony a seknesse,   *sickness*
Dispite, debate, angre, and envye,   *Spite (Resentment)*
Repreve and shame, untrust and jelosye,   *Disgrace; distrust*
175 Pride and myschefe, povert and wodenesse. *wickedness, poverty; madness*

"What? Lovyng is an office of dispaire,   *a task*
And oon thing is therin that ys not faire;
For who that geteth of love a lytil blysse,   *gets (begets)*

| | But he be alway ther by, ywysse, | *Unless he is always by it (i.e., paying attention to it)* |
| 180 | He may ful sone of age have his eire. | *right away have his heir come of age* |

	"And therfor, nyghtyngale, holde thee nye,	*stay nearby*
	For leve me wel: for al thy loude crie,	*believe; despite*
	Yf thou fer or long be fro thi make,	*If; from; mate*
	Thou shalt be as other that be forsake,	*are forsaken*
185	And then shalt thou hoten as do I."[1]	

	"Fye," quoth she, "on thi name and on thee!	
	The God of Love let thee nevere ythe!	*let you never prosper*
	For thou art wors a thousand folde then wode,	*worse; crazy*
	For mony is ful worthie and ful good,	*many*
190	That had be noght ne had Love ybe.[2]	

	"For Love his servant evermore amendeth,	*Love always improves/corrects his servant*
	And fro al tachches him defendeth,	*vices/faults protects him*
	And maketh him to brenne as eny fire,	
	In trouthe and in worschipful desire,	*fidelity; honorable (virtuous)*
195	And whom him likes, joy ynogh him sendeth."[3]	

	"Ye, nyghtyngale," he seyde, "holde thee stille!	
	For Love hath no reson but his wille;	*reason; will*
	For ofte sithe untrew folke he esith,	*frequently; unfaithful; pleases*
	And trew folke so bittirly displesith,	*faithful; cruelly*
200	That for defaute of grace hee let hem spille.	*lack; he lets them (causes them to) die*

	"With suche a lorde wolde I never be,	
	For he is blynde and may not se.	*see*
	And when he lyeth he not, ne when he fayleth;	*lies; does not know, nor; misses*
	In this court ful selde trouthe avayleth,	*very seldom does being in the right do any good*
205	So dyverse and so wilful ys he."	

---

[1] *And then will you be called by the same name as I am (i.e., a cuckold)*

[2] *That would have been nothing [if] Love had not existed*

[3] *And sends plenty of (enough) joy to whomever he likes (lit., to whom it pleases him)*

Then toke I of the nyghtyngale kepe.   *took; heed*
She kest a sighe out of her hert depe,   *heaved; heart deep*
And seyde, "Alas, that ever I was bore!   *born*
I can for tene sey not oon worde more."   *sorrow say*
210   And ryght with that she brast on for to wepe.   *burst into tears*

"Alas!" quoth she, "my hert wol tobreke,   *heart will shatter*
To her thus this fals birdde to speke   *hear; bird*
Of Love, and of his worshipful servyse.   *honorable service*
Now, God of Love, thou helpe me in summe wise,   *in some way*
215   That I may on this cukkow ben awreke."   *get revenge*

Me thoght then that I stert out anone,   *arose from sleeping right away*
And to the broke I ran and gatte a stone,   *brook; got*
And at the cukkow hertly I cast,   *vigorously*
And he for drede flyed awey ful fast,   *flew*
220   And glad was I when that he was gone.

And evermore the cukkow as he fley,   *flew*
He seyde, "Farewel, farewel, papyngay,"   *parrot*
As thogh he had scorned, thoght me.   *mocked [us]*
But ay I hunted him fro tre to tre,   *I kept hunting; tree to tree*
225   Till he was fer al out of syght away.

And then come the nyghtyngale to me   *came*
And seyde, "Frende, forsoth I thanke thee,   *Friend, truly*
That thou hast lyked me thus to rescowe,   *chosen thus to rescue me*
And oon avowe to Love I avowe,   *vow; make*
230   That al this May I wol thy singer be."

I thanked her, and was ryght wel apayed.   *pleased*
"Yee," quoth she, "and be thou non amayed,   *not at all afraid*
Thogh thou have herde the cukkow er then me,   *earlier than*
For, if I lyve, hit shal amended be
235   The next May, yf I be not affrayed.   *if; alarmed (afraid)*

And oon thing I wol rede thee also: *will advise*
Ne leve not the cukkow, Loves fo,   *Do not believe; Love's foe*
For al that he hath seyde is strong lesing."   *flagrant lying*

"Nay," quoth I, "ther shal nothing me bring
240   Fro Love, and yet he doth me mekil wo."   *even though; great*

"Yee, use thou," quoth she, "this medecyne: *medicine*
Every day this May er that thou dyne,   *before you dine*
Goo loke upon the fressh flour, the daysye,   *flower; daisy*
And thogh thou be for wo in poynt to dye,   *on the point of dying*
245   That shal ful gretly thee lyssen of thy pyne.   *relieve you of your pain*

And loke alwey that thou be good and trewe,   *see*
And I wol singe oon of thy songes newe.
For love of thee, as loude as I may crie."
And then she began this songe ful hye: *loudly*
250   "I shrewe hem al that be to Love untrewe."   *curse*

And when she had songen hit out to the ende,   *it*
"Now fairewel," quoth she, "for I most wende.   *must go my way*
And God of Love, that can ryght wel, and may,
As mekil joy sende yow this day,   *much*
255   As ever yet he eny lover sende!"   *sent*

Thus toke the nyghtyngal her leve of me.   *took; leave*
I prey to God He alwey with her be,
And joy of love He sende her ever more,
And shilde us fro the cukkow and his lore,   *shield*
260   For ther is non so fals a bridde as he.   *none; bird*

Forthe she fley, the gentil nyghtyngale,   *flew; courteous (noble)*
To al the briddes that were in the vale,   *birds*
And gat hem all into a place yn fere,   *got; together*
And besoght hem that they wolde here   *would hear*
265   Her dysese, and thus began her tale: *suffering*

"Yee knowe wel, hit is not fro yow hidde,   *You; hidden*
How that the cukkow and Y have chidde   *I; argued*
Ever sithe hit was dayes lyght.   *since; daylight*
I prey yow al that ye do me ryght
270   Of that foule, fals, unkynde bridde."   *foul, deceitful, unnatural bird*

Then spake oon brid for al by assent: *bird for all*
"This mater asketh good avysement,   *matter demands; counsel*
For we be fewe briddes her in fere;   *birds here in a flock (together)*
And soth hit ys the cukkow is not here,   *it is true [that]*
275   And therfore we wol have a parlement.   *an assembly*

And therat shal be the egle our lorde,   *eagle*
And other perys that ben of recorde;   *nobles; are officially members of parliament*
And the cukkow shal be after sent,   *sent for afterwards*
And ther shal be geven the jugement,   *given*
280   Or elles we shul make summe acorde.   *else; some settlement*

And this shal be, withouten any nay,   *denial*
The morowe of Seynt Valentynes day,   *morning*
Under the maple that is feire and grene,
Before the chambre wyndow of the quene,   *window of the queen's chamber*
285   At Wodestok, upon the grene lay."   *Woodstock; lawn*

She thanketh hem and then her leve toke,   *leave took*
And fleye into an hawthorn by the broke,   *flew; brook*
And ther she sate and songe upon the tre: *sat; tree*
"Terme of lyve, Love hath withholde me"   *[For the] term of life; retained*
290   So loude that with that songe I awoke.

Explicit liber Cupidinis   *Here ends the book of Cupid*

Explanatory Notes to *The Boke of Cupide, God of Love*

Abbreviations: see Textual Notes.

1–2   These two lines are produced from Chaucer's Knight's Tale (*CT* I[A]1785–86). For details of the many resonances with The Knight's Tale, see Chamberlain and Rutherford, respectively.

3–5   *For he can . . . make fre.* Compare Chaucer's Knight's Tale: "For he kan maken, at his owene gyse, / Of everich herte as that hym list divyse" (*CT* I[A]1789–90). Compare also Gower's *CA*: "he that hihe hertes loweth / With fyri dartes whiche he throweth, / Cupide, which of love is godd" (ed. Peck, 4.1273–75). *For he can make of low hertys hie* (line 3) is proverbial (see Whiting L530).

1–20   Sc notes that such descriptions of "the irresistible power of the god of love" are conventional, citing *RR* (lines 865–906), Froissart's *Cour de may* (lines 699–761), and Machaut's *Dit du vergier* (lines 246–324). Sc adds that "[i]f these lines were derived directly it may have been from *Le Dit du Vergier*, for lines 3, 6–8, 9–10, 11–12, 13, 14, 16–17, 18–19 may all be paralleled there; but all are commonplace" (p. 81n1–20). The idea that "love is master" is proverbial (Whiting L518). See, for example, the opening to Book 1 of Gower's *CA*, where love is characterized as so powerful that "ther is no man / In al this world so wys, that can / Of love tempre the mesure," and "[i]t hath and schal ben everemor / That love is maister wher he wile" (ed. Peck, 1.21–23, 34–35).

9–10   *He can bynde . . . and unbounde.* An allusion to Matthew 16:18–19, the prooftext that defines the pope's powers: "And I say to thee: That thou art Peter; and upon this rock I will build my church, and the gates of hell shall not prevail against it. And I will give to thee the keys of the kingdom of heaven. And whatsoever thou shalt bind upon earth, it shall be bound also in heaven: and whatsoever thou shalt loose on earth, it shall be loosed also in heaven." The God of Love similarly acts as a kind of "pope" over lovers. Also proverbial: "love binds" (Whiting L497). Compare Gower's description of Venus in *CA* as "sche which mai the hertes bynde / In loves cause and ek unbinde" (ed. Peck, 8.2811–12). See Whiting for further citations.

20   *in May*. Springtime is a conventional setting for many medieval narratives, and May in particular is a time of year traditionally associated with lovers and love. See the opening to *RR*, where the narrator dreams that he awakens in May, filled with joy and thinking of love. In Book 1 of Gower's *CA*, Amans tells of "[h]ow love and I togedre mette" (1.85) in May:

> This enderday, as I forthferde   *other day; went forth*
> To walke, as I yow telle may,
> And that was in the monthe of Maii,
> Whan every brid hath chose his make   *bird; mate*
> And thenkth his merthes for to make
> Of love that he hath achieved.   *obtained*
>   (ed. Peck, 1.98–103)

Compare also the opening lines of *QJ* and Lydgate's *CLL*, as well as Chaucer's General Prologue to *CT*. Chamberlain less convincingly connects the recurrence of the word May throughout the poem with Chaucer's Merchant's Tale (pp. 45–46). For discussion of the depiction and significance of the different seasons in medieval art and literature, see Pearsall and Salter's chapter, "The Landscape of the Seasons," pp. 119–60.

26–30   *For when they mow her the briddes sing . . . lusty thoghtes ful of grete longynge.* The sound of the birds singing in *RR* inside the Garden of Diversion (*Déduit*) makes the narrator long to enter the garden (lines 497 ff.). Compare the opening lines of Chaucer's *CT*, where springtime causes restlessness in the birds and "[t]hanne longen folk to goon on pilgrimages" (I[A]12). See also the Prologue to *LGW*: "whan that the month of May / Is comen, and that I here the foules synge, / And that the floures gynnen for to sprynge" (F.36–38; see also G.36–38, which reads similarly).

31–35   *of that longynge . . . grete distresse.* A description of lovesickness, typically accompanied by outward signs of sorrow, including sighing, complaining, and changing of color. Sc (p. 81n30–33) suggests a comparison with Arcite's lovesickness in Chaucer's Knight's Tale (*CT* I[A]1356–79). Compare *CLL*, lines 215–16; *QJ*, lines 95–98; and Roos' *BDSM*, lines 127–28. For a review of lovesickness in the Middle Ages, see Wack, especially pp. 40, 62–66, 101–02, and 135–39. For a discussion of lovesickness in medieval medical discourse, see John Livingston Lowes, "The Loveres Maladye of Heroes," *Modern Philology* 11 (1913–14), 491–546.

37   *althogh I be olde and unlusty.* As Sc notes, both Chaucer, in *Lenvoy de Chaucer a Scogan* (lines 29-36), and Gower (*CA* 8.2403) claim they are too old for love (p. 81n37). Chamberlain argues that, while the first several stanzas appear to establish "the narrator as one who is ironically praising Cupid," the narrator's age and susceptibility to love in the eighth stanza reveal him instead to be "old and nearly impotent" (p. 44).

39   *Bothe hote and colde, an accesse every day.* The narrator describes his suffering from lovesickness as a fever that burns hot and cold by turns. Compare the extended description of the lover's fever in *CLL* (lines 229–45). In Chaucer's *TC* 2.809–11, Criseyde suffers similarly. See also Gower's *CA*, where Amans describes his love-drunkenness: "In cold I brenne and frese in hete" (ed. Macaulay, 6.249). Sc (p. 82n39) points out that this is the "standard terminology for referring to the cotidian fever" mentioned in Trevisa 7.38: "furst þe colde and þeraftir þe hete, and euery day axesse, ȝit wers, for som day comeþ double axesse" (p. 386/20–21).

41   *feveres white.* See *MED, fever*, 3 (a), which explains that "blaunche fever" is "a stage of lovesickness analogous to chills." Gower describes it in *CA* 6.239–46. Compare Pandarus' discussion of lovers' symptoms in *TC*, including "a blaunche fevere" (1.917). *The Riverside Chaucer* adds that this is "a French technical term for a form of lovesickness, characterized by paleness and chills" (p. 1030n916). For further discussion, see David G. Byrd, "Blanche Fever: The Grene Sekeness," *Ball State University Forum* 19.3 (1978), 56–64.

42   *Of al this May yet slept I but a lyte.* Compare the Prologue to Chaucer's *LGW*, where the narrator imagines he might "[d]uellen alwey, the joly month of May, / Withouten slep, withouten mete or drynke" (F.176–77).

43–45   *hit is unlyke for to be . . . his firy dart wol smyte.* The God of Love shooting arrows into the lover is a common trope that stems from classical traditions. In *RR* the God of Love stalks the lover with his bow drawn and shoots him a number of times through the eye into the heart (lines 1679–2008; *Romaunt*, lines 1715–2100). Compare Gower's *CA*, where Amans reports that, in answer to his prayer to Cupid, "[a] firy dart me thoghte he hente / And threw it thurgh myn herte rote" (ed. Peck, 1.144–45; see also 4.1274 and 7.1910). Chaucer uses the image frequently, as in The Knight's Tale, where Arcite complains, "Love hath his firy dart so brennyngly / Ystiked thurgh my trewe, careful herte" (*CT* I[A]1564–65); and in *A Complaint to His Lady*, lines 36–37: "Thus am I slayn with Loves fyry

55

dart! / I can but love hir best, my swete fo." Chamberlain contends that the narrator's susceptibility to Cupid's dart reveals that "[i]nstead of the seemingly wise observer of stanza one, we have an old, shaking, libidinous invalid" (p. 44), whose "derogatory" reading of the cuckoo is not to be trusted (p. 51).

46   *as I lay this other nyght wakyng.* The narrator's sleeplessness is a commonplace of medieval dream visions and love complaints. See, for example, Chaucer's *BD*, where the narrator explains that he has not been able to sleep because of a "sicknesse" he has "suffred this eight yeer" (lines 36–37).

47–50   *lovers had a tokenyng . . . leude cukkow syng.* Proverbial; see Whiting N111. The cuckoo is also characterized as "lewde" in lines 90 and 103 (see explanatory notes to lines 90 and 270).

55   *the thirde nyght of May.* An unlucky day for lovers (see the Introduction to *BC*, p. 24n19). Chamberlain gives a more detailed discussion of May 3 in *The Boke of Cupide* in comparison to Chaucer (p. 46). For more on Chaucer's use of the date, see John P. McCall, "Chaucer's May 3," *Modern Language Notes* 76 (1961), 201–05; and Robert C. Cox and Alfred L. Kellog, "Chaucer's May 3 and Its Contexts," in Kellog, 1972, pp. 155–98.

58–60   *into a wode . . . on a broke syde.* The *locus amoenus* of medieval dream visions. This convention is borrowed from classical tradition and is typically a garden, but often the forest or even a building can perform the same function, as when Chaucer's narrator of *HF* finds himself in "a temple ymad of glas" (line 120). For a more detailed discussion of the convention, see Curtius, pp. 195–202, and Howes, pp. 16–18. An influential instance in medieval poetry is the opening of *RR*, lines 103 ff. (*Romaunt*, lines 110 ff.). Compare the opening of Chaucer's *PF*, lines 183 ff.; the beginning of *Pearl*; *QJ*, lines 19 ff.; *BDSM*, lines 22–25; and *CLL*, lines 15 ff.

63   *poudred with dayse.* Compare Chaucer's Prologue to *LGW*, where the lover/narrator discards his books (F.36–39) and, rising to "doon . . . alle reverence" to the daisy, "of alle floures flour" (F.52–53), afterwards goes out to hear birdsong while the daisies declare lays of love under the warm sun, singing, "Blessed be Seynt Valentyn" (F.145).

67 ff.   The narrator listening to the melody of birds in the pleasant landscape or enclosed garden is a frequent trope in the love complaint or dream vision. Compare Chau-

cer's *BD*, where the narrator dreams he is awakened by "smale foules a gret hep / That had affrayed me out of my slep" (lines 295–96); and *PF*: "On every bow the bryddes herde I synge, / With voys of aungel in here armonye" (lines 190–91). For detailed discussion of the birdsong in the poem and its relationship to Chaucer's use of the same, see Chamberlain, pp. 47–50. In this volume, see *CLL*, lines 43 ff.

70   *ther houres.* Devotions or prayers at set times of the day (i.e., canonical hours). In this case, given that the birds are "joyful of the dayes lyght" (line 69), this probably refers to prime, the second of the canonical hours, recited at sunrise, especially given its association with beginnings (e.g., spring; prime is also the division of the day from 6 to 9 a.m.). It could refer to matins, which, along with lauds, was the first canonical hour, said at midnight or early morning. By the fifteenth century, this is a common description of birdsong. Compare William Dunbar's *The Thistle and the Rose*: "lusty May . . . maid the birdis to begyn thair houris" (poem 52, lines 4–5) and *The Golden Targe*: "Full angellike thir birdis sang thair houris" (poem 59, line 10).

78–80   *And evermore two . . . Seynt Valentynes day.* The *Riverside Chaucer* suggests that "[t]he tradition of St. Valentine as patron of mating birds (and humans) may have been an invention of Chaucer and his literary circle. . . . [T]here is no convincing evidence of a prior popular cult, or of other connection between any of the several Saint Valentines and the subject of erotic love or fertility before Chaucer" (p. 999 n309). See also Robert C. Cox and Alfred L. Kellog, "Chaucer's St. Valentine: A Conjecture," in Kellog, 1972, pp. 108–45; Jack B. Oruch, "St. Valentine, Chaucer, and Spring in February," *Speculum* 56 (1981), 534–65; and Henry Ansgar Kelly, *Chaucer and the Cult of Saint Valentine* (Leiden: E. J. Brill, 1986). Compare Chaucer's *Complaint of Mars*, where a bird offers to sing Mars' complaint in honor of Valentine's Day; see also *PF*, lines 309–10 and 386–89; *Complaynt D'Amours*, lines 85–91; the Prologue to *LGW* F.145–47; Gower's *Cinkante Balades* 34 and 35; and Dunbar's *The Tretis of the Tua Mariit Wemen and the Wedo* (poem 3, line 206). For discussion of *In Marche*, see textual note to line 80.

81–85   *the ryver that I sat upon . . . myght be herd of eny man.* Compare the description of birdsong in Chaucer's *PF*, lines 197–203. In Chaucer's *BD*, the narrator describes how the birds

    . . . al my chambre gan to rynge
Thurgh syngynge of her armonye;
For instrument nor melodye

Was nowhere herd yet half so swete,
Nor of acord half so mete. (lines 312–16)

See also explanatory note to lines 67 ff.

90   *the lewde cukkowe.* A common characterization of the cuckoo in medieval literature because it is a bird that lays its eggs in other birds' nests (for more on this, see explanatory note to line 270). The cuckoo is also called "lewde" in lines 50 and 103. Compare *PF*, line 616, where the Merlin enjoins the cuckoo: "Go, lewed be thow whil the world may dure." More specifically, the narrator here, at the beginning of his dream, sets up the initial opposition between the "ill-mannered" (or simply "crude") cuckoo and the more "refined" nightingale that is played out in the birds' debate with one another.

The cuckoo is often associated with a fear of cuckoldry (see Whiting C603), but see Chamberlain's argument on the cuckoo's connection with Christ in the poem and Clanvowe's development of "a virtuous cuckoo" (p. 53) as an alternative tradition in medieval poetry (see especially pp. 50–55). Chamberlain concludes that "Clanvowe has humorously presented a virtuous cuckoo, embodying Christian truth in the tradition of 'Sumer is icumen in'" (p. 59), a thirteenth-century song that calls on the cuckoo to sing in praise of the rejuvenation of the natural world: "Murie sing, cuccu! / Cuccu! cuccu! / Wel singes thu, cuccu; / Ne swik thu naver nu!" (Middle English and Latin texts, as well as translation of the Latin, available online from Bella Millett, English Department, University of Southampton, <http://www. soton.ac.uk/~wpwt/harl978/sumer.htm>.)

98–100   *A nyghtyngale . . . grene wode wide.* On the power of the nightingale's song, see Albertus Magnus, who explains that the nightingale "would sooner give up its life than lay down its song defeated. It is small of body, but its breathing has such a great vital force that it wondrously gives forth its melodious and complex song" (23.137). See also "Philomena" (or "Philomela"), the Latin poem probably by John Peckham (*Philomena: A Poem, the Latin Text with an English Version*, ed. and trans. William Dobell [London: Burns, Oates and Washbourne, 1924]). Compare Lydgate's *CLL*, lines 43–49, in which the birds sing so loudly "that al the wode ronge, / Lyke as hyt sholde shever in pesis smale" (lines 45–46) and the nightingale "[w]yth so grete myght her voys gan out wrest, / Ryght as her hert for love wolde brest" (lines 48–49). Although the narrator favors the nightingale, Chamberlain argues that the nightingale is "wholly partisan to Cupid, vengeful, willful, and not at all spiritual or mystical" (p. 58; see also pp. 55–59).

112–15   *good cukkow, go . . . Thy songes be so elynge.* The cuckoo's song is tedious perhaps because of its repetitive nature; proverbial sayings about the cuckoo include that it can sing only one song (Whiting C600) and that it sings only of itself (Whiting C601), both of which would make for repetitious listening.

118–20   *my songe is bothe trewe and pleyn . . . As thou dost in thy throte.* The owl makes a similar claim about his song in *The Owl and the Nightingale* (lines 260–65) and complains of the nightingale's constant trilling (lines 335–40). Albertus Magnus describes the nightingale's song as

> melodious and complex. . . . Now it is drawn out long in a continuous breath and then it is varied as if with the breathing of an inflected voice. Then it is punctuated with an abrupt sound and is finally linked to a convoluted breathing. The sound is full, low, high, complex and drawn out, exalted and depressed, imitating almost every musical instrument. (23.137)

He adds that it "responds and sings back to [singers] as if trying to be victorious" and that nightingales "also provoke one another to sing in this way" (23.137), which perhaps explains its use in debate poetry.

Sc (p. 83n118–20) suggests that the contrast here is between plainsong (i.e., monophonic music), represented by the cuckoo's *pleyn* singing (line 118), and polyphonic music, corresponding to the nightingale's ability to *breke* the song in her *throte* (lines 119–20). Given the cuckoo's complaint that the nightingale sings incomprehensibly in French (see explanatory note to lines 123–25), the contrast might also be between courtly French and *pleyn* (i.e., "unembellished") English.

123–25   *mony a nyse, queynt crie . . . what that shuld be?* The descriptors *nyse* and *queynt* (line 123) point to the unfamiliarity of the nightingale's cry. The cuckoo questions the nightingale's use of words that cannot be readily understood, as evident in her cry *Ocy! Ocy!* (line 124), which is, as Sc notes, "[a] fairly frequently used imitation of the nightingale's song, though this seems to be its first use in English. . . . *ocy* was usually taken to be the imperative of [French] *occire* 'to kill'" (p. 84n124–35). The difficulty in understanding the cry masks the violent nature of love that it would otherwise reveal, though the hidden meaning of the song might also allude to the story of Philomela that lies behind the nightingale in classical traditions (detailed in explanatory note to *CLL*, line 374). In addition, the word *queynt*, with its potential pun, is perhaps a reminder that the nightingale's song is not just of love, but also of sex.

127–30   *When that I sey . . . agen Love amys.* The nightingale's explanation illustrates that her cry requires an interpreter in order to be understood.

136   *this is a queynt lawe.* See explanatory note to lines 123–25 for discussion of the adjective *queynt.*

157   *Semelyhed.* According to the *MED*, the more common meaning of *semelihed(e)* n. is "beauty, attractiveness," but the *MED* cites this line from *BC* as the sole example for meaning (b) "?propriety; ?graciousness."

160   *Wer lother to be schamed then to dye.* Proverbial: "better to die with honor than live in shame" (see Whiting D239). Compare lines 492–96 and 525–26 in *QJ*; and lines 546–48 in *BDSM* (see explanatory note to line 492 in *QJ* for more details).

166–67   *Nyghtyngale, thou spekest . . . is the contreyre.* Sc points to *The Owl and the Nightingale*, lines 839–44, for a similar ploy (p. 84n166–67).

178–80   *For who that geteth of love a lytil blysse . . . have his eire.* "Whoever gets (begets) a little bliss of love, / Unless he is always by it (i.e., paying attention to it), indeed, / May have his heir come of age right away." These lines hint at the cuckoo's final pronouncement on the matter of love (lines 183–85): that leaving one's mate will turn one into a cuckold. See explanatory note to line 185, for more on the cuckoo's connection to cuckoldry.

185   *then shalt thou hoten as do I.* In other words, the nightingale will be called a cuckold, as is the cuckoo; i.e., those who follow Love will find themselves cuckolded. Presumably the cuckoo knows this from experience, as the proverbial pun on cuckoo/cuckold implies (see Whiting C603). For further discussion of the cuckoo's traditional associations, see especially David Lampe. Gregory Roscow takes the position that "there is no evidence that *cuckoo* and *cuckold* could mean the same thing at this time" (p. 183), adding that "Clanvowe in his conventional courtly treatment of romantic love steers well clear of adultery or cuckoldry as a possible consequence of the nightingale's advocacy of love" (pp. 183–84).

197   *no reson but his wille.* The dichotomy between reason and will was common in the Middle Ages, and is a key component of a number of medieval works, including William Langland's *Piers Plowman*, Gower's *CA*, Jean de Meun's section of *RR*, and Christine de Pizan's *The Book of the City of Ladies*. Will was the faculty that encouraged lovers to love, while reason usually counseled restraint. For the proverbial saying "love puts reason away," see Whiting L533. The cuckoo's argument echoes Gower's *CA*, where love's lack of reason is attributed to his connection to Fortune (also frequently depicted as blind):

> For if ther evere was balance
> Which of fortune stant governed,
> I may wel lieve as I am lerned   *believe; taught*
> That love hath that balance on honde,
> Which wol no reson understonde. (ed. Peck, 1.42–46)

202   *he is blynde and may not se.* Proverbial: "love is blind" (Whiting C634). Cupid, the God of Love, is frequently depicted as blind. See, for example, *Romaunt*, lines 3702–03: "Cupide, / The God of Love, blynde as stoon"; and Gower's *CA*: "For love is blind and may noght se" (ed. Peck, 1.47). See Whiting for further citations.

204   *ful selde trouthe avayleth.* Compare the Prologue to *LGW*, where Alceste argues that the God of Love's court is full of liars and slanderers (F.352–56; G.327–32).

205   *So dyverse and so wilful ys he.* Proverbial: "love changes oft"; see Whiting L502.

209   *I can for tene sey not oon worde more.* Sc (pp. 84–85n209) writes, "This is tantamount to an admission of defeat on the nightingale's part, for it was the rule of medieval school's debate that whoever argued his adversary into silence was the victor," suggesting comparisons with *The Owl and the Nightingale* (lines 391–410, 665–66) and *Dispute between a Good Man and the Devil* (lines 949–52).

222   *papyngay.* "Parrot." Clearly an insult. The comment perhaps carries an accusation of licentiousness, since the parrot is characterized by Chaucer as promiscuous (see *PF*, line 359: "The popynjay, ful of delicasye [wantonness]"). On another level, a parrot speaks without reason, only able to repeat what it learns by rote, perhaps hinting that this is the case with those who follow love. According to Trevisa, "some bestes beþ y-ordeynede for mannes mete, as scheep, hertes, and oþre suche; and [som] serueþ for seruyce of mankynde, as horse, asses, oxen, and cameles, and oþere suche; and some for mannes merþe, as apes and marmusettes and popyngayes" (p. 1110/19–23), which implies a kind of uselessness, as of a creature whose only reason for existence is to provide entertainment. In Langland's *Piers Plowman*, the peacock and the parrot "with here proude federes / By-tokneþ ryght riche men" (C.15.173), which points to a connection with vanity. Lee Patterson sums up these characteristics in his suggestion that this is "a shrewd critique," noting that the "parrot is a quintessential courtly bird," designating not only "the courtier but . . . the courtly over-achiever" because of "its gaudy plumage, its status as a plaything of the rich, and its ability to rehearse, with mindless enthusiasm, the phrases it has been laboriously taught," all of which make it "an apt symbol of the

fawning, too-perfect courtier" (pp. 22–23). Eustache Deschamps' balade, "Plaintes d'amoureux" (3.296–97, no. 476), also associates the nightingale with the parrot in opposition to the cuckoo, as the narrator complains that even though it is May, he cannot hear much of the nightingale or the parrot, only the cuckoo's song: "Car l'en oit poy rossignol, papegay, / Fors seulement que le chant du cucu" (lines 23–24, "Because one hears little of the nightingale, parrot, / But only the song of the cuckoo").

241–45   *this medecyne . . . the daysye . . . lyssen of thy pyne*. Compare the Prologue to *LGW* F.40–209 (see explanatory note to line 63). For more on the courtly cult dedicated to the daisy and Chaucer's *LGW*, see John L. Lowes, "The Prologue to the *Legend of Good Women* as Related to the French *Marguerite* Poems, and the *Filostrato*," *PMLA* 19 (1904), 593–683. See also Peter W. Travis, "Chaucer's Heliotropes and the Poetics of Metaphor," *Speculum* 72 (1997), 399–427.

270   *that foule, fals, unkynde bridde*. Sc notes, "For a long account of the cuckoo's evil nature see *La Messe des Oiseaus* 381–416, and *The Parliament of Fowls* 358, 612–16" (p. 86n270). Albertus Magnus explains that "[t]he chicks of the cuckoo are never found in their own nests, nor is the cuckoo ever found to carry them to the nest, for its custom is to lay in the nests of other birds" (6.52), adding that "they first suck out the eggs of those birds and then put their own in their place. Therefore almost all other birds fight against the cuckoos" (6.53). See also 17.6. In another discussion of the cuckoo, he suggests that the cuckoo leaves its egg to be incubated by other birds, and

> [t]he bird whose nest it is incubates all the eggs, its own and that of the cuckoo, until the shell of the cuckoo's egg cracks open. It is said that the cuckoo's egg opens faster than the others and that then the bird no longer incubates the other eggs, but it feeds the cuckoo chick instead. This, as it gradually grows, incubates the other eggs and hatches out the chicks of the bird that is feeding it. . . . Others say, however, that the eggs hatch together and then the mother kills her own chicks and gives them as food to the cuckoo. This is because the cuckoo chicks are prettier and larger than her own and she therefore despises her own and kills them. (8.91)

275 ff.   *we wol have a parlement*. The nightingale asks the birds for judgment against the cuckoo, and they agree to form a parliament to decide the cuckoo's fate within this official legal setting. The birds in Chaucer's *PF* hold a yearly parliament on Valentine's Day (lines 320–22).

276   *the egle our lorde*. In *PF*, Nature identifies "[t]he tersel egle . . . / The foul royal" (lines 393–94) as the preeminent bird.

284–85 *the quene, / At Wodestok*. Given the probable date of the poem, most likely Richard II's Queen Anne (of Bohemia), "who was at Woodstock with Richard II in 1389 and almost certainly other times as well" (Sc, p. 86n284–85).

287   *an hawthorn*. Sc (p. 86n287) observes that the hawthorn is linked to steadfastness in love, citing *The Court of Love* (lines 1353–54) and Lydgate's *Temple of Glass* (lines 510–22) as examples. See also line 71 of *CLL*.

289   *Terme of lyve, Love hath withholde me*. Patterson suggests that *withholde* here means "retain" and that the line should be read "I have been retained for life by Love," reading this as an allusion to the fact that, beginning in 1389, "Richard [II] began to indulge, systematically and extensively, in life-retaining" ("Court Politics," p. 10). The *MED* suggests the word should be understood as "sustained" or "supported" (see *withholden* v., 4 [c]).

290   Compare *PF*, where the narrator awakens similarly at the end of the poem "with the shoutyng, whan the song was do / That foules maden at here flyght awey" (lines 693–94); and *BD*, where the narrator dreams he is awakened by "smale foules a gret hep / That had affrayed me out of my slep / Thorgh noyse and swetnesse of her song" (lines 295–97); and *TC*, when Pandarus is roused from sleep by the song of the swallow (2.64–70).

Textual Notes to *The Boke of Cupide, God of Love*

Abbreviations: **B** = Bodleian Library MS Bodley 638, fols. 11v–16r; **Ff** = Cambridge University Ff.1.6 (Findern MS), fols. 22r–28r; **F** = Bodleian Library MS Fairfax 16, fols. 35v–39v [base text]; **S** = Bodleian Library MS Arch. Selden. B. 24, fols. 138v–141v; **Sc** = V. J. Scattergood; **Sk** = Walter W. Skeat; **T** = Bodleian Library MS Tanner 346, fols. 97r–101r; **Th** = William Thynne (1532).

title	F, B: *The boke of Cupide god of love.* Ff: *Geffrey Chaucer's Poem of the Cuckow and the Nightingale* (in later hand). T: *Of þe Cuckow & þe Nightingale* (in later hand). Th: *Of the Cuckowe and the Nyghtyngale.*
3	*hertys.* F: *herty,* though the stroke above the *y* may indicate that *s* should be added. Sc's emendation.
4	*high hertis low.* Ff, S, T: *of hye lowe.* Sc emends: *highe lowe.*
7	*ful.* T, Th: omit
12–13	T, Th transpose these lines.
14	*in.* T, Th: omit.
19	*don him laugh or siketh.* Ff, T: *he laugethe or sigheth.* S: *laughith or he sikith.* Th: *he loweth or syketh.* Sc emends: *he laugheth or he siketh.*
20	*he sheweth.* T, Th: *he shedeþ.*
24	*morenynge.* Ff, T, Th: *some mornynge.*
25	*grette.* T, Th: *mych.*
26	*when.* F: *then.* Sc's emendation.
28	*bringes.* F: *burges.* Sc's emendation.
29	*ease.* F, B: *case.* Sc's emendation.
33	*And for.* B: *For.* S: *And all for,* which Sc follows (*And al for*).
	that that. F, B, Ff: *that.* S: *it þat.* Sc's emendation.
39	*an.* T, Th: *and.*
41	*slayn.* Ff, S, T, Th: *shaken.* Sc reads F, B as *alayn* and emends to *shaken.*
43	*is unlyke for to be.* Ff, T, Th: *is not like to me.* S: *naught likith vnto me.* Sc emends: *is vnlyke to me.*
50	*leude.* Ff: *lowde.*
54	*I non had herd.* Ff, Th: *had y non herde.* T: *herd I none.*
55	*was.* Ff, S, T, Th: *was tho,* which Sc follows.
59	*prively.* Ff, T, Th: *boldly.*

63–64	B transposes these lines.
64	*gras.* Ff, T, Th: *grenes.* S: *greses.*
	al ilike hie. Ff, T, Th: *lyke hye*, which Sc follows (*ilike hie*).
67	*the.* F: *thee.* Sc's emendation.
	crepe. Ff, T, Th: *trippe.* S: *flee.*
70	*of.* S: *on.*
	May. F, B, S: *Mayes.*
	to don ther houres. F, B: *ben ther houres.* S: *vse thair houris.* T, Th: *forto done houres.* Sc's emendation (*to don her houres*).
71	*that.* Ff, T: *nat.*
73	*loude.* Ff: *lowe.*
75	*a lowde.* Ff: *all the ful*, which Sc follows (*al the fulle*). S: *all full.* T, Th: *þe ful.*
76	*hem.* Ff: *hym.*
	gay. Ff: *gay gay.*
79	*they.* Ff: *the.*
80	*Marche.* T, Th: *Feuirȝere.* Sc notes that, although it was more usual for St. Valentine's Day to fall in February, it could occur in March (p. 83n80). Sk notes that "it ruins the scansion, unless we adopt the reading *March*. It looks as if the author really *did* write *Marche*!" (p. 527n80).
86	*delyte.* Ff, S: *delite ther of*, which Sc follows (*delyte therof*).
87	*swowe.* B, S: *slow.*
90	*lewde.* Ff: *lowde.* Sc emends: *lewede.*
94	*foule.* T, Th: *lewde.*
96	*gan chide.* Ff: *now gan chyde.* S: *gan to chide.* T, Th: *þus gan chide*, which Sc follows (*thus gan chide*).
97	*busshe.* F: *busshes.* S: *beugh.* Sc's emendation.
	me. Ff, S, T, Th: omit.
99	*voys.* F: *woys.*
100	*grene wode.* Ff: *grenes of the wode.*
103	*lewde.* Ff, T: *lowde.* Sc emends: *lewede.*
104	*then thou.* Ff, S, T, Th: *thanne hastowe*, which Sc follows (*then hast thou*).
105	*him.* S, Th: *hir.*
111	*And then.* T: *And þere.* Th: *There.*
112	*thy wey.* Ff, T, Th: *aweye.*
113	*here.* T: *he.*
115	*Thy.* Ff: *The.*
116	*What.* S: *Quhat bird.*
	he. F, B: *she.* Sc's emendation, which I follow here and at line 164. The context makes it clear that the cuckoo is speaking, thus the masculine rather than the

feminine pronoun is needed. Although the first two pronoun references to the cuckoo in F and B use "she," all other references (lines 196, 219–225, 238, 240, and 260) make it clear that the cuckoo is male. Perhaps the scribe or the scribe's exemplar mistook the nightingale as the speaker of this line and line 164.

119	*breke hit.* Ff: *crake.* S, T, Th: *crekill.*
123	*nyse, queynt.* F, B: *queynt.* S: *queynt feyned.* Sc's emendation (*nyse, queynte*).
127	*that.* Ff: *than.*
131	*were.* Ff, T, Th: *had the.*
135	*crede.* S: *cryed.* B, Ff, T, Th: *gred*, which Sc follows (*grede*), but *crede* is a legitimate variant (see *MED, greden* v.).
136	*ywis.* Ff, S, T, Th: omit, followed by Sc.
137	*eyther shal I.* Ff, S, T, Th: *euery wight shall.*
	elles be slawe. Ff, T, Th: *bene to drawe.*
139	*neyther.* Ff, T, Th: *not.*
	for to dye. F: *dye.* Sc's emendation.
140	*Ne.* Ff, Th: *Ne neuer.* S: *nor.* T: *Ne neþir.*
	yoke. F: *loke.* Sc's emendation.
141	*lyven.* Ff, S, T, Th: *bene.*
	on. F: *of.* Sc's emendation.
142	*most unthrive.* F: *most and vnthrive.* Sc's emendation.
144	*at the last, failen of her.* Ff, T, Th: *lest feelen of.* S: *alderleste haue felyng of.*
146	*What.* S: *Quhat brid.*
147	*cherles hert.* Ff, Th: *cherlnesse.* S: *cherlich hert.* T: *clerenes.*
151	*goodnesse.* Ff: *gladnesse.*
153	*al.* F, B: omit. Sc's emendation.
	hertys. F: *hurtys.* Sc's emendation, which I follow to avoid confusion, though this is a legitimate variant of *hertys* (see *MED, herte* n.).
154	*trust.* Ff: *liste.*
156–57	T, Th: transpose the second halves of the lines.
157	*largenesse.* Ff, S, T, Th: *largesse*, which Sc follows.
158	B: omits, but includes as line 161, with marginal notation that the line should go before 159.
	and. Ff, T, Th: omit.
160	*to$_2$.* Ff: *do.*
161	*that ys.* T, Th: *þat þis is.*
	al that. Ff, T, Th: *that.* S: *all þat euer.* Sc's emendation (*alle that*).
162	*bothe.* T, Th: omit.
163	*rede I thee, that thou.* Ff: *I rede thou.* T, Th: *I rede þat þou.* S: *rede I þat thou*, which Sc follows.

164   *he.* F, B: *she.* Sc's emendation. See textual note to line 116.

      God. T, Th: omit.

167   *the sothe is the.* Ff, T, Th: *ys the soth.*

168   *in yong folke is.* B, Ff, S, T, Th: *is yn yonge folke,* which Sc follows (*is in yonge folke*).

169   *olde.* T, Th: *old folk.*

171   *disese and.* F, B: *mony an.* Sc's emendation.

172   *Sorow.* Th: *So sorowe.*

      a. Ff, S, T, Th: *a grete,* which Sc follows.

174   *Repreve.* Ff: *Disproue.* T, Th: *Deprauyng.*

      and₁. T, Th: omit.

      untrust. F: *to trust.* Sc's emendation (*vntrust*).

175   *and₁.* B, Ff, T, Th: omit.

176   *What.* Ff, T, Th: omit.

179   *But he.* Ff, S, T, Th: *But yf he,* which Sc follows (*But if he*).

180   *eire.* F, B: *crie.* Sc's emendation: "The F. B. reading fails to give a true rhyme or adequate sense" (p. 84n180).

182   *loude.* Ff, S, T, Th: *queynt.*

183   *fer or long be.* F: *fer of long be.* Ff, T, Th: *be ferre or longe,* which Sc follows (*be fer or longe*). S: *be long and fer.*

184   *Thou.* B: *Then.*

187   *let.* S: *now lat.* Ff, T, Th: *ne let,* which Sc follows.

189   *mony is.* Ff, T, Th: *many on ys,* which Sc follows (*mony oon is*). S: *mony one ar.*

191   *Love his.* Ff: *loues.*

      servant. Ff, S, T, Th: *seruaunteȝ.*

192   *tachches.* Ff, T, Th: *euel tacches,* which Sc follows (*euel tachches*) S: *euell scathis.*

      him. Ff, S, T, Th: *hem.*

193   *him.* Ff, S, T, Th: *hem.*

      as. Ff, T: *ryght as.* Th: *right in.*

194   *and in worschipful.* S: *honour and worschip to.*

195   *whom.* Ff, T, Th: *whanne.*

      him₁. T, Th: *hem.*

      joy. S: *I seye.*

      him₂. Ff, T, Th: *hem.* S: *he.*

196   *Ye.* Ff, S, T, Th: *Thou.*

      holde thee. Th: *he.*

197   *his.* T, Th: *it is.*

198   *untrew.* Ff: *ful vntrewe.*

200   *That.* F, B: *And.* Sc's emendation.
       grace. Th: *corage.*
201–05 T, Th: omit.
202   *not.* Ff: *nothyng.*
203   *And when.* Ff: *And whome.* S: *Quhom.*
       lyeth. Ff: *hit.* S: *hurtith.*
       when₂. Ff, S: *whome.*
       fayleth. S: *helith.*
207   *She.* Ff: *And she.* T, Th: *Hou she.*
       sighe. Ff: *syght.*
       hert. Ff, T, Th: omit.
208   *ever I.* F, B: *I ever.* Sc's emendation.
209   *I can.* S: *And gan.*
210   *that.* Th: *þat worde.*
212   *fals.* Th: *leude.*
216   *I.* Th: *he.*
       out. Ff, S, T, Th: *vp,* which Sc follows.
217–19 T, Th: omit.
218   *I.* Ff: omits.
220   *when.* T, Th: omit.
223   *thoght me.* T, Th: *me aloone.*
224   *fro tre to tre.* Ff: *fro the tre.*
224–25 T, Th: omit.
228   *thus.* Ff, T, Th: omit.
229   *oon avowe.* S: *rycht anon.*
       I avowe. Ff: *I wol a vowe.* S: *I wole allowe.* T, Th: *make I now.*
230   *That.* T: *And.*
232   *amayed.* T, Th: *dismaied.*
233   *cukkow.* S: *false cukkow.*
       er then. S: *greue.* T: *syng erst þan.*
237   *leve.* F, B: *love.* Ff, Th: *loue thou.* S: *leue thou.* T: *love þeir.* Sc's emendation.
       Loves. Ff: *the loues.* T, Th: *ne his louys.*
239   *nothing.* T: *noman.*
240   *Fro.* Ff, T, Th: *For.*
       yet he doth. T, Th: *it haþ do.*
241   *Yee, use thou.* Ff, T, Th: *Ye vse.* S: *ȝa thou schalt vse.*
243   *flour, the daysye.* Ff, T, Th: *daysy.* S: *flour dayeseye,* which Sc follows (*flour daysye*).
245   *That.* Ff: *Thal.*

245	*gretly.* S: *mekle.*
	thee lyssen. Ff, T, Th: *lyssen the,* which Sc follows. S: *lessen.*
247	*thy.* Ff: *my.* T, Th: *þe.*
247–90	This final section of the poem is missing in S.
250	*to.* Ff, T, Th: *of.*
251	*out.* Ff, T, Th: omit, followed by Sc.
254	*day.* Ff: *may.*
255	*ever yet he eny lover.* T, Th: *eny ʒit louer he euer.*
257	*with.* Ff: *whele.*
262	*were.* F: *werne.*
	vale. F: *wale.* Ff, T, Th: *dale.*
266	*Yee knowe wel.* Ff: *Ye wyten well for.* T, Th: *The cukko wel.*
	is not fro yow hidde. Ff: *may not be yhydde.* T, Th: *is not forto hide.*
267	*have.* Ff, T, Th: *fast haue,* which Sc follows.
271	*by.* Ff, T, Th: *by onne.*
273	*fewe.* Th: omits.
276	*shal be the egle.* Ff, T, Th: *shall the Egle been,* which Sc follows (*shal the egle be*).
277	*recorde.* Ff: *O record.*
280	*make summe.* Ff: *maken.* T, Th: *fynalli make.*
281	*any nay.* T: *may.* Th: *nay.*
282	*of.* Ff, T, Th: *after.*
285	*grene.* Ff: *grete.*
286	*and.* Ff: omits.
	then. F: *the.* Sc's emendation.
287	*fleye.* T, Th: omit.
	hawthorn. F: *hawthornes.* Sc's emendation.
290	*awoke.* Ff: *began awake.*
colophon	B: *Explicit the boke of Cupyde god of loue.* Ff: *Explicit Clanvowe,* followed by two seven-line stanzas on the verso side of the folio. T, Th: *Explicit,* followed by three stanzas addressed to the book and an envoy of one stanza; in T this is followed by *Explicit þe Cuck. & þe Nighting.* in the same hand that added the title.

A Complaynte of a Lovers Lyfe or The Complaint of the Black Knight

Introduction

John Lydgate's *Complaynte of a Lovers Lyfe* (also called *The Complaint of the Black Knight*) begins, like many medieval love-narratives, by introducing a narrator whose own story is not the main subject of the poem but who is spurred by unhappiness or dissatisfaction to tell another's melancholy tale. The cause of the narrator's discontent is likely to be unclear, perhaps little more than the stirring of some anxiety. Usually the anxiety will have to do with love, which attracts the narrator to some particular event, the recounting of which then forms the core of the poem. The frame of the narrative may overtly serve to establish some occasion for the poem's composition, but its conventional status in medieval poetry also signals to readers a richly layered garden of love-delights, with two intertwined lovelorn voices, a palimpsest of lovers who mourn one atop the other: narrator and lover. Readers of *The Romance of the Rose* or Chaucer's *Book of the Duchess* would expect the ideal garden setting in Lydgate's poem to yield a narrator whose dreaming provides an escape, both for himself and for those readers who follow him into the landscape. Lydgate is not slow to satisfy these desires in some measure, but the dream vision conventions invoked here lead to slightly different pleasures than the ones readers might anticipate from such a "Chaucerian" poet.

A Complaynte of a Lovers Lyfe begins conventionally in spring (May), "when Flora, the fressh lusty quene" (line 1), has covered the ground with burgeoning plants, and Lucifer, the morning star, has chased away the night to bid lovers stir from sleep. During this time, Nature invites lovers to rise and make merry, and Hope also beckons them out to take the air. Accordingly, the narrator sighs himself awake and, despite feeling heartsick, goes into the woods to hear the birds sing. He walks by a river and comes upon a small park enclosed by a wall. Going inside, he hears the birds singing loudly, especially the nightingale, who sings "[r]yght as her hert for love wolde brest" (line 49).

In the park, the ground is covered with Nature's tapestries, canopied by green boughs to protect the flowers from the hot sun, and the air is mild. This is the setting of love visions and dreams, decked out in the sumptuous array of the *locus amoenus* — here the narrator and reader will expect the easing of hearts and minds. Accordingly, under the trees (some of them named for ill-fated lovers) is a well that, unlike the wells of Narcissus, Pegasus, or Diana, has the virtue of soothing lovers or any in distress. The narrator drinks from the well and feels refreshed. Wandering further in the park, he comes upon an arbor where he sees a pale man dressed in black and white lying amidst the flowers with fresh wounds, shaking from fever. Hiding in the bushes, the narrator listens to the knight's complaint and promises to do his best to write it down, even though he is not much of a writer and has no personal experience to help him along. It is in this voyeuristic position that the rest of the poem unfolds, with reader atop narrator in a new arrangement, both hiding from and spying on the lover.[1]

The knight's fever poises him between cold and heat, and he suffers because Envy and Male-Bouche (Slander), among others, have conspired to overthrow Truth and put Falsehood in his place. Truth, the knight says, was falsely accused and condemned out of hand by Cruelty, who urged Disdain to execute the sentence right away, and the knight does not understand how God, who is Lord of Truth, can stand to witness this. The knight realizes that "[t]his blynde chaunce, this stormy aventure" (line 309), is what most lovers experience in matters of love. He himself has been in love for so long that he cannot give up to save his life, even though he knows that "evere sithe that the worlde began" (line 323) stories have related how "the trwe man" was hindered while "the falshede [deceitful] / I furthered was" (lines 325–27); Love never cares about protecting the true and lets "the fals goth frely at her large" (lines 329). He notes the stories of lovers who have suffered, as well as those who were false. As these stories show, lovers never get anything for their troubles, no matter what bold feats they accomplish, because ultimately the beloved lacks mercy and pity, and instead "hath joy to laughen at my peyn" (line 448).

The knight then complains against unseeing Cupid, who is willful and unstable, shooting blindly and making "the seke for to crie and calle / Unto his foo for to ben his leche [doctor]" (472–73). This is the situation in which he finds himself. The knight wishes he had never been born, especially since Nature made the lady so attractive and so resistant to his appeals that Compassion and Pity are exiled from her court, while "Dispite now haldeth forth her reyn / Thro hasty beleve of tales that men feyn" (lines 510–11). The knight concludes that if his lady does not have mercy on him, he will die, but adds that he is willing to die whenever she wishes, if that is her desire. He tells God, "yf I dye, in my testament / My hert I send and my spirit also, / Whatsoever she list with hem to do" (lines 558–60).

Tears rain from the narrator's eyes upon witnessing such suffering. Soon the knight gets up and goes into a nearby dwelling, where he is wont to spend each May complaining of his keen pains. Evening is falling, and the narrator quickly takes up his pen, "[t]he woful pleynt of this man to write, / Worde be worde as he dyd endyte" (lines 599–600). He says that if anything is wrong, blame his lack of ability as a poet. As the narrator is writing, he seems to see Venus rising in the distance and prays to her on behalf of the lovesick knight: "O lady Venus, so feire upon to se, / Let not this man for his trouthe dey" (lines 619–20). He appeals to her for the sake

---

[1] In *The Medieval Poet as Voyeur*, A. C. Spearing provides a detailed study of the trope of secret watching in medieval literature. He discusses *Complaynte* in Chapter 11, pp. 218–30.

of the love she had for Mars and Adonis to uphold the truth and ease the sorrowful, especially "[t]he trew man that in the erber lay" (line 637), and to encourage the knight's "lady him to grace take, / Her hert of stele to mercy so enclyne" (lines 640–41).

When the evening star has set, the narrator goes to bed himself and prays for those who are faithful to be eased. Too sleepy to stay awake, he then bids true (faithful) lovers farewell, hoping they will defeat Jealousy and be reconciled to their ladies. The narrator asks in his envoy: "Princes [Princess], pleseth hit your benignité / This litil dité to have in mynde" (666–67) in hopes that she will have pity and mercy on the narrator, her "trew man" (line 669). Finally he sends his little book "unto my lyves quene / And my verry hertis sovereigne" (lines 674–75) but is himself left behind, not knowing to whom to complain, since "Mercie, Routhe, Grace, and eke Pité / Exiled be" (lines 679–80).

Unlike *The Boke of Cupide*, whose focus seems to be on the type of language appropriate to poetry, *A Complaynte of a Lovers Lyfe* questions the virtue of poetic effort more generally. The setting within the restorative powers of spring and the shift from night to day that takes place in the first stanzas, though entirely conventional, produce at first an encouraging outlook towards love and its capacity to transfigure lovers. The narrator's allusions to stories of metamorphosis in his description of the garden he encounters on his walk extend this transformative theme in a way that at once holds out hope that transformation is possible and reveals the concern that such changes may not be desirable. The narrator's role as watcher and recorder of the knight's sorrows would seem to provide a complete and unmodified version of someone else's personal experience, and his appeal to those present who have suffered from love to heed the knight's story offers the possibility that listening to the knight (or reading the poetic account the narrator provides) may prove therapeutic. But within the garden lie stories that throw doubt on both the narrator's position and the coercive force of love, even as the narrator's own behavior casts suspicion on his role in the narrative. And in the knight's tale bleak stories of lovers lurk to remind devotees of love what their own fate might be. Ultimately, the poem's preoccupation with deadly tales of metamorphosis and thwarted love suggests anxiety about the transformational power of poetry — regarding both its capacity to transform and the nature of that alteration.

The narrator's description of the garden and the well in its center gives us our first hint of the theme of transformation. In the midst of restorative trees, such as pine, myrrh, cedar, ash, and oak (lines 65–73), all of which have medicinal and protective properties, the narrator explains that he "sawe ther Daphene, closed under rynde, / Grene laurer" (lines 64–65), and "[t]he philbert eke, that lowe dothe enclyne / Her bowes grene to the erthe doune / Unto her knyght icalled Demophoune" (lines 68–70). The narrator here not only identifies the trees (laurel and filbert/hazelnut tree) but also explicitly mentions the unfortunate love stories that lie behind their names: Daphne was chased by Apollo until Zeus turned her into a laurel tree to save her; Phyllis hanged herself for love of Demophon when he never returned to her and was afterwards pitied by the gods, who changed her into a nut tree. Both these stories point to the destructive nature of love. In Daphne's case, metamorphosis "saves" her from love, but in so doing changes her very nature, in effect ending her human life. For Phyllis, presumably the transformation is intended as a recompense for the rejection by Demophon, who had previously promised her love, but it is clear that life as a tree is no compensation — either for lost love or for life. In both these tales metamorphosis enables the wronged woman to live on in a shape alien to her own, suggesting that love has the capacity to transform but at the cost of one's identity — perhaps this is a transformation that should be feared instead of desired.

At the well the narrator is refreshed, but at the same time, the stories of Narcissus and Acteon to which he alludes anticipate the narrator's own position as secret watcher and suggest the dreadful possibilities of what can happen to such witnesses. The reference to the tale of Narcissus as presented here draws a renewed picture of the destructive force of love. Although the well is "[n]at lyche the welle wher as Narcisus / Islayn was thro vengeaunce of Cupide" (lines 87–88), the very mention of the story serves as a reminder of it. The presentation of Narcissus' fate as the result of the "vengeaunce of Cupide" emphasizes the fact that Narcissus' pride, which caused him to refuse all other potential suitors, doomed him to fall in love with a reflection of himself. As watcher of that likeness, he is condemned to death, for he cannot bear to leave his own image and so wastes away on the brink of the pool (after which he becomes a flower). Further, the story of Narcissus is bound up in that of Echo, who observed him from afar, fell in love, and then faded away until only her voice was left after Narcissus rebuffed her. The fates of these two suggest that no matter which side of love's equation one is on, rejected suitor or cold beloved, death will result, and in each case it is looking that has led to that end. The narrator's reference to the story of Acteon also leaves no doubt about the dire consequences of spying. As the narrator explains, when Acteon accidentally stumbled on Diana, goddess of the hunt and chastity, bathing in a pool in the forest, Diana turned him into a stag, and his own hounds chased him down and tore him to pieces. If that is the fate of one who looks unintentionally, what will the narrator's fate be, or that of his readers, who are deliberate voyeurs with him? Though the narrator hastens to tell us that this well was not like the ill-fated ones he mentions, both stories highlight the fact that secret watching can lead to death, with transformations that turn out either not to be redemptive (as with Echo and Narcissus), or to be downright destructive (as in the case of Acteon).

Bringing up these stories thus serves as a warning about the narrator's own behavior when he encounters the grieving knight. Furthermore, the narrator's remark that the well that refreshes him is not "lyche the pitte [spring] of the Pegacé / Under Parnaso, wher poetys slept" (lines 92–93) casts doubt on his own ability as a poet even before he tells us that he has none. Pegasus' well, the fountain Hippocrene, is the source of poetic inspiration, but its placement between the well of Narcissus and that of Diana links death with poetic achievement in a way that suggests lovers may have to suffer in order to produce poetry. The description of the ideal garden thus not only indicates that this narrator is no poet, but also highlights the problems inherent in his voyeurism. It is not perhaps enough to watch suffering — one must experience it. The culmination of the stories alluded to in the prelude to the knight's complaint suggests that spying on love will not teach one anything about it, but simultaneously cautions that the experience of love leads at best to transformation, at worst to death. These dire predictions about love then play out in the body of the poem, as the narrator attempts to offer the poem as a soothing draft to his audience.

The narrator's voyeuristic placement in the bushes for the whole of the poem means that, unlike the nobleman-lover in Guillaume de Machaut's *Dit de la fonteinne amoureuse*, the knight here has no say over the status of his words, the efficacy of his complaint, or even whether or not (or how) his voice is reproduced. In *Fonteinne amoureuse* the narrator similarly overhears a lament from a hidden vantage point but afterwards goes outside to find the man whose words he wrote down. This lover then asks the narrator to record his complaint, only to find it has already been done, at which point the lover has the opportunity to read and approve his complaint. In Machaut's poem, this process brings narrator and lover together, a companionship cemented by their sharing a dream at the end of the poem. Similarly, Chaucer's *Book of the Duchess* offers its narrator a chance to interact with the suffering knight due to its dream setting, where concerns of rank do not hold sway.[2] These encounters serve in part to legitimate the narrator's account of the suffering he witnesses, but in *Complaynte* there are no opportunities for the narrator to interact with the knight; there is no dream, either as frame or otherwise, that enables the narrator to bridge the gap between himself and the otherwise unreachable lover. This departure from what readers have come to expect may seem like a small detail — evidence perhaps of an anemic relationship to its precursor, Chaucer's *Book of the Duchess* — but it is in fact a crucial change, for the potential healing that narrators in the earlier poems offer the sufferers they witness depends on the interaction between the two. The question Lydgate's poem seems to pose is whether writing can substitute for that interaction once the narrator discards his active role.

In Lydgate's hands, the conventional setting, reminiscent of poems such as *The Romance of the Rose*, Machaut's *Jugement dou Roy de Behaingne*, and Chaucer's *Book of the Duchess*, now takes on a new, unconventional life as the knight makes his complaint and the narrator settles in passively to hear it. This complaint is one over which the knight no longer has control; it has left his own mouth to come out of another's. The lament as the narrator tells it must ultimately fail to represent what the knight really said, since it is no longer his own dream the narrator recounts, over which he might have some authority, but the distress of a "real" lover who does not know he is being recorded, whose record is made by one who admits — even dwells on — his inadequacy for such a task. The narrator lacks the personal experience of love that would enable him to empathize with the lover he watches. Though he admits that "who that shal write of distresse / In partye nedeth to know felyngly / Cause and rote of al such malady" (lines 187–89), he then acknowledges his own lack of such qualifications:

---

[2] See Spearing (1993), p. 220.

> But I, alas, that am of wytte but dulle   *wit*
> And have no knowyng of suche mater
> For to discryve and wryte at the fulle   *describe*
> The wofull compleynt which that ye shul here.   *hear*
>   (lines 190–93)

Without a guide to "interpret" the events of the poem for the narrator, his ineptitude becomes more than simply an expected rhetorical flourish: it now constitutes a source of anxiety for both narrator and readers. Readers must now depend on this inadequate rendition of the knight's grief, as if the narrator were the guide who has the key to open the poem's meaning. And the narrator's claims that he will write out the complaint exactly, "wythout addissyon / Or disencrese, outher mor or lesse" (lines 201–02), do not adequately reassure us on this point.

Thus the narrator is the only one left who can lead readers through the poem's examination of personal consciousness, but we fear he may not be adequate to the task. The narrator is himself in need of therapeutic treatment for his "bitter langour" (line 109) and "the brynnyng that sate so nyghe [his] hert" (line 114) — treatment that he receives at the "holsom" well that is able to ease and refresh all those "fallen in distresse" (lines 100, 105). Now that he is healed of his own distress, the task of refreshing his readers would seem to fall to him, since his voyeuristic handling of the situation makes him the sole authority of the narrative (though he claims to be but a "skryvener" writing "as his maister beside dothe endyte" — lines 194, 196). But the narrator's inadequacy for comforting anyone in distress, whether lover within the poem or readers outside it, becomes clear from his reaction to the discovery of a man prostrate on the ground, and so "destreyned [tormented] with sekenesse" that "Hyt was a deth for to her him grone" (lines 134, 140). Though he notices that the knight "had no felowe" and says he "coude no wyght with him se" (lines 143–44), the narrator's response is not to approach the poor knight to offer him comfort or even bring him water from the "holsom" well, despite his claims he "had routhe and eke pité" for the unhappy knight (line 145). Instead, he says, "I gan anon, so softly as I coude, / Amonge the busshes me prively to shroude" (lines 146–47). Will the narrator thus retreat from his readers too? In fact, he does, sitting back as the knight relates the whole complaint and not offering much in the way of a gloss on it.

But perhaps this lack of help from the narrator has the potential to be therapeutic itself by forcing readers to look into their own hearts even as they watch another's situation through the narrator's eyes. If Chaucer's narrator in *The Book of the Duchess* can perform a restorative role in his seemingly stumbling questions, which lead the suffering knight there into a "talking cure," this narrator's incompetence could conceivably lead to a similar cure for readers, if not for the knight of the tale. Seeing another's pain detailed, readers might find the tale as "holsom" as the well was to the narrator. And at first, it seems that the knight's complaint will help with such a task. The knight's physical state, described by the narrator, bears testament to his turmoil. At the beginning of his complaint, the knight then draws connections between his body and the interior emotions that inhabit it:

The thoght oppressed with inward sighes sore,	*inner (mental); painful*
The peynful lyve, the body langwysshing,	*existence; suffering*
The woful gost, the hert rent and tore,	*spirit; torn*
The petouse chere, pale in compleynyng,	
The dedely face lyke asshes in shynyng,	*deathly; pale like ashes (i.e., lifeless)*
The salt teres that fro myn yen falle,	*eyes*
Parcel declare grounde of my peynes alle.	*To some degree proclaim [the] foundation*
(lines 218–24)	

This connection between body and "inward sighes sore" elides the differences between mental and physical suffering, and sets up a metonymic relationship between both the physical and metaphysical aspects of the lover and his internal state of being, so that "the body langwysshing," "hert rent and tore," "petouse chere," "dedely face," and "salt teres" all become representative of his sickness as easily as his "thoght," "inward sighes," "peynful lyve," or "woful gost."

The knight's appeal to both his inner turmoil and the outward signs of it as evidence of his pain suggests the importance of personal experience, and extends the hope that the connection between suffering and complaint could in turn be transferred to the reader. But after moaning briefly, in a few token stanzas, about his fever and chills, he turns his appeal away from personal experience into the ethereal atmosphere of allegory, which takes place as a kind of courtroom drama in which the usual allegorical figures appear to sharpen their swords, file their arrows, and conspire maliciously "agens al ryght and lawe" to slay Truth (lines 258–59). Further attacks manage to damn Truth, with no recourse to his attorney, so that "Falsnes now his place occupieth" (line 266). The knight's appeal to the allegorical figures of *The Romance of the Rose* sets the stage for both his complaints against the injustice of the god of love and Fortune, and his turn to stories of love — all of which end violently — as proof of his own suffering. The source of his anguish is the arrows of blind Cupid, and the authority for his pain, he seems to suggest, is his similarity to those other lovers, such as Hercules, Pyramis, or Tristram, who suffered and died so spectacularly: "Lo, her the fyne [conclusion] of lovers servise!" (line 400). The knight's rehearsal of these tragic stories of love warns against getting involved in love at the same time as they expose his own false position as a lover, despite his attempts to align himself with Truth, because the fact that he is not himself dead or transformed undercuts the very comparisons the knight attempts to draw. Instead of emphasizing his own experience, the knight seeks to justify his distress on the basis of a connection to dead/transformed lovers that ultimately fails.

Finally, the knight's revelation that he spends *every* May complaining of his pains also lessens the importance of his grief and implies that talking about lovesickness does not "cure" it. His familiarity with the stories of other lovers points out that simply learning about such fellow sufferers does no good to relieve his pain either. The knight's recurring complaint in fact indicates that he is not really suffering at all, for those who truly love do not talk endlessly — as the knight's own rehearsal of stories makes clear; talking is instead a prelude to death and/or transformation. True lovers either kill themselves, waste away to death, or are killed or otherwise radically transformed by outside forces because of their love. The layering of the story, while seeming to provide the unadulterated account of a "real" lover, in fact shows the inadequacy of a "real" lover who cannot experience his own suffering except through allegory and old stories of former lovers' suffering. *A Complaynte of a Lovers Lyfe* finally suggests that neither talking about nor listening to tales of love-agony can provide the therapy readers desire. For one thing, the poem seems to imply, those who are still around to complain must not really be in pain (otherwise they would be dead or transformed); for another, whoever is well enough to pay attention to another's suffering instead of ending his/her own must not really need the transformative power of poetry. In any event, listening to such an inadequate lament will not ease distress — and if it does, the transformation may prove deadly.

The reference to secret watching in the narrator's prayer to Venus at the end of the poem, once the knight's complaint is finished, offers a final model for the narrator's role, and it is one that proves destructive for the lovers being watched. Vulcan, the narrator reminds us, captured his wife Venus in bed with Mars with an invisible net and invited the rest of the gods to witness their disgrace:

For that joy thou haddest when thou ley	*For [the sake of]; lay*
With Mars thi knyght, whom Vulcanus founde	
And with a cheyne unvisible yow bounde	*chain*
"Togedre both tweyne in the same while,	
That al the court above celestial	*[So] that*
At youre shame gan laughe and smyle.	
(lines 621–26)	

This image puts the narrator-as-spy in less danger himself, but suggests his role may be a nefarious one, detrimental to lovers. If this is the transformation the narrator has experienced — from Narcissus and Acteon to Vulcan — we can assume that he has progressed from innocent watching to the type of jealous surveillance that brings to mind Genius' warning to Amans in Gower's *Confessio Amantis* that those who "ben noght able as of hemselve / To gete love, and for Envie / Upon alle othre thei aspie" (ed. Peck, 2.98–100). Thus, the narrator as failed lover proves to be the worst kind of guide, offering models of destruction for lovers that suggest no redemption is possible through poetry.

Lydgate presents his dire exposition on the dangers of poetry to lovers within a frame that is, despite its modifications, recognizably Chaucerian, and it is no surprise that *A Complaynte of a Lovers Lyfe* shares many of the same manuscript contexts as John Clanvowe's *Boke of Cupide*. *Complaynte* appears, like Clanvowe's poem, in the closely related group comprised of Oxford, Bodleian Library MSS Fairfax 16, Tanner 346, and Bodley 638,[3] as well as in the Scottish compilation Oxford, Bodleian Library MS Arch. Selden. B. 24, where it is attributed to Chaucer.[4] In addition to these, there are copies in Oxford, Bodleian Library MS Digby 181; Cambridge, Magdalene College MS Pepys 2006; one of John Shirley's manuscripts (London, British Library MS Additional 16165); the Bannatyne manuscript (Edinburgh, National Library of Scotland MS 1.1.6); and the Asloan manuscript (Edinburgh, National Library of Scotland MS 16500).

The contents of Fairfax 16, Tanner 346, and Bodley 638 lean heavily towards Chaucer's dream visions, complaints, and shorter poems (as well as works by Lydgate, Hoccleve, and Clanvowe), while Digby 181 includes *Troilus and Criseyde* and *The Parliament of Fowls*, and Hoccleve's *Letter of Cupid*.[5] A. S. G. Edwards sees two strains of Chaucer compilation operating in the selection of Chaucer's poetry for these collections, one represented by Fairfax 16, Tanner 346, and Bodley 638, which display "a primary interest in Chaucer's dream visions and lyrics" and those, like Digby 181, that include *Troilus and Criseyde*, "occasionally in conjunction with other shorter works by or associated with Chaucer."[6] Arch. Selden. B. 24 combines these two "strands of earlier fifteenth-century manuscript compilation" by including Chaucer's *Troilus and Criseyde*, plus a selection of dream visions and shorter poems, such as *The Legend of Good Women*, *The Complaint of Mars*, *The Complaint of Venus*, and *Truth*.[7]

Pepys 2006 represents another Chaucerian anthology, comprised of "two originally quite distinct manuscripts."[8] The first of these is the pertinent one: it begins with *A Complaynte of a Lovers Lyfe*, followed by Lydgate's *Temple of Glass*, Chaucer's *Legend of Good Women*, *An ABC*, *The House of Fame*, *The Complaint of Mars*, *The Complaint of Venus*, *Fortune*, and *The Parliament of Fowls*. Like Fairfax 16, Tanner 346, and Bodley 638, the focus here is on dream

---

[3] Julia Boffey and John J. Thompson discuss the relationships of many of the following manuscripts, pp. 280–83.

[4] As *The Maying and Disport of Chaucere*. See the introduction to the facsimile volume, Julia Boffey and A. S. G. Edwards (1997), p. 1. The Introduction to *The Boke of Cupide*, above, provides a more detailed discussion of the contents of these four manuscripts (pp. 26 ff.).

[5] Edwards (1996), p. 56. Edwards explains that manuscripts like Digby 181 derived from Cambridge University Library MS Gg.IV.27, "the first attempt to create an anthology of Chaucer's works" (p. 56).

[6] Edwards (1996), p. 56.

[7] Edwards (1996), p. 56.

[8] See Edwards' introduction to the facsimile volume (1985), p. xvii.

visions, complaints, and lyrics, though Edwards points out in his introduction to the facsimile volume that the two manuscripts that make up Pepys 2006 both "suggest the broadening of the audience for Chaucer's works, since they seem clearly aimed at an audience very different from the courtly, sophisticated ones generally postulated for such Chaucer anthologies as Fairfax 16 or Tanner 346, one content with less elaborate and hence less expensive manuscripts."[9]

The Shirley manuscript, BL Add. 16165, probably the earliest, has a less cohesive organization than these Chaucerian anthologies.[10] Margaret Connolly explains that, despite the long prologue describing the contents that begins the collection, which "encourages us to receive it as an ordered and coherent entity[,] . . . the volume's vacillations between prose and verse, and its mixture of philosophy, instruction, and court poetry, seem to make little sense."[11] The compilation has relatively little by Chaucer — it begins with *Boece* (Chaucer's translation of Boethius' *De consolatione philosophiae*) and includes two selections from *Anelida and Arcite* somewhat later (separated from one another). John Trevisa's translation of *The Gospel of Nicodemus* follows *Boece*, after which comes Edward of York's treatise on hunting, *Master of Game*. After these prose works, *A Complaynte of a Lovers Lyfe*, here attributed to Lydgate,[12] is followed by another prose text, the Latin *Regula Sacerdotalis*, "a tract concerned with the duties and obligations of priests,"[13] then Lydgate's *Temple of Glass*, and a number of short lyrics and ballads, some anonymous, including a cluster of short poems by Lydgate near the end.[14] Connolly argues that the manuscript was compiled in at least three separate sections, which explains its eclectic contents.[15] The most coherent of these sections seems to have been the final one, which contains what Connolly calls "mostly an anthology of Lydgate's poetry," six of the eight Lydgate items.[16]

The final two manuscripts, Bannatyne and Asloan, are both sixteenth-century Scottish collections. Bannatyne is best known for containing large numbers of William Dunbar's works. The copy of *Complaynte* in Bannatyne is a Scottish version in 21 rhyme royal stanzas, while

---

[9] Edwards (1985), p. xvii.

[10] Boffey and Thompson discuss Shirley's manuscript collections, pp. 284–87.

[11] Connolly, p. 28.

[12] Connolly, p. 37.

[13] Connolly, p. 28.

[14] The poems by Lydgate are: "St. Anne," "Departure of Thomas Chaucer," "My Lady Dere," "Beware of Doublenesse," "A Lover's New Year's Gift," and "The Servant of Cupid Forsaken"; Connolly lists the contents of the manuscript in Table 1, pp. 30–31.

[15] Connolly, p. 28.

[16] Connolly, p. 40.

the Asloan text was copied from the Chepman and Myllar print. Unlike Arch. Selden. B. 24, these manuscripts do not illustrate an extensive interest in Chaucer, but rather in verse composed by Scots writers, such as William Dunbar and Robert Henryson, though in both cases, the poem is attributed to Chaucer, as it is in the Chepman and Myllar print.[17]

In his relationship to the king and court, Lydgate differs from Chaucer, Gower, and other Ricardian poets who were willing to criticize, "even though the advice they proffer usually turns out to be ultimately complicit with the prince's program."[18] David Wallace points out that Lydgate "emerges as the only poet in this period, c. 1399–1547, to enjoy meaningful, official recognition *as* an English poet at court."[19] Derek Pearsall's recent *Bio-Bibliography* gives the details of Lydgate's life and his relationship to the court. John Lydgate was a Benedictine monk at Bury St. Edmunds in Suffolk, not far from where he was born in about 1371 in the town of Lydgate, from which he took his name. He probably became a novice at age 15, professing as a full monk at 16. He later became a sub-deacon, then deacon, then priest over the course of eight years from 1389–97, before attending Oxford in the early years of the fifteenth century, though he does not seem to have taken a degree. Beginning as early as his years at Oxford, Lydgate came, as a poet, under the patronage of the Prince of Wales, later King Henry V.[20] Pearsall suggests that

> Henry had his attention drawn to Lydgate's facility as a versifier, recognised his promise as a future Lancastrian propagandist, and perhaps saw too the possibilities for a kind of high-style religious poetry in English that would embody his own austerely orthodox piety, fulfil his desire to promote the English language as an engine of nationhood, and preempt the claims of the Lollards on the vernacular as a language of religion.[21]

---

[17] In the Asloan MS and the Chepman and Myllar print under a variation of the title in Arch. Selden. B. 24. For a description of Bannatyne, see William Dunbar, *The Poems of William Dunbar*, ed. Priscilla Bawcutt, 1.6–7; for Asloan, see 1.5–6; for the Chepman and Myllar print, see 1.4–5. For Bannatyne's contents, see the introduction to the facsimile volume by Denton Fox and William A. Ringler, pp. xviii–xl. For the contents of Asloan, see W. A. Craigie, ed., *The Asloan Manuscript: A Miscellany in Prose and Verse, Written by John Asloan in the Reign of James the Fifth*, Scottish Text Society first ser. 14, 16 (Edinburgh: W. Blackwood and Sons, 1923–25). It is now possible to view images of the Chepman and Myllar print online at <http://www.nls.uk/digitallibrary/chepman/page.htm>, part of the National Library of Scotland's digital library (includes transcriptions of each page and a table of contents).

[18] Strohm, p. 657.

[19] See the introduction to "Before the Reformation," in Wallace, 1999, pp. 637–39, at p. 637; italics in original.

[20] For the above details, see Pearsall (1997), pp. 12–17.

[21] Pearsall (1997), p. 17.

The first big commission was *Troy Book*, a translation of the lengthy *Historia destructionis Troiae* of Guido della Collona, which fit as "part of Henry's policy of encouraging the use of English, in the writing of official documents as well as in the writing of poetry, as a way of consolidating national unity and identity."[22] Henry also appears to have continued his patronage after he became king, commissioning *A Defence of Holy Church*, *The Life of Our Lady*, and other poems. Lydgate continued to serve Henry until Henry's death in 1422, after which he became prior of Hatfield Broad Oak from 1423–30. There he wrote poetry supporting Henry VI but was also commissioned to write a variety of works for a diverse group of patrons. He seems to have spent time in Paris in 1426, receiving commissions from the earls of Warwick and Salisbury,[23] after which he returned to England to begin a very prolific three years, which Pearsall describes as "the apogee of his public career as a poet."[24] Pearsall associates many of the London poems with this period, also stating that Lydgate fulfilled many commissions at this time, both royal and for lesser aristocratic patrons. Lydgate returned to Bury in late 1433 (at the time of a royal visit, after which he seems to have stayed on), where he remained until his death in c. 1449, continuing a fairly steady stream of poetic output through the 1430s (including *The Fall of Princes*), slowing to only a few poems in the 1440s.[25]

A Complaynte of a Lovers Lyfe is presumed to be Lydgate's on the basis of the heading in the Shirley manuscript (BL Add. 16165).[26] Pearsall considers it one of the three poems "which are amongst Lydgate's most significant achievement" and adds that the poem "is one of

---

[22] Pearsall (1997), pp. 18–19.

[23] For the above details, see Pearsall (1997), pp. 18–27.

[24] Pearsall (1997), p. 27.

[25] For the above details, see Pearsall (1997), pp. 28–40. In 1439 he was finally granted an annuity for his royal service (p. 36). For further details of Lydgate's life, see Pearsall (1970, 1997). For more on the fifteenth-century, see V. J. Scattergood, *Politics and Poetry in the Fifteenth Century* (London: Blandford Press, 1971).

[26] See also Eleanor Prescott Hammond's discussion of the manuscripts (1908, pp. 413–15, especially p. 414). Shirley's is the only attribution to Lydgate; other manuscripts provide no information as to author, with the exception of Arch. Selden. B. 24, which attributes the poem to Chaucer (see the facsimile volume, intro. Boffey and Edwards, 1997, fol. 129v). Shirley's "rubrics in his Lydgate manuscripts are an important source of information (and misinformation) for the dates and occasions of Lydgate's poems," according to Pearsall, who adds that "his attributions are nearly all well supported by other external evidence and/or by strong internal evidence of style, syntax, and metre," but recommends evaluating Shirley's information on a case by case basis (1997, pp. 17–18). See Boffey and Edwards (1998), for further discussion of Shirley's collections. Without going into detail, Alain Renoir and C. David Benson remark that "[a]lthough the authorship has been questioned, this poem is generally assumed to be Lydgate's" (p. 1823).

Lydgate's best."[27] Some scholars have advanced an early date, possibly from the Oxford years, for *Complaynte*. For example, Walter F. Schirmer dates it at 1400–02, Lois A. Ebin calls it "one of his earliest poems," and John Norton-Smith argues in his notes to the poem that it should be considered an early work (from 1398 to 1412) because "it clearly belongs to a period of Lydgate's development characterized by close Chaucerian imitation and use of the *persona* of an actual lover," adding that later "the *persona* of the poet in Lydgate's work becomes less conventional, more autobiographical, and more religiously assertive," attributing this to Lydgate's experience in writing *Troy Book*.[28] But Pearsall cautions against assuming that the *Complaynte* and other "undated love-poems" were composed in this early period, claiming that "[s]uch poems would have been appropriate for Lydgate to write only when he had secured a measure of freedom from monastic restraint, in the 1420s."[29] Pearsall suggests in particular the three-year period of close affiliation with the court (1427–29) as the most likely time for writing of these poems.[30]

Scholarship on Lydgate, like that on much fifteenth-century poetry, has typically reflected a strong admiration of Chaucer, of whom Lydgate and many of his contemporaries were said to be imitators. The notion that Lydgate's value should be measured primarily by his resemblance to Chaucer, embedded as it was in the idea of Lydgate as imitator rather than innovator, condemned his writing as second class in the view of critics who not only privileged originality and inventiveness but had also already decided that Lydgate lacked such qualities. Martin J. Duffell sums up the situation in a recent article:

> Most modern critics and editors of John Lydgate's work feel it necessary to address the problem of his reputation as a versifier: why did his contemporaries rate him so highly when twentieth-century writers regard him, at best, as idiosyncratic and, at worst, as incompetent? Thus, for example, [George] Saintsbury dismissed him as "a doggerel poet with an insensitive ear" and [Eleanor Prescott] Hammond demonstrated that Lydgate's roughness was due, not to ignorant copyists, but to an ignorant poet; "The study of Lydgate's mentality," she concluded, "may not be worth the student's candle." In the last sixty years a number of writers . . . have made important contributions to our understanding of Lydgate's metrics, but have not succeeded in making us

---

[27] Pearsall (1970), pp. 84 and 97.

[28] Schirmer, p. 31; Ebin, p. 22; Norton-Smith (1966), p. 161.

[29] Pearsall (1997), p. 14.

[30] Pearsall (1997), p. 31.

admire his versification. Yet he was the most prolific and admired versifier in England during his own lifetime and for a century after his death.[31]

Pearsall made a similar assessment in 1970 about the nineteenth century, saying that Joseph Ritson's condemnation of Lydgate in his 1802 *Bibliographia poetica* as "this voluminous, prosaick and driveling monk" has "put paid to the possibility of any cool and discriminating consideration of Lydgate's work," adding that "in modern times strings of literary historians have vied with each other to heap ridicule upon his head."[32] Yet Pearsall's own insistence on emphasizing and accounting for the charges leveled against Lydgate still directs the focus away from the appeal of Lydgate's verse for contemporary audiences.[33] And Duffell's comments that "Lydgate's verse design was different from Chaucer's and was more conservative," which he says "is perhaps not surprising, since Chaucer's was so revolutionary" are no more inclined to endear him to twentieth- and twenty-first-century ears than Hammond's comment about the waste of a student's candle.[34]

Lydgate's prolific production of an estimated 145,000 lines of poetry[35] suggests one reason for him to be maligned, the assumption being that a writer who could produce so much must not be producing much of quality.[36] As Pearsall puts it, "[i]n more recent times he has been more or less universally contemned and become the butt of every jibe, especially for his prolixity and the great bulk of his writing. He now appears like a great whale helplessly beached on the shore of reputation."[37] Indeed, according to critical complaints, Lydgate's was a poetic of excess, for not only was he too prolific, but he was also too prolix, too dull, too

---

[31] Duffell, p. 227. The comments he cites from Hammond are in *English Verse between Chaucer and Surrey* (Durham, NC: Duke University Press, 1927), p. 152.

[32] Pearsall (1970), pp. 3–4 (Ritson qtd. on p. 3).

[33] Pearsall (1970), for example, still describes Lydgate as "prolific, prolix and dull" despite his own attempts to account for these qualities (see pp. 4–14). See also Pearsall (1990), p. 39.

[34] Duffell, p. 247.

[35] Renoir and Benson, p. 1809.

[36] As Pearsall puts it, "No one who wrote so much can be anything but a hack, we may think, and protect ourselves from what looks like an unrewarding task by simply dismissing the man and his work as unworthy of our attention" (1970, p. 4). Pearsall goes on to point out the problems with this view, arguing that we should not conflate our expectations for poetry with those of the Middle Ages (p. 4). For Lydgate "poetry is a public art, its existence conditioned and determined by outer needs and pressures, not by inner ones"; thus, looking at Lydgate's poetry as an example of the development of "poetic personality," for example, would be irrelevant (p. 5).

[37] Pearsall (1990), p. 39.

ornate, too superficial, and too politically conventional, always ready to write (too) glowing verse in support of his patrons and king.[38]

In addition to these charges might be added that he was too dependent on Chaucer — along with a kind of critical insistence on keeping him there. Pearsall, for example, though acknowledging correspondences "with the French love-vision poems of Machaut, Deschamps, and Froissart," concludes that "the parallels are general to an infinitely familiar tradition, and it is rarely necessary to go beyond Chaucer for Lydgate's specific borrowings."[39] Similarly, for classical models "Chaucer, as always, provides the focus of the tradition for Lydgate."[40] But these views of Lydgate's singular reliance on Chaucer backfire when it becomes clear that his poetry does not provide the same pleasures as Chaucer's verse, with the consequence that Lydgate inevitably suffers by comparison to his precursor in the modern critical eye. When Pearsall, one of Lydgate's staunchest longtime defenders, says that *Complaynte* privileges "the profusion of surface ornament at the expense of inner significance," or that it is "fundamentally . . . an easy poem, almost a template of a poem,"[41] he is still reacting to it in terms of a Chaucerian aesthetic, despite his acknowledgment of the problematic nature of such reactions.[42]

Ebin sees the surface ornamentation as deliberate, remarking that Lydgate "moves the complaint genre away from narrativity and realism toward artifact," while his amplification of "a single moment or moments in time" attempts "to create an intricate surface of words and sounds."[43] The emphasis on "artifact" and "surface" suggests an ossified poetic that does not cater to modern tastes, not only because it does not tell a realistic story, but also because of its

---

[38] Paul Strohm explains that "throughout his poetry, Lydgate does what he can to see that obstinate circumstances and putative enemies voluntarily adjust themselves to the requirements of the Lancastrian solution" (p. 656). He argues, "Jettisoning the stance of the loyalist critic, Hoccleve and Lydgate address Henry V and Henry VI in the voice of the wholehearted ally determined in no respect to offend" (p. 657), going on to add, "If the characteristic Ricardian pattern was to chide the monarch even while assenting in the end to things he wants done, the characteristic Lancastrian pattern moves in the opposite direction: an extreme surface deference to the monarch's aims and an attempt to accommodate all aspects of his programme eventuates in a text that straddles crisis after crisis of argumentative consistency" (p. 659). See also Lee Patterson, "Making Identities in Fifteenth-Century England: Henry V and John Lydgate," *New Historical Literary Study: Essays on Reproducing Texts, Representing History* (Princeton: Princeton University Press, 1993), pp. 69–107.

[39] Pearsall (1970), p. 84.

[40] Pearsall (1970), p. 85.

[41] Pearsall (1970), pp. 86, 95.

[42] Pearsall (1970) explicitly argues that "Chaucer, in fact, as this study will make plain more than once, is not a very representative medieval poet" (p. 6).

[43] Ebin, p. 21.

interest in formal design.[44] Ebin goes on to emphasize this impression by arguing that Lydgate uses "formal and stylistic devices" to "transform emotion into design."[45] This ultimately suggests that we must move beyond the understanding of Lydgate that has informed much of twentieth-century scholarship on his poetry in order to understand what made Lydgate's poem compelling enough to be "widely imitated in the fifteenth century."[46]

If Lydgate's poetry is not to suffer, in other words, we must think beyond his relationship to Chaucer, despite the fact that he was considered "in his own life-time . . . the principal inheritor of the Chaucerian poetic tradition."[47] It should be possible to acknowledge the different pleasures offered by Chaucer's verse and by the Chaucerian poetry that both followed and modified or added to it. But critical preference for Chaucer has made it difficult to understand what medieval audiences may have appreciated about Lydgate, despite the fact that he was perceived "by his contemporaries [to be] an equal and, in some cases, a superior poet to Chaucer."[48] Pearsall is no doubt right to point out that this "difference of opinion, so stark and inexplicable, is a challenge," and, in Pearsall's view, critical explanations have put forth either "extremely derogatory estimates of the good sense of Lydgate's fifteenth-century admirers, or else unlikely suggestions as to the merit of his verses."[49] He suggests that

> In taking up the challenge, again, one would not want to become embroiled in further debate about whether Lydgate's poetry is any good. There is no need for a debate: it is not very good. It is often dull, especially in long stretches, and it usually comes in long stretches. It is hard work to read, and the most skilful reader, however optimistic he is about Lydgate's versification, will stumble every few lines.[50]

The explanation Pearsall offers for the stark differences between medieval and modern reception of Lydgate's work is that "it is all Chaucer's fault."[51] In one sense this is true, but in another sense, it is also the fault of scholars' persistence in discussing the merits of Lydgate's poetry in aesthetic terms — i.e., it is either "good" or "bad." It may be more useful to think instead of the pleasures he may have offered his audiences.

---

[44] Pearsall (1970) points out at great length the differences between medieval and modern aesthetic expectations with a view to explaining Lydgate's medieval popularity (pp. 8–11).

[45] Ebin, p. 21.

[46] Pearsall (1970), p. 84.

[47] Pearsall (1997), p. 9.

[48] Ebin, preface.

[49] Pearsall (1990), p. 39.

[50] Pearsall (1990), p. 39.

[51] Pearsall (1990), p. 39.

In a more recent article, Pearsall points to at least two possibilities for audience enjoyment when he shows that Lydgate was an innovator in his persistent use of "new and rare words,"[52] and in his activity in "responding to . . . commissions and also to requests of all kinds for occasional poems, especially those that were needed to accompany some kind of visual display."[53] This perhaps offers some explanation for the tendency towards surface ornamentation noted by both Pearsall and Ebin. Recently Sue Bianco has suggested that a fresh look at Lydgate's relationship to Chaucer should be instigated. She argues that *Complaynte*, instead of existing merely as an imitation of Chaucerian verse, may have been influenced by French poetry more than has been previously acknowledged, suggesting that we should not look so narrowly upon the field of influence. Ultimately Bianco argues that a particular occasion most likely existed for the composition of English love-complaints, since these poems were modeled on French poems that were generically heavily invested in occasion, and suggests that Lydgate's *Complaynte of a Lovers Lyfe* may have had a topical genesis itself.[54]

New approaches to Lydgate scholarship need not focus on recovering the source of a poem's inspiration, and Bianco's discussion of the occasional nature of this type of verse in fact points to one of the pleasures Lydgate's verse might have offered its contemporaries — that of figuring out who the characters might represent and the situation for which a poem might have been composed. Bianco points, for example, to the way in which the portrait of the lady in Lydgate's *Temple of Glass* "mutates" from copy to copy; the colors she wears and the mottos associated with her differ in some manuscripts, suggesting that she was adopted for different patrons and/or occasions.[55] Some of the marginalia in the copy of *The Temple of Glass* from Bodley 638 suggest that medieval readers may have been attempting to figure out such associations: "*hic vsque nescio quis*" ("up to this point I do not know who [this might be]"), and "who in all godly pity maye be."[56] Bianco interprets these marginal comments to mean that "the writer of these remarks may have been trying in vain to work out the lady's identity," adding that "Charles d'Orléans, Lydgate's contemporary, used anagrams . . . to conceal the personalities behind his characters; the fourteenth-century 'game' of deciphering identity from

---

[52] Pearsall (1992), p. 9. Pearsall acknowledges the seeming contradiction in his "offer to write on Lydgate as an innovator," adding: "it is a view of his poetic achievement apparently quite contrary to the views I myself have put forward in the past" (p. 5).

[53] Pearsall (1992), p. 21.

[54] Bianco initially presents this argument in "A Black Monk in the Rose Garden: Lydgate and the *Dit Amoureux* Tradition" and extends it in "New Perspectives on Lydgate's Courtly Verse."

[55] Bianco (1999), pp. 64–65.

[56] At line 847 (fol. 29v) and line 972 (fol. 31v), respectively. These marginal notations are discussed in J. Schick's edition of *The Temple of Glas*, p. xx; and in Bianco (1999), p. 65 (both put the second phrase at line 970).

symbolic representation was alive and well in the first half of the fifteenth century."[57] Such attempts to decipher clues in *The Temple of Glass* point more generally to the inherent interest occasional poetry could engender for its audiences. It would seem that Lydgate's style thus works well with the type of verse that made up so much of his poetic output: as a poet of presentation and commissioned works, Lydgate knew how to produce a properly ornamental setting for a proper occasion.

Note on the text

A Complaynte of a Lovers Lyfe appears in the nine manuscripts discussed above and listed in detail below. The poem was also popular among early printers, forming part of the repertoire of Walter Chepman and Androw Myllar and Wynkyn de Worde, as well as making its way into editions of Chaucer by William Thynne, John Stow, and Thomas Speght. John Norton-Smith and E. Krausser each offer discussions of the manuscripts and their relationships,[58] which can be classified into two rough groups. The Shirley manuscript is the earliest (c. 1420) and "is a unique (probably earlier) version of the poem," but is missing the prayer to Venus; Arch. Selden. B. 24, a manuscript from the late fifteenth or early sixteenth century, is also missing some lines though it descends from another early copy. These two are more closely related than the remaining manuscripts and share a number of bad readings.[59] Fairfax 16, Bodley 638, Tanner 346, Digby 181, and Pepys 2006 form another group that can again be subdivided, with Fairfax 16 and the acephalous Bodley 638 sharing a closer relationship than the others, while Pepys 2006 is probably the worst of these, "marred by excessive mechanical mistakes and omissions."[60] Fairfax 16 and Tanner 346 would both make good choices, and here I follow previous editors in preferring the Fairfax 16 manuscript for its slightly earlier date.[61] Emendations and some alternate readings from selected manuscripts are recorded in the textual notes, according to the principles laid out in the General Introduction. I have taken the horizontal stroke above a word such as *rec forte* (line 8) to be an abbreviation of a nasal consonant (*n/m*) and have expanded accordingly. Other strokes and flourishes are disregarded as otiose.

---

[57] Bianco (1999), p. 65.

[58] See Norton-Smith (1966), pp. 160–61; and Krausser, pp. 216–23.

[59] Norton-Smith (1966), p. 160.

[60] Norton-Smith (1966), pp. 160–61.

[61] Norton-Smith (1979) gives a description of the manuscript in his introduction to the facsimile volume.

Indexed in

IMEV 1507.

Manuscripts

London, British Library MS Additional 16165 (Shirley MS), fols. 190v–200v (c. 1420s). [Missing the narrator's prayer to Venus, lines 610–51.]

Oxford, Bodleian Library MS Fairfax 16 (*SC* 3896), fols. 20v–30r (1430–50). [Base text for this edition.]

Oxford, Bodleian Library MS Tanner 346 (*SC* 10173), fols. 48v–59r (mid- to late fifteenth century).

Oxford, Bodleian Library MS Digby 181 (*SC* 1782), fols. 31r–39r (second half of fifteenth century).

Cambridge, Magdalene College MS Pepys 2006, pp. 1–17 (second half of fifteenth century).

Oxford, Bodleian Library MS Bodley 638 (*SC* 2078), fols. 1r–4v (late fifteenth century). [Missing lines 1–467 because the manuscript is defective at beginning.]

Oxford, Bodleian Library MS Arch. Selden. B. 24 (*SC* 3354), fols. 120v–129v (late fifteenth or early sixteenth century). [Missing lines 113–26.]

Edinburgh, National Library of Scotland MS 16500 (Asloan MS), fols. 243r–246v, 293r–300v (early sixteenth century). [Copied from the Chepman and Myllar print.]

Edinburgh, National Library of Scotland MS 1.1.6 (Bannatyne MS), fols. 281r–283v (1568). [Scottish version in 21 rhyme royal stanzas (lines 302–434, 456–69), attributed to Chaucer, and possibly copied "from the edition of c. 1545–50,"[62] STC 5071–74.]

---

[62] See the introduction to the facsimile volume, Fox and Ringler, p. xxxviii, no. 371. The version is different enough to be listed separately in *IMEV* (3911.5).

Early printed editions

Chepman, Walter, and Androw Myllar, eds. and printers. *The Maying or Disport of Chaucer*. Edinburgh, 1508. [STC 17014.3 (formerly 5099). Originally printed as a booklet together with *When by Divine Deliberation*, but later bound together with other Chepman and Myllar prints.]

Wynkyn de Worde, ed. and printer. *The Cōplaynte of a Louers Lyfe*. London, ?1531. [STC 17014.7].

Thynne, William, ed. *The Workes of Geffray Chaucer Newly Printed: With Dyuers Workes Whiche Were Neuer in Print Before*. London: T. Godfray, 1532. [STC 5068. Rpt. 1542, STC 5069; ?1550, STC 5071.]

Stow, John, ed. *The Workes of Geffrey Chaucer: Newly Printed, With Diuers Addicions, Whiche were Neuer in Printe Before: With the Siege and Destruccion of the Worthy Citee of Thebes, Compiled by Jhon Lidgate*. London: J. Wight, 1561. [STC 5075. Based on Thynne.]

Speght, Thomas, ed. *The Workes of our Antient and Lerned English Poet, Geffrey Chavcer, newly Printed*. London: G. Bishop, 1598. [STC 5077. Rpt. 1602, STC 5080; 1687. Based on Thynne.]

A Complaynte of a Lovers Lyfe or
The Complaint of the Black Knight

	In May when Flora, the fressh lusty quene,	*bright invigorating*
	The soyle hath clad in grene, rede, and white,	*soil*
	And Phebus gan to shede his stremes shene	*began to shine; bright rays*
	Amyd the Bole wyth al the bemes bryght,[1]	
5	And Lucifer, to chace awey the nyght,	*i.e., the morning star*
	Agen the morowe our orysont hath take[2]	
	To byd lovers out of her slepe awake,	*bid; their*
	And hertys hevy for to recomforte	*sorrowful hearts; ease*
	From dreryhed of hevy nyghtis sorowe,	*Of misery; night's*
10	Nature bad hem ryse and disporte	*bade them rise; make merry*
	Ageyn the goodly, glad, grey morowe;	*morning*
	And Hope also, with Seint John to borowe,	*Saint John as his guarantor*
	Bad in dispite of Daunger and Dispeyre	*Bade; spite; Resistance; Despair*
	For to take the holsome, lusty eyre.	*wholesome, invigorating air*
15	And wyth a sygh I gan for to abreyde	*sigh; began to awake*
	Out of my slombre and sodenly out stert,	*sleep; awakened abruptly*
	As he, alas, that nygh for sorowe deyde —	*Like one; who nearly; died*
	My sekenes sat ay so nygh myn hert.[3]	
	But for to fynde socour of my smert,	*find relief for; suffering*
20	Or attelest summe relesse of my peyn	*at least some relief*
	That me so sore halt in every veyn,	*sorely afflicted*
	I rose anon and thoght I wolde goon	*right away; would go*
	Unto the wode to her the briddes sing,	*wood; hear; birds*
	When that the mysty vapour was agoon,	*foggy mist; gone*

---

[1] *In the midst of the Bull (i.e., the zodiacal sign Taurus) with all the beams bright*

[2] *Shortly before the morning hour (i.e., dawn) has pierced [the] horizon (celestial vault)*

[3] *My sickness sat always so near my heart (i.e., affected me deeply)*

25	And clere and feyre was the morownyng.	*light; pleasant; morning (dawn)*
	The dewe also, lyk sylver in shynyng	*like silver; brilliance*
	Upon the leves as eny baume suete,	*leaves; any sweet balm*
	Til firy Tytan with hys persaunt hete	*i.e., the sun; piercing heat*
	Had dried up the lusty lycour nyw	*fresh dew*
30	Upon the herbes in the grene mede,	*plants; meadow*
	And that the floures of mony dyvers hywe	*flowers; many different colors*
	Upon her stalkes gunne for to sprede	*their; began to open*
	And for to splay out her leves on brede	*spread out their; wide*
	Ageyn the sunne, golde-borned in hys spere,	*Under; gold-burnished; sphere*
35	That doun to hem cast hys bemes clere.	*bright beams*
	And by a ryver forth I gan costey,	*river; went alongside*
	Of water clere as berel or cristal,	*beryl*
	Til at the last I founde a lytil wey	*little path*
	Touarde a parke enclosed with a wal	*surrounded by*
40	In compas rounde; and, by a gate smal,	*All around; by [means of]*
	Hoso that wolde frely myght goon	*Whoever wished; go*
	Into this parke walled with grene stoon.	
	And in I went to her the briddes songe,	*hear; birds' song*
	Which on the braunches, bothe in pleyn and vale,	*field and valley*
45	So loude songe that al the wode ronge,	*sang; wood rang*
	Lyke as hyt sholde shever in pesis smale.	*it; shatter into small pieces*
	And, as me thoght, that the nyghtyngale	*it seemed to me*
	Wyth so grete myght her voys gan out wrest,	*intensified her voice*
	Ryght as her hert for love wolde brest.	*as [if]; burst*
50	The soyle was pleyn, smothe, and wonder softe,	*flat; soil*
	Al oversprad wyth tapites that Nature	*covered; tapestries (carpets)*
	Had made herselfe, celured eke alofte	*canopied also aloft*
	With bowys grene, the flores for to cure,	*boughs; flowers; shield*
	That in her beauté they may longe endure	*their*
55	Fro al assaute of Phebus fervent fere,	*From; assault; heat*
	Which in his spere so hote shone and clere.	*hot*
	The eyre atempre and the smothe wynde	*mild (temperate) air*
	Of Zepherus amonge the blosmes whyte	*blossoms*

	So holsomme was and so norysshing be kynde	*nourishing by nature*
60	That smale buddes and rounde blomes lyte	*shoots (buds); round little blooms*
	In maner gan of her brethe delyte	*After a fashion did; breath delight*
	To gif us hope that their frute shal take,	*give; will begin to grow*
	Agens autumpne redy for to shake.	*Toward; ready to fall*

	I sawe ther Daphene, closed under rynde,	*Daphne; within bark*
65	Grene laurer, and the holsomme pyne,	*laurel; pine*
	The myrre also, that wepeth ever of kynde,	*myrrh; by nature*
	The cedres high, upryght as a lyne,	*cedars; perfectly upright*
	The philbert eke, that lowe dothe enclyne	*filbert (hazel nut tree)*
	Her bowes grene to the erthe doune	*earth*
70	Unto her knyght icalled Demophoune.	*Demophon*

	Ther saw I eke the fressh hawthorne	
	In white motele that so soote doth smelle;[1]	
	Asshe, firre, and oke with mony a yonge acorne,	*fir; oak*
	And mony a tre mo then I can telle.	*more*
75	And me beforne I sawe a litel welle	*before me; spring*
	That had his course, as I gan beholde,	*beheld*
	Under an hille with quyke stremes colde.	*flowing streams (springs)*

	The gravel golde, the water pure as glas,	
	The bankys rounde the welle environyng,[2]	
80	And softe as velvet the yonge gras	
	That therupon lustely gan spryng.	*vigorously did*
	The sute of trees about compassyng	*row; extending all around*
	Her shadowe cast, closyng the wel rounde	*Their; enclosing the spring*
	And al th'erbes grouyng on the grounde.	*the plants growing*

	The water was so holsom and so vertuous	*full of power (virtuous)*
85	Throgh myghte of erbes grouynge beside —	*Through [the] virtue of plants growing*
	Nat lyche the welle wher as Narcisus	*Not like; where Narcissus*
	Islayn was thro vengeaunce of Cupide,	*Slain*
	Wher so covertely he did hide	*subtly (secretly)*

---

[1] *In white motley (i.e., the flowers of the hawthorn) that smells so sweet*

[2] *The circular earthworks surrounding the spring; or, The earthworks encircling the spring on all sides*

90	The greyn of deth upon ech brynk	*seed (grain); death; each side (edge)*
	That deth mot folowe, who that evere drynk;	*must*
	Ne lyche the pitte of the Pegacé	*Nor like; spring; Pegasus*
	Under Parnaso, wher poetys slept;	*Parnassus*
	Nor lyke the welle of pure chastité,	
95	Whiche as Dyane with her nymphes kept	*Diana*
	When she naked into the water lept,	
	That slowe Atteon with his houndes felle	*slew Acteon; deadly hounds*
	Oonly for he cam so nygh the welle.	*Only because; came so near*
	But this welle that I her reherse	*here discuss (give an account of)*
100	So holsom was that hyt wolde aswage	*it; sooth (assuage)*
	Bollyn hertis, and the venym perse	*Swollen [i.e., with anger]; destroy the venom*
	Of pensifhede with al the cruel rage,	*Of anger*
	And evermore refresh the visage	
	Of hem that were in eny werynesse	
105	Of gret labour or fallen in distresse.	
	And I that had throgh Daunger and Disdeyn	*Resistance*
	So drye a thrust, thoght I wolde assay	*thirst; attempt*
	To tast a draght of this welle, or tweyn,	*taste; drink; two*
	My bitter langour yf hyt myght alay;	*sickness if it; alleviate (allay)*
110	And on the banke anon doune I lay,	*bank*
	And with myn hede into the welle araght,	*reached (stretched)*
	And of the watir dranke I a good draght.	
	Wherof me thoght I was refresshed wel	*relieved*
	Of the brynnyng that sate so nyghe my hert	*From; burning; sat; near*
115	That verely anon I gan to fele	*truly; feel*
	An huge part relesed of my smert;	*alleviated (eased)*
	And therwithalle anon up I stert	*in response to that*
	And thoght I wolde walke and se more	*see*
	Forth in the parke and in the holtys hore.	*dark woods*
120	And thorgh a launde as I yede apace	*as I went quickly through a clearing*
	I gan about fast to beholde,	*to look around intently*
	I fonde anon a delytable place	*found; delightful*
	That was beset with trees yong and olde	*covered*

94

(Whos names her for me shal not be tolde),   *here*
125   Amyde of which stode an erber grene   *In the middle of; garden (arbor)*
        That benched was with clourys nyw and clene.   *was furnished with seats of turfs fresh*

        This erber was ful of floures ynde,   *deep blue flowers*
        Into the whiche, as I beholde gan,   *In which; saw/observed*
        Betwex an hulfere and a wodebynde,   *holly; honeysuckle (woodbine)*
130   As I was war, I sawe ther lay a man   *I noticed*
        In blake and white colour, pale and wan,
        And wonder dedely also of his hiwe,   *deathly; complexion*
        Of hurtes grene and fresh woundes nyw.   *recent injuries; recently inflicted (new)*

        And overmore destreyned with sekenesse   *moreover tormented*
135   Besyde, as thus he was ful grevosly,   *Besides; very severely*
        For upon him he had a hote accesse   *fever*
        That day be day him shoke ful petously,   *shook*
        So that, for constreynyng of hys malady   *because of [the] affliction*
        And hertly wo, thus lyinge al alone,   *heartfelt anguish*
140   Hyt was a deth for to her him grone.   *It; hear; groan*

        Wherof astonied, my fote I gan withdrawe,   *Astonished by that; foot*
        Gretly wondring what hit myght be   *why it*
        That he so lay and had no felowe,   *companion*
        Ne that I coude no wyght with him se,   *Nor; person*
145   Wherof I had routhe and eke pité;   *compassion*
        I gan anon, so softly as I coude,   *right away, as*
        Amonge the busshes me prively to shroude;   *myself secretly; hide*

        If that I myght in eny wise espye   *[To see] if; discover*
        What was the cause of his dedely woo,
150   Or why that he so pitously gan crie   *did cry out*
        On hys fortune and on his eure also,   *Against; fate also*
        With al my myght I leyde an ere to   *paid attention*
        Every worde to marke what he sayed   *to take note of*
        Out of his swogh among as he abreyde.   *swoon at intervals; recovered*

155   But first, yf I shal make mensyon   *mention*
        Of hys persone and pleynly him discrive,   *fully; describe*
        He was in sothe, without excepcion,   *truth*

95

To speke of manhod, oon the best on lyve —   *one [of]; alive*
Ther may no man agein trouthe stryve —   *argue with [the] truth*
160   For of hys tyme, and of his age also,
He proved was ther men shuld have ado.[1]

For oon the best ther of brede and lengthe,   *in every respect*
So wel ymade by good proporsion   *formed*
Yf he had be in his delyver strengthe;   *been; full*
165   But thoght and sekenesse wer occasion   *were [the] cause*
That he thus lay in lamentacion,
Gruffe on the grounde in place desolate,   *Face down; uninhabited*
Sole by himself, awaped and amate.   *Alone; stunned; exhausted (overcome)*

And for me semeth that hit ys syttyng   *because it seems to me; appropriate*
170   His wordes al to put in remembraunce,
To me that herde al his compleynyng   *lamenting*
And al the grounde of his woful chaunce,   *source; misfortune*
Yf therwithal I may yow do plesaunce,   *with that; please you*
I wol to yow, so as I can, anone
175   Lych as he seyde reherse everychone.   *Like; every one*

But who shal helpe me now to compleyn?
Or who shal now my stile guy or lede?   *pen (stylus) guide or control*
O Nyobe! Let now thi teres reyn   *Niobe; tears rain*
Into my penne and eke helpe in this nede,   *pen*
180   Thou woful mirre that felist my hert blede   *stream; feels*
Of pitouse wo, and my honde eke quake,   *compassionate; hand; tremble*
When that I write for this mannys sake.   *man's*

For unto wo acordeth compleynyng,   *complaining is fitting for misery (sorrow)*
And delful chere unto hevynesse;   *a sorrowful (doleful) expression to grief*
185   To sorow also, sighing and wepyng
And pitouse morenyng unto drerynesse;   *wretched lamentation; grief*
And who that shal write of distresse
In partye nedeth to know felyngly   *part; sympathetically*
Cause and rote of al such malady.   *root*

---

[1] *He was experienced [in those things] in which men should have involvement (concern)*

190	But I, alas, that am of wytte but dulle	*wit*
	And have no knowyng of suche mater	
	For to discryve and wryte at the fulle	*describe*
	The wofull compleynt which that ye shul here,	*hear*
	But even like as doth a skryvener	*precisely; professional scribe*
195	That can no more what that he shal write	*knows*
	But as his maister beside dothe endyte,	*dictate*

	Ryght so fare I, that of no sentement	*personal experience/feeling*
	Sey ryght noght, as in conclusion,	*absolutely nothing*
	But as I herde when I was present	
200	This man compleyn wyth a pytouse son;	*voice*
	For even lych, wythout addissyon	*exactly; addition [i.e., of words]*
	Or disencrese, outher mor or lesse,	*subtraction [i.e., of words], either*
	For to reherse anon I wol me dresse.	*devote myself*

	And yf that eny now be in this place	
205	That fele in love brennyng or fervence,	*passion; ardor*
	Or hyndered were to his lady grace	*slandered*
	With false tonges that with pestilence	*wickedness*
	Sle trwe men that never did offence	*Ruin faithful (true)*
	In worde ne dede, ne in their entent —	*nor*
210	Yf eny such be here now present,	

	Let hym of routhe ley to audyence	*[out] of pity pay attention*
	With deleful chere and sobre contenaunce	*sorrowful*
	To here this man, be ful high sentence,	*hear; with complete seriousness*
	His mortal wo and his perturbaunce,	*severe; agitation*
215	Compleynyng, now lying in a traunce	*faint*
	With loke upcast and reuful chere,	*glance turned upward; sorrowful face*
	Th'effect of which was as ye shal here.	*hear*

Compleynt

	"The thoght oppressed with inward sighes sore,	*inner (mental); painful*
	The peynful lyve, the body langwysshing,	*existence; suffering*
220	The woful gost, the hert rent and tore,	*spirit; torn*
	The petouse chere pale in compleynyng,	
	The dedely face lyke asshes in shynyng,	*pale like ashes (i.e., lifeless)*

The salt teres that fro myn yen falle,   *eyes*
Parcel declare grounde of my peynes alle.   *To some degree proclaim [the] foundation*

225   "Whos hert ys grounde to blede on hevynesse,   *crushed; bleed in misery*
The thoght resseyt of woo and of compleynt,   *[the] receptacle*
The brest is chest of dule and drerynesse,   *breast; [the] repository; grief*
The body eke so feble and so feynt.
With hote and colde my acces ys so meynt[1]
230   That now I shyver for defaute of hete,   *shiver; lack*
And hote as glede now sodenly I suete: *hot as [a] live coal; sweat*

"Now hote as fire, now colde as asshes dede,   *cold (i.e., lifeless)*
Now hote for colde, now cold for hete ageyn,
Now colde as ise, now as coles rede   *ice; fiery embers*
235   For hete I bren; and thus betwext tweyn   *burn; between two*
I possed am, and al forcast in peyn,   *pushed; tossed about*
So that my hete pleynly, as I fele,   *completely*
Of grevouse colde ys cause everydele.   *in every respect*

"This ys the colde of ynwarde high dysdeyn,   *cold (i.e., lack of feeling); scorn*
240   Colde of dyspite, and colde of cruel hate;   *contempt*
This is the colde that evere doth besy peyn   *does his best (takes pains)*
Agens trouthe to fight and debate;   *strive*
This ys the colde that wolde the fire abate
Of trwe menyng, alas, the harde while;   *faithful (pure) intention; difficult time*
245   This ys the colde that will me begile.

"For evere the better that in trouthe I ment
With al my myght feythfully to serve,
With hert and al to be dilygent,   *attentive*
The lesse thanke, alas, I can deserve.   *thanks; did*
250   Thus for my trouthe Daunger doth me sterve,   *loyalty Resistance; kill*
For oon that shuld my deth of mercie let   *[out] of pity prevent*
Hath made Dispite now his suerde to whet   *Defiance; sword to sharpen*

---

[1] *With sensations of heat and cold my feverous malady (i.e., lovesickness) is so mingled*

"Agens me and his arowes to file   *file (i.e., sharpen)*
To take vengeaunce of wilful cruelté;
255   And tonges fals throgh her sleghtly wile   *false; their sly wiles*
Han gonne a werre that wol not stynted be;   *have begun a war; stopped*
And fals Envye of wrathe, and Enemyté   *Hatred; Hostility*
Have conspired agens al ryght and lawe,
Of her malis, that Trouthe shal be slawe.   *their malice; Truth (Constancy in love) slain*

260   "And Male-Bouche gan first the tale telle   *Slander (lit., "Bad-Mouth")*
To sclaundre Trouthe of indignacion,   *slander; [out] of anger*
And Fals-Report so loude ronge the belle[1]
That Mysbeleve and Fals-Suspecion   *Skepticism (Mistrust)*
Have Trouthe brought to hys damnacion,   *ruin*
265   So that, alas, wrongfully he dyeth,   *dies*
And Falsnes now his place occupieth

"And entred ys into Trouthes londe   *has asserted ownership of Truth's estate*
And hath therof the ful possessyon.
O ryghtful God, that first the trouthe fonde,   *founded*
270   How may Thou suffre such oppressyon,
That Falshed shuld have jurysdixion   *Falsehood; power/authority*
In Trouthes ryght, to sle him giltles?   *slay; unjustly*
In his fraunchise he may not lyve in pes.   *freedom; peace*

"Falsly accused and of his foon forjuged,   *by his enemies convicted/sentenced*
275   Without unsuer while he was absent   *Without opportunity to defend himself in court*
He damned was and may not ben excused,   *convicted*
For Cruelté satte in jugement   *held court (sat in judgment)*
Of hastynesse, without avisement,   *In undue haste; consideration*
And bad Disdeyn do execute anon   *enforce*
280   His jugement in presence of hys fon.   *sentence/punishment; enemies*

"Atturney non ne may admytted ben   *be permitted [to plead in court]*
To excuse Trouthe, ne a worde to speke;
To feyth or othe the juge list not sen;   *formal pledge; oath; does not want to see*
Ther ys no geyn, but he wil be wreke.   *help; ruined*

---

[1] *And False-Report so loudly rang the bell (i.e., spoke so slanderously)*

285	O Lorde of Trouthe, to Thee I calle and cleke:	*hold fast*
	How may Thou se thus in Thy presence	
	Without mercy mordred Innocence?	*Innocence mercilessly destroyed*
	"Now God that art of Trouthe sovereyn	
	And seest how I lye for trouthe bounde,	*faithfulness bound*
290	So sore knytte in Loves firy cheyn,	*fettered; chain*
	Even at the deth, thro-girt wyth mony a wounde	*pierced through*
	That lykly ar never for to sounde,	*heal*
	And for my trouthe am damned to the dethe,	
	And noght abide but drawe alonge the brethe,[1]	
295	"Consider and se in Thyn eternal sight	
	How that myn hert professed whilom was	*pledged formerly/once*
	For to be trwe with al my ful myght	
	Oonly to oon, the which now, alas,	
	Of volunté, withoute more trespas,	*Arbitrarily/Willingly; [suffering] any injury*
300	Myn accusurs hath taken unto grace	*Has received my accusers with good will*
	And cherissheth hem my deth for to purchace.	*incites them to seek my death*
	"What meneth this? What ys this wonder ure	*strange fate [ordained]*
	Of purveance, yf I shal hit calle,	*providence (foreknowledge)*
	Of God of Love that fals hem so assure,	*[the] false are so confident*
305	And trew, alas, doun of the whele be falle?	*off the wheel [of Fortune] are fallen*
	And yet, in sothe, this is the worst of alle:	*truly*
	That Falshed wrongfully of Trouth hath the name,	
	And Trouthe, agenwarde, of Falshed bereth the blame.	*on the other hand*
	"This blynde chaunce, this stormy aventure,	
310	In love hath most his experience,	
	For who that doth with Truth most his cure	*duty/effort*
	Shal for his mede fynde most offence,	*reward; annoyance*
	That serveth Love with al his diligence;	
	For who can feyne under loulyhede	*whoever; feign; humility*
315	Ne fayleth not to fynde grace and spede.	*prosperity/luck*

---

[1] *And do not delay [it] but [merely] prolong my breathing*

"For I loved oon ful longe sythe agoon   *[a] long time ago*
With al my hert, body, and ful myght,
And to be ded my hert cannot goon   *to save my life; turn away*
From his hest, but hold that he hath hight.   *its vow; [to] that [which] it has promised*
320   Thogh I be banysshed out of her syght   *driven out*
And by her mouthe damned that I shal deye,   *condemned to death*
Unto my behest yet I wil ever obeye.   *promise*

"For evere sithe that the worlde began,
Whoso lyste loke and in storie rede,   *desires; read*
325   He shal ay fynde that the trwe man   *ever find; true (devoted)*
Was put abake, wheras the falshede   *hindered; deceitful [one]*
Ifurthered was, for Love taketh no hede   *Was advanced; is not concerned about*
To sle the trwe and hath of hem no charge,   *Killing; offers them no protection*
Wheras the fals goth frely at her large.   *boldly without restriction*

330   "I take recorde of Palamides,   *cite the case of Palomedes*
The trwe man, the noble worthy knyght,
That ever loved, and of hys peyne no relese;   *forever; relief*
Notwithstondyng his manhode and his myght,   *valor*
Love unto him did ful grete unright,   *wrong*
335   For ay the bette he did in chevalrye,   *ever the better; feats of arms*
The more he was hindred by envye;   *ill-will*

"And ay the bette he dyd in every place
Throgh his knyghthode and besy peyn,   *prowess; constant effort*
The ferther was he fro his ladys grace,
340   For to her mercie myght he never ateyn,
And to his deth he coude hyt not refreyn   *to save his life; restrain himself*
For no daunger, but ay obey and serve
As he best coude, pleynly til he sterve.   *unreservedly (completely); died*

"What was the fyne also of Ercules,   *end; Hercules*
345   For al his conquest and his worthynesse,   *victory*
That was of strengthe alone pereles?   *Who; peerless (unequaled)*
For, lyke as bokes of him list expresse,   *are pleased to relate*
He set pilers thro his high prouesse   *pillars; great might*
Away at Cades for to signifie   *Cadiz*
350   That no man myght hym passe in chevalrie;   *surpass*

101

"The whiche pilers ben ferre by-yonde Ynde   *far beyond Asia*
Beset of golde for a remembraunce.   *Covered*
And, for al that, was he sete behynde   *despite all that*
With hem that Love list febly avaunce;[1]

355   For him set laste upon a daunce   *he finally set himself of a course of action*
Agens whom helpe may no strife —   *struggle*
For al his trouth, he lost his lyfe.   *Despite; devotion*

"Phebus also, for al his persaunt lyght,   *piercing*
When that he went her in erthe lowe   *here*
360   Unto the hert with Venus sight   *the sight of Venus*
Ywounded was thro Cupides bowe;
And yet his lady list him not to knowe,   *wished*
Thogh for her love his hert did blede;
She let him go and toke of him non hede.   *made; notice*

365   "What shal I say of yong Piramus?   *Pyramus*
Of trwe Tristram for al his high renoune?
Of Achilles or of Antonyas?   *Antony*
Of Arcite or of him, Palamoune?   *Palamon*
What was the ende of her passion   *their*
370   But after sorowe, dethe, and then her grave?   *afterwards*
Lo, her the guerdon that lovers have!   *here; reward*

"But false Jasoun with his doublenesse,   *Jason; faithlessness*
That was untrwe at Colkos to Medé;   *unfaithful; Colchis; Medea*
And Tereus, rote of unkyndenesse;   *root of unnaturalness (ingratitude)*
375   And with these two eke the fals Ené.   *Aeneas*
Lo, thus the fals ay in oon degré   *in the same way*
Had in love her lust and al her wille,   *their desire; their will*
And save falshed ther was non other skille.   *except for*

"Of Thebes eke the fals Arcite,
380   And Demophon eke for his slouthe,   *sloth*
They had her lust and al that myght delyte   *their enjoyment*
For al her falshede and grete untrouthe.   *their*

---

[1] *With those whom Love half-heartedly desires [to] promote*

Thus ever Love, alas, and that is routhe,   *[a] pity*

His fals legys furthereth what he may   *attendants*

385   And sleeth the trwe ungoodly day be day.   *slays; unjustly*

"For trwe Adon was slayn with the bore   *Adonis; boar*

Amyde the forest in the grene shade,

For Venus love he felt al the sore.

But Vulcanus with her no mercy made;

390   The foule cherle had many nyghtis glade,   *churl; pleasant nights*

Wher Mars, her worthi knyght, her trewe man,

To fynde mercy, comfort noon he can.   *favor, gratification/pleasure*

"Also the yonge, fressh Ipomones,   *Hippomenes*

So lusty fre as of his corage,   *pleasingly noble; heart*

395   That for to serve with al his hert ches   *chose*

Athalans, so feire of her visage.   *Atalanta; fair*

But Love, alas, quyte him so his wage   *paid; due*

With cruel daunger pleynly at the last,

That with the dethe guerdonlesse he past.   *unrewarded; passed*

400   "Lo, her the fyne of lovers servise!   *conclusion*

Lo, how that Love can his servantis quyte!   *does; repay*

Lo, how he can his feythful men dispise   *does*

To sle the trwe men and fals to respite!   *spare*

Lo, how he doth the suerde of sorowe byte   *sword; pierce*

405   In hertis suche as must his lust obey   *desire*

To save the fals and do the trwe dey!   *cause the faithful (true) to die*

"For feythe nor othe, worde ne assuraunce,[1]

Trwe menyng, awayte, or besynesse,   *service, or diligence/devotion*

Stil port, ne feythful attendaunce,   *Quiet demeanor; attention (homage) paid*

410   Manhode, ne myght in armes, worthinesse,

Pursute of wurschip, nor high prouesse,   *Pursuit of honor; might*

In straunge londe rydinge ne travayle —

Ful lyte or noght in love dothe avayle.   *little; nothing*

---

[1] *For formal pledge nor oath, word of honor (promise) nor pledge of loyalty*

"Peril of dethe, nother in se ne londe,   *neither in sea nor land*
415   Hungre ne thrust, sorowe ne sekenesse,   *thirst*
Ne grete emprises for to take on honde,   *chivalric enterprises (deeds)*
Shedyng of blode, ne manful hardynesse,   *bold courage (daring)*
Nor ofte woundynge at sawtes by distresse,   *repeated; raids (assaults)*
Nor jupartyng of lyfe, nor dethe also —   *risking*
420   Al ys for noghte, Love taketh non hede therto.

"But Lesynges with her fals flaterye,   *Lies; their; flattery*
Thro her falshed and with her doublenesse,   *duplicity*
With tales new and mony feyned lye,   *many [a]; lie*
By false semlaunce and contrefet humblesse,   *pretense; counterfeit humility*
425   Under colour depeynt with stidfastnesse,   *Under guise of loyalty*
With fraude cured under a pitouse face,   *dishonesty concealed*
Accept ben now rathest unto grace,   *Are most easily taken into good graces*

"And can hemself now best magnifie   *exalt*
With feyned port and presumpsion.   *appearance/demeanor*
430   They haunce her cause with fals surquedrie,   *advance their; pride*
Under menyng of double-entencion,   *double-purpose*
To thenken on in her opynyon   *one [thing]; their opinion*
And sey another, to set hemselfe alofte
And hynder Truthe, as hit ys seyn ful ofte.

435   "The whiche thing I bye now al to dere,   *purchase; too dearly (i.e., at too high a price)*
Thanked be Venus and the god Cupide,
As hit is seen by myn oppressed chere   *evident; expression*
And by his arowes that stiken in my syde,   *arrows; are embedded*
That, safe the dethe, I nothing abide   *[So] that, except for; await*
440   Fro day to day — alas, the harde while!   *difficult time*
Whenevere hys dart that hym list to fyle,   *he wishes to file (sharpen)*

"My woful hert for to ryve atwo   *rip in two*
For faute of mercye and lake of pité   *want; lack*
Of her that causeth al my peyn and woo
445   And list not ones of grace for to see   *cares never*
Unto my trouthe throgh her cruelté.
And most of al I me compleyn
That she hath joy to laughen at my peyn

"And wilfully hath my dethe sworone   *sworn*

450   Al giltles and wote no cause why,   *unjustly; [I] know*

Safe for the trouthe that I have hade aforne   *formerly*

To her allone to serve feythfully.

O God of Love, unto thee I crie

And to thy blende, double deyté   *blind, duplicitous deity (i.e., Venus)*

455   Of this grete wrong I compleyn me,

"And unto thy stormy, wilful variaunce,   *fickle; instability*

Imeynt with chaunge and gret unstablesse: *Mingled; inconstancy*

Now up, now down, so rennyng is thy chaunce   *so rapid*

That thee to trust may be no sikernesse,   *surety*

460   I wite hit nothinge but thi doublenesse;   *blame it [on]*

And who that is an archer and ys blynde

Marketh nothing, but sheteth by wenynge.   *Takes aim at; shoots; guessing*

"And for that he hath no discrecion   *because*

Withoute avise he let his arowe goo,   *heed*

465   For lak of syght and also of resoun,

In his shetyng hit happeth oft soo   *shooting, it happens*

To hurt his frende rathir then his foo.   *than; foe*

So doth this god with his sharpe flon   *arrows*

The trwe sleeth and leteth the fals gon.

470   "And of his woundyng this is the worst of alle:

When he hurteth he dothe so cruel wreche   *cruelly punish/injure*

And maketh the seke for to crie and calle   *sick [person]*

Unto his foo for to ben his leche;   *be his doctor (leech)*

And herd hit ys for a man to seche   *hard; seek*

475   Upon the poynt of dethe in jupardie   *In danger of death*

Unto his foo to fynde remedye.

"Thus fareth hit now even by me,   *it is happening*

That to my foo that gaf my hert a wounde   *gave*

Mot axe grace, mercie, and pité,   *[I] must ask*

480   And namely ther wher noon may be founde,   *none*

For now my sore my leche wol confounde;   *wound; doctor will trouble*

And God of kynde so hath set myn ure   *nature; fate*

My lyves foo to have my wounde in cure.   *in [her] power*

        "Alas the while now that I was borne

485   Or that I ever saugh the bright sonne!   *saw*

        For now I se that ful longe aforne,   *see; very long ago*

        Er I was borne, my destanye was sponne   *Before; determined (spun)*

        By Parcas sustren, to sle me if they conne,   *Parcae sisters (i.e., the three Fates)*

        For they my dethe shopen or my shert,   *shaped (ordained) before; shirt*

490   Oonly for trouthe I may hit not astert.   *escape*

        "The myghty goddesse also of Nature,

        That under God hath the governaunce

        Of worldly thinges commytted to her cure,   *care*

        Disposed hath thro her wyse purveaunce   *Has ordained; foresight*

495   To give my lady so moche suffisaunce   *great [an] abundance*

        Of al vertues and therwithal purvyde   *by means of that planned (plotted)*

        To mordre Trouthe hath taken Daunger to guyde.   *destroy; Resistance as guide*

        "For bounté, beauté, shappe, and semelyhed,   *loveliness*

        Prudence, wite, passyngly fairenesse,   *wit, surpassing*

500   Benigne port, glad chere with loulyhed,   *Gentle deportment; face; humility*

        Of womanhed ryght plenteuous largesse,   *womanliness; generosity*

        Nature in her fully did empresse   *put*

        Whan she her wroght, and altherlast Dysdeyne   *made (wrought); last of all Disdain*

        To hinder Trouthe she made her chambreleyne,

505   "When Mystrust also, and Fals-Suspecion   *Distrust*

        With Mysbeleve, she made for to be   *Skepticism (Mistrust)*

        Chefe of counseyle, to this conclusion:

        For to exile Routhe and eke Pité,   *ban Compassion*

        Out of her court to make Mercie fle,

510   So that Dispite now haldeth forth her reyn   *reign (rule)*

        Thro hasty beleve of tales that men feyn.   *belief*

        "And thus I am for my trouthe, alas,

        Mordred and slayn with wordis sharp and kene,   *acrimonious*

        Giltles, God wote, of al trespas,   *knows*

515   And lye and blede upon this colde grene.   *bleed*

        Now mercie, suete, mercye my lyves quene!   *sweet; soul's*

        And to youre grace of mercie yet I prey,

        In your servise that your man may dey.   *die*

"But and so be that I shall deye alagate,   *But if [it] so; in any event*
520   And that I shal non other mercye have,
      Yet of my dethe let this be the date   *Then*
      That by youre wille I was broght to my grave.   *[On] which*
      Or hastely, yf that ye list me save,   *quickly; wish to save me*
      My sharpe woundes that ake so and blede   *ache*
525   Of mercie charme, and also of womanhede.   *[Out] of*

      "For other charme pleynly ys ther noon,
      But only mercie, to helpe in this case;
      For thogh my wounde blede evere in oon,   *continually*
      My lyve, my deth, stont in your grace;   *stand*
530   And thogh my gilt be nothing, alace,
      I axe mercie in al my best entent
      Redy to dye yf that ye assent.   *ask*

      "For theragens shal I never strive   *in defiance of that; offer resistance*
      In worde ne werke, pleynly I ne may,   *work*
535   For lever I have then to be alyve   *I would rather; than*
      To dye sothely, and hit be her to pay;   *truly, if it would be her pleasure*
      Ye, thogh hit be this ech same day,   *Yea; very*
      Or when that ever her lust to devyse,   *she wishes*
      Sufficeth me to dye in your servise.   *[It] satisfies*

540   "And God, that knowest the thoght of every wyght
      Ryght as hit is in everything Thou maist se,   *see*
      Yet er I dye, with al my ful myght
      Louly I prey, to graunte unto me   *Humbly (lowly)*
      That ye, goodly, feir, fressh, and fre,
545   Which sle me oonly for defaut of routhe,   *Who; lack*
      Er then I die, may know my trouthe.   *Before I*

      "For that in sothe suffiche me,   *in truth satisfies*
      And she hit knowe in every circumstaunce,   *If*
      And after I am welpayed that she,   *pleased*
550   Yf that her lyst, of deth to do vengeaunce   *If she wishes*
      Unto me that am under her legeaunce;   *authority*
      Hit sitte me not her doom to dysobey   *judgment*
      But at her lust wilfully to dey.   *desire willingly*

	"Wythout gruching or rebellion	*objection*
555	In wil or worde holy I assent,	*wholly*
	Or eny maner contradixion,	
	Fully to be at her commaundement.	
	And yf I dye, in my testament	
	My hert I send and my spirit also,	
560	Whatsoever she list with hem to do.	*wishes*

	"And alderlast to her womanhede	*at the last*
	And to her mercy me I recommaunde,	
	That lye now here betwext hope and drede,	*between; fear*
	Abyding pleynly what she list commaunde;	*Awaiting unreservedly*
565	For utterly — this nys no demaunde —	*certainly — there is no question about it*
	Welcome to me while me lasteth brethe,	*I can still breathe (i.e., while I am still alive)*
	Ryght at her chose, wher hit be lyf or dethe.	*choice, whether*

	"In this mater more what myght I seyn,	
	Sithe in her honde and in her wille ys alle:	*Since*
570	Bothe lyf and dethe, my joy and al my peyn.	
	And fynally my hest holde I shall	*promise*
	Til my spirit be destanye fatal	*by predestined fate*
	When that her list fro my body wynde.	*i.e., die*
	Have her my trouthe, and thus I make an ynde."	*here; end (i.e., finish speaking)*

575	And with that worde he gan sike as sore	*sigh*
	Lyke as his hert ryve wolde atweyne	*would break in pieces*
	And holde his pese and spake a worde no more.	*peace*
	But for to se his woo and mortal peyn,	
	The teres gan fro myn eyen reyn	*eyes rain*
580	Ful piteusly, for verry inwarde routhe	*for sincere (heartfelt)*
	That I hym sawe so languysshing for his trouthe.	*suffering*

	And al this wile myself I kep close	
	Amonge the bowes and myself gunne hide,	*boughs; did*
	Til at the last the woful man arose	
585	And to a logge went ther besyde	*building (?summer house)*
	Wher al the May his custom was to abide,	
	Sole to compleyn of his peynes kene	*sharp*
	Fro yer to yer under the bowes grene.	

	And for because that hit drowe to the nyght,	*drew [near]*
590	And that the sunne his arke diurnall	*daily path (arc)*
	Ipassed was, so that his persaunt lyght,	*Had traversed*
	His bryght bemes, and his stremes all	
	Were in the wawes of the water fall,	*waves*
	Under the bordure of our occean	*edge*
595	His chare of golde his course so swyftly ran;	*chariot*

	And while the twilyght and the rowes rede	*beams red*
	Of Phebus lyght wer deaurat a lyte,	*gilded a little*
	A penne I toke and gan me fast spede	
	The woful pleynt of this man to write,	*lament*
600	Worde be worde as he dyd endyte:	*tell*
	Lyke as I herde and coude him tho reporte	*then*
	I have here set, your hertis to dysporte.	*amuse*

	Iff oght be mys, leyth the wite on me,	*anything; wrong, lay; responsibility*
	For I am worthy for to bere the blame	
605	Yf enything mysreported be	
	To make this dité for to seme lame	*poem; halting*
	Thro myn unkynnyng. But for to sey the same,	*lack of skill (knowledge)*
	Lyke as this man his compleynt did expresse,	
	I axe mercie and forgevenesse.	

610	And as I wrote me thoght I sawe aferre	*at a distance*
	Fer in the west lustely appere	*pleasantly*
	Esperus, the goodly bryght sterre,	*Hesperus; star*
	So glad, so feire, so persaunt eke of chere:	
	I mene Venus with her bemys clere	
615	That hevy hertis oonly to releve	
	Is wont of custom for to shew at eve.	*show; evening*

	And I as fast fel doun on my kne	
	And even thus to her I gan to preie:	*began to pray*
	"O lady Venus, so feire upon to se,	*fair to look upon*
620	Let not this man for his trouthe dey,	
	For that joy thou haddest when thou ley	*For [the sake of]; lay*
	With Mars thi knyght, whom Vulcanus founde	
	And with a cheyne unvisible yow bounde	*chain*

109

"Togedre both tweyne in the same while,

625   That al the court above celestial   *[So] that*

At youre shame gan laughe and smyle.

O feire lady, wel-willy founde at al,   *benevolent (propitious); in every way*

Comfort to carefull, O goddesse immortal,   *to [the] wretched*

Be helpyng now and do thy diligence   *relief; exert yourself to the utmost*

630   To let the stremes of thin influence   *rays of your*

"Descende doune in furtheryng of the trouthe,   *promotion*

Namely of hem that lie in sorow bounde:

Shew now thy myght and on her wo have routhe   *their*

Er fals Daunger sle hem and confounde.   *Before*

635   And specialy let thy myght be founde

For to socour, whatso that thou may,   *relieve*

The trew man that in the erber lay.   *garden*

"And al trew further for his sake,   *all [who are]*

O glad sterre, O lady Venus myn,

640   And cause his lady him to grace take,

Her hert of stele to mercy so enclyne   *steel*

Er that thy bemes go up to declyne,   *Before; to [your] setting*

And er that thou now go fro us adoune

For that love thou haddest to Adon."   *for Adonis*

645   And when she was goon to her rest

I rose anon and home to bed went

For verry wery, me thoght hit for the best,   *On account of weariness*

Preyng thus in al my best entent

That al trew that be with Daunger shent   *overcome*

650   With mercie may, in reles of her peyn,   *relief; their*

Recured be er May come eft agen.   *Restored; once more*

And for that I ne may noo lenger wake,

Farewel, ye lovers al that be trewe,

Prayng to God, and thus my leve I take,

655   That er the sunne tomorowe be ryse newe,

And er he have agen his rosen hewe,   *rosy hue*

That eche of yow may have such a grace

His oune lady in armes to embrace.   *own*

	I mene thus: that in al honesté,	
660	Withoute more, ye may togedre speke	
	Whatso yow list at good liberté,	*Whatever; wish uninhibitedly*
	That eche may to other her hert breke,	*their hearts open*
	On Jelosie oonly to be wreke,	*avenged*
	That hath so longe of his malice and envie	*ill-will*
665	Werred Trouthe with his tiranye.	*Persecuted; overriding dominance*

L'envoye

	Princes, pleseth hit your benignité	*Princess, may it please your graciousness*
	This litil dité to have in mynde,	*poem*
	Of womanhede also for to se,	*see*
	Your trew man may summe mercie fynde,	*[So that] your*
670	And pité eke that longe hath be behynde	*been in the rear*
	Let him agein be provoked to grace.	*restored to favor*
	For, by my trouthe, hit is agens kynde	*nature*
	Fals Daunger to occupie his place.	

L'envoye de quare

	Go, litel quayre, go unto my lyves quene	*poem*
675	And my verry hertis sovereigne,	*true heart's*
	And be ryght glad for she shal thee sene —	*see*
	Such is thi grace, but I, alas, in peyne	
	Am left behinde and not to whom to pleyn,	*do not know; complain*
	For Mercie, Routhe, Grace, and eke Pité	
680	Exiled be, that I may not ateyne	
	Recure to fynde of myn adversité.	*A way out; from*

Explanatory Notes to *A Complaynte of a Lovers Lyfe*

Abbreviations: see Textual Notes.

1   *In May.* See explanatory note to line 20 of Clanvowe's *BC*, for discussion of the convention of love complaints set in spring. Compare also the opening lines of *QJ* and the General Prologue to Chaucer's *CT*.

1–2   *Flora, the fressh lusty quene . . . in grene, rede, and white.* Lydgate uses an amplified version of this setting in the beginning of *The Siege of Thebes* (lines 13–16):

Whan that Flora the noble myghty quene	*(the goddess of flowers)*
The soyl hath clad in newe tendre grene,	
With her floures craftyly ymeynt,	*artfully combined*
Braunch and bough with red and whit depeynt.	*painted*

Chaucer pairs Flora with Zephirus, the west wind, in *The Book of the Duchess*, line 402, and the Prologue to *LGW*, F.171. The phrase *fressh lusty quene* echoes Chaucer's description of Dido in *LGW* as "this lusty freshe queene" (line 1191), while *grene, rede, and white* may reflect *TC* 2.51: "fresshe floures, blew and white and rede." Lydgate often uses the conjunction of green, red, and white, sometimes with other colors: see, for example, his description of the garden of Cupid in *Reson and Sensuallyte*, where the fruits change colors, being "[s]ommtyme grene, somtime rede, / Sommtyme white as cloth of lake" (lines 3940–41); the discussion of the mutability of the world in *Beware of Doubleness*, where "fresh somer floures, / White and rede, blewe and grene, / Ben sodeynly with wynter shoures / Made feynt and fade with-oute wene" (lines 11–14); or the report about burgeoning flowers in the garden that Medea's powers create in the midst of winter in *Troy Book*: "With many colour schewyng ful diuerse, / Of white and rede, grene, ynde, and pers" (1.1661–62).

3–5   *Phebus . . . bemes bryght . . . chace awey the nyght.* Phebus is the sun, while Lucifer is the morning star. Compare Chaucer's *TC* 2.54–55: "Whan Phebus doth his bryghte bemes sprede / Right in the white Bole, it so bitidde." See also *Romaunt*, lines 2636–38: "A, slowe sonne . . . / Sped thee to sprede thy beemys bright, / And chase the derknesse of the nyght." NS notes that line 5 particularly resonates with *Boece* 3.m.1.9–10: "Lucifer, the day-sterre, hath chased awey the dirke nyght" (p. 163n5–6). In *Boece* we learn that Hesperus, the evening star, and Lucifer, the morning star, are the same (1.m.5.11–16).

12 *Hope*. In *RR*, Hope comforts and encourages lovers (lines 2601 ff.). See *Romaunt*, lines 2760 ff.

  with Seint John to borowe. The *MED* entry for *borgh* n., 2b (d) cites this line and translates: "St. John be your sponsor or protector; — usually as a farewell," but the gloss of the phrase in *The Riverside Chaucer*, "with St. John as my guarantor" (*CT* V[F]596), makes more sense in the context. The use of the phrase in *The Kingis Quair* points to its status as a formulaic goodbye: "With mony 'fare wele' and 'sanct Iohne to borowe'" (line 59 [st. 23]). As the several citations in Whiting (S22) indicate, the expression is a fairly common one, used repeatedly by Chaucer, Gower, and Lydgate, among others. See, e.g., Chaucer's Squire's Tale (*CT* V[F] 596) and *Complaint of Mars* (line 9); Gower's *CA* 5.3416; and Lydgate's *Troy Book* 1.3082.

13 *Daunger*. In *RR*, *Dangier* ("Standoffishness/Resistance") guards the roses from lovers' attempts to pluck them (see for example *RR*, lines 2807 ff. and 14787 ff.; *Romaunt*, lines 3011 ff. and 3130 ff.). Compare *QJ*, line 541, and Roos' *BDSM*, lines 175–80.

15 ff. The narrator of a medieval love complaint frequently travels to a pleasant scene in nature, such as woods, fields, or a garden, to grapple with problems. For more on the *locus amoenus* tradition, see explanatory note to lines 58–60 of *BC*. See also *QJ*, lines 19 ff.; and *BDSM*, lines 22–25.

17 *As he, alas, that nygh for sorowe deyde*. NS (p. 163n17) points to *TC*, where Troilus, hearing of Criseyde's betrayal, "neigh for sorwe deyde" (4.432).

18 *My sekenes sat ay so nygh myn hert*. The narrator appears to be suffering from lovesickness, though he later claims not to know much of "suche mater" (line 191). For more on lovesickness, see explanatory note to lines 31–35 of *BC*.

22–23 *thoght I wolde goon / Unto the wode to her the briddes sing*. Compare the opening of *RR*, where the narrator dreams he awakens in May and longs to get out of town to where he can hear the birds sing. Similarly, in *BC* the narrator desires to go out and hear a nightingale sing: "I wolde goo somme whedir for to assay / Yf that I myght a nyghtyngale here" (lines 52–53).

26–30   *dewe also, lyk sylver in shynyng . . . in the grene mede.* NS (p. 163n25–30) suggests a comparison with Chaucer's Knight's Tale, where the sun's rays "dryeth in the greves / The silver dropes hangynge on the leves" (*CT* I[A]1495–96).

28   *firy Tytan.* A variation of the description of the sun as "fiery Phoebus"; compare Chaucer's Knight's Tale, where "firy Phebus riseth up so bright / That al the orient laugheth of the light" (*CT* I[A]1493–94); and *The Complaint of Mars*, line 27: "Phebus with his firy torches rede."

34   *golde-borned.* The *MED* cites only this instance of the compound, which it defines as "shining like burnished gold" (see *gold* n., 5 [b]).

36   *by a ryver forth I gan costey.* Compare *Romaunt*, where the narrator walks "thorough the mede, / Dounward ay in my pleiyng, / The river syde costeiyng" (lines 133–35).

36–42   *by a ryver forth . . . a parke . . . walled with grene stoon.* The narrator makes his way through a pleasant landscape (*locus amoenus*) of flowered meadows and a river to an enclosed garden (*hortus conclusus*). See the opening of *RR*, with its descriptions of woods and flowered meadows in May as the narrator's dream-self travels along a riverbank to the walled Garden of Diversion (*Déduit*). For more on the *locus amoenus* tradition, see Curtius, pp. 195–202. For more on the convention of the enclosed garden, see Howes, pp. 18–19; and Pearsall and Salter's chapter, "The Enclosed Garden," pp. 76–118, which provides a detailed discussion of the convention in medieval art and literature (for discussion of landscape in *CLL*, see p. 193; for *RR*, "the most famous and influential of all garden poems of the Middle Ages" [p. 83], see pp. 83–96). Pearsall (1970) notes that the description of the landscape is particularly indebted to *RR* and Chaucer's *PF* (pp. 84 ff.). The *grene stoon* (line 42) recalls Chaucer's *PF*, where the narrator encounters "a park walled with grene ston" (line 122).

43 ff.   Birdsong is a conventional part of the *locus amoenus*; see *BC*, explanatory note to lines 67 ff. In *RR* (lines 497 ff.) the sound of the birds singing in the Garden of Diversion (*Déduit*) heightens the narrator's longing to enter the garden. Lines 45–46 echo Chaucer's *PF*: "The noyse of foules . . . / So loude rong . . . / That wel wende I the wode hadde al to-shyvered" (lines 491–93).

52–56   NS (p. 164n52–56) notes that "[t]he roof of boughs which protects the flowers from the sun's heat is an optional feature of the *locus amoenus*," drawing parallels with *Romaunt* (lines 1395–1400), Horace (*Odes* 2.15.9–10), Statius (*Silvae* 2.1.154–55), Claudian (*De raptu Proserpinae* 2.105–06), and Achilles Tatius (*Clitophon and Leucippe* 2.A.24–25).

57–59   *The eyre atempre and the smothe wynde / Of Zepherus . . . / So holsomme was.* Zephirus is the gentle west wind, conventionally invoked as a sign of spring. See, for example, Chaucer's *BD*, line 402, and the General Prologue, *CT* I(A)5. Lydgate uses a very similar set of phrases in *The Siege of Thebes*, lines 1054–56: "Zephyrus with his blowing softe / The wedere made lusty, smoth, and feir, / And right attempre was the hoolsom eir." The temperate air is a common image; see, for example, Chaucer's *PF*, lines 204–05: "Th'air of that place so attempre was / That nevere was grevaunce of hot ne cold." NS (p. 164n57) points out parallels with Lydgate's *King Henry IV's Triumphal Entry into London*, line 19: "The eyre attempred, the wyndis smoth and pleyn"; and *Romaunt*, line 131.

        Trevisa (*De vento orientali et eius collateralibus*, 11.3) identifies Zephirus as the southwest wind: "The secounde cardynale and chief wynde is *Fauonius*, þe west-erne wynde. . . . And þis wynd haþ bysides hym tweye wyndes. Þe on hatte *Circius*, þe west northwest wynde; þe oþir hatte *Zephirus*, þe west souþwest wynde" (p. 574/13–17).

64 ff.   The convention of cataloguing frequently used by medieval writers derives from classical tradition. Compare Chaucer's catalogue of trees in *PF* (lines 176–82). See Curtius' discussion of the "mixed forest" catalogue, pp. 194–95, and Howes, pp. 19–20.

64–65   *Daphene, closed under rynde . . . / Grene laurer.* A reference to the story of Daphne and Phebus (Apollo, god of the sun). Phebus pursued Daphne relentlessly, even though she continually refused his advances. Attempting to escape ravishment, Daphne prayed to Zeus (or her father in some versions) for help and was turned into a laurel tree. See Ovid, *Metam.* 1.452 ff., Parthenius, *Love Stories* 15, Pausanias 8.20.1–4, Hyginus, *Hyg. Fab.* 203, *Vat. Myth.* I (115) and II (33). See also Boccaccio, *Gen. deo.* 7.29. Gower tells a version of the story in *CA* 3.1685–1720, and Chaucer refers to the story briefly in *TC* 3.726–28, and in The Knight's Tale (*CT* I[A]2062–64), where the story appears as one of those depicted on the walls of Diana's temple.

        Trevisa discusses the laurel under *De daphiri* in 17.48 and again very briefly under *De lauro* in 17.59. The laurel is said to be protection against lightning (p.

941/24 ff.) and to represent victory (pp. 940/28 ff., 941/11 ff.). Its leaves are said to heal bee and wasp stings, as well as keep moths and worms away from clothes and books (p. 942/11–15); the fruit is good in medicines and "[o]f bayes is ymade precious oyle þat helpeþ aʒeins many yueles and colde passiouns" (p. 942/19–21).

65   *the holsomme pyne.* Trevisa (*De pino*, 17.121) says that the pine "is good to alle þyng þat is þervnder" (p. 1017/14–15), and its fruit (i.e., the pine nut; *De pinea*, 17.122) has the medicinal properties of clearing, opening, and cleansing the lungs; soothing coughs; helping those with a wasting disease of the lungs (such as tuberculosis); and stimulating the blood (p. 1019/7–10).

66   *myrre.* Trevisa discusses the myrrh in 17.102 (*De mirra*), saying that it is good for embalming, adding that it keeps its properties for a long time. It helps with digestion and the lungs, works against runny mucus, and purges phlegm ("glemy humours") (p. 994/10–15). It also heals problems with gums and lips, "conforteþ þe brayn," helps conception, and "sleeþ wormes in þe eeren," among other things (p. 994/16 ff.).

67   *cedres.* Trevisa discusses the cedar in 17.23 (*De cedro*). It has some similar properties to myrrh. According to Trevisa, cedar wood lasts forever and books that are varnished with the gum (resin) of the tree are not eaten by worms and do not disintegrate with age (p. 920/32, 34–36). The gum or resin of the cedar "wypeþ away dymnesse of yhen, and," like myrrh, "sleeþ wormes of eeren," as well as helping with toothache and snakebite, among other things (p. 921/14–15). Similarly to myrrh, it also "kepiþ and saueþ neisshe fleissch fro rotynge" and "[t]he cedre tree anoynt wiþ his owne gomme kepeþ and saueþ fro rotynge dede bodies þat beþ yleyde þerinne" (p. 921/18–20).

68–70   *philbert . . . Demophoune.* An allusion to the story of Demophon and Phyllis as Gower tells it in *CA* 4.731–878. The tale tells of King Demophon of Athens (son of Theseus), who, blown ashore in a storm, seeks help from Phyllis, the queen of Thrace, the country where he has landed. He speaks of love to Phyllis, who believes him and awaits his return after he sails away with promises to return in a month's time. When he does not come back, she hangs herself in a tree. The gods take pity on her and she is "schape into a notetre . . . / And after Phillis philliberd / This tre was cleped in the yerd," (ed. Peck, 4.867–70). According to NS (p. 165n68– 70), in classical versions she turns into an almond tree, not a filbert tree as here, which seems to have been Gower's invention. The story appears in Ovid, *Heroides* 2 and *Remedia amoris*, lines 591–604; Hyginus, *Hyg. Fab.* 59; *Vat. Myth.* I (156) and II

(258); and Boccaccio, *Gen. deo.* 10.52 and 11.25. There is also a brief mention of the story in *RR*, lines 13211 ff., and Chaucer tells the tale in *LGW*, lines 2394–2561. Compare also Lydgate's *Temple of Glass*, lines 86–90, where the story of how Phyllis "was honged vpon a filbert tre" (line 90) because of Demophon's "falshed" and "trepas" (line 88) is one of those depicted on the walls of the temple of glass.

Trevisa discusses the filbert in *De auellana* (17.109), noting that the skin of the nut mixed with honey helps keep hair from falling out as well as making it grow (p. 1000/21–22).

71   *hawthorne.* In Lydgate's *Temple of Glass* Venus answers the lady's prayer for a steadfast lover with hawthorn branches: "Venus cast adoune / Into hir lap, braunchis white & grene / Of hawthorn" (lines 503–05). According to Venus, love should be like the leaves of the hawthorn, "þe which mai not die / Þuruȝ no dures of stormes þat be kene, / Nomore in winter þen in somer grene" (lines 514–16). In *Romaunt*, Shame and Dread find Resistance (Daunger) "[l]iggyng undir an hawethorn" asleep (line 4002). See also explanatory note to *BC*, line 287.

73   *Asshe.* According to Trevisa (*De fraxino*, 17.62), ash is good for spears, its leaves help against venom, and the juice of the leaves, squeezed and drunk, helps against venomous snakes, which will not even go into the shade of an ash tree, morning or evening, and which would rather flee into fire than into the leaves of an ash tree (p. 951/32–37).

firre. Trevisa (*De abiete*, 17.4) says that the fir is good for building because of its height and straight growth (see pp. 904–05).

oke with mony a yonge acorne. Trevisa (*De quercu*, 17.134) notes that the oak endures a long time and is good for making masts, while acorns help against venom by blocking "weyes and poris" so that venom cannot pass quickly to the heart (p. 1028/29–31). See also Trevisa, *De ilice* (17.83).

75–77   *a litel welle . . . quyke stremes colde.* In *Romaunt* the narrator washes his face in a river that "from an hill that stood ther ner / Cam doun . . . ful stif and bold" (lines 114–15). Compare *RR*, lines 108–09.

78   *The gravel golde, the water pure as glas.* In *Romaunt* the well of Narcissus has "clere water" and "gravell, which that shoon / Down in the botme as silver fyn" (lines 1555–57). Compare *RR*, lines 1523–25.

80   *softe as velvet the yonge gras.* NS (p. 165n80) draws a comparison with *Romaunt*, lines 1417–20: "About the brinkes of these welles . . . / Sprang up the grass, as thicke set / And softe as any veluët."

83   *shadowe cast.* The well Narcissus drinks from in *Romaunt* is "shadowid . . . with braunches grene" (line 1511). See also *RR*, lines 1476–77.

87–88   *Narcisus / Islayn was.* An allusion to the story of Echo and Narcissus, told in *RR* (lines 1437 ff.; lines 1469 ff. in *Romaunt*). As a young man, Narcissus was full of pride and did not love anyone. Echo, who could not speak except to repeat what was said to her, fell in love with Narcissus, but he spurned her, after which she faded away until only her voice was left. In answer to the prayer of another rejected lover, the goddess Nemesis caused Narcissus to fall in love with his own reflection in a spring of water. He then pined away for love of himself and was turned into a flower after his death. Ovid tells the story in *Metam.* 3.342 ff. See also Boccaccio, *Gen. deo.* 7.59, and Gower, *CA* 1.2275–358. In The Knight's Tale Narcissus is one of those depicted on the walls of the temple of Venus (*CT* I[A]1941); see also The Franklin's Tale (*CT* V[F]951–52). Gower mentions Narcissus in his company of lovers, *CA* 8.2542.

87–91   *Nat lyche the welle wher as Narcisus . . . deth mot folowe, who that evere drynk.* In *RR*, the narrator sits by the well where Narcissus died (lines 1436 ff.), but in Lydgate's poem, as Spearing (1993) points out, p. 222, the narrator is careful to note that the well from which he drinks is *Nat lyche the welle wher as Narcisus / Islayn was thro vengeaunce of Cupide* (lines 87–88). Spearing points to this and other changes as evidence that Lydgate "has been careful to alter some of [the] most problematic features [of *The Romaunt of the Rose*] in such as way as to dissolve potentially dangerous clashes between courtliness and orthodox morality" (p. 222). Lydgate says Cupid hid *The greyn of deth upon ech brynk* of the well, in contrast to lines 1616–18 of *Romaunt*, where "Venus sone, daun Cupido, / Hath sowen there of love the seed." Here, Spearing says, Lydgate "simplifies the moral issue by stating that in the fountain of Narcissus Cupid had sown 'The greyn of deth'" rather than that of love (p. 222). NS suggests that Lydgate makes the change as a rejection of "the erotic tendencies encouraged by *fine amour*," adding: "Much of Lydgate's love ethic borrows imagery and ideas from the *Roman*, but Lydgate always recoils from any erotic implications" (pp. 166–67n90).

92–93   *the pitte of the Pegacé . . . wher poetys slept.* According to the *MED*, Pegasus' well is "the fountain Hippocrene, sacred to the Muses" (see *Pegase* n., [a]). *The Oxford*

Classical Dictionary elaborates: "Pegasus was said to have created various springs from the earth by a stamp of his hoof, including Hippocrene on Mt. Helicon near the Muses' sacred grove, and another spring of that name at Troezen," referencing Pausanias 9.31.3 and 2.31.9 (p. 1131). See also Ovid, *Metam.* 5.256 ff.

94–98   *the welle of pure chastité . . . nygh the welle.* An allusion to the story of Acteon's death. Acteon happened upon Diana, goddess of the hunt and chastity, as she was bathing in a pool in the forest. Offended at his seeing her naked, Diana turned Acteon into a stag. He was then chased down and torn to pieces by his own hounds. See Ovid, *Metam.* 3.138 ff., Hyginus, *Hyg. Fab.* 180 and 181, and *Vat. Myth.* II (103). In Chaucer the story is one of those depicted on the walls of Diana's temple in The Knight's Tale, *CT* I(A)2065–68, and Emelye also refers to the story in her prayer to Diana (I[A]2302–03). Gower tells the story in *CA* 1.333 ff. NS (p. 167n91–92) notes:

> Lydgate seems to be following Hyginus's account of the myth of Diana and Actæon. Ovid, *Metamorphoses* III. 161, does not name the fountain or identify it with a moral quality. Hyginus . . . *Fabulæ*, 181, identifies the fountain as Parthenius in Gargaphia in Boeotia. The association of the spring with chastity may have been suggested to Lydgate by Servius's note on Mount Parthenius (*ad Ecl.* x. 57 [i.e., from Servius' commentary on Virgil's *Eclogues*]).

111–12   *And with myn hede . . . a good draght.* NS (p. 167n111–12) notes a similarity to the portrayal of Narcissus drinking from the fountain in *Romaunt*: "And forth his heed and necke he straughte / To drynken of that welle a draughte" (lines 1515–16; compare *RR* 1479–80).

122–26   Compare the description of the garden where Antigone sings her song in Chaucer's *TC* 2.820–22: "This yerd was large, and rayled alle th'aleyes, / And shadewed wel with blosmy bowes grene, / And benched newe." The *MED* explains that in the context of a garden *benched* adj., (b), means "furnished with turf-covered mounds used for seats." NS suggests that Chaucer's Prologue to *LGW* (G.203–04) uses a similar setting (p. 167n125–26).

124   *Whos names . . . not be tolde.* NS notes a comparison to Chaucer's *PF*, line 229, though the contexts are quite different (p. 167n124).

129   *hulfere and a wodebynde.* NS suggests that the symbolism here "is vague," and that these "plants are probably meant to suggest no more than the idea of constancy" (p. 168n129). In Chaucer's Knight's Tale, Arcite goes to make himself "a gerland of

the greves [branches], / Were it of wodebynde or hawethorn leves" as part of his "observaunce to May" (*CT* I[A]1507–08, 1500). In *TC* the embracing of Troilus and Criseyde is compared to the woodbine: "as aboute a tree, with many a twiste, / Bytrent and writh the swote wodebynde, / Gan ech of hem in armes other wynde" (3.1230–32), which would suggest that it may not represent steadfastness, since Criseyde betrays Troilus afterwards. Medieval herbals and surgery manuals give the woodbine a number of curative properties.

130 *I sawe ther lay a man.* For discussion of the narrator as "the silent watcher and listener," who is in the position of "voyeur and *écouteur*," see Spearing (1993), pp. 223 ff. (the discussion of the poem begins on page 218). See also the Introduction to *CLL*, especially pp. 73 ff.

131 *In blake and white colour.* NS suggests that white represents the knight's chastity and black his anguish, citing Lydgate's *My Lady Dere*, lines 99 ff. (p. 168n130–31) to support this reading. Compare the knight in Chaucer's *BD*, who wears black to symbolize his grief (line 445), or the lover in *BDSM*, whose clothes are also "[a]lle blake" with "noo devise" (i.e., unmarked by any heraldic device that could reveal his identity, line 130).

 pale and wan. A common expression to indicate suffering (see *MED*, *wan* adj., 2 [a]). Chaucer uses the phrase to describe John the carpenter in The Miller's Tale after he has fallen into the street and broken his arm at the end of the tale (*CT* A[I]3828), and to illustrate Troilus' distress when he has learned of Criseyde's betrayal: "Upon his beddes syde adown hym sette, / Ful lik a ded ymage, pale and wan" (4.234–35).

146–53 *I gan anon . . . marke what he sayed.* The narrator here hides himself at a vantage point from which he can see while remaining unseen. Such setups are commonplace in medieval poetry. For example, *QJ* and *BDSM* feature similar circumstances in which the narrator's eavesdropping provides fodder for his tale. See also explanatory note to line 130.

151 *hys fortune and on his eure.* NS (p. 168n151) remarks that this phrase "enjoyed some popularity" after Lydgate's use of it, citing *The Kingis Quair* (line 65 [st. 10]) and *The Court of Love* (line 634) as examples.

162 ff.   The lover is often described, as here, as robust and attractive but laid low by lovesickness. Compare, for example, the description of the knight in Chaucer's *BD*, lines 151 ff.

167   *Gruffe on the grounde.* NS (p. 168n167) points to Chaucer's Prioress' Tale: "And gruf he fil al plat upon the grounde" (*CT* VII[B²]675).

168   *awaped and amate.* Apparently a favorite pairing of Lydgate, since he uses it in several places. Compare *The Temple of Glass*, "That þei wiþ derknes were waped and amate" (line 401), and *Troy Book* 3.1608–09, where the Trojans, "of long fiȝt awaped and amat, / Gan with-drawe, faynted in bataille."

176–77   NS (p. 168n176–82) suggests this is an imitation of The Monk's Tale, *CT* VII(B²) 2663–64: "Who shal me yeven teeris to compleyne / The deeth of gentillesse and of franchise[?]"

178   *O Nyobe! Let now thi teres reyn.* Niobe is a symbol of grief. Mother of fourteen children, Niobe considered herself superior to goddess Leto, who only had two: Apollo and Artemis (Diana). Apollo and Artemis, at Leto's bidding, then killed Niobe's children as punishment for her boasting. Niobe's grief was immortalized when she was changed into a rock with water running constantly down its surface. See Ovid, *Metam.* 6.146 ff. Pausanias (1.21.3) claims to have seen the rock: "This Niobe I myself saw when I had gone up to Mount Sipylus. When you are near it is a beetling crag, with not the slightest resemblance to a woman, mourning or otherwise; but if you go further away you will think you see a woman in tears, with head bowed down."

180–82   NS (p. 169n176–82) suggests these lines are a reworking of Chaucer's *TC* 4.12–14: "For which myn herte right now gynneth blede, / And now my penne, allas, with which I write, / Quaketh for drede of that I moste endite."

183–86   *For unto wo . . . unto drerynesse.* Proverbial; see Whiting W254.

190 ff.   *I, alas, that am of wytte but dulle.* The narrator's disclaimer about his abilities as a writer is common in medieval writing. See *QJ*, lines 160–62 and 185 ff., and *BDSM*, lines 17 ff. Compare Chaucer's Retraction to *CT*, as well as the Prologue to *LGW*, where the narrator complains:

> Allas, that I ne had Englyssh, ryme or prose,
> Suffisant this flour to preyse aryght!

But helpeth, ye that han konnyng and myght,
Ye lovers that kan make of sentement. (F.66–69)

215–16   *Compleynyng . . . reuful chere.* A brief picture of lovesickness. For more on lovesickness, see *BC*, explanatory note to lines 31–32.

218–24   NS (p. 169n218–23) notes the opening lines to Chaucer's *PF* as the source of this "rhetorical scheme, *anaphora, parison, suspensio*," suggesting that "[i]n Lydgate's hands it turns into a kind of catalogue."

218–28   In these lines at the beginning of the lover's complaint, a number of words have been underlined in F: *thoght* (line 218), *lyve* (line 219), *gost* (line 220), *chere* (line 221), *face* (line 222), *teres* (line 223), *hert* (line 225), *thoght* (line 226), *brest* (line 227), *body* (line 228). All of these appear to sum up the significant parts of a lover, as they pertain to the physical and affective attributes appropriate to one suffering from lovesickness.

222   *lyke asshes in shynyng.* The image is of an extremely pale face, but the phrase has an oxymoronic quality about it, since *shininge* is normally used to mean something like luminous, clear, radiant, bright, shiny, glossy, brilliant, or gleaming (see *MED, shinen* v.). Unlike coals, whose gleaming signals that there is life in the fire yet, ashes do not glow and would seem to suggest lifelessness, since they are what remains once the fire has burned itself out. Compare line 232, which contrasts the heat of fire to the cold of ashes: "Now hote as fire, now colde as asshes dede."

229–45   This is an extended description of the lover's *acces* (line 229), a fever that keeps him burning with sensations of heat and cold. Compare Lydgate's *Temple of Glass*, lines 356 ff., for a similar description of a love fever. See also *BC*, explanatory note to line 39, for further literary resonances. NS comments that "[t]he paradox of hot and cold probably derives from *Troilus* I. 420: 'For hete of cold for cold of hete I dye'" (pp. 169–70n233) and also suggests a comparison with Gower's *Cinkante Balades* 9.

248   *With hert and al.* NS (p. 170n248) points to *Romaunt*, line 1883: "To serve his love with herte and alle."

250–59   *Daunger . . . Trouthe shal be slawe.* See explanatory note to line 13.

257   *fals Envye of wrathe, and Enemyté.* See the portrait of Envy on the wall of the
       Garden of Diversion in *RR*, lines 235 ff. (*Romaunt*, lines 247 ff.). In *CA* Gower
       discusses Envy in Book 2 and Wrath in Book 3.

260–68   *And Male-Bouche . . . the ful possessyon. Male-Bouche* is often translated as "Foul
          Mouth" ("Slander"). In *RR* Foul Mouth ("Wykked-Tonge" in Chaucer's transla-
          tion), Shame, Fear, and Resistance (*Dangier*) are the four companions who guard
          the roses from lovers' attempts to pluck them. Foul Mouth's role is to prevent the
          lover's approach by spreading tales to discredit him. See *RR*, lines 2817 ff., and
          Romaunt, lines 3024 ff.

260–87   Love punishing the true and favoring the false is a common trope. In *BC* the cuckoo
          argues that in Love's court "ful selde trouthe avayleth / So dyverse and so wilful ys
          he [Love]" (lines 204–05). The dramatic courtroom scene in which Trouthe is
          placed on trial and condemned so that Falness can take his place is akin to Fals'
          displacement of Truthe through vigorous legal discourse in *Piers Plowman* B,
          Passus 3–4. Compare also Chaucer's *Lak of Stedfastnesse*. NS explains, "The
          property into which Falsnes has entered is the person of the knight in the lady's
          estimation — in the allegory, a land which Truth has a right to, since he is what he
          is, not what the lady imagines him to be" (p. 170n267).

260–62   *And Male-Bouche . . . And Fals-Report so loude ronge the belle.* Compare *QJ*:
          "Jelousye hath evir suich a tong / That from the malice of his hert procedith, / By
          quhich that sclander wyde quhare is rong" (lines 394–96).

290   *Loves firy cheyn.* See, for example, line 288 of *BDSM*, where the lover is chased by
       Love into the lady's "chayne." In The Knight's Tale Chaucer refers to "that faire
       cheyne of love" (*CT* I[A]2991), and he uses the phrase laced in "loves cheyne" in
       Romaunt (line 3178), expanding on this idea later, when Reason warns against love:

       > If love be serched wel and sought,
       > It is a syknesse of the thought
       > Annexed and knet bitwixe tweyne,
       > Which male and female, with oo cheyne,
       > So frely byndith that they nyll twynne,
       > Whether so therof they leese or wynne. (lines 4809–14)

       See also Lydgate's *Temple of Glass*: "nov of nwe within his [Love's] fire cheyne /
       I am enbraced" (lines 574–75), and *Troy Book*, "Venus sone so felly can prouyde
       / His arwys kene to perce nerf & veyne, / And hem enlacen in his firy cheyne"
       (4.1550–52).

In addition to its literary resonances, this image of love occurs in religious texts. See, for example, *Book to a Mother*, which warns that "fleshlich men" will often seem to be bound "wiþ chaynes and fetres of loue and drede, to holde Godis hestis," but "aftur Ester þei breken þer bondus and unyuen þer affecciones, folewinge here lustis as þei weren hogges" (*Book to a Mother: An Edition with Commentary*, ed. James Adrian McCarthy [Salzburg: Institut für Anglistik und Amerikanistik, Universität Salzburg, 1981], 12.12–18, p. 97).

291   *thro-girt wyth mony a wounde.* Compare The Knight's Tale, where after the battle between Theseus and Creon, Palamon and Arcite are discovered in a heap of dead bodies, "Thurgh-girt with many a grevous blody wounde" (*CT* I[A]1010).

302   *What meneth this? What ys this wonder ure.* Compare Mars' questions about God's purpose in making people fall in love in Chaucer's *Complaint of Mars*: "What meneth this? What is this mystihed?" (line 224). This is a common rhetorical flourish; see *QJ*, line 121 and explanatory note.

303   *purveance.* Throughout Book 5 of *Boece* Chaucer uses this word to define God's omniscience: see, e.g., 5.pr.3.8–12.

305   *doun of the whele be falle.* A reference to the wheel of Fortune. One was either on the top or bottom (i.e., enjoying good fortune or suffering bad), or headed in one direction or the other, depending on Fortune's whims. Boethius, in his *Consolation of Philosophy*, especially Book 2, argues that one should rely on philosophy rather than Fortune, if one seeks constancy.

309   *This blynde chaunce, this stormy aventure.* See explanatory note to line 456.

311–15   On Love punishing the true and rewarding the false, see lines 260–87 and explanatory note.

323–29   See also lines 260–87 and explanatory note. Compare the cuckoo's condemnation of Love for much the same reasons in *BC*, lines 198–200: "For ofte sithe untrew folke he esith, / And trew folke so bittirly displesith, / That for defaute of grace hee let hem spille."

330   *Palamides.* One of Arthur's knights, Palomedes "the Saracen," also called "the Knight of the Questing Beast," who is in love with Isolde. See the entry in Chris-

topher W. Bruce, *The Arthurian Name Dictionary* (New York: Garland, 1999), pp. 390–91.

330–99   Catalogues of lovers were common in medieval texts. Compare Gower's companies of lovers in *CA* 8.2545 ff. NS observes that these lines catalogue two types of lovers: "true lovers unrewarded" and "false lovers rewarded" (p. 171n330–99).

344   *Ercules.* Hercules (Heracles), "the greatest of Greek heroes," according to *The Oxford Classical Dictionary* (p. 684), and famous for his Labors. See explanatory note to line 357, for details on his relevance as an exemplary lover.

348   *pilers.* During his quest for the cattle of Geryon, Hercules created the pillars, the rocky promontories on either side of the Strait of Gibraltar. In some versions he erected the pillars to narrow the passage as protection against sea-monsters; in others he broke through a mountain range to connect the Mediterranean Sea with the Atlantic Ocean. Guido delle Colonne's *Historia destructionis Troiae* explains that Hercules set the pillars up at Gades (now Cadiz, Spain) (ed. Griffin, p. 9; trans. Meek 1.183). See also Boccaccio, *Gen. deo.* 8.1, and Chaucer's Monk's Tale, *CT* VII(B^2)2117–18.

354–55   The dance of Love is proverbial; see Whiting L535, "Love's old dance." Whiting D14 cites line 355, *For him set laste upon a daunce*, as the sole example of the proverbial expression "to set someone last upon a dance," though the *MED* reads the phrase as reflexive, that is, Hercules sets *himself* on a course of action. See Chaucer's *HF*, "Thou maist goo in the daunce / Of hem that hym [Love] lyst not avaunce (lines 639–40), and *TC*, "Now, thanked God, he may gon in the daunce / Of hem that Love list febly for to avaunce" (1.517–18). Chaucer also uses the phrase "old dance" frequently: in *TC*, "Pandarus . . . wel koude ech a deel / Th' olde daunce, and every point therinne" (3.694–95), in *Romaunt* Jealousy is an old hag who "knew all the olde daunce" (line 4300), and the portrait of the Wife of Bath from the General Prologue to *CT* explains: "Of remedies of love she knew per chaunce, / For she koude of that art the olde daunce" (I[A]475–76). See also The Physician's Tale, where the daughters of lords who have "falle in freletee, / . . . knowen wel ynough the olde daunce" (*CT* VI[C]78–79).

357   *For al his trouth, he lost his lyfe.* Hercules is one of the lovers featured on the walls of Venus' temple in Chaucer's *PF*; see also Pyramus (line 365), Tristan (line 366), and Achilles (line 367). Gower mentions the story of Hercules and his wife Deianira in his company of lovers, *CA* 8.2559–62. Deianira, believing Hercules desired Iole,

wanted to recapture his love. To this end, she sent him a tunic dipped in the blood of the centaur Nessus. Nessus had tried to take Deianira from Hercules years before, and as a result Hercules killed him. Nessus had told Deianira the tunic would rekindle diminishing love when he gave it to her as a gift, but the garment instead poisoned Hercules. Burning from the poisoned tunic, which could not be removed, Hercules finally built his own funeral pyre and burned himself upon it to end his misery. Ovid's version of the tale (*Metam.* 9.136 ff.) explains that Hercules was not really in love with Iole, but "Rumour, who loves to mingle false and true and, though very small at first, grows huge through lying . . . reported that [Hercules] was enthralled by love of Iole. The loving wife believes the tale, and completely overcome by the report of this new love, she indulges her tears" (p. 13). See Ovid, *Metam.* 9.8–272, and *Heroides* 9; Hyginus, *Hyg. Fab.* 34–36; *Vat. Myth.* I (58); and Boccaccio, *Gen. deo.* 9.17. Chaucer's Monk tells the tale in a way that emphasizes the idea that Deianira may have known the tunic was poisoned, *CT* VII(B^2)2119–35, though he claims "I wol hire noght accusen" (VII[B^2]2129). Gower also tells the story in *CA* 2.2145 ff., where "Deianara is more clearly a victim than she is in the sources" (ed. Peck, p. 345n2145).

358–64   This stanza alludes to the story of Phebus and Daphne, discussed in explanatory note to lines 64–65.

365   *Piramus.* A reference to the story of Pyramus and Thisbe, whose parents would not let them marry, despite their love for each other. They communicated secretly by talking through a chink in the wall that separated their family dwellings. Deciding to run away together, they agreed to sneak out at night and meet at Ninus' tomb. Thisbe arrived first and saw a lioness coming to drink at a nearby spring, her jaws dripping blood from the cattle she had just killed. At this sight, Thisbe fled, leaving behind her cloak, which the lioness mauled with her bloody mouth. Pyramus arrived on the scene to find Thisbe's bloody and torn cloak and concluded that she had been killed. He drew his sword and killed himself. Returning to find him dead, Thisbe killed herself with his sword in turn. The story of Pyramus and Thisbe appears in Ovid, *Metam.* 4.55 ff. Chaucer tells the story in *LGW*, lines 706 ff., and Gower in *CA* 3.1331 ff. Pyramus is one of the representative lovers on the walls of Venus' temple in Chaucer's *PF*; see also Hercules (line 345), Tristan (line 366), and Achilles (line 367). Gower mentions Pyramus in his company of lovers, *CA* 8.2543, and Thisbe in 8.2578–82.

366   *Tristram.* A favorite Arthurian tale, the story of Tristan and Isolde appears in numerous medieval versions. See, for example, Gottfried von Strassborg's *Tristan*,

Eilhart von Oberge's *Tristrant*, Béroul's *Roman de Tristran*, Thomas of Britain's *Tristran*, the anonymous Middle English *Sir Tristrem*, and the Old Norse *Tristrams saga* (translated as *The Saga of Tristram and Isönd* by Paul Schach [Lincoln: University of Nebraska Press, 1973]). Tristan is sent by his uncle, King Mark of Cornwall, to bring Isolde from Ireland to be Mark's bride. On the boat, Tristan and Isolde mistakenly drink the love potion intended for Mark and Isolde on their wedding night and fall in love. Isolde marries Mark, but she and Tristan carry on a secret affair, finally running away to together to live for a time in the woods in most versions. Tristan is one of the lovers depicted on the walls of Venus' temple in Chaucer's *PF*; see also Hercules (line 345), Pyramus (line 365), and Achilles (line 367). Gower mentions Tristan in his company of lovers, *CA* 8.2500–01.

367   *Achilles.* Lydgate tells the story of Achilles' love for Polyxena, daughter of Priam and Hecuba, in *Troy Book* 4.630 ff. The story is a late addition to the myth. See, for example, Hyginus, *Hyg. Fab.* 110; Dictys Cretensis, *De bello Trojano* 3.2–3; Dares Phrygius, *De exidio Trojae* 27; Joseph of Exeter, *De bello Trojano*, 6.81–85; Guido delle Colonne, *Historia destructionis Troiae* (ed. Griffin, pp. 184 ff.; trans. Meek 23.110–60); *Gest Hystoriale* 23.9541 ff. Benoît tells an elaborate version of the story in his *Roman de Troie*, lines 17511–18472, 20691–812, and 21838–22334. Chaucer mentions the story in *BD*, lines 1067–71, and Gower in *CA* 4.1693–1701. Achilles is one of the exemplary lovers who appears on the walls of Venus' temple in Chaucer's *PF*; see also Hercules (line 345), Pyramus (line 365), and Tristan (line 366). Gower mentions Achilles in his company of lovers, *CA* 8.2545.

367   *Antonyas.* Chaucer tells the famous story of Antony and Cleopatra in *LGW*, lines 580–705, and Gower alludes to the story in his company of lovers, *CA* 8.2571–77.

368   *Of Arcite or of him, Palamoune.* An allusion to Chaucer's Knight's Tale, adapted from Boccaccio's *Teseida delle nozze d'Emelia*, which tells the story of two cousins of noble blood who are captured by Theseus after the war with Creon over Thebes. Imprisoned together in Athens, Palamon and Arcite both fall in love with Emelye, but Palamon is the one who gets to wed her at the end of the tale. It is therefore puzzling that Lydgate would include Palamon in his catalogue of wronged lovers here. Chaucer also alludes briefly to the story in the Prologue to *LGW* (F.420–21).

371   *Lo, her the guerdon that lovers have!* Set in the midst of pagan figures, both those who suffered from love and those who themselves caused pain, this line and lines 400–06 evoke Chaucer's *TC* 5.1849–55, where the narrator contrasts "payens corsed olde rites" (5.1849), which prove false, with the true love of Christ, "hym the

which that right for love / Upon a crois, oure soules for to beye, / First starf, and roos, and sit in hevene above; / For he nyl falsen no wight" (5.1842–45). *Lo, her the guerdon that lovers have!* and "[l]o, her the fyne of lovers servise!" (line 400) echo *TC* 5.1852–53 in particular: "Lo here, the fyn and guerdoun for travaille / Of Jove, Appollo, of Mars, of swich rascaille!" Compare also *TC* 5.1828–32, discussed in the explanatory note to lines 400–06.

372   *Jasoun*. In his *Troy Book* Lydgate tells the story of Jason and Medea (1.1823 ff.), detailing Jason's betrayal of Medea in 1.2868 ff. The story is told in Ovid, *Metam.* 7.1–403 and *Heroides* 12; Hyginus, *Hyg. Fab.* 22–26; and Guido delle Colonne, *Historia destructionis Troiae* 1–3. Chaucer tells the tale in *LGW*, lines 1580 ff., and Gower in *CA* 5.3247–4222. Gower mentions Medea's story in his company of lovers, *CA* 8.2563–66, but also lists Jason as a true lover of Creusa in 8.2504–05.

374   *Tereus*. Tereus raped Philomela, his wife Procne's sister. He then cut out Philomela's tongue to keep her silent about the crime. Philomela sent her story to her sister in a piece of weaving. Procne then killed Itys, her son by Tereus, and served him as a meal to his father in revenge. All three were turned into birds. See Ovid, *Metam.* 6.424–674. Chaucer's version of the tale is in *LGW*, lines 2288 ff. Gower tells the tale in *CA* 5.5551 ff. and also mentions the story in his company of lovers, *CA* 8.2583–86.

375   *Ené*. For the story of Dido and Aeneas, see Virgil's *Aeneid*, books 1–4. Dido was queen of Carthage, where Aeneas landed after fleeing the destruction of Troy. Dido fell in love with Aeneas, but he, feeling the call of destiny, left to found Rome. Dido then killed herself in despair, after cursing Aeneas and his descendants. See also Ovid, *Heroides* 7; and Hyginus, *Hyg. Fab.* 243. There were numerous medieval adaptations of the story, especially the twelfth-century French *Roman d'Eneas*. Chaucer tells the tale in *LGW*, lines 924 ff., and *HF*, lines 240 ff.; Gower in *CA* 4.77 ff. Gower also mentions Dido in his company of lovers, *CA* 8.2552–53.

379   *Arcite*. An allusion to Chaucer's *Anel.*, in which the Theban knight Arcite wins the love of Anelida, queen of Armenia, who is visiting Thebes. Even though he does not love her, Arcite not only woos Anelida, but also pretends to be jealous of her interactions with other men. Finally he betrays her for "another lady, proud and newe" (line 144). As *The Riverside Chaucer* points out, although Chaucer attributes the story to "ancient Latin sources," in fact "the tale of Anelida and the 'false' Arcite seems to have been his own invention" (p. 375).

380   *Demophon.* See explanatory note to lines 68–70. Gower mentions the story of Demophon and Phyllis in his company of lovers, *CA* 8.2554–55.

386   *For trwe Adon was slayn with the bore.* The story of Venus and Adonis is told in Ovid, *Metam.* 10.542 ff., with Adonis' death and transformation narrated in 10.708 ff. Venus loved Adonis and warned him against the dangers of wild beasts. He ignored her and was slain by a boar in the forest. Overcome with grief, Venus changed him into a flower, the anemone. Compare Chaucer, *TC*: "Adoun, that with the boor was slawe" (3.721).

389–92   *Vulcanus . . . noon he can.* The story of the adulterous relationship between Mars and Venus was frequently retold; lines 621–26 further elaborate the details of Vulcan's reaction (see also explanatory note to these lines). See Ovid, *Metam.* 4.169 ff. and *Ars amoris* 2.561–92; Hyginus, *Hyg. Fab.* 148; *Vat. Myth.* II (144); *Patrologia Latina*, ed. Migne, 78.551; and Boccaccio, *Gen. deo.* 9.3. Gower tells the story in *CA* 5.651–97. Chaucer's *Complaint of Mars* tells of the love between Mars and Venus.

393–99   *Ipomones . . . guerdonlesse he past.* The allusion is to the story of Atalanta and Hippomenes. Warned by the oracle that a husband would prove her undoing, Atalanta avoids marriage. She agrees to marry only the man who can defeat her in a footrace, if he is willing to risk the death that will be his reward should he lose. After several men die, Hippomenes manages to trick Atalanta into losing by throwing golden apples onto the path, thus pulling ahead and defeating her when she stops to pick them up. The two were turned into lions as punishment for making love in the temple of Cybele. Ovid tells the story in *Metam.* 10.560–707; see also Hyginus, *Hyg. Fab.* 6.

400–06   The repetition of *Lo* in these lines echoes *TC* 5.1849–55 (discussed in explanatory note to line 371), but the emphasis on Love's preference of the false over the true also suggests a comparison to *TC* 5.1828–32, where the narrator laments the sorrowful end of Troilus:

    Swich fyn hath, lo, this Troilus for love!
    Swich fyn hath al his grete worthynesse!
    Swich fyn that his estat real above!
    Swich fyn his lust, swich fyn hath his noblesse!
    Swych fyn hath false worldes brotelnesse!

404   *suerde of sorowe byte.* Compare Chaucer's *Anel.*, "Thogh that the swerd of sorwe
        byte / My woful herte" (lines 270–71). "Sword of sorrow" is a phrase most com-
        monly used in religious contexts, especially as an expression of the anguish of the
        Virgin Mary at Christ's sufferings. See, for example, the lyric "The Knight of
        Christ," line 12: "Mi sheld shal be þe swerd of sorwe" (in *Religious Lyrics of the
        XIVth Century*, ed. Carleton Brown [Oxford: Clarendon Press, 1924; second ed.,
        rev. G. V. Smithers, 1957], pp. 223–25); and the lyric "Stabat Mater Dolorosa," line
        4: "Þe swerd of sorowe þyne hert kitte" (in *Religious Lyrics of the XVth Century*,
        ed. Carleton Brown [Oxford: Clarendon Press, 1939] pp. 22–25). A homily from
        The Northern Homily Cycle (ed. Saara Nevanlinna, vol. 1 [Helsinki: Société Néo-
        philologique, 1972]) recounts the prophesy to Mary by Saint Simeon (Luke 2:35)
        from which the phrase arises: "Þat for sorow þat þou sal se / Þe swerde of sorow sal
        pas thurgh þe" (lines 3665–66). Mary's lines in *Ludus Coventriae* (p. 268, lines
        1065–67) enact that same prophesy: "Ffor þese langowrys may I susteyn / Þe swerd
        of sorwe hath so thyrlyd my meende / Alas what may I do" (in *Ludus Coventriae or
        the Plaie Called Corpus Christi*, ed. K. S. Block, EETS e.s. 120 [London: Oxford
        University Press, 1922; rpt. 1960]), while a Middle English translation of Aelred of
        Rievaulx's *De institutione inclusarum* (ed. John Ayto and Alexandra Barratt, EETS
        287 [London: Oxford University Press, 1984], pp. 1–25) demands empathy with it
        on the part of the faithful Christian: "Miȝt þu be wit-owte sobbyngge and whep-
        yngge, whanne þu sikst a swerd of so scharp sorwe renne þorouȝ here tendre herte?"
        (p. 49/951–53).

421   *Lesynges.* "Lesynges" ("Lies") is one of the personifications represented on the wall
        of Venus' temple in Chaucer's Knight's Tale (*CT* I[A]1927).

425   *Under colour depeynt with stidfastnesse.* Perhaps a variation on the proverbial idea
        "under color of kissing is much old hate" (Whiting C374).

426   *With fraude cured under a pitouse face.* Similar to a proverbial expression Lydgate
        uses to characterize Fortune's changeable nature in *Troy Book*: "Feyth in hir face
        & fraude ay in þe tail" (1.3314; he also describes her as having "forhed pleyn and
        [a] false visage," 1.3310; brackets in original). See Whiting F5. Whiting also lists
        a number of proverbial expressions that indicate concern over what a face may hide,
        such as "deem not after the face" (F1), "the face may fail to be the heart's token"
        (F2), "the face of treason is black within and white without" (F3), "he that makes
        the fairest face shall soonest deceive" (F4), "in the face peace, in the heart war"
        (F7), as well as several having to do with a "double face" (F8, F12, and F13). For

discussion of similar proverbial expressions about a false appearance hiding one's true nature, see explanatory note to *BDSM*, lines 389–94.

429   *feyned port.* A common image in discussions of love. Compare *BDSM*, where the lover claims that a true lover (one who is really hurt) complains much better, since "fayned chere is harde to kepe in mewe" (line 338).

431–34   Compare *Romaunt*, where "fals lovers . . . in herte cunne thenke a thyng, / And seyn another in her spekyng" (lines 2538–42; *RR*, lines 2394–97). See also the lady's assessment in *BDSM* of lovers' fair words in wooing, lines 325–32, and her description of love: "Love is sotill and hath a gret awayte, / Sharpe in worching, and in gabbyng [lying] gret plesaunce" (lines 341–42). *To thenken on in her opynyon / And sey another* (lines 432–33) is a proverbial expression that Lydgate also uses in *Troy Book* 2.4280. See Whiting T189 for further literary citations.

441   *hys dart that hym list to fyle.* The image of Cupid filing his arrows also occurs in Chaucer's *PF*, line 212: "Cupide, oure lord, his arwes forge and file."

448   *she hath joy to laughen at my peyn.* A common complaint against the beloved. Compare Chaucer's *Anel.*, where Anelida makes a similar criticism of Arcite after he has transferred his affection to another: "Ryght as him list, he laugheth at my peyne" (line 234).

449–50   *wilfully hath my dethe sworone / Al giltles.* Compare Aurelius' prayer to Apollo in Chaucer's Franklin's Tale, where he complains that Dorigen does not love him: "Lo, lord! My lady hath my deeth ysworn / Withoute gilt" (*CT* V[F]1038–39).

454   On Venus' blindness, NS suggests a comparison with Robert Henryson's *Testament of Cresseid*, lines 134–35, and notes that Henryson's portrait makes clear that Venus' blindness "has not been transferred from Cupid to Venus, but from the traditional account of Fortune" (p. 173n454).

456   *unto thy stormy, wilful variaunce. Stormy* is an image of love used in Lydgate's *Troy Book*: 2.2544–45: "Þe trowble and aduersite / Þat is in Loue, and his stormy lawe"; and Chaucer's *TC* 2.778: "love is yet the mooste stormy lyf."

456 ff.   The characterization of Cupid as capricious, shooting lovers at random and favoring the false over the true, is typical. See explanatory note to line 461.

461   *and ys blynde.* "Love is blind" is proverbial; see Whiting C634. Cupid, the God of Love, is frequently depicted as blind. See, for example, *Romaunt*, lines 3702–03: "Cupide, / The God of Love, blynde as stoon"; and Gower's *CA*: "love is blind and may noght se" (ed. Peck, 1.47). Compare also line 202 in *BC*. See Whiting for further citations.

470–83 The idea of the love-object as enemy or foe is commonplace. See, for example, Chaucer's *TC*, where Troilus exclaims, "Thanne is my swete fo called Criseyde!" (1.874; see also 5.228); and The Knight's Tale, where Arcite says, "Fare wel, my sweete foo, myn Emelye!" (*CT* I[A]2780). See also *Complaint to His Lady*, line 37; and *Anel.*, line 272.

473   *his leche.* The beloved as the doctor or cure is typical. Compare *BDSM*, line 201: "His leche was nere, the greter was his thought."

487–88 *Er I was borne, my destanye was sponne / By Parcas sustren.* The three goddesses of Fate (the Parcae) were held to spin the thread of life. See also explanatory note to line 489.

489   *my dethe shopen or my shert.* "My death was shaped (ordained) before my shirt." Proverbial; see Whiting D106, as well as *MED*, *shapen* v., 8 (a), for citations. This is perhaps a strange pun, where the Fates' spinning leads to death rather than the more usual item of cloth. See also a similar expression in Whiting, "to be nearer than one's shirt" (S255). Compare Chaucer's Knight's Tale, *CT* I(A)1566; *TC* 3.733–35; and *LGW*, lines 2629–30.

491   *Nature.* Nature as God's agent is typical. See, for example, *RR*, lines 16752 and 19476 ff.; Chaucer's *PF*, line 379; and The Physician's Tale, *CT* VI[C]9 ff.

495–511 The idea of the lady's virtues enabling her to resist the black knight's advances is a commonplace. Compare *Romaunt*, lines 3011 ff. (*RR*, lines 2807 ff.), where Daunger, Wykked-Tonge, Shame, Chastite, and so on keep the lover at bay. Pity in particular is the traditional enemy of Daunger (Resistance). In *Romaunt*, lines 3499 ff. (*RR*, lines 3231 ff.), Pite and Fraunchise (Liberality) try to reason with Daunger to let the lover pass.

512 ff. The lover's claim that he will die of unrequited love is typical. Compare the lover's complaint in *Romaunt* that "lyf and deth, withouten wen, / Is in his [Love's] hand" (lines 4596–97). In Chaucer's *Legend of Cleopatra*, the narrator avers that women,

not men, die from true love in his discussion of Antony: "Ye men that falsly sweren many an oth / That ye wol deye if that youre love be wroth, / Here may ye sen of wemen which a trouthe!" (*LGW*, lines 666–68), and he maintains an equally skeptical attitude towards Jason in *The Legend of Hypsipyle and Medea*: "O, often swore thow that thow woldest dye / For love, whan thow ne feltest maladye / Save foul delyt, which that thow callest love!" (*LGW*, lines 1378–80). Although the lover seems to think he is going to die, it is more often the woman who dies in love laments, becoming a proper object for unrequited love/desire. See, for example, Chaucer's *BD* or Charles of Orleans' fifteenth-century balade sequence. Compare *BDSM*, however, where the lover does die (lines 717–24, 812), though the narrator of *BDSM* explains that *he* is suffering because his lady has died (lines 57 ff.).

516   *my lyves quene.* Compare line 674. See also Chaucer's *Complaint to His Lady*: "Myn hertes lady and hool my lyves quene" (line 54).

540–46 Such appeals are common in love complaints. See, for example, lines 781–88 of *BDSM*, where the lover complains to God when he realizes grace from his lady is not forthcoming. Compare also Troilus' appeal to the god of love in Chaucer's *TC* 4.290 ff.: "O god . . . / That knowest best myn herte and al my thought," etc.

551   *that am under her legeaunce.* It is common to discuss the lover and his lady as vassal and lord respectively. Compare, for example, lines 253 ff. of *BDSM*.

558–59 *yf I dye, in my testament . . . my spirit also.* This uses the conventional language of the medieval will, where a person generally began by leaving the soul to God. See Lydgate's translation of Guillaume de Deguileville's *Pilgrimage of the Life of Man*, where Christ leaves his "soule vn-to [his] Fader dere" (line 4783), his "body . . . / To the sepulkre for dayes thre" (lines 4794–95), and his heart "To all that [his] commaundëment / Kepe" (lines 4803–04). Compare also *Romaunt*, lines 4610 ff., for a secular context.

569–70 *Sithe in her honde . . . al my peyn.* Compare *Romaunt*, where the narrator admits to the God of Love, "My lyf, my deth is in youre hond; / I may not laste out of youre bond" (lines 1955–56).

576   *hert ryve wolde atweyne.* A conventional expression. See line 799 of *BDSM*: "His woful hert, almoost it brast atwayne." Compare also Lydgate's *Siege of Thebes*, where the women's "hertys felt almost ryve asonder" (line 4500) when Creon forbids the bodies of the dead to be buried or burned; and King Lamedoun's grief

at the sacking of Troy in *Troy Book* 1.4268–70: "Þan for to se þe wo he dide make, / It wolde haue made a pitus hert as blyue / Of verray dool asondre for to rive." See also the effect of Pride's anger in *The Pilgrimage of the Life of Man*, lines 14092–93: "Myn hertë wolde for Ire tremble, / Ryve atwo almost for tene."

578–81   The narrator's sympathy to the lover is conventional. Compare, for example, *QJ*, lines 107 ff.

590–91   *the sunne his arke diurnall / Ipassed was*. Compare the line "Parfourned hath the sonne his ark diurne" in Chaucer's Merchant's Tale (*CT* IV[E]1795).

592–97   NS (p. 174n594) suggests a comparison with the description of the setting sun in *Troy Book*:

> The hour whan he made his stedis drawe
> His rosen chariet lowe vnder the wawe
> To bathe his bemys in the wawy see,
> Tressed lyche gold, as men my3t[e] see,
> Passyng the bordure of oure occian. (Prol. 127–31; brackets in original)

595   *chare of golde*. A reference to Phebus, the sun, driving his chariot across the sky.

596–97   *the rowes rede / Of Phebus lyght*. Compare Chaucer's *Complaint of Mars*: "Lo, Venus, rysen among yon rowes rede!" (line 2); and Lydgate's *Troy Book*: "the lusty rowes rede / Of Phebus char" (1.1199–1200).

597   *deaurat*. A neologism, from Latin *deauratus*, p. ppl. of *deauro, deaurare*. The *MED* cites only this line in its entry for *deaurat*.

603–09   The narrator's self-deprecation is conventional. See explanatory note to lines 190 ff. Compare lines 607–09 to the narrator of Chaucer's *TC*, who conversely suggests that he is *not* to blame: "Disblameth me if any word be lame, / For as myn auctour seyde, so sey I" (2.17–18).

610–16   Compare Lydgate's description of Venus as the evening star in *The Temple of Glass*, lines 326–31. For *Esperus* (line 612) as the evening star, see Chaucer's *Boece* 1.m.5.11–13: "the eve sterre, Hesperus, whiche that in the first tyme of the nyght bryngeth forth hir colde arysynges." (See also explanatory note to lines 3–5.) Venus is often described as "clear" — see Trevisa: "among alle sterres Venus schiniþ most comfortabilly and whitly, and þerfore he is iclepid 'cleernesse', for he sendiþ fro himself clere bemes of liȝt" (p. 482/6–9).

619 ff.   Compare the prayer to Venus in Lydgate's *Temple of Glass*, lines 321 ff., and *Reson and Sensuallyte*, lines 2213 ff. See also the proem to Book 3 of Chaucer's *TC* (3.1 ff.), Palamon's prayer to Venus in The Knight's Tale (*CT* I[A]2221 ff.), and the narrator's appeal in The Nun's Priest's Tale on behalf of Chauntecleer (*CT* VII[B²] 3342–46). See also Amans' prayer to Cupid and Venus in Gower's *CA* 1.124 ff.

621–26   *when thou ley . . . smyle*. While married to Vulcan, Venus had an affair with Mars. When Vulcan learned that Mars and Venus were lovers, he devised a plan to catch them in the act. Fashioning an invisible net to ensnare them, he caught the two in an intimate embrace, then invited the rest of the gods to witness their disgrace. Arcite makes a similar appeal in his prayer to Mars in The Knight's Tale, *CT* I(A)2383–92. See explanatory note to lines 389–92 for further classical and medieval references to the story of the affair. Gower's version (*CA* 5.651–97) is sympathetic to the lovers.

627   *wel-willy*. Compare Troilus' designation of Venus as "the wel-willy planete" in Chaucer's *TC* 3.1257.

634   *fals Daunger*. See explanatory note to lines 250–59.

644   *that love thou haddest to Adon*. A reference to the story of Venus and Adonis. See explanatory note to line 386 for details.

645 ff.   Curtius identifies the topos of ending "because night is coming on" (p. 90) as conventional and discusses its origins (pp. 90–91).

653 ff.   *Farewel, ye lovers al*. Addressing lovers and/or ladies at the end of love complaints is conventional. Compare, for example, the apostrophes to lovers at the ends of *QJ* (lines 582 ff.) and *BDSM* (lines 813–20) and to ladies in the latter (lines 821–28).

674 ff.   The "envoy de quare," an envoy addressed to the book or poem, is used by Chaucer at the end of *TC*: "Go, litel bok, go, litel myn tragedye" (5.1786). NS gives a very detailed account of the history of this literary trope, borrowed from classical poets (pp. 174–75n674 ff.).

679–81   Compare line 508.

Textual Notes to *A Complaynte of a Lovers Lyfe*

Abbreviations: **A** = British Library MS Add. 16165 (Shirley MS), fols. 190v–200v; **B** = Bodleian Library MS Bodley 638, fols. 1r–4v; **Ch** = Chepman and Myllar Print; **D** = Bodleian Library MS Digby 181, fols. 31r–39r; **F** = Bodleian Library MS Fairfax 16, fols. 20v–30r [base text]; **K** = E. Krausser; **M** = Henry Noble MacCracken; **NS** = John Norton-Smith; **P** = Cambridge, Magdalene College MS Pepys 2006, pp. 1–17; **S** = Bodleian Library MS Arch. Selden. B. 24, fols. 120v–129v; **Sk** = Walter W. Skeat; **T** = Bodleian Library MS Tanner 346, fols. 48v–59r; **Th** = William Thynne (1532); **W** = Wynkyn de Worde.

title	F, B, W: *The Complaynte of a louers lyfe.* F: omits *The*; in F another hand has added *or of the blake knight*; in B, which is missing the first 467 lines, this is the running title. A (at bottom of fol. 190r): *And here filowyng begynneþe a right lusty amerous balade made in wyse of complaynt of a right worshipful knyght þat truly euer serued his lady enduryng grete disese by fals envye and malebouche made by Lydegate* (with various running titles). D: *the man in þe erber.* P, T, Th: *The complaynt of þe blak Knyght.* S: omits (but see colophon). Ch: *Here begynnys the mayng or disport of Chaucer.*
1	*fressh.* D: omits.
4	*al the bemes bryght.* A: *bemys of delyte.*
5	*awey the nyght.* A: *þe night als tyte.*
7	*lovers.* F, T, W: omit. In F a later hand has written *louwers* or *loueuers* in margin with caret to mark point of insertion. I follow previous editors in emending.
9	*dreryhed.* W: *sluggerdy.*
	hevy. A: omits. P: *any.*
11	*goodly.* W: omits.
15	*I.* F: omits. I follow previous editors in emending.
16	*out stert.* D, P, T, S, Ch: *vpstert.* Sk, NS emend. I follow K, M in retaining F.
17	*nygh.* P: *night.*
18	*hert.* D: *smert.*
19	*of my.* W: omits.
20	*my.* F, W: omit. I follow previous editors in emending.
21	*halt.* A: *haldeþe.* P, S, Ch, W: *held.*
22	*anon.* A: *als swiþe.* W: *me vp.*
	wolde goon. F: *wol goon.* W: *wyll anone.* I follow previous editors in emending.

23	*Unto.* A, P, S, T, Ch, Th: *In to.* K emends. I follow M, NS in retaining F.
25	*morownyng.* S, Ch: *dawing.*
26	*lyk.* F: *lykyng.* W: *lyenge lyke.* I follow previous editors in emending.
30	*the₂.* F: omits. W: *euery.* I follow previous editors in emending.
32	*her.* F: *the.* I follow previous editors in emending.
34	*golde-borned.* A: *as golde.*
35	*hem.* D: *hym.*
42	*with grene.* A: *so with.* D: *with grete.*
44	*bothe in.* A: *and þe.* S: *and in.*
	and. F, A, D, S, T, Ch: omit. I follow previous editors in emending.
45	*songe.* A: *were.*
	wode. F: *world.* A: *park.* Ch: *londe.* I follow previous editors in emending.
46	*hyt.* T: *his.*
48	*wrest.* S: *brest.*
52	*celured.* A: *syloured.* D, P, W *coloured.* S, Ch: *siluered.* T, Th: *couered.*
53	*cure.* P: *couer.*
54	*That in.* T: no longer legible.
	they. T: *the.*
	longe. F, P, T, W: *not longe.* I emend, following K, NS. M retains F's reading.
58	*Zepherus.* A: *feyre Phebus.* S, Ch: *Phebus.*
60	*buddes.* A, S: *briddes.*
	lyte. T: *white.*
61	*brethe.* A: *birthe.* P: *bright.*
62	*that.* F, D, P, T, Th, W: omit. I follow previous editors in emending.
	their. S, Ch: *thai.* W: *the eyre.*
64	*ther.* A, D, P, S, T, Ch, Th: *the.*
	closed under. D: *clothir.*
	rynde. A: *lynde.*
69	*Her.* S: *His.*
70	*her.* S: *his.*
71	*the.* F: omits. I follow previous editors in emending.
73	*oke with.* D: *eke.*
	yonge. T: *fressh.*
75	*And me beforne.* A: *Þat hade his.*
76	*That.* T: *And.*
78	*golde.* D: *colde.* S, Ch: *like golde.*
80	*velvet.* P: *violet.*
81	*gan spryng.* F: *gan syng.* D, P, T, Th: *came spryngyng* (D: corrected from *game*), followed by NS, Sk. I emend, following K, M.

82	*sute.* S, Ch: *nowmer.*
87	*Nat.* F: *That.* A: *Nought.* I follow previous editors in emending.
	Narcisus. F, D, T, W: *Narcius.* P: *Marcius.* I follow previous editors in emending.
89	*Wher so.* S: *Quharfor.*
	covertely. Ch: *coniunctly.*
	hide. A, S, Ch: *abyde.*
90	*greyn.* A: *greef.*
	of deth. S: *of cruell deth.*
	ech. A: *euer yche a.* P, S, Ch: *the.*
92	*of the Pegacé.* F: *of the Pegate.* A: *vnder purgatorye.* I follow previous editors in emending.
93	*Under.* A: *Or of.*
	slept. F: *splept.* I follow previous editors in emending.
94	*pure.* F, W: omit. I follow previous editors in emending.
95	*as.* A: *þat.* Th: *ye.* W: omits.
97	*Atteon.* A: *Akoun.* D: *Actioun.* P, T, Th, W: *Acteon.* S: *Arceon.* Ch: *Anceon.*
	his. A, D, S, Th: *hir.*
	houndes. F: *hondes.* A, D, W: *handes.* I follow previous editors in emending.
101	*Bollyn.* S, Ch: *Belyng.* W: *Swollen.*
	perse. F: *perysh.* I follow previous editors in emending.
104	*werynesse.* Ch: *heuinesse.*
106	*had.* F: omits. I follow previous editors in emending.
107	*thoght.* F: *thogh,* corrected to *thought* by later hand.
108	*welle.* D, P, T: omit.
111	*araght.* A, D, P, S, T, Ch, Th, W: *I raught,* which K, M follow (*I raght*). I follow NS in retaining F.
113–26	S, Ch: omit.
117	*therwithalle.* P: *yer with alon.*
121	*I.* A, D, P, T, Th: *And.* K, NS emend. I follow M in retaining F.
126	*clourys.* F, A, D, P, T, Th: *colours.* W: *turues.* Emended for sense, following NS, who points out that "[i]t is impossible to bench with colors. The word should be the ME n. *clour,* 'turf'" (p. 167n126). K, M, Sk retain *colours.*
127	*ynde.* F: *rende.* A, S, Ch: *of ynde.* Th: *gende.* W: *rynde.* I emend, following previous editors.
129	*hulfere.* A: *haselle.* S: *lorere.* Ch: *hoser.*
130	*As I was war, I.* A: *So was I ware and.*
	ther. A, D, P, S, T, Ch, Th, W: *wher.* K, NS emend. I follow M in retaining F.
131	*white.* D: *with.*
132	*also.* S, Ch: *was he also.*

133   *fresh.* A: *fresshly.*

134   *overmore.* P, S, Ch, W: *euermore.*

135   *as thus.* A, D, P, S, T, Ch, Th: *al þis.* K, M emend. I follow NS in retaining F.

          ful. F, W: omit. I follow previous editors in emending.

136   *hote.* A: *harde.* S, Ch: *grete.*

          accesse. S: *excesse.*

138   *for.* P: omits. Ch: *sore.*

          constreynyng. S, Ch: *constreynt.* Other editors emend to *constreynt,* but the *MED* cites this line under *constreininge* ger. 2.

          malady. T: *lady.*

140   *her.* F, W: *se.* I follow previous editors in emending, although *grone* could be a variant of *grene* adj. 1 (b), meaning "of the skin or complexion: green; also, pale, colorless, livid"; as a verb, *gronen* v. 3 can mean "sicken" or "die" (see *MED*).

145   *routhe.* P, S: *gret rowthe.*

146   *I.* A: *An.* D, P, S, T, Ch, Th: *And,* which previous editors follow.

          gan. A: *þanne.*

147   *me prively.* T: *me peyuyly.*

151   *eure.* W: *feuer.*

157   *without.* P: *with.*

158   *speke.* D: *take.*

          on lyve. F, P: *of lyve.* I follow previous editors in emending.

159   *trouth.* P: *through.*

167   *Gruffe.* W: *Grouelynge.*

          in place. T: omits.

168   *Sole.* T: *So.*

          awaped. W: *awaked.* S, Ch: *he wept.*

173   *I.* A: *hit.*

          yow. W: omits.

174   *to yow, so.* S, Ch: *his wordis ryght.*

176   *helpe me now.* F: *now helpe me now.* I follow previous editors in emending.

178   *O Nyobe.* D: *Caliope.* S, Ch: *O eyen two.*

182   *When.* P: *What.*

187   *of.* F: *to.* I follow previous editors in emending.

192   *discryve.* A, S, Ch: *discerne.*

          wryte. A: *wit.*

206   *Or.* A: *So.*

207   *that.* A: *and.* S, Ch: *or.*

209   *ne$_2$.* A: *neuer.* S: *as.* Ch: omits.

213   *high.* A: *his.* D: *wofull.* W: omits.

214	*perturbaunce.* S: *grete perturbance.*
216	*and.* A, S: *and with ful.* Ch: *and wyth.* Other editors emend for meter: K, M add *with ful*; Sk adds *with ruful.* NS changes *loke* to *lokes,* based on D, P, T, Th, and adds *with.*
217	*Th'effect.* W: *The fytte.*
217a	*Compleynt.* F: in margin at line 219.
218	Marginalia in F: *nota.*
	sighes. D: *thoughtis.*
218–228	A number of words in these lines have been underlined in F: see explanatory note.
220	*and.* W: *and and.*
221	P: omits this line.
223	*falle.* W: *shall.*
224	*Parcel.* Ch: *Playn can.*
	declare. F: *declared,* with the *d* added by another hand.
225	*grounde.* D: *grownded.* S: *bound.*
226	*resseyt.* A: *resort.*
230	*shyver.* A: *cheele.* S, Ch: *chill.*
233	*now cold.* F, W: omit. I follow previous editors in emending.
234	*now₂.* S, Ch: *now hote.*
	coles rede. D: *firy glede.*
236	*possed.* W: *passed.*
	am. T: omits.
237	*hete.* F, A, D, P, S, T, Ch, W: *colde.* I follow previous editors in emending.
	as I fele. A: *euery dele.*
238	*grevouse.* S, Ch: *greuance.*
	colde. D: *hert.*
	everydele. A: *of myn vnseele.*
239	*dysdeyn.* S, Ch: *distresse.*
241	*evere.* S, Ch: omit.
	besy peyne. A: *his peyne.* D, P, Th: *his besy payne.* S, Ch: *besynesse.* T: *his bysy hate.* K emends to *his besy peyne.* I follow M, NS in retaining F.
243	*This.* F: *Thus.* I follow previous editors in emending.
246	*that in trouthe I.* A: *þat I in trouthe.* S: *þat I treuth.* W: *the trouth I.*
248	*be.* P: omits.
250	*me sterve.* Ch: *desterue.*
252	*now.* P, T, Th: *newe.*
254	*of.* P: *and.*
255	*sleghtly.* P: *sely.*
256	*Han.* P: *Thanne.*

257   *of wrathe.* Th: omits *of,* followed by Sk. NS emends to *[and] Wrathe.* I follow K,
       M in retaining F.

259   *Trouthe.* A: *right.* S, Ch: *throw I.*

       slawe. P: *drawe.*

261   *Trouthe of.* P: *through on.*

263   *Suspecion.* P: *enspicioun.*

273   *lyve.* T: *lyen.*

274   *accused . . . forjuged.* A: *forjuged . . . accused.*

279   *do.* D: *to.* Ch: *be.*

281   *admytted.* A: *accepted.*

282   *ne a worde.* S: *now inward.* W: omits *ne.*

283   *othe.* S: *soth.*

284   *ys no geyn.* A: *gayneþe nought.*

285   *cleke.* F, A, P, T, Th, W, Ch: *clepe.* D: *speke.* I emend for rhyme, based on S. K,
       M, Sk retain *clepe.* NS emends to *creke.*

287   *mordred.* D: *to mordir.* S: *murder.*

290   P: omits this line.

291   *thro-girt.* A: *hurt.* S, Ch: *ouergirt.*

292   *ar.* W: *am.*

294   *but.* A: *and.*

       the. A: *my.* S, Ch: *thy.*

295   Marginalia in F: *nota.*

       sight. A: *light.* D, P, S, T, Ch, Th: *right.*

299   *more.* T: *eny.*

301   *hem.* W: *hym.*

302   *What.* A: *That.*

       meneth. D: *movith.*

303   *Of.* A: *Or.*

304   *Of₁.* A: *On.* S, Ch: *O.*

       hem. W: *hym.*

307   *wrongfully.* A: *wronge.*

308   *Trouthe.* A: *truwe.*

       of Falshed. D, P, T: omit.

319   *his.* A: *hir.* S, Ch: *my.*

       he hath. A, S, Ch: *I haue.*

319–20 A: transposes these lines.

320   *banysshed.* A: *banned.*

321   *that I shal.* A: *for to.*

327   *no.* Ch: *now.*

328	*the.* P: omits.
	hem. A, W: *him.*
329	*her.* P, S, Ch: *his.*
331	*the noble worthy.* P: *and the nobyl.*
332	*of hys peyne no relese.* A: *neuer hade relees.*
334	*Love.* W: *None.*
338	*his.* W: *his hye.*
	besy. A, D, P, S, T, Ch: *his bisy.* Previous editors emend.
340	*mercie.* A: *grace.*
341	*not refreyn.* T: *neuyr attayne.*
342	*no.* W: *to.*
	obey. F: *wey.* I follow previous editors in emending.
345	*worthynesse.* F: *worchynesse.* I follow previous editors in emending.
347	*of him list.* S: *can of him.*
348	*pilers.* F: *periles.* P: *peyrles.* I follow previous editors in emending.
	high. D: omits.
349	*Away.* A: *So fer.* P, W: *Alwey.*
	Cades. P: *Goddes.*
351	*pilers.* Th: *pyles.*
	ben. P, Th: omit.
355	*him.* A: *he him.* Previous editors emend.
	daunce. P: *chance.*
356	*whom.* S, Ch: *quhois.*
357	*he.* A: *for loue he.*
358	*al.* F: *as.* I follow previous editors in emending.
359	*he.* P: *she.*
360	*hert.* W: *erthe.*
	Venus. A: *goddes Venus.* S: *fresch Venus.* T: *Phebus.*
363	*Thogh.* S: *Though hit.*
	her. A: *his.* P: omits.
	love. S: omits.
364	*let.* A: *bade.*
365	*Piramus.* A, D, W: *Pryamus.*
366	*trwe.* D: *Troy.*
	high. A: omits. D: *grete.*
371	*lovers.* A, D, P, S, T, Ch, Th: *þees louers.*
373	*at Colkos to Medé.* A: *and al so ymodee.*
374	*Tereus.* A, P, S, T, Th: *Theseus.* D: *the Thesus.* Ch: *Thecius.* W: *Terens.*
375	*Ené.* P: *gne.*

379	*the*. A: *loo þe*.
380	*his*. A: *his foule*.
382	*grete*. A: *hir gret*.
383	*ever*. A: omits.
	alas, and that. S: *in that allace*. Ch: *allace in that*.
	routhe. A: *gret routhe*.
385	*ungoodly*. F: *ungooly*. I follow previous editors in emending.
387	*shade*. W: *shadowe*.
389	*with her no mercy*. A: *no mercy with him*.
390	*had*. F, W: *and*. I follow previous editors in emending.
391	*her*. S: *the*.
	worthi. F, A, D, P, T, Ch, Th, W: omit. I follow previous editors in emending.
	trewe. F, A, D, P, T, Ch, Th, W: omit. I follow previous editors in emending.
393	*Ipomones*. Th: *Ypomedes*.
394	*fre*. D: *and fre*.
	as. A: *was*. P: omits. W: *and*.
	his. A, P, S: *hir*.
395	*ches*. A, D, P, S, T, Ch, Th, W: *he ches*.
396	*Athalans*. D: *Atlans*.
	her. A: *his*.
399	*guerdonlesse*. P: *grewusly*.
400	*lovers*. A, D, P, S, T, Ch, Th: *louys*.
	servise. A: *hye servyce*.
401	*that Love can*. A, S, Ch: *he can*.
404	*byte*. P: *smyte*.
405	*must*. A: *doþe*. D, P, S, T, Ch, Th: *moste*.
	his. P: omits.
	lust. D: *love*.
414–20	A: omits these lines.
415–16	P: omits these lines.
419	*jupartyng*. F, P, S, T, Ch, Th, W: *in partyng*. D: *jupardy*. I follow previous editors in emending.
421	*Lesynges*. Ch: *losingeris*.
	fals. D, P, S, T, Ch: omit.
426	*pitouse*. S: *double*.
427	*Accept*. A: *Accepted*. Ch: *Excep*.
	rathest. T: *accepte ben ratheste*.
428	*best*. W: omits.
429	*and*. S: *and false*.

430	*haunce.* P, Th: *haunt.* A, S, Ch, W: *chaunge.*
433	*another.* S, Ch: *they aught.*
	hemselfe. F: *hymselfe.* K, M retain F's reading. I follow NS's emendation.
445	*of.* D: *my.*
446	*throgh.* P: *trwe.* S, Ch: *for.*
452	*feythfully.* A: *hir feythfully.* S, Ch: *most feithfully.*
453	*of Love.* A, D, P, S, T, Ch: *abowe.*
	I crie. A: *I calle and crye.*
457	*unstablesse.* A: *doublenesse.*
458	*is.* S, Ch: *in.*
458–59	P: *Now vp now downe* ~~*that the to trust may be no sekyrnes*~~ / *Soyr rynnyng is thy chaunce.* (I.e., line 459 is written as the last half of 458, canceled, then rewritten in its proper sequence before line 460; the last half of line 458 is written as 459.)
460	*I.* P: *And.*
	hit. D, P, T: omit.
462	*by wenynge.* S: *as he wend.* Th: *by wende.* Ch: *be the weynd.*
464	*he.* P: omits.
	let his arowe goo. A: *holdeþe his bowe gode.*
466	*shetyng.* P: *settyng.*
470	*is.* Th: omits.
471	*When.* A: *Whome þat.* P: *Wham.*
	hurteth he dothe. A: *hurteþe doþe.* D: *hurt doth and.* T, Th: *hurteth doth to so.*
473	*Unto.* F: *Wnto.* K, M retain F's reading. I follow NS's emendation.
475	*of dethe in.* A: *of a.*
	jupardie. F: *pardie.* P: *jupard.* I follow previous editors in emending.
477	*even.* S, Ch: *evinly.*
478	*gaf.* F: *yaf.*
479	*axe grace.* A: *me graunt.*
480	*wher.* B, W: omit.
483	*my₂.* P: omits.
	wounde. S, Ch: *wo.*
488	*By.* A: omits.
	sustren. A: *suffre.*
493	*to.* A: *to do.*
	cure. D: omits.
494	*wyse.* A, B, W: omit.
	purveaunce. T: omits.
497	*taken.* A: omit.
499	*wite.* A, D, T: *with.*

501	*plenteuous.* W: *plenteous and.*
502	*her.* A: *hir persone.*
505	*When Mystrust.* Ch: *Quham to myscheyf.*
507	*this.* Th: *his.*
508	*Routhe.* S, Th, W: *truthe.*
	Pité. S: *pietee.*
509	*Out.* W: *But.*
510	*her.* D, P, T: *the.* S, Ch: *his.*
514	*al.* A, S: *al manere.*
519	*and.* T: *if.*
522	*wille.* T: omits.
523	*Or.* F: *Er.* I follow previous editors in emending.
	yf that. D: omits.
524	*so.* P: *so sore.*
525	*charme.* W: *charyte.*
526	*charme.* W: *maner.* A: *medecyne.*
527	*mercie.* T: omits.
	to helpe in. A: *lady.* S: *in.* Ch: *in to.*
	this. S: *this wofull.*
528	*evere.* P: *ouer.*
534	*I ne.* P: *yif I.*
536	*hit.* P: *if.*
	her to. A, S: *ʒowe to.*
561	*alderlast.* A: *euermore.*
562	*mercy.* P: omits.
566	*me lasteth brethe.* A: *she lasteþe brethe.* P: *that lastyth my breth.* T: *lasteth deth.*
570	*dethe, my.* D: omits.
571	*hest.* W: *herte.*
572	*my.* F, B, W: *be my.* I follow previous editors in emending.
	fatal. F: *fal.* I follow previous editors in emending.
573	*When.* P: *What.*
	her. S: *it.*
575	Marginalia in F, B, W: *Nota perseveranciam amantis,* "Note the lover's constancy."
579	*myn.* D: *his.*
580	*verry.* F: *werry.* K, M retain F's reading. I follow NS's emendation.
581	*That.* A: *While.*
	languysshing. W: *languysshe.* B: *sangvisshing.*
	his. A, S, Ch, Th: omit. T: *her.*

583	*bowes.* Ch: *leves.*
593	*Were.* F, P: *Wher.* I follow previous editors in emending.
595	*swyftly.* T: *swythely.*
599	*pleynt.* D, P: *payne.*
600	*Worde.* A: *Right worde.*
602	*to.* S, Ch: *in.*
603	*wite.* W: *faute.*
606	*seme.* W: *feyne.*
607	*sey.* F, B, S, T, Ch: *seme.* K, M retain F's reading. I follow NS in emending. Sk follows Th: *seyn.*
610–51	A: omits these lines.
619	*to se.* S, Ch: *the see.*
622	*whom.* D, P, T, Th: *whan.* S, Ch: *quhen þat.*
	founde. T: *you founde.*
623	*cheyne.* W: *reyne.*
625	*above.* W: *aboute.*
627	*wel-willy.* Th: *wylly.*
628	*O.* F: *Of.* I follow previous editors in emending.
632	*lie.* F: *he.* I follow previous editors in emending.
634	*Er.* W: *Theyr.*
	hem. P, S: *hym.*
635	*be.* P: omits.
638	*further.* Ch: *men thou furthyr.*
639	*glad.* S, Ch: *goodly.*
640	*cause.* F: omits. I follow previous editors in emending.
	take. B: *call.*
644	*Adon.* D: *Adamoun.* W: *downe.*
647	*verry wery.* F: *werry wery.* S, Ch: *verily.* D, P, T, Th: *wery.* K, M retain F's reading. I follow NS's emendation.
648	*thus.* S: *rycht thus.*
649	*trew.* W: *true louers.*
650	*may in relese.* P: *thou relese.*
651	*Recured.* D, P, S, Ch: *Recouered.*
656	*er.* A: *as.*
	he. T: *ȝe.*
	his. P, S, T, Th: omit.
659	*thus.* S: *rycht thus.*
	that. T: omits.
660	*togedre.* S: *with othir.*

663   *Jelosie*. A, D, P, T, Th: *jalousyes*.

     oonly. A: *and*.

664   *his*. A, B, P, W: omit.

666   *L'envoye*. D, P, S, T, Ch: omit.

     hit your. A, D, P, Th: *hit to your*. S, Ch: *to your*. T: *hit to you of youre*.

667   *mynde*. A: *your mynde*.

668   *also*. A: *oonly*.

669   *trew*. D, Th: omit.

     summe. W: omits. Th: *your*.

670   *be behynde*. F: *be hynde*. I follow previous editors in emending.

671   *him*. F, B, W: omit. I follow previous editors in emending.

     provoked. D: *promited*.

672   *by my trouthe*. S: *trewely*.

674   *L'envoye de quare*. A, D, P, S, T, Ch, Th: omit.

676   *shal*. D: *hath*.

679   *Routhe*. W: *trouthe*.

681   *Recure*. A, D, S, Ch: *Rekouer*.

     myn. F: *hym*.

colophon F: omits. A, P, T, Th: *Explicit*. B: *Explicit the Compleynt of a loveres life*. D: *Explicit Edorb qd* [for *quod*]. S: *Here endith the maying and disport of Chaucere*. Ch: *Explicit. Heir endis the maying and disport of chaucer Imprentit in the south gait of Edinburgh be Walter chepman and Androw myllar the fourth day of aperile the yhere of god. M.CCCCC. and viii. yheris.* W: *Imprynted at London in the Flete strete at the sygne of the Sonne by Wynkyn de Worde.*

The Quare of Jelusy

Introduction

The single surviving copy of *The Quare of Jelusy* appears in a late-fifteenth- or early-sixteenth-century manuscript of Scottish provenance, Oxford, Bodleian Library MS Arch. Selden. B. 24.[1] The poem is anonymous, although some earlier editors attributed it to James Afflek, an otherwise unknown poet mentioned in William Dunbar's *Lament for the Makaris* (poem 21, line 58).[2] *The Quare of Jelusy* survives in a collection of mainly Middle English verse (albeit to some degree Scotticized)[3] and in some respects recalls *The Kingis Quair*, with its strong Chaucerian and Boethian influences. Even so, the poem does not impart a particularly Chaucerian flavor, although there are echoes of Chaucer's works, most notably The Knight's Tale, *Anelida and Arcite*, and especially *Troilus and Criseyde*. The poem also strongly recalls the anonymous *Lancelot of the Laik* and has some resonances with Lydgate's poetry. It may owe something of its plot to Lydgate's *Temple of Glass*, where the narrator listens to a woman's complaint during his dream. The view of *The Quare of Jelusy* as a less successful imitation of Chaucer may explain in part its neglect by critics. The poem has usually

---

[1] For discussion of the date, see the facsimile volume, intro. Julia Boffey and A. S. G. Edwards (1997), pp. 3–4; and R. J. Lyall, "Books and Book Owners in Fifteenth-Century Scotland" in *Book Production and Publishing in Britain, 1375–1475*, ed. Jeremy Griffiths and Derek Pearsall (Cambridge, UK: Cambridge University Press, 1989), pp. 250–52.

[2] This identification was based on the colophon, of which only *au* and the top of a nearby ascender which follows are still legible. The edition in *The Bannatyne Miscellany*, which Norton-Smith and Pravda suggest was transcribed and edited by David Laing, records the first six letters as *auchin*, while Alexander Lawson and J. T. T. Brown read *auch*, which they interpreted as the beginning of the name Auchinleck (a variant spelling of Afflek), following Laing's conjecture. While agreeing that *au* is clearly visible, J. Norton-Smith and I. Pravda make a detailed argument against the *chin* reading, claiming that, the paper being "worn to a thin transparency," these letters are the reverse images of letters from the recto side of the folio (see p. 15; for Norton-Smith and Pravda's full discussion, see pp. 15–16). As the leaf is now missing the edge in question, it is not possible to draw a firm conclusion.

[3] Norton-Smith and Pravda suggest that the second Selden scribe is more consistent in the use of Scots forms than the first one, a characterization confirmed by Boffey and Edwards (1999, pp. 181–82). Boffey and Edwards identify the poem as one of those in Selden "that are uniquely or peculiarly Scottish" (1999, p. 180).

been ignored altogether or, when mentioned, maligned as lacking in literary merit, and John MacQueen's assessment of it as "possess[ing] a certain complexity and power" seems to be a minority view.[4]

Like *A Complaynte of a Lovers Lyfe*, *The Quare of Jelusy* begins with a dissatisfied narrator who finds an outlet for his own anxiety in the observation and telling of another's troubles. In this case, the target of the narrator's observation is a woman, rather than a man, and her suffering is caused by Jealousy, not unrequited love. After a conventional evocation of springtime, followed by a brief lament on "this warldis changeing and his wo" (line 24), the narrator of *The Quare of Jelusy* promises to remain silent on the subject of his own suffering. Instead, looking towards the sun, he discovers a new object of attention in a lady who suddenly appears "among the levis grene" (line 35). At this point the narrator hides himself so that he can discreetly observe the woman who has strayed into his view, another recurrent trope in medieval poetry. As A. C. Spearing writes in *The Medieval Poet as Voyeur*,

> Within medieval love-narratives, secret observers, concealed from the lovers as the lovers are from society at large, are frequently represented as responsible for exposing private experience to the public gaze; as readers of or listeners to such narratives, we too can be made to feel that we are secret observers; and, in the later Middle Ages especially, the love-poet is often realized as one who looks and tells, himself a secret observer of experiences in which he does not participate.[5]

To this we might add "or understand." In *The Quare of Jelusy*, as in many such narratives, the narrator observes not the lady's direct experiences but, rather, the signs of her internal suffering derived from past incidents that the narrator does not himself witness and cannot fully grasp. He can therefore only relate her story at second hand, albeit empathetically.

As the narrator watches, camouflaged by leaves, from his secret space, the woman weeps, sighs, and complains, while, in her sorrow, "[h]ir coloure . . . changit oft, and wexit pale and grene" (lines 97–98). Such symptoms usually signal lovesickness, although when this woman voices her complaint it turns out to be not a lament for a lost or unrequited love but a rant against Jealousy, from which she claims to suffer unjustly. In the course of the lady's monologue, we learn that she has newly entered into marriage, which she considers to be the

---

[4] MacQueen, p. 63. R. D. S. Jack ignores it entirely in his introductions to *The History of Scottish Literature* and *The Mercat Anthology of Early Scottish Literature, 1375–1707* (Edinburgh: Mercat Press, 1997), while Gregory Kratzmann calls it "the least memorable of all the Scots poems in the courtly allegorical mode," suggesting that it "illustrates a much more derivative handling" of Lydgate's *Temple of Glass* than any relationship to *The Kingis Quair*. He finishes by describing the "metres" as "reminiscent of Lydgate's at their most awkward" (*Anglo-Scottish Literary Relations, 1430–1550* [Cambridge, UK: Cambridge University Press, 1980], p. 20).

[5] Spearing (1993), p. 1.

cause of her distress: a surfeit of love (in the form of a jealous husband) rather than a lack of it. After calling on Hymen to take pity on her, on Diana for help "agayn this waryit chance" (line 80), and on Jupiter to defend her, the woman frequently curses Jealousy and asks to be delivered from "this warldis chance" (line 90), before her passionate pleas finally dissolve into tears.

Moved by her weeping, the narrator plans to reveal himself and offer the lady comfort, but before he can make his move, another lady comes along, and the two of them walk off together. The narrator then mulls over everything that he heard the first woman say and decides to write down her complaint. Having made his decision to complain against Jealousy on behalf of the lady, the narrator hopes that he says nothing to offend lovers, but as for jealous people, "quhethir [whether] thay flete [float] or into hell synk, / Yit schall I writen efter as I think" (lines 177–78). This first section ends with the narrator's promise: "Thus I begyn, and on this wise I say" (line 190).

The nine-line stanza that takes over in line 191 begins an apostrophe to women, whom the narrator addresses as "tendir youth, that stant in innocence, / Grundid on treuth, sadnes, and pacience" (lines 191–92). The narrator proceeds with an explanation of the blameless and long-suffering nature of women, and the contemptibility of those who would accuse them unjustly before moving into a kind of history of Jealousy, in which he explains how Jealousy was perceived "in the tyme . . . of oure elderis old" (line 254) as "abhominable" (line 255) and a cause for shame, but complains that "now thai mon thame uttirly dispone / To duell as doth the anker in the stone" ("now they [i.e., women] must wholly incline themselves / To live as does the recluse in the stone [cell]," lines 266–67) in order to avoid Jealousy's false accusations. The poem then advances swiftly into the narrator's "trety in the reprefe of Jelousye" (after line 316). This section, composed in rhyme royal, draws heavily on exempla from biblical sources, but is also indebted to a thirteenth-century French book of knowledge, *Sidrac* (or more probably to its Middle English translation, *Sidrak and Bokkus*), and to Jacobus de Voragine's *Legenda Aurea*. The tone here is rather calm — almost clinical — as the narrator details how the jealous "[f]rom worldis joy and hevinly companye / Excludit ar thus throu thair false invye" (lines 376–77). In addition, because of their jealousy, they often suffer misfortunes, of which, he says, "I coud ane hundreth samplis [examples] tell / Of stories olde the quhich I lat ourego [pass by]" (lines 380–81).

The poem's return to the nine-line stanza signals a shift from a discourse about jealousy to a direct address that condemns Jealousy, now personified, with all the fiery oratory of a sermon. "O wofull wrech and wickit, evill consate!" (line 464), he begins, going on in the next few lines to call Jealousy a false suspicion nourished full of hate, a cruel serpent always lying in ambush, and a slanderous tongue. Here the narrator rebukes Jealousy for giving love the responsibility for his own possessive behavior and enumerates the harm Jealousy's "cursit violence" (line 482) does to innocent women. Moved to anger, the narrator exclaims, "Fy on thee, wrech! Fy on thee, lufis fo!" (line 497), before going on to explain the reasons why the jealous person is doomed to suffer. Jealousy loses him his lady's heart and her love, makes her his enemy, and makes her wish she were dead. For the same reason, the jealous lover is doomed to suffer his "wrechit, cursit life" (line 547) in anger and woe, eternally fretting: laid waste, burned, and burning, tormented by thoughts of jealousy that make life a hell and doom the jealous to eternal suffering (lines 556–62).

The variation in rhyme scheme from the first set of nine-line stanzas implies that the treatise operates as a mechanism of change, since the new rhyme resembles a mingling of the first type of nine-line stanza with a rhyme royal stanza. The differences in the two sections also suggest a movement from defense to attack, as if the weight of the examples in the treatise galvanizes the narrator into an ardent assault on jealousy. His aggression leads finally to an unequivocal appeal to "every god that regnyth" (line 597), who "mycht or power hath to done vengeance" (line 601), to ensure

That quho thir ladyis likith to annoye,	*whoever likes to oppress these ladies*
Or yit thare fame or yit thaire ese engrewe,	*injure*
Mote suffryn here and fallyn grete mischewe	*May suffer; come [to] great misfortune*
Into this erth — syne with the falouschip of hell	*On; afterwards; fellowship*
In body and soule eternaly mot duell.	*may [they] dwell eternally*
(lines 603–07)	

Such a fiery resolve offers, indeed, a passionate release with which the agitated narrator may conclude his asseverations.

The poem's elaborate scheme of formal divisions in the narrative linked to shifts in content or tone points to an experiment in verse forms that looks forward to the increasing number of complex poetic forms prized by early modern poets. The first 190 lines are composed in heroic couplets, followed by fourteen nine-line decasyllabic stanzas rhyming *aabaabbab* (lines 191–316). These are succeeded in turn by "the trety in the reprefe of Jelousye," containing twenty-one rhyme royal stanzas (*ababbcc*; lines 317–463). The poem then returns to the nine-line stanza, but with a variation on the rhyme scheme: *aabaabbcc* (twelve stanzas, lines 464–572), followed by one ten-line stanza (*aabaabbcbc*; lines 572–81), before finally returning to heroic couplets for the remaining twenty-six lines (lines 582–607). In each case the shift in verse style signals a shift in the narrative. The section of heroic verse that begins the poem acts as a prologue, where the narrator frames his story and explains his reasons for writing. The section of nine-line stanzas which follows is headed by an apostrophe to women, which gives way to a defense of women against Jealousy. Following this, the "trety" acts almost as a sermon, supporting its condemnation of Jealousy through the use of numerous biblical and other exempla. The second set of nine-line stanzas forms a long apostrophe to Jealousy. The ten-line stanza which ends the apostrophe to Jealousy concludes the narrator's attempt to persuade the jealous person to give up his narrow way of life to live instead in "ese and in prosperitee / And love, and eke with ladies lovit be" (lines 577–78). In the concluding heroic couplets the narrator once again addresses his audience, identified here as "[y]ou loveris" (line 582), and finally asks the gods to bring destruction upon those who are jealous.

The topic of the narrator's discourse, jealousy, is necessarily double. It can be understood in two ways: in its positive aspect as devotion or love that gives rise to an impulse to guard or take care of the beloved; or, when this is taken to extremes, in its negative, destructive aspect as a desire to possess and restrict the beloved, characterized by suspicion, mistrust, and fear of lost affection. The lady's cursing of "[t]he cruell vice of causeles Jelousye" (line 56) points out that jealousy is to be understood here in its guise as suspicious and mistrustful possessiveness. Thus it is no surprise when the lady describes marriage as a "dangerouse bound" (line 60), a phrase that contains a complicated resonance that must be unpacked in order to understand the lady's grievance. Like jealousy, "bound" has positive and negative implications. On the one hand, it can be a simple tie, on the other, a "fetter or shackle (to hold a prisoner)" or "confinement, imprisonment." It can refer to a "mutual agreement or obligation undertaken at marriage," or to feudal ties between lord and vassal. It can mean a unifying force, such as love, but it can also be a "force that dominates, controls, compels, constrains, or restrains."[6] The word "dangerouse" at once suggests "hard to please," "aloof," "stingy," "domineering," and "risky," qualities which in turn point up the different facets of jealousy.[7] Its aloof or standoffish attribute might be likened to the guarded stance of jealousy in its positive role as protector, while the rest of the "dangerouse" traits suggest the prickliness of a suspicious lover who fears at any moment to be ousted.[8] In the context of marriage, the phrase "dangerouse bound" might suggest either a mutual agreement to love and protect one another or a tyrannical shackle tying one to an overbearing person impossible to please. The complications of this phrase in a sense embody not only the complaints that the lady expresses against jealousy, but also the conflicts evident in the narrator's attempts to tell another's story. The lady's demand to know "[q]uhich be the cause that I / Am turment thus, withoutyn cause or quhy" (lines 61–62) is in a sense already answered by her foregoing characterization of marriage as a "dangerouse bound."

The tensions that characterize the lady's comments on Hymen's "dangerouse bound" also predominate in her plea to Diana: "O Dyane! Goddesse of fredome and of ese, / Under quhom I have bot thraldome and disese, / Litill of treuth, of gladnese, or plesance" (lines 77–79). If the "dangerouse bound" of Hymen[9] is the source of her trouble, then Diana, as goddess of

---

[6] See *MED, bond* n.

[7] See *MED, daungerous* adj.

[8] In *The Romance of the Rose*, it is the job of Dangier ("Danger/Resistance") to protect the roses from any lovers who attempt to pluck them (see for example lines 2823 ff.).

[9] I.e., marriage; Hymen is the god of marriage (usually male, but in this case represented as female).

chastity, would appear to represent the freedom of the unmarried state,[10] but instead the lady appears to suffer as much under Diana's influence as under Hymen's, a fact that leads to renewed grief and the narrator's mellifluous praises as, moved by her tears, he waxes lyrical in his appeals for sympathy towards her, likening "the teris upoun hir fresch hewe" (line 106) to the hail which descends "from the ayr abone / Upoun the lusty colourit rose in June, / Quhen thai ar fairest on thair stalkis newe" (lines 103–05). These overblown images, like the extravagant praises on her appearance that begin in line 36, place the narrator in the position of hopeful lover who reserves the right to compare her to "Dyane or sum hie goddesse" (line 44), a rose, or the sun ("als fresch in hir beautee and array / As the bricht sonne at rising of the day" [lines 37–38]). But, as Anne M. McKim points out, the narrator's impulse to hide himself after comparing her to Diana "suggests that he himself resembles Actaeon whose voyeurism was summarily punished when he was hunted and torn to pieces by his own hounds" and casts doubt on the narrator's right to observe her.[11]

Like the compliments he pays, the narrator's observation of a woman alone would usually put him in the position of lover stricken with desire, as it does in the case of the narrator of *The Kingis Quair*, or both Palamoun and Arcite in Chaucer's Knight's Tale. But there are also famous cases where being stricken in such a manner leads to unrequited love and thence to jealousy when another is chosen by the beloved. In fact, it is the narrator's position of secret watcher of a woman in distress that suggests his potential to become a jealous lover himself. At the beginning of the Tale of Acis and Galatea in Book 2 of Gower's *Confessio Amantis* (2.97–200), Genius explicitly warns against those who spy on others because they cannot get love themselves (ed. Peck, 2.97–100):

> Ther ben of suche mo than twelve,
> That ben noght able as of hemselve
> To gete love, and for Envie
> Upon alle othre thei aspie.   *spy*

These lines anticipate the Cyclops Polyphemus' spying on Galatea and his jealous rage when she instead falls in love with Acis. The narrator of *The Quare of Jelusy* finds himself in a similarly compromising position, and his attitudes towards the woman he watches suggest the possibility that he may be displaying signs of the jealousy he condemns so vociferously at the end of the poem.

---

[10] Compare Emelye's prayer to Diana in which she protests that she wants to be neither "love ne wyf," adding, "I am, thow woost, yet of thy compaignye, / A mayde" (*CT* I[A]2307–08).

[11] McKim, p. 37.

That the narrator's attempt to "confort hir and counsele of hir wo" (line 110) is deflected by the fleet foot of "one othir lady" (line 111) who arrives before he can show himself suggests that the narrator's role as lover is usurped by the second woman. In effect, the hidden position that makes possible his surveillance of the lady and that should enable him to emerge just at the point where she is most vulnerable backfires. The other woman's route is "[t]he nerrest way unto" the lady (line 112), indicating that the narrator's loss of such an opportunity is partly due to his own distance. What this distance means in terms of the narrator's ability to rehearse the lady's story is not clear; what is clear is that the narrator does not share the intimacy of the two ladies, both initially alone, who pair up and walk off together: "one [direction] thai tuo ysamyn gan to fare" (line 113). His inability even to see where they go — "Bot quhens thai past I can nocht you declare" (line 114) — suggests that the narrator's ability to speak against Jealousy in this woman's cause is suspect, since he cannot even observe her destination once she passes out of his immediate purview. But even more, the fact that his role remains that of observer in the manner of Polyphemus suggests that his motives cannot be trusted either.

In the face of the impenetrable unit of the "tuo ysamyn," the narrator is unable to enact his role as the lady's comforter and potential lover and is left to insert himself into the narrative by taking on the woman's complaint, an act that may itself be a sign of jealousy. Ultimately this interjection is his attempt to thrust his way between the two women, just as his elaborate compliments on the lady's appearance (lines 36 ff.) act to reinscribe heteronormative relations by placing her in the position of love-object and asserting his own viability as a possible lover. But the narrator's initial lack of comprehension at the lady's plight points to his inability to represent her complaint adequately. Although at first his "goste hath take in sad remembering / This ladies chere and wofull compleynyng" ("spirit absorbed in sober memory of / This lady's expression and sorrowful complaining," lines 117–18), he does not, finally, understand what her problem is. He thinks that "sche, for fairhede and for suete-having, / Mycht wele accorde for ony wicht lyving" (lines 133–34); that is, because she is so fair and of such a pleasant demeanor, he thinks she should be compatible with anyone, so at first he does not understand why she should be suffering. After thinking on this problem for a while, he has an epiphany: "tho it fell into my fantasy / How sche so oftsyse cursit Jelousy" (lines 135–36). But the "fantasy" that motivates the narrator to tell the woman's story in the first place is suspect, for it is not clear what the difference is between the kind of "fantasy" the narrator experiences and the "fantasy" of the jealous person who

And sett sche loke or speke unto no wy,	*Even though; speaks; person*
Yit evill he demith in his fantasy;	*Yet; assumes; fancy (deluded imagination)*
And be sche glad or wele besene in oucht,	*dressed at all*
This tyrane saith it is nat do for nocht.	*tyrant; not done for no reason*
(lines 275–78)	

"Fantasy" is here equivalent to "fancy" or "imagination," which in the case of the narrator seems to be benign or even good, while in the jealous person it becomes tyrannical. Yet the narrator's descriptions of the lady clearly reveal his attraction to her and suggest the possibility that he could become jealous in his turn.

It is his moment of "fantasy" that motivates the narrator to decide that "for this ladies sak" (line 153) he will compose something in condemnation of Jealousy, no matter what anyone thinks ("quho be wroth, or quho be blith" [line 157]). Again this points to the narrator's insistent insertion of himself into the woman's story — he will write against Jealousy perhaps despite her feelings on the matter, could she express them.[12] Just as the narrator is excluded from the scene of female-bonding in a way that suggests his potential unsuitability for this tale, his motives for telling this story may be suspect, for what the narrator's "fantasy" shows is that women are bound together, not by mutual agreements or oppressive shackles, such as men and women are, but by shared experience — "Under thraldome and mannis subjectioun" (line 200). This is a reading that again provides a heteronormative explanation for the two women leaving together as "tuo ysamyn," for this ensures that they are bound together in their grievances towards male lovers, rather than for any homoerotic reason.

The narrator's seeming defense of women is as fraught as his relationship to jealousy and the woman whose complaint he purports to represent. In the introduction to their 1976 edition of the poem, J. Norton-Smith and I. Pravda remark on the "trety" as "gain[ing] obsessional momentum," suggesting that, "after the conventional passages of abstract ethical discussion, Christian moralizing, schematic polish and exemplifying lessons[,] the poet reaches an emotional pitch where he ... paints a vivid picture of destructive jealousy in its psychological aspect," a vision that "owes little to Ovid, Guillaume de Lorris or Chaucer."[13] The two editors conclude instead that the "poet is aggressively and irrationally pro-feminist."[14] It is true that the narrator explicitly steers away from any negative mention of women: "From viciouse women passith my matere, / Thai most all gone apoun one othir dance" (lines 225–26). But his very mention of "viciouse women" signals their existence and throws at least some doubt on the narrator's reliability or his sincerity in this attempt to defend women from "the cruel vice of causeless Jealousy." This is similar to the narrator's earlier determination to speak of this woman's suffering — "quho be wroth, or quho be blith" — in a way that calls into question

---

[12] This is one of the tensions of the framed narrative: the narrator's appropriation of the woman's complaint in a sense gives a voice to the woman only to take it away at the same time, since it is not she who speaks, but the narrator — and the narrator chooses to speak for her without giving her a choice. As McKim puts it, "the *Quare of Jelusy* is a poem *about* speaking for women, and appropriating the female voice is one means of doing so" (p. 36).

[13] Norton-Smith and Pravda, p. 8.

[14] Norton-Smith and Pravda, p. 9.

his motives and suitability for such a task. The narrator's insistence in writing against Jealousy on behalf of this woman may in fact be motivated by his need to assert himself as a potential lover in light of the arrival of the second woman, since her presence obviates any need on the lady's part for the comfort or counsel he wishes to offer her. His rant against Jealousy then becomes, in this reading, a kind of male insecurity, deflecting the same-sex alliance of the women "tuo ysamyn" by projecting another male rival in the figure of the jealous lover/husband, the source of the causeless Jealousy against which the lady rails.

The reaction of Norton-Smith and Pravda points to the way in which the intense nature of much of the poem's rhetoric forces its readers to react by attempting to explain its ardent pitch. This intensity also takes attention off of the unsupportable confusion of the narrator and elides the question of whether or not he is qualified to speak "for this ladies sak" (line 153). It is not easy to ascertain whether the poem is a credible effort to champion women or if the tone of it signals instead a kind of ridiculous escalation of vitriol that is meant to poke fun at an advocate who wishes to defend the indefensible. As Derek Pearsall points out in his introduction to *The Assembly of Ladies*, "The theme of . . . truth and loyalty of women and, generally speaking, the neglect and unfaithfulness of men . . . is a conventional one in the love poetry of the period, and bears the same relation to reality as the opposed theme of women's lasciviousness and fickleness."[15]

Such difficulties of interpretation punctuate the narrative throughout. For example, in his initial apostrophe to women, although ostensibly praising their innocence and long-suffering nature, the narrator injects a seed of doubt by his use of the phrase "Wommen I mene":

O tendir youth, that stant in innocence,	*tender; stands*
Grundid on treuth, sadnes, and pacience	*Established*
(Wommen I mene), all vicis contempnyng,	*vices spurning*
That void ibene of every violens,	*empty are; all violence*
And full of pitee and benevolence,	*pity*
Humble and wise, rycht sobir and benig,	*gracious*
And full of merci unto everything.	
(lines 191–97)	

The narrator's depiction of women as youthful and innocent is somewhat belied by his need to define his subject — "Wommen I mene" — implying that such an equation is not self-evident. Not only must the narrator define who he is talking about, but he must also go on to catalogue women's virtues, as if these qualities were so uncommon in women as to need definition. Nevertheless, it is difficult to know exactly how to read this, since such a list probably *was* uncommon, and this move could be seen as a parallel to the kinds of defenses

---

[15] Pearsall (1990a), pp. 29–30.

of women mounted by Christine de Pizan in her *Epistre au Dieu d'Amours* and *Cité des dames*. The characterization of women "[f]ull paciently into this erth lyving / Under thraldome and mannis subjectioun" (lines 199–200) that follows the amplification of their honorable qualities is a marked contrast to the narrator's portrayal of Jealousy: "Ofe evill condicioun evirmore is he, / As the Devill, ay birnyng into hate, / Full of discorde and full of frese consate [cruel judgment]" (lines 150–52). But if doubt is cast on the characterization of the one (women), then it is also thrown on the representation of the other (Jealousy). Further, many of the remarks on Jealousy reflect those of Chaucer's Criseyde, such as when the narrator hears the lady complain of "the cruel vice of causeless Jealousy," echoing Criseyde's complaint to Troilus about his jealousy: "noot I for-why ne how / That jalousie, allas, that wikked wyvere, / Thus causeles is cropen into yow" (*Troilus and Criseyde* 3.1009–11). But in this case, Troilus' jealousy turns out not to be unfounded, since Criseyde does betray him later on. This and other such resonances (detailed in the explanatory notes) appear to undercut the narrator's claims to excuse women by suggesting that no matter how he defends them, they will turn out, like Criseyde, to be traitors.

But the identification of the lady with Criseyde does not necessarily imply that the poem's defense of women is not to be taken seriously. Whatever the reason, the narrator's vigorous defense of the lady he observes, and of women more generally, from any culpability and his emphasis on what he terms "the cruel vice of causeless Jealousy" seems antithetical to the frequent stereotypes of women in medieval literature as inconstant, willful, and manipulative. The poem at points suggests a tone not unlike that of Chaucer's *Legend of Good Women*, in which Chaucer, supposedly writing legends of good women to make up for his translation of *The Romaunt of the Rose* and for his portrayal of Criseyde as an unfaithful lover in *Troilus and Criseyde*, effectively exposes the ridiculousness of the notion that "good" women would rather die than lose their reputations, a position that ultimately implies less a condemnation of Criseyde than of those who object to her.

In Chaucer's *Legend of Good Women*, the narrator follows to the letter his instruction from Queen Alceste to tell stories of good women (that is, women who are true to men at all costs) but in such an exaggeratedly one-sided way that doubt is cast not only upon the narrator's sincerity but also on the viability of the project as Queen Alceste defines it. Alceste's "goode wymmen, maydenes and wyves, / That weren trewe in lovyng al hire lyves" (Prologue, F.484–85) are ones, it seems, who have suffered distress at the hands of men, a conclusion that ironically insinuates in its most extreme version that the only "good" woman is a dead woman. The deadly outcome of Alceste's definition of a good woman in turn raises another question: why *should* women continue to be faithful under conditions that cost them their lives?

The narrator of *The Quare of Jelusy* perhaps takes a page from Alceste's book when he claims that "every lady of honour and of fame / Lesse settith of hir deth than hir gud name" (lines 491–92), going on to argue that many experiences show "mony o lady quhich . . . / Rather chesyn can [did] thair deth than blame" (lines 494–95). In fact, the narrator goes one step further in suggesting that a woman might choose death not only over dishonor, but also over marriage to a jealous husband: "A lady rather schuld hir deth ytak / Than suich a wrech till have onto hir mak" (lines 525–26). In this way, the tensions present in the lady's complaint about Hymen's "dangerouse bound" are finally resolved by the narrator, whose claim stands in contradistinction to the lady's own demand that Jupiter make her life follow "ane othir dance, / Or me delyvir of this warldis chance; / Quhich is to say that efter as I deserve / That I may lyve or sodaynly to sterve" (lines 89–92). The lady's desire to live or die (i.e., be judged) according to what she deserves, rather than at the hands of an arbitrary Fortune, suggests that she is not, in fact, willing to die for honor, but only for dishonor (i.e., if she deserves it).

As discussed in the Introduction to *The Boke of Cupide*, the arrangement of the manuscript is heavily "Chaucerian," containing for the most part works by and attributed to Chaucer, suggesting a preoccupation with Chaucerian authorship not shared by earlier manuscript collections of Chaucerian verse.[16] Of the first 14 items, 6 are by Chaucer, another 5 are inaccurately identified as his, while only 3 remain unattributed.[17] The Chaucerian contents are heavily front-loaded, taking up nearly the first four-fifths of the manuscript, and represent the probable first two stages of the manuscript's construction. In "The 'Scotticization' of Middle English Verse," Julia Boffey and A. S. G. Edwards point out that "[p]hysical details of the manuscript's construction suggest that it was copied in several stages and systematically upgraded over time."[18] According to Boffey and Edwards, the transcription of *Troilus and Criseyde* represented the first stage, "followed — probably at some interval — by the rest of the major Middle English contents of the manuscript."[19] *The Kingis Quair* (item 15) and other Scots poems comprise the last fifth of the manuscript; this section was "seemingly a later project," probably added to the manuscript in its final stage of compilation, and was "primarily the work of a second scribe who began his stint towards the end of *The Kingis Quair*."[20] This second scribe is the one responsible for copying *The Quare of Jelusy*.

In his introduction of nearly a century ago to *The Kingis Quair*, Alexander Lawson notes that "[p]oints of resemblance in artificiality of language in the *Kingis Quair*, *Lancelot of the Laik* and the *Quare of Jelusy* have long been noted by students of philology," going on to argue that

---

[16] See p. 35. Edwards (1996) suggests that the preference for ascribing works to Chaucer that Arch. Selden. B. 24 displays is unusual, for earlier Chaucerian anthologies tended "to underascribe works to Chaucer" (p. 59).

[17] See the contents in the facsimile volume, intro. Boffey and Edwards (1997), pp. 1–3.

[18] Boffey and Edwards (1999), pp. 166–67.

[19] Boffey and Edwards (1999), p. 167.

[20] Boffey and Edwards (1999), p. 167.

"there is a closer affinity than a common artificiality of language" between the three.[21] He catalogues resemblances between *Lancelot* and *The Kingis Quair*,[22] "little similarities of phrase" between *The Kingis Quair* and *The Quare of Jelusy*,[23] and "numerous" links between *Lancelot* and *The Quare of Jelusy* (among other things the reproduction of an entire line), which lead him to conclude that the three poems must be closely related, perhaps even authored by the same poet.[24] He does not trace links with *The Quare of Jelusy* and other Scots poetry, however. Matthew P. McDiarmid (who also thought *The Quare of Jelusy* and *Lancelot* were authored by the same person) suggests that *The Quare of Jelusy* shows the influences of several of William Dunbar's poems and Blind Hary's *The Wallace*.[25] MacQueen also notes similarities of style between *Lancelot of the Laik* and *The Quare of Jelusy*, although he agrees with M. M. Gray, an early editor of *Lancelot*, who rejects the claim that *The Kingis Quair* and *Lancelot* may have been authored by the same poet.[26]

In contrast, Norton-Smith and Pravda persistently deny *The Quare of Jelusy* any significant place in Scottish literary history. They dismiss as untenable the older idea that "the poet consciously borrow[ed] from James I's poem [*The Kingis Quair*]," arguing instead that *The Quare of Jelusy* "reflects what had been already written and circulated in England at the time when James left for Scotland to resume the responsibilities of government."[27] They further see the "faint resemblances between the *Quare* and later Scottish verse" as "traceable to earlier and more widely available English poetic material."[28] Finally, they conclude, "*The Quare of Jelusy* is a uniquely preserved, sometimes skilful, Scottish imitation of Chaucerian and Lydgatian poetic form and ethical concerns composed just prior to the later, more accomplished, fifteenth- and sixteenth-century literary development beyond the Tweed which has come to be

---

[21] Lawson, p. lxvi.

[22] Lawson, p. lxviii–ix.

[23] Lawson, p. lxix.

[24] Lawson writes: "we ask what conclusion may be drawn as to the relation of the three poems? Have we, as tradition has it, three poets — King James writing in 1423 or 1424, and two Scottish subjects writing later who knew his work and used it? Have we two poets — a poet of the *Kingis Quair*, and one poet of two later poems, as Professor Skeat privately assures me he is able to prove? There is a third possible solution — that we have but one poet" (p. lxxiii).

[25] Matthew P. McDiarmid, ed., *The Kingis Quair of James Stewart* (Totowa, NJ: Rowman and Little-field, 1973), p. 4.

[26] MacQueen, p. 60.

[27] Norton-Smith and Pravda, p. 9.

[28] Norton-Smith and Pravda, p. 9.

called 'Chaucerian.'"[29] This view defines the value of Scots poetry through its relationship to English poetry. Further, the assessment of *The Quare of Jelusy* as less "accomplished" in its imitation of English "poetic form and ethical concerns" suggests that it cannot be either significantly influenced by or have a notable influence on "more accomplished" Scots verse. The notion that the Scottish poem's value lies solely in its status as an "imitation"of English poetry, whether by Lydgate or Chaucer, unfortunately suggests that the relationship of *The Quare of Jelusy* is one of Scottish "imitation" to English "master" text, with all of the negative implications inherent in such a comparison. It seems worthwhile to point out that, whether or not the poem draws directly on *The Kingis Quair*, and whether or not it is a source of immediate influence upon later Scottish writers, it nevertheless forms part of the literary culture which thrived in Scotland in the fifteenth century.

Note on the text

The text of the poem is based on the single copy in Arch. Selden. B. 24, discussed above. Emendations are recorded in the textual notes, following the rationale explained in the General Introduction. In cases where a horizontal mark above a vowel might indicate a nasal consonant (*n*/*m*), I have expanded only in places where the stroke is more intensified in thickness and curvature (e.g., *cōnyng*, line 162) than the scribe's usual hairline strokes, and this would seem to reflect the scribe's usage in spelled-out forms. Other strokes and flourishes are disregarded as otiose. I follow Norton-Smith and Pravda's readings in cases where the manuscript has sustained further damage than when they examined it for their edition. After line 475, the edges of the pages along the binding have deteriorated significantly, so that many letters or words are missing at the beginnings of lines on the verso side of folios and at the end of lines on the recto side.[30] The Bannatyne Club edition, a nineteenth-century publication put out by the Bannatyne Club of Edinburgh in 1836 and probably transcribed and edited by David Laing,[31] is the earliest, and thus useful in its recording of some readings that are no longer legible. Norton-Smith and Pravda explain that "a comparison of the 1836 evidence and that of the 1910 edition [by Alexander Lawson] and the manuscript" shows that "the text deteriorated by 2 to 4 mms along the inner margins between 1836 and 1910."[32] Except in places where Norton-Smith and Pravda have argued convincingly that the Bannatyne Club reading is wrong,

---

[29] Norton-Smith and Pravda, p. 9.

[30] In their introduction to the facsimile volume, Boffey and Edwards (1997) give a detailed description of the manuscript.

[31] This is Norton-Smith and Pravda's speculation, p. 36.

[32] Norton-Smith and Pravda, p. 36.

The Quare of Jelusy

	This lusty Maii, the quhich all tender flouris	*invigorating (life-giving); which; flowers*
	By nature nurisith with hir hote schouris,	*nourishes; her warm showers*
	The felde oureclad hath with the tender grene,	*field has covered over; green*
	Quhich all depaynt with diverse hewis bene,	*emblazoned; colors is*
5	And everything makith to convert	*makes everything turn*
	Agayn the stroke of winter, cold and smert.	*Away from (Against); harsh*
	The samyn moneth and the sevynt ide,	*[In] this same month; seventh ides*
	The sonne, the quhich that likith not to hyde	*sun, which does not like to hide*
	His course, ascending in the orient	*east*
10	From his first gree, and forth his bemys sent,	*degree; sent his beams forth*
	Throu quhich he makith every lusty hert	*Through; joyful heart*
	Out of thair sleuth to walkyn and astert	*sluggishness; awaken; leap up*
	And unto Maii to done thair observance.	*May; do*
	Tho fell it me into remembrance	*Then*
15	A thing the quhich that noyith me full sore,	*which troubles; very keenly*
	That for to rest availith me no more;	*[So] that*
	Bot walking furth upoun the new grene,	*forth*
	Tho was the ayer sobir and amene,	*Then; air calm (mild); pleasant*
	And solitare, allone without my fere,	*alone; companion*
20	Unto a bonk, quhare as a small ryvere	*bank; where*
	Makith his course doun by a woddis side,	*wood's*
	Quhois levis fair did all the bewis hyde,	*Whose leaves; boughs hide*
	I past me furth remembring to and fro,	*went on reflecting*
	All on this warldis changeing and his wo,	*world's inconstancy; its misery*
25	And namely on the suffrance and the peyne	*suffering; grief*
	Quhich most hath do my carefull hert constreyne,[1]	
	The quhich as now me nedith not report.	*I need not (it is not needful for me to) report*
	For thare is non that likith to support,	*there; none who wants to assist [me]*
	Nor power has; quharefor I will sustene,	*wherefore; be strong*
30	And to no wicht I will compleyne nor mene,	*person; complain; lament*

---

[1] *That most have distressed my miserable heart*

Bot suffering furth, as I have done tofore,[1]   *My sorrow (misfortune); anguish; what*
Myn hevynes and wo: quhat is thare more?   *My sorrow (misfortune); anguish; what*
Wele long I walkit there, till at the last   *Very; walked*
Myn eye estward agayne the sonne I cast,   *eastward towards*

35   Quhare as I saugh among the levis grene   *Where; saw; green*
A lady, quhich that was rycht wele besene,   *very well-dressed (good-looking)*
And als fresch in hir beautee and array   *as youthful (fresh); appearance*
As the bricht sonne at rising of the day.   *bright*
Of coloure was sche lik unto the rose,   *she like*

40   Boith quhite and red ymeynt; and I suppose   *Both white; mingled; think*
One gudliar that Nature nevir wrocht;   *better [than]; never made*
Of lustyhede ne lakkit sche rycht nocht.[2]
My spirit coud nocht resemble hir, nor gesse,   *could not; compare; consider*
Bot unto Dyane or sum hie goddesse.   *Except to Diana; some exalted*

45   And prevely I hid me of entent   *secretly; myself on purpose*
Among the levis to here quhat sche ment.   *hear; said*
And forth a passe sche walkit sobirly   *while; walked quietly*
There as I was and passing cam so ny   *Where; near*
That I persavit have upoun hir chere   *perceived; face*

50   The cristall teris falling from hir eyne clere.   *crystal (shining) tears; eyes bright*
It semyt wele that wo hir hert constreynit,   *seemed very much; heart distressed*
Sche sorowit, sche sikit, sche sore compleynit;   *lamented; sighed; complained*
So sobirly sche spak that I no mycht   *spoke; might*
Not here one word quhat that sche said arycht.   *hear; clearly (aright)*

55   Bot wele I herd, sche cursit prevaly   *cursed in private*
The cruell vice of causeles Jelousye.   *cruel; causeless (i.e., unfounded)*
Sche wepit so a quhile, till at the last   *wept; while*
With that hir voce and eyne to hevin sche cast   *voice; eyes*
And said, "Goddesse Imeneus, thou rewe   *Hymen; take pity*

60   Of me, into thy dangerouse bound of newe   *On me; domineering bond recently*
Ycome. Allace! Quhich be the cause that I   *Come. Alas! What is the reason*
Am turment thus, withoutyn cause or quhy,   *tormented; without; reason*
So sudaynly under youre strong lowe,   *suddenly; law*
For it the quhich is unto me unknowe?   *For something that is unknown to me*

65   As als sekirly here in thy presence,   *also surely*

---

[1] *But go on suffering, as I have done up to now*

[2] *Of beauty she lacked absolutely nothing*

	Geve evirmore I did in suich offence,	*If at any time; such*
	The scharp deth mote perce me throuch the hert[1]	
	So that on fute from hens I nevir astert.	*foot; here; never escape*
	Nor nevirmore it was in myn entent;	
70	Thareof I am both hole and innocent.	*Of that [offense]; free from blame*
	And, gif I say false, Pluto that is king,	*if*
	Quhich the derk regioun hath in his governyng,	*dark region (Hades); under his rule*
	Mote me into his fyry cart do ta,	*May; fiery cart; take*
	As quhilom did he to Proserpina,	*once*
75	And thare my body and my soule also	*there*
	With him ay duell in torment and in wo.	*always live (stay)*
	O Dyane! Goddesse of fredome and of ese,	*Diana; freedom; tranquility*
	Under quhom I have bot thraldome and disese,	*whom; only servitude; suffering*
	Litill of treuth, of gladnese, or plesance,	*Little; joy (pleasure)*
80	So helpith me agayn this waryit chance,	*beleaguered circumstance*
	For of this gilt thou knowis wele my part;	*accusation (offense); know*
	And Jupiter, that knowith every hart,	*who; heart*
	Wote that I am sakelese — me defende!	*Know; blameless; defend me*
	Ne for no want, nor for to have commend,	
85	Not say I this, for here nys non bot ye,	
	Of thilk hid thing, that knowith the veritee;[2]	
	And sen thou wote that my complaynt is treuth,	*since*
	Of pitee, than, compassioun have and reuth;	
	My life to gone mak on ane othir dance,[3]	
90	Or me delyvir of this warldis chance;	*Or [else] deliver me from; world's fortune*
	Quhich is to say that efter as I deserve	*according to what I*
	That I may lyve or sodaynly to sterve."	*suddenly; die*
	And thus apoun the goddis can sche crye,	*upon; gods did she cry*
	And evir among sche cursit Jelousye;	*continually*
95	With that sche sichit with a rycht pitouse chere;	*sighed; piteous expression*
	Allace, gret reuth hir pleynyng was to here.	*[a] great pity; complaining; hear*
	Hir coloure, quhich that was so fair to sene,	*see*

---

[1] *May sharp death pierce me through the heart*

[2] Lines 84–86: *Neither for any desire, nor in order to be commended, / Do I say this, for here [there] is not any (none) but you, / Who knows the truth of this hidden thing*

[3] Lines 88–89: *Then [out] of pity have compassion — and sympathy; / Cause my life to follow a different course*

	It changit oft, and wexit pale and grene.	*changed often; turned (waxed); green*
	Hir to behold, thare was no gentill hert	
100	Than ne schuld have compassioun of hir smert,[1]	
	To sene from hir lusty eyne availle	*bright eyes drop*
	Tho glettering teris, als thik as ony haile	*Those; thick; any*
	As thai descendet from the ayr abone	*air above*
	Upoun the lusty colourit rose in June,	*Upon; brightly colored*
105	Quhen thai ar fairest on thair stalkis newe;	*they (i.e., roses) are; new stems (stalks)*
	So was the teris upoun hir fresch hewe.	*were; complexion*
	Allace, hir chere! Allace, hir countenance!	*Alas; expression (face)*
	For to behald it was a grete pennance.	*hardship (penance)*
	And, as I was uprising for to go	*getting up*
110	To confort hir and counsele of hir wo,	*comfort*
	So come one othir lady, hir allone,	*another; alone (i.e., by herself)*
	The nerrest way unto hir is sche gone;	*quickest (nearest)*
	And one thai tuo ysamyn gan to fare,	*one [direction] they two together began to take*
	Bot quhens thai past I can nocht you declare.	*But where; went; tell*
115	Bot quhen that thai out of my sicht were gone,	*sight*
	And I in wod belevit me allone,	*wood left by myself alone*
	My goste hath take in sad remembering	
	This ladies chere and wofull compleynyng,[2]	
	Quhich to my hert sat full very nere;	*near (close)*
120	And to myselfe I thocht in this manere:	*thought*
	Quhat may this mene? Quhat may this signifye?	*mean*
	I can nocht wit quhat is the cause or quhy	*understand; reason*
	This lady suffrit this strong adversitee;	*suffered*
	For, as me think, in erde suld nothing be	*as it seems to me, on earth should*
125	Possible to ony wicht of wele-willing,	*benevolence*
	As ony richesse or hertis cherising,	*[Such] as; wealth; heart's affection*
	And everything according to plesance,	*conforming; desire (pleasure)*
	Than sche thareof suld have full suffisance[3]	
	To gladin hir and plesyn with thair chere,	*gladden; please; mirth*

---

[1] Lines 99–100: *To behold her, there would be no noble heart / That would not have compassion about her pain*

[2] Lines 117–18: *This lady's face (expression) and sorrowful lamentation / Has absorbed my spirit in sober (pensive) reflection*

[3] *But that she should have full sufficiency thereof*

130	Bot deth of lufe or deth of frendis dere,	*Except death of loved [one]; dear friends*
	Quhich is inpossible for to bring ageyn.	*impossible; back*
	For thing possible, me think, sche suld nocht pleyne;[1]	
	For sche, for fairhede and for suete-having,	*because of beauty; pleasant demeanor*
	Mycht wele accorde for ony wicht lyving.	*be compatible with*
135	Bot tho it fell into my fantasy	*then; imagination*
	How sche so oftsyse cursit Jelousy.	*often*
	Than thoucht I thus: gife lyvis ony wicht	*Then; if any person lives*
	Quhich fynd into his cherlisch hert mycht	*Who finds in his churlish heart [the]*
	Thus for to turment suich one creature,	*Thus to torment such a*
140	To done hir wo, to done hir payne endure,	*do her injury; make her endure suffering*
	Now wele I wote — it is no questioun —	
	Thare lyveth none into this erth adoun,	*none [such] down on this earth*
	Bot he be cummyn of sum cherlisch kynd,	*Unless; is a descendent; some churlish race*
	For othir wayis, forsuth, I can nocht fynd,	*ways, in truth (forsooth)*
145	He suich one lady wold in ony way displese,	*a; would*
	Or harme do to hir honour or hir ese.	*pleasure*
	Be as be may, yit my consate me gevith	*yet my mind tells me*
	This Jelousye, the quhich that sche reprevith,	*blames (condemns)*
	Annoyith hir, and so it may wele be	*Troubles (Harasses)*
150	Ofe evill condicioun evirmore is he,	*Of wicked character*
	As the Devill, ay birnyng into hate,	*Devil, forever burning in*
	Full of discorde and full of frese consate.	*cruel judgment*
	Howevir it stonde, yit for this ladies sak	*stands; lady's sake*
	Sa mekle occupacioun schall I tak	*I will take very great pains*
155	Furthwith for to syttyn doun and writt	*Right away; sit; write*
	Of jelouse folk sumthing into dispitt;	*jealous people; in contempt*
	And quho be wroth, or quho be blith, here I	*whoever; angry; happy (blithe)*
	Am, he the quhich that sett nothing thareby.	*he who takes no account of that*
	For ladyes schall no cause have, gif I may,	*if*
160	Thame to displese for nothing schall I say,	*To be displeased by anything I will say*
	And gif I do, it is of negligence	*[because] of*
	And lak of connyng and of eloquence,	*lack of skill (knowledge)*
	For it is nothing into myn entent	*in my*
	To say the thing schall mak thame discontent;	*[that] shall make them*
165	Nor yit no faithfull lover to displese,	

---

[1] *For something possible, it seems to me, she should not complain*

	Nor schewe nothing in contrare of thair ese,	*show; contrary to*
	Nor of no wicht of gude condycioun,	*character*
	Bot of this wickit ymaginacioun,	*Except; wicked imagination (inventiveness)*
	Quhich by his name is clepit Jelousye,	*called*
170	That every lovere hatith of invy.	*That hates every lover [because] of enmity*
	And thouch all suich were wode in thair entent	*though; mad; purpose*
	As Herculese, quhen he himselven brent,	*when he burnt himself*
	Or cursit Nero, quhen he his perile sawe,	*peril saw*
	Of his own hond ymurderit and yslawe,	*hand murdered; slain (i.e., suicide)*
175	Ne rek I not, nor geve I of thame charge — [1]	
	Lat thame go saile all in the Devillis barge!	*Devil's*
	And quhethir thay flete or into hell synk,	*whether; float; sink*
	Yit schall I writen efter as I think.	*write according to what*
	And ye loveris that stondith furth in treuth,	*continue to be steadfast in devotion*
180	Menyt eke, compassioun have and reuth	*Lamented also*
	How ladies evill demanit ar oftsyse[2]	
	By this foule wrech. Go! Helpith him dispise,	*wretch (Jealousy); [to] despise him*
	And to compleyne thair treuth and innocence,	*proclaim; integrity*
	That mekle suffrith throuch thair owin pacience.	*suffer greatly; own*
185	And of my termes and my rude endite	*phrases; unlearned verses*
	Excusith me sett thai be inperfyte,	*although; imperfect*
	Beseking you at Lovis hie reverence,	*Beseeching; by Love's high*
	Takith gude will instede of eloquence.	*good*
	For as I can, non othir wyse I may.	*other way*
190	Thus I begyn, and on this wise I say:	*begin; in this way*
	O tendir youth, that stant in innocence,	*tender; stands*
	Grundid on treuth, sadnes, and pacience	*Established*
	(Wommen I mene), all vicis contempnyng,	*vices spurning*
	That void ibene of every violens,	*empty are; all violence*
195	And full of pitee and benevolence,	*pity*
	Humble and wise, rycht sobir and benig,	*gracious*
	And full of merci unto everything	
	In suffrance, scant of mony grete offense,	*tolerance, free*
	Full paciently into this erth lyving	*on*

---

[1] *I do not count them, nor do I give them importance*

[2] *[On] how ladies are many times maliciously mistreated (demeaned)*

200	Under thraldome and mannis subjectioun,	*servitude; man's subjection*
	And mekly suffrith thair correctioun.	*meekly endure; punishment*
	Allace, the wo! Allace, the sad grevance!	
	Ye, suffering men of evill condicioun,	*You, putting up with; bad character*
	Quhich hath no pitee and lakkith discrecioun,	*Who have; pity; lack*
205	And bene ysett under thair govirnance,	*are placed*
	Youre suffering thare is mony one hard mischance,	*many a; misfortune*
	Youre fairhede goth, your youth is brocht adoun	*beauty goes; brought*
	With weping teris ay full of strong penance.	

	Loveris compleyne, and every gentill wicht	*gentle (i.e., noble)*
210	Help for to mene, help for to waill arycht;	*complain (moan); lament well*
	Compassioun have and reuth upoun the nede,	*when necessary*
	In helping and supporting at your mycht	*by*
	Thame quhich that of youre gladnese is the licht,	*Those whom; light*
	That is to say, all lusty womanhede,	*delightful (beautiful) womankind*
215	Quhich you in lufe and chevalry doth fede,	*Whom; love; chivalry do sustain*
	But quhom this warldis gladnese from his hicht	*Without; world's; its height*
	Schold sone avale and fallyn out of drede	*Should soon drop; fear*

	Into this erth; quhat is oure gladnese here,	
	Iff that we lak the presence and the chere	*kindness*
220	Of thame that bene this worldis hole plesance?	*those who (i.e., women); whole*
	Quhat ar we worth, gif that thair help ne were?	*if their help (favor) did not exist*
	All vertuouse womman Salamon holdith dere,	*virtuous women Solomon holds dear*
	And mekle worth of thair govirnance.	*much*
	Thai ar oure ese; thai ar oure suffisance.	*delight; satisfaction*
225	From viciouse women passith my matere,[1]	
	Thai most all gone apoun one othir dance.	*must; go upon a different*

	Allace, the wo — quho can it specify?—	
	That wommen suffren ay withoutyn quhy	*suffer always without reason*
	Into this erth in dangere and in vere.	*In; fear*
230	And to recist agaynis tyranny	*resist against*
	Is no defense; thai have to pas thareby	*[Offers] no defense; pass*
	Bot weping with the teris of thair chere,	*Only; faces*

---

[1] *My [subject] matter passes over immoral women*

	With syking, wailling, pleynyng, and prayere;	*sighing, wailing, complaining*
	And evirich thing sustene thai paciently:	*every; bear*
235	Thus livith ay thir sely women here.	*these innocent*

	This mene I: all be wickit men oftsyse	
	That giltles dooth thir ladies to supprise[1]	
	Withoutyn cause of ony maner thing,	*Without*
	And namely, by thair varyit tyrannyis,	*various tyrannies*
240	The cruelteis, the wikkitnes that lyis	*cruelties; wickedness; lies*
	In Jelousy and false ymagynyng,	*treacherous (untrustworthy) imagination*
	Quhich harmyth all this world by his demyng,	*harms; its judgment*
	Of quhom I think sumthing to devise	*plan something*
	And schewe to you here, eftir my connyng.	*according to my knowledge (ability)*

245	Quho schall me help, allace, for to endite,	*compose*
	For to bewaill, to compleyne, and to write	
	This vice that now so large is, and common?	*is now so widespread*
	Quhat sall I say? Quhom sall I awite?	*What shall; accuse*
	For hie nor low is non estate to quyte,	*rank to be acquitted*
250	Now all hath fele of thilke poysoun.	*[the] feeling of this poison*
	Allace, this false and wickit condicioun	
	The lustyhede and every glade delyte	*joyfulness; glad delight*
	Hath of this world full nere ybrocht adoun.	*very nearly brought*

	For in the tyme was of oure elderis old,	*time; elders*
255	Quhen Jelousy abhominable was hold,	*When; held (considered)*
	Quhareofe eschamith every noble wy,	*Of which was ashamed; person*
	Than was thir ladies ever in honour hold,	*Then were these ladies; held*
	Thair lustyhede, quhich causith monyfold	*joyfulness; abundant*
	Fredome, gentrise, disport, and chevalry;	*generosity, courtesy, entertainment*
260	Thai syng, thai dance, and makith company.	
	Thame to defame was non that durst nor wold,	*none; dared; would*
	As now thai do withoutyn cause or quhy.	

---

[1] Lines 236–37: *This is what I have in mind: all are wicked men commonly / Who unjustly abuse (oppress) these ladies*

	And yit I wote thir ladies bene echone	*each one*
	Als trew and sad as ony tyme aygone,	*faithful and sober as [at]; past*
265	And ar to blame als litill or repreve;	*culpable*
	Bot now thai mon thame uttirly dispone	*must wholly incline themselves*
	To duell as doth the anker in the stone,	*live; recluse; stone [cell]*
	Yf that thai think undemyt for to leve;	*If; uncondemned; live*
	So fast encressyn can this false beleve	*expanded has; belief*
270	That in this world fewe ladyis ar, or none,	*[there] are*
	Quhich schall unsclanderit from his tong escheve.	*unslandered; tongue escape*
	For ife sche makith chere or company,	*entertains*
	As they were wount, he raisith up his cry;	*wont*
	And yfe sche loke, he jugith of hir thocht;	*looks*
275	And sett sche loke or speke unto no wy,	*Even though; speaks; person*
	Yit evill he demith in his fantasy;	*Yet; assumes; fancy (deluded imagination)*
	And be sche glad or wele besene in oucht,	*dressed at all*
	This tyrane saith it is nat do for nocht.	*tyrant; not done for no reason*
	Allace! By him the harm withoutyn ony quhy	*reason*
280	Is every day into this world ywrocht.	*in; done*
	And ife a spouse stant with this vice, iwys,	*if; sides with; indeed*
	All thing is said, all thing is wrocht amys	*done amiss*
	In his consate; and gif that ony way	*if any*
	Fro home he goth, his spy he schall nocht mys,	*From; goes; miss*
285	That feynith tailis — nothing as it is —	*Who makes up tales (i.e., the spy)*
	To plesyn him, for sumthing mon he say.	*please him (i.e., the spouse); must*
	Than goth all rest, than goth all pes away;	*goes; peace*
	Farewele of lufe the gladnese and the blis,	*Farewell the gladness and the bliss of love*
	Fro he cum home als ferfuth as he may.	*When; quickly*
290	And yit to hir is double wo and grame,	*grief*
	For thouch that he be gilty in the same	*guilty*
	Full mony a lady nothing dare sche say;	
	And yit thir ladies in Jelousy to blame	
	Ar nocht as men, for men haith now no schame	*have; shame*
295	To be in love as double as thai may —	*duplicitously*
	Thir ladies thus full mony a cause have thay.	

And thouch he speke, it hynderit nocht his name;[1]
And ife sche loke, it harmith hir allway.   *Yet; forever*

    This may be clept a wrech intill his mynd,   *called; in his mind*
300 For, as we may in old bukis fynd,   *books find*
In lak of hert ay stant this maladeye   *This malady ever consists of lack of courage*
To him the quhich supposith aye behynd   *who believes [himself] always behind*
And verreis to stond in lufis kynd.   *hesitates to be steadfast in love's nature*
For Salamoun saith, "Ane noble hert nor eye   *A noble heart*
305 Haith to enquere of ladis, nor espye,   *Has [neither] to investigate ladies; spy*
Nor thame misdeme into thair treuth unkinde,"   *misjudge in; faithfulness impiously*
As doth this wrech, that hot is Jelusye;   *is called*

    Of quhom into contempnyng and dispite   *in scorn; contempt (defiance)*
My will is gude for to declare and write.   *desire; good (strong)*
310 Suppose of wit I empty be and bare,
Thou Ecco, quhich of chiding is perfyte,   *who; perfect*
I thee beseke thou helpith me to flyte,   *beseech; attack/rail*
And Thesiphone, thou lord of wo and care,   *Tisiphone (one of the three Furies)*
So helpith me this mater to declare
315 On Jelousy his malice to acquyte   *repay*
With the supplee of every trewe lufare.   *assistance; true (faithful) lover*

Here efter folowis the trety in the   *treatise*
reprefe of Jelousye.   *condemnation*

    The passing clerk, the grete philosophoure   *surpassing (preeminent)*
Sydrake, enspirit of hevinly influence,   *Sidrak, inspired by heavenly*
Quhich holdyn was into his tyme the floure   *Who was held in; flower*
320 Of clergy, wisedome, and intelligence,   *Of knowledge (doctrine)*
Into his bukis declarith this sentence   *In; books declares this wisdom*
To Bokas King, amang his doctrinis sere,   *King Boctus, among his various doctrines*
Of Jelousy, and saith in this manere:

    He clepith it foly of one ignorant,   *calls; [the] folly of an ignorant person*
325 The quhich evill humoris makith to procede,

---

[1] *And though he speak [i.e., to another woman], it harms (hinders) not his reputation*

172

As hert corrupt, or quho it list to hant;[1]
Malancholy it raisith up but drede,   *It (Jealousy) raises up melancholy without fear*
That lust of slepe, of mete or drink, of ded;   *desire for; food or drink; death*
And wit of man confusith it all plane   *it (Jealousy) confuses fully*
330   With this hote fevir that is cotidiane.   *hot (intense) fever; recurring*

And suth it is by resoun, as we fynd,   *truly*
That this suspicioun and this Jelousye
Is and cummith of the veray kynd   *arises from; true nature*
Of Herubus, the quhich that of Invye   *Envy*
335   The fader is, and be this resoun quhy   *father; [the] reason why*
For evirmore in rancoure and in ire,   *rancor*
As Ethena, he birnyth in the fyre.   *Like Etna; burns*

Thus with the cheyne of sorow is he bound   *chain*
Furth in this world full of adversitee,
340   His frendschip to no wicht it schall be found.
Quhy in himself ay at debate is he?
Withoutyn lufe, withoutyn cheritee,   *charity*
In his consate and his ymagynyng
Ay to the worst he demith everything,   *judges (believes)*

345   That in this erth lyveth thare no wicht   *[Such] that; there lives*
Of no condicioun nor of no degree,   *rank*
In his presence that wisedome has, nor micht,   *might*
To reule himself in ony wyse than he   *conduct; way but that he (i.e., Jealousy)*
Schall deme thareof amys, ysett he be   *judge (think); wrong, even if (although)*
350   Als chaste, als trew, and reule himself als wele
As evir hath do the prophete Daniele.   *ever did*

For every thocht and luke and countenance   *look*
Suspect he holdith into his demyng,   *in; judgment*
And turnyth all to harm and to mischance.
355   This tygir with his false ymagynyng   *tiger*
Lith as a devill into this erth lyving,   *Lurks as a devil living on this earth*

---

[1] Lines 325–26: *Which causes destructive humors to continue / [Such] as [a] sinful heart, or whoever chooses to practice (dwell morbidly on) it (jealousy)*

Contenyng aye in anger and in hate —   *Persisting*
Both with himself and otheris at debate.   *at odds*

But cheritee thus evirmore he levith,
360   Quhich Crist of wedding clepith the habyte,
But quhilk of hevin every wicht belevyth,
But of the blisse and of the fest is quyte.[1]
And Paule thus to the Corinthies doth writ   *Corinthians*
Of faith, of hope, and eke of cheritee;   *charity*
365   The last the most he clepith of the thre.   *greatest; calls*

And he declarith in the samyn chapture   *same chapter*
That thouch men be as angelis eloquent,   *[as] eloquent as angels*
Or all thair gudis gyvith to the pure,   *goods give; poor*
Or yit for Crist ysuffering suich turment
370   To be yslawe, ymarterit, or brent,   *slain, martyred*
Or doth all gude the quhich that may be wrocht,   *good which; done (wrought)*
And lakkith cheritee, all it availit nocht.   *lacks; helps not at all (does no good)*

And every wicht that hath discrecioun wote   *who has moral judgment*
That quho thus lyvith into Jelousye,   *lives in*
375   In ire and malice birnyth ay full hote,   *burns; very intensely (hotly)*
From worldis joy and hevinly companye   *world's; heavenly*
Excludit ar thus throu thair false invye;   *hatred (malice)*
And oft thareof cummith mischance,   *comes trouble*
As strife, debate, slauchter, and vengeance;   *[Such] as; murder (destruction)*

380   Quhareof I coud ane hundreth samplis tell   *Whereof I could a hundred examples*
Of stories olde the quhich I lat ourego;   *let pass by*
And als that in this tyme present befell,   *also [stories]; present time happened*
Amongis quhilk we fynd how one of tho   *Amongst which; find; those*
His lady sleuch and syne himselfe also   *killed; afterwards*
385   In this ilk lond withoutyn ony quhy   *same land; reason*
But onely for his wickit gelousy.   *only because of; jealousy*

---

[1] Lines 359–62: *Without charity thus evermore he lives, / Which Christ calls the wedding garment, / Without which every person turns away from (forgoes) heaven, / And of the bliss and of the feast is destitute*

Of quhich full mony ensample may we fynde   *many example[s]*
Of olde ygone and new experiment,   *observation*
That quho this gilt hauntith in his mynd,   *sin practices (dwells on); mind*

390   It hath bene cause quhy mony one were schent;[1]
Sum sleuch himself, and sum of evill entent
From innocentis bereving oft the lyfe;   *Often took the life of innocents*
Sum sleuch his lady, and othir sum his wife.

And Jelousye hath evir suich a tong   *always*

395   That from the malice of his hert procedith,   *arises from the malice of his heart*
By quhich that sclander wyde quhare is rong,   *slander widely there; rung (sounded)*
And Crist he saith, "That quhom of sclander dredith,   *fears*
Wo be to him!" and, more, unto him bedith   *bids*
Away the sclanderouse member for to kerve,[2]

400   Quhich dampnyth you eternaly to sterve.   *damns; eternally; die*

And the first verteu, as poetis can declare,   *virtue; poets know how to declare*
Is tong with wysedome to refreyne and stere,   *[the] tongue; restrain; command (steer)*
Quhich unto God is nerest evirmare;   *nearest*
And Salamoun saith, "Fer better that it were   *Far*

405   Allone to duell with lyouns than be nere   *Alone; dwell; lions; near*
A sclanderouse tong of chiding and of hate,"
So odiouse he holdith suche debate.   *he (Solomon)*

A poete saith that nevirmore is pes,   *peace*
Quhare suich a tong hath dominacioun,   *dominion*

410   Nor yit the tong the quhich that can nocht ces,   *which cannot cease*
Ay schewing his evill ymaginacioun,   *making known*
And hath of langage no more discrecioun
Than he the quhich that talkith in his slepe;   *Than he who*
Nor unto him aucht no wicht takyn kepe.   *ought; heed*

415   Approvit is by resoun and scripture   *It is proved*
Of Crist and His apostlis evirilkone,   *apostles every one*
By prophetis, doctouris, poetis, and Nature,

---

[1] *It has been [the] cause why many were ruined*

[2] *To cut (carve) away the offending (slanderous) member*

	Of quhom this vice, of quhom this gilt is tone,	*sin; derived (conceived)*
	And quhens he cummith, and quhider he schall gone;	*whence; whither*
420	Quhich is to say that Jelousy, at schort,	*Which; in short*
	Commyth of the devill, and thedir schall resort.	*Comes; thither; return*

	As onys of one emperoure we rede,	*once; an; read*
	One haly man, and clepit was Henry,	*A holy; called*
	In prayer, fasting, and in almouse dede;	*works of charity*
425	And for no cause bot for his Jelousye,	*except*
	The quhich he caucht, and for non othir quhy,	*conceived (caught); no; reason*
	Upoun his lufe trew and innocent,	*Upon*
	Efter his deth he come to jugement.	*After; came*

	And thare, as into revelacioun	*there (i.e., at judgment); in divine communication*
430	Till one of oure faderis old was sene,	*To; fathers; seen*
	He had ressavit his owin dampnacioun	*would have received; own damnation*
	For the ilk gilt of Jelusy I mene,	*very sin*
	Had nocht Laurence the blisfull marter bene	*blissful martyr*
	By merci of oure blisfull Salvioure:	*mercy; Savior (i.e., Christ)*
435	Suich is the fyne of all this false erroure.	*conclusion*

	And quhareof long it hath bene said or this	*has been; before*
	"That of hote lufe ay cummith Jelousye,"	*hot; comes*
	That sentence is interpret to amys,	*proverb is greatly misinterpreted*
	And, schortly said, nocht understand the quhy.	*the reason not understood*
440	For it is nocht for to presume thareby	*not [appropriate]; thereby*
	That Jelousye, quhich is of vice the ground,	*foundation*
	Is into lufe or in a lufar found.	*in*

	For jelousy, the quhich of lufe that risith,	*which rises from*
	Is clept nothing bot of a simple drede,	*called; blameless fear*
445	As quhen thir lufaris remembreth and avisith,	*lovers reflect; deliberate*
	Sum of thair wo and sum apoun thair nede,	*need*
	And sum of gladnese, that doth of lufe procede,	
	Throuch quhich thair hertis brynt ar in the fyre,	*Through; hearts are burned*
	Sum of grete raddoure, and sum of hote desire.	*terror*

| 450 | Than everything thai dout that may thame make | *Then; fear* |
| | Of lufe the grettest plesance to forgo, | *Forego the greatest pleasure of love* |

Throuch quhich sum lufaris hath suich drede ytake — *some lovers; taken*
That it to thame is hevynes and wo;
Bot, natwithstonding, ay thai reule thame so — *control themselves so [that]*
455 Thair drede it is to every wicht unknowe —
Thame likith not to sclander nor to schowe. — *It pleases them neither; reveal*

Thir jelousyis full diverse ar of kynd. — *jealousies; different; in nature*
The tone, it harmith to no creature, — *The one*
Bot secrete ded and symple, as we fynd, — *secret deeds and blameless [ones]*
460 That lufaris into lufing most endure; — *lovers in loving must*
That othir bereth all one othir cure: — *other (i.e., Jealousy) has; another concern*
He sclanderith, feynyth, defamith, and furth criyth, — *cries out*
And lufe and every lufar he invyith. — *lover; feels ill-will toward*

O wofull wrech and wickit, evill consate! — *deplorable wretch*
465 O false suspicioun nurist full of hate, — *nourished*
In hevyn and erth thi harm is boith ywritte! — *heaven; your; written*
O cruell serpent aye lying in awayte! — *ambush*
O sclanderouse tong, fy on thy dissayte! — *fie; deceit*
Quhare that thou lovith thou feynyth, that ypocrite; — *love; feign, who [are a] hypocrite*
470 That thou art jelouse, lufe thou gevith the wyte — — *give the responsibility*
Thou leis thareof, as that I schall declare — *lie about that*
To understand to every trewe lufare.

For every wicht that is with lufe ybound,
And sad and trewe in every faith yground, — *Both sober*
475 Syne likith nocht to varye nor eschewe; — *Afterwards does not like to change; flee*
Rather suffer schall he the dethis wound — *death's*
Than into him schall onything be found — *anything*
That to this lady may displese or greve, — *grieve*
Or do to hir or to hir fame reprefe, — *reputation disgrace*
480 For his desire is althir most to se — *most of all to see*
Hir stand in honoure and in prosperitee.

And contrair this thy cursit violence — *against*
Staunt ay for quhy; thi sclanderouse offense — *Stands; for this reason; your*
Harmith thy lady most of ony wy, — *anyone*
485 Quhich stryvith evir agayn hir innocence, — *struggles/fights always against*
That hath no suerd bot suffrance and pacience — *sword except endurance*

177

	For to resist agaynis hir inymy,	*enemy*
	The quhich thou art; and be this resoun quhy:	*for this reason*
	Thou uirkith that quhich may hir most annoye,	*do (work)*
490	That is to say, hir worschip to distroye.	*honor*

	For every lady of honour and of fame	
	Lesse settith of hir deth than hir gud name;	*Sets less store by; good*
	Oft be experiment previth it is so	*by observation demonstrates*
	Of mony o lady quhich done the same,	*many a; who did*
495	Rather chesyn can thair deth than blame,	*did choose (chose)*
	So lovyn thai thair honoure evirmo.	*So do they forever love their honor*
	Fy on thee, wrech! Fy on thee, lufis fo!	*Fie; love's foe*
	That for to sclander hath no schame nor drede	*reluctance (hesitation); fear*
	The innocence and fame of womanhede.	

	Quhat helpith thee be clepit hir lovare,	*What [does it] help you [to] be called*
500	Syne doith all thing that most is hir contrare?	*Since [you] do; against her*
	Quhat servyth it? Quhat vaillith it of ocht?	*What good does it do*
	Forgo thy lady schall thou nevirmare,	*You shall never give up your lady*
	And set hir corse be thine, yit I declare	*But even though her body*
505	Hir hert is gone, it servyth thee of nocht,	*heart*
	Thare is no lufe quhare that such thing is wrocht;	*where; done (wrought)*
	And thouch sche wold, it is, as thou may fynd,	*would like [to give it]*
	Contrair to lufe, to resoun, and to kynd.	*Contrary; nature*

	Thus of thi lady makis thou thy fo,	*your lady you make your enemy*
510	Quhois hert, of resoun, most thou nede forgo	*Whose heart; you must needs forfeit*
	Be thyne owin gilt, may nothing it appese;	*By your own sin*
	And every othir lady schall also	
	Ensample tak to adventure evirmo	*Be warned against risking ever again*
	Under thine hond thair honour or thair ese;	*hand*
515	And yfe thai do suppose thai have disese,	*think; suffering*
	Quho schall thame mene of weping, eve and morowe,	
	Quhich seith tofore, syn rynnyth on thair sorowe?[1]	

---

[1] Lines 516–17: *Who shall pity them in their weeping, evening and morning, / Those who see beforehand, yet afterwards hasten towards their sorrow (see note)*

To every lady schortly I declare
That thare thou art beith thare nevirmare   *wherever you are [there will] be nevermore*
520   Rest nor quyete, treuly to conclud,   *quiet, truly*
Nor grace, nor ese, nor lyving in welfare,   *comfort; living in security*
Bot everything of gladnese in his contrare.
For barane ay thou art and destitud   *barren; destitute*
Of everything that soundith unto gude;   *has a tendency towards*
525   A lady rather schuld hir deth ytak   *take*
Than suich a wrech till have onto hir mak.   *to have as; mate*

Quhare is thi wit or thy discrecioun,
Quhich be thine evill ymaginacioun
In sewing thingis the quhich that bene unknewe?   *pursuing bizarre things*
530   Quhat helpith thee thy false suspicioun?   *What does your false suspicion do to help you*
Or quhat availith thy wickit condicioun   *what use is*
To sayne or done that thou most efter rewe?[1]
O nyce foole, thine owin harm for to schewe!   *ignorant; own ruin*
Drink nat the poysoun sene tofore thine eye,   *poison; before*
535   Lest thou corrupt and venymyt be thareby.   *contaminated; poisoned*

For yf thee lestith as thou hath begonne   *it pleases you; begun*
Of Jelusy to drinkyn of the tonne,   *drink; cask*
Thare thy confusioun sene is thee before,   *There*
Thou wo yneuch unto thyself hath wonne.   *enough; won*
540   Farewele of lufe, thy fortune is yronne;   *luck has run out*
Thy ladyis dangere hath thou evirmore,   *lady's resistance (disdain)*
For thy condicioun greveth hir so sore,   *oppresses*
And all thi lufe furth drivyth in pennance   *pursues*
With hevynes and suffering grete mischance.

545   For it hath bene and aye schall be also,   *been*
Thou Jelousy in angir and in wo
Enduryn schall thy wrechit, cursit life,   *Shall endure; wretched*
Yfret rycht by the suerd of cruell syte a two,   *Pierced; sword; anguish in*
Thy stormy thocht ay walking to and fro
550   As doth the schip among the wawis dryve,   *ship; waves drive*

---

[1] *To say or do that [which] you must afterwards regret*

And not to pas and note quhare to arryve,[1]
Bot ay in drede furth sailith eve and morowe, *in fear keeps sailing*
So passith thou thy worldis course in sorowe. *will you spend; world's*

For scharp wo doth so thi dredfull goste bete *fearful spirit scourge (beat)*
555 That, as the tree is by the wormis frete, *worms devoured*
So art thou here ay wastit and ybrent *wasted (laid waste)*
And birnyng as the tigir ay in hete. *burning; tiger; heat*
Quho lyvth nowe that can thi wo repete? *Who lives now; repeat*
Bot in thiselfe thou sufferith such torment,
560 Leving to deth ay in thin owen entent; *Living; own mind (thought)*
Thyne owin harm consumith thee, and annoyith, *consumes*
And both thi body and thi soule distroyith.

Bot sith it is thou failith not one of two:[2]
That is to say, into this erth in wo *on*
565 Ay to endure, or efter to be schent *afterwards; destroyed*
Eternaly withoutyn ony ho, *pause*
And wele accordith it for to be so. *is it very just*
Quho is thi lord? The fader of haterent, *father of hatred*
And quhens that cummith every evill entent, *whence; comes*
570 Quhois love thou ay full besyly conservith, *Whose; diligently maintain*
For thi desert rewardith thee and servith.

Thus may thou fynd that proffit is thare non *profit; none*
In Jelousy. Tharefore thou thee dispone, *therefore make yourself ready*
My counsele is, playnly and forsee *and fully prepare*
575 This fantasy to leve quhich thou hath tone[3]
And furth among gud falouschip thou gone, *good fellowship; go*
Lyving in ese and in prosperitee
And love, and eke with ladies lovit be; *loved*
Gif so thee likith not, I can no more. *If*
580 Thus I conclude schortly, as for me,
Quho hath the worst I schrew him evirmore. *curse*

---

[1] *And does not know where it is going, nor where it will come ashore*

[2] *But since it is [that] you will not lack one [or another] of two [things]*

[3] *To leave this fantasy that you have conceived*

You loveris all rycht hertly I exhort *lovers; earnestly*
This litill write helpith to support; *composition*
Excusith it, and tak no maner hede *take no kind of heed*
585 To the endyte, for it most bene of ned. *poetic form; must be of necessity*
Ay simpill wit furth schewith sympilnese, *lack of sophistication*
And of unconnyng cummith aye rudnese. *ignorance; lack of skill*
Bot sen here ar no termes eloquent, *since; phrases*
Belevith the dyté and takith the entent, *Turn away from; poem; thought (intent)*
590 Quhich menyth all in contrair lufis fo, *declares all against love's foe*
And how thir ladies turment bene in wo *are tormented*
And suffrith payne and eke gret violence *suffer pain*
Into thair treuth and in thair innocence, *In*
As daily be experience may be sene; *by*
595 The quhich, allace, grete harm is to sustene. *endure*
Thus I conclude with pitouse hert, and meke: *compassionate heart; meek*
To every god that regnyth, I beseke, *reigns; beseech*
Above the erth, the watir, or the aire,
Or on the fire, or yit in wo and care, *whether*
600 Or yit in turment, slauchter, or mischance, *torment, strife (destruction)*
Or mycht or power hath to done vengeance *Has either might or power to do*
Into this erth, or wickitnese distroye, *On; wickedness*
That quho thir ladyis likith to annoye, *whoever likes to oppress these ladies*
Or yit thare fame or yit thaire ese engrewe, *injure*
605 Mote suffryn here and fallyn grete mischewe *May suffer; come [to]; misfortune*
Into this erth — syne with the falouschip of hell *On; afterwards; fellowship*
In body and soule eternaly mot duell. *may [they] dwell eternally*
        Explicit quod au . . . *(see textual note)*

Explanatory Notes to The Quare of Jelusy

Abbreviations: see Textual Notes.

1   *lusty Maii.* A common way to characterize spring and May in particular. Compare William Dunbar's *Thistle and the Rose*: "lusty May, that mvddir is of flouris" (poem 52, line 4). In the anonymous *Lancelot of the Laik*, it is April which is termed "lustee" (line 1). See also descriptions of May as "lusty" in Chaucer's *PF* (line 130) and The Knight's Tale (*CT* I[A]2484), as well as in Gower's *CA*, where Genius explains the properties of the astrological signs and the months that correspond to them. According to this schema, Genius explains, May belongs to Gemini:

> His propre Monthe wel I wot
> Assigned is the lusti Maii,
> Whanne every brid upon his lay
> Among the griene leves singeth. (ed. Macaulay, 7.1044–47)

1 ff. For the conventional opening in spring, see Clanvowe's *BC*, explanatory note to line 20. Compare especially the opening lines of *Lancelot of the Laik*. Lydgate's *CLL*, Gavin Douglas' *Palis of Honoure*, and Dunbar's *Golden Targe* (poem 59) and *Merle and the Nightingale* (poem 24), have similar openings.

3   *oureclad. The Dictionary of the Older Scottish Tongue* lists *overclethe* as to "clothe or cover over (with verdure)," but the *MED* does not include a similar meaning for the past participle of *overclothen*. Compare the use of "ourgilt" in Dunbar's *The Golden Targe*: "The purpur hevyn, ourscailit in silver sloppis, / Ourgilt the treis branchis, lef, and barkis" (poem 59, lines 26–27); and "overspred" in Douglas' *Palis of Honoure*: "The fragrant flouris, blomand in their seis, / Overspred the leves of Naturis tapestreis" (lines 19–20).

6   *Agayn the stroke of winter, cold and smert.* Possibly an echo of Chaucer's Squire's Tale, where the birds find protection in spring "[a]gayn the swerd of wynter, keene and coold" (*CT* V[F]57), or the Prologue to *LGW*: "Forgeten hadde the erthe his pore estat / Of wynter, that hym naked made and mat, / And with his swerd of cold so sore greved" (F.125–17; compare G.113–15). See also explanatory note to line 548.

7   *sevynt ide*. 9 May. The ides are the fifteenth of March, May, July, October, or the thirteenth of any other month. Thus, *sevynt ide* would be the seventh day before the ides (counting backwards from, and including the ides). In *Lancelot of the Laik* it is the "kalendis of May" (line 12) that is mentioned (i.e., 1 May).

8–13   Compare the description of the sun early in *Lancelot of the Laik*, lines 4–12.

13   *unto Maii to done thair observance*. Compare Chaucer's *TC*, where Pandarus says to Criseyde, "rys up, and lat us daunce, / And lat us don to May som observaunce" (2.111–12); and Chaucer's Knight's Tale, where Arcite goes out into the fields "for to doon his observaunce to May" (*CT* I[A]1500). Similarly, in Douglas' *Palis of Honoure* the narrator explains: "In May, I rays to do my observance" (line 6).

18   *Tho was the ayer sobir and amene*. Compare Dunbar's *The Golden Targe*: "The air attemperit, sobir and amene" (poem 59, line 249); and *Lancelot of the Laik*, where "the lusty aire" is rendered "soft, ameyne, and faire" by the coming of morning (lines 63–64).

19 ff.   The narrator's walk alongside a river bank where he meditates on some source of private grief after which he spies a beautiful woman is a variant of the conventional opening to the medieval amatory complaint. Consider, for example, the openings of *CLL* and the prologue to *Lancelot of the Laik*. For more on the *locus amoenus* tradition, see explanatory note to lines 58–60 of *BC*.

23   *I past me furth remembring to and fro*. Compare the narrator's walk in *Lancelot of the Laik*: "Thus in the feild I walkith to and froo" (line 43).

24   *All on this warldis changeing and his wo*. The narrator's concern for the world's inconstancy is conventional and recalls the Prologue to Gower's *CA*, where the narrator laments, "The world is changed overal, / And therof most in special / That love is falle into discord" (ed. Peck, Prol.119–21). See Curtius' discussion of the theme, "The World Upsidedown," pp. 94–98.

39–40   *Of coloure was sche lik unto the rose, / Boith quhite and red ymeynt*. White and red is a common way of describing medieval beauty. See Whiting R199, "As red as (a, any, the) rose," and L285, "As white as (any, a, the) lily-flower." Dunbar characterizes Margaret Tudor similarly in *The Thistle and the Rose*: "the fresche Ros of cullour reid and quhyt" (poem 52, line 142).

44   *Dyane.* Goddess of chastity and the hunt. Perhaps likening the woman to Diana serves to emphasize the unjustness and irrationality of "causeles Jelousye" (line 56). The narrator compares the woman to Diana while he hides himself, essentially spying on her (lines 45–46), recalling the story of Acteon, who saw Diana bathing naked in the woods and was killed by his own hounds once the goddess had turned him into a stag as punishment. For literary citations on Acteon, see explanatory note to lines 94–98 of *CLL*.

47–52 The description of the lady's tears, accompanied by her sorrowing, sighing, and complaining is a common portrait of one suffering from love-longing. Compare lines 95–98 (and see explanatory note).

50   *The cristall teris falling from hir eyne clere.* As with the comparison to Diana in line 44, the images of *cristall* and *clere* are perhaps used to emphasize the lady's purity. The image of *cristall teris* is not Chaucerian, but rather seems to be a somewhat popular descriptive phrase among Middle Scots poets, perhaps following Lydgate. Compare Venus' description of her own tears in *The Kingis Quair*: "of my cristall teris that bene schede / The hony flouris growen vp and sprede" (lines 816–17 [st. 117]); Aurora's (the dawn's) tears when she weeps at parting from Phebus (the sun) in Dunbar's *Golden Targe*: "Hir cristall teris I saw hyng on the flouris" (poem 59, line 17); and "the most [moist] schowris" in *Lancelot of the Laik* that "[a]s cristoll terys withhong [hung] upone the flouris" (lines 61–62). Aurora has "cristall ene" in Dunbar's *Thistle and the Rose* (poem 52, line 9); as does Cresseid in Robert Henryson's *Testament of Cresseid* (line 337).

    The ballade "As Ofte," sometimes attributed to Lydgate, makes use of the phrase in its opening lines: "As ofte as syghes ben in herte trewe, / And cristall teres on dolefull chekes trill" (lines 1–2; H. N. MacCracken, "Lydgatiana," *Archiv* 127 [1911], 323–27). Lydgate uses the image in *Troy Book* to describe the tears of Cassandra and other women of Troy, who cry upon sight of their lords' wounds: "Wher men may seen the cristal teris meynt / Of her wepinge in ther woundes grene" (4.6382–83). See also Lydgate's *Life of Saint Alban and Saint Amphibal*, where Alban weeps "bitter teeris from his eyen tweyn / Lik cristal wellis encresyng as a flood" (lines 1661–62; ed. J. E. Van Der Westhuizen [Leiden: E. J. Brill, 1974]).

55–56 *sche cursit prevaly / The cruell vice of causeles Jelousye.* Compare Criseyde's complaint to Troilus about his jealousy in Chaucer's *TC*: "noot I for-why ne how / That jalousie, allas, that wikked wyvere, / Thus causeles is cropen into yow" (3.1009–11). See also *Romaunt* where Drede says to Shame: "Jelousie hath us blamed, / Of mystrust and suspecioun, / Causeles, withoute enchesoun" (lines 3980–82).

59–92 In her speech, the lady calls on pagan gods and goddesses to judge her and find her innocent. In this way she is similar to Henryson's Cresseid (in *The Testament of Cresseid*), who complains to the pantheon of gods that she has been mistreated by Cupid and Venus and demands the gods' judgment in the matter.

59 *Goddesse Imeneus*. Hymen is the god of marriage and is normally represented as male rather than female. See, for example, Chaucer's *TC* 3.1258–60. NS&P (p. 64n59 ff.) remark that the address to Hymen shows that the lady has only recently been married, since she has come under his purview "of newe" (line 60).

71–72 *Pluto that is king, / Quhich the derk regioun hath in his governyng*. The god Pluto is king of Hades, the underworld. Although the woman's speech here depicts Hades as a place of punishment only, where body and soul will "ay duell in torment and in wo" (line 76), Virgil describes Hades as containing places of both reward (Elysian Fields) and punishment (Tartarus). The phrase *derk regioun* (line 72) echoes Chaucer's description of Pluto's kingdom in The Knight's Tale: "Ther Pluto hath his derke regioun" (I[A]2082); and in The Franklin's Tale, where Aurelius wishes "to synken every rok adoun / Into hir owene dirke regioun / Under the ground, ther Pluto dwelleth inne" (V[F]1073–75).

73–76 *Mote me into his fyry cart do ta, / As quhilom did he to Proserpina . . . ay duell in torment and in wo*. Proserpina is the daughter of Ceres, goddess of the harvest. Having fallen in love with Proserpina, Pluto abducts her and brings her to the underworld to be his bride. Once in Hades, Proserpina makes the mistake of eating pomegranate seeds, enabling Pluto to keep her in Hades for part of the year, while she continues to dwell with her mother for the remainder. Winter thus represents Ceres' grief at the loss of her daughter while Proserpina lives with Pluto; spring and summer occur during the time Proserpina spends with Ceres, who celebrates her daughter's return each year with the bounty of the earth. The story is recorded in *Vat. Myth.* I (7), Ovid, *Fasti* 4.417 ff., and Hyginus, *Hyg. Fab.* 146. Chaucer alludes to Pluto's rape of Proserpina in The Merchant's Tale (*CT* IV[E]2229 ff.). In Book 4 of *TC*, Troilus uses the image of spending eternity with Proserpina as a way to emphasize his faithfulness to Criseyde (4.472–76).

77–81 *O Dyane! . . . wele my part*. The woman calls upon Diana as goddess of chastity to vouchsafe her innocence. Compare Chaucer's Knight's Tale, where Emelye prays to Diana to keep her chaste (*CT* I[A]2304–11). See also explanatory note to line 44.

82–83   *Jupiter . . . me defende.* Jupiter is king of the gods. Chaucer's Criseyde also calls on Jupiter (Jove) to defend her from jealousy when she tells Troilus, "Jove hym [i.e., jealousy] sone out of youre herte arace!" (3.1015). However, Jupiter himself is depicted as a womanizer and adulterer in Gower's *CA*:

> For Jupiter was the secounde,
> Which Juno hadde unto his wif;
> And yit a lechour al his lif
> He was, and in avouterie
> He wroghte many a tricherie;
> And for he was so full of vices,
> Thei cleped him god of delices. (ed. Macaulay, 5.870–76)

Among other affairs, Jupiter begat Cupid on his sister Venus (mentioned in *CA* 5.1404–05).

87–88   The syntax of line 88 emphasizes its final word, *reuth*. The same construction and rhyme are repeated in lines 179–80, with the phrase *compassioun have and reuth* of line 88 repeated in line 180 and at the beginning of line 211 ("compassioun have — and reuth"). *Reuth* ("pity/compassion") comes up frequently in the poem as a defining quality for both those who are noble and the true (faithful) lover. Jealousy lacks this quality completely, which suggests that nobility or true love and jealousy are mutually exclusive qualities. The connection with the Christian virtue of compassion becomes explicit later in the poem in the section called "the trety in the reprefe of Jelousye" (after line 316). The poet's rhyme of *treuth* (line 87) with *reuth* (line 88) echoes lines 1309–10 at the end of *BD*: "'She ys ded!' 'Nay!' 'Yis, be my trouthe!' / 'Is that youre los? Be God, hyt ys routhe!'"

89–92   *My life to gone mak . . . sodaynly to sterve.* In Book 3 of *TC*, Criseyde expresses a similar sentiment to that of the lady here: "if that I be giltif, do me deye!" (3.1049).

95–98   *With that sche sichit . . . pale and grene.* As in lines 49–52, the lady's sighing, *pleynyng*, and changing of color are a typical depiction of the lovesick sufferer. See the description of the lovesick knight in *BD*, whose "hewe chaunge and wexe grene / And pale" (lines 497–98). For more on lovesickness, see *BC*, explanatory note to lines 31–32.

102   *glettering teris, als thik as ony haile.* Compare Dunbar's description of the Dawn's tears (dew) as "cristall haile" in *A Ballat of the Abbot of Tungland* (poem 4, line 1).

107 *Allace, hir chere! Allace, hir countenance!* Compare lines 202 and 227. See also Chaucer's Knight's Tale, *CT* I(A) 2771 and I(A)2773–75, for similar rhetorical flourishes.

121 *Quhat may this mene? Quhat may this signifye?* L points out that this line is the same as line 160 of *Lancelot of the Laik* (p. 150n121). Compare also the phrase "quhat may this be?" repeated in lines 78, 249, and 253 (st. 12, 36, 37) of *The Kingis Quair*. See also Chaucer's *Complaint of Mars*, line 224, and *CLL*, line 302.

135 *Bot tho it fell into my fantasy.* The narrator's use of fantasy and imagination recurs throughout the poem. See the Introduction for further discussion, pp. 155–56. The two other uses of the word "fantasy" occur with negative overtones in reference to the jealous lover's imagined slights; in line 276 it is the jealous lover (represented as Jealousy personified) who "evill . . . demith in his fantasy," imagining unjustly that his lady has been unfaithful; in lines 575–76 the narrator urges the jealous one: "This fantasy to leve quhich thou hath tone [conceived] / And furth among gud falouschip thou gone." Here, "fantasy" refers to the lover's jealous imagination that keeps him from "gud falouschip" and love. These images of Jealousy echo Gower's depiction of lovers in *CA*, who "thurgh here oghne fantasie . . . fallen into Jelousie" (ed. Macaulay, 5.441–42). See also explanatory note to lines 168–69.

160–62 *Thame to displese . . . lak of connyng and of eloquence.* Compare lines 185 ff. The narrator's modesty is conventional. For more on this trope, see *CLL*, explanatory note to lines 190 ff.

168–69 *wickit ymaginacioun, / Quhich by his name is clepit Jelousye.* This negative view of Jealousy also goes hand in hand with imagination elsewhere in the poem; see, for example, lines 240–42. (For more on wicked jealousy, see explanatory note to lines 240–41.) For jealousy's association with imagination or fantasy, see, for example, Lydgate's *Banner of St. Edmund* 2.548; Chaucer's Prologue to *LGW*, where the narrator tells Alceste that her court is full of liars who "tabouren in youre eres many a thyng / For hate, or for jelous ymagynyng" (G.330–31; compare F.354–55, which reads somewhat differently); and Gower's *CA*, where Genius informs Amans,

>Riht so this fieverous maladie,
>Which caused is of fantasie,
>Makth the Jelous in fieble plit
>To lese of love his appetit

Thurgh feigned enformacion
Of his ymaginacion. (ed. Macaulay, 5.589–94)

For further discussion of the poem's treatment of "fantasy" see explanatory note to line 135.

172   *Herculese, quhen he himselven brent.* See explanatory note to line 357 of *CLL* for details of the story and literary references. The narrator continues his extended metaphor of Jealousy "ay birnyng into hate" from line 151. The comparison to Hercules' self-immolation foreshadows the narrator's later claim in lines 559–62 that the jealous lover consumes himself with his jealousy. The image of Jealousy burning forever in a hell of its own making also contrasts with the lady's claim of innocence in lines 71–76, where she imagines herself abducted into Hades by Pluto should she "say false" (line 71).

173–74   *cursit Nero, quhen he his perile sawe, / Of his own hond ymurderit and yslawe.* Chaucer tells the story of Nero in The Monk's Tale, *CT* VII(B²)2463–2550. It also appears in *Boece* (2.m.6). Gower discusses Nero in *CA* 6.1151 ff., but without mentioning the story of his death.

176   *saile all in the Devillis barge.* NS&P observe, "The extended allegory of Envy's barge in [*CA*] (II.1882–1909) points to a well-known convention. Invidia's barge never reaches port but sails on ceaselessly with attending tempests. Our poet is thinking precisely of this allegory in lines 549–53 in the ship similitude there — where the jealous person's mind is so compared" (p. 66n176).

177   *quhethir thay flete or into hell synk.* Chaucer frequently uses a variant of this phrase (always omitting *into hell*). See, for example, The Knight's Tale, *CT* I(A)2397; *The Complaint unto Pity*, line 110; *Anel.*, line 182; and *PF*, line 7.

185 ff.   Compare lines 160–62. For more on the convention of modesty, see explanatory note to lines 190 ff. of *CLL*.

187   *at Lovis hie reverence.* Compare Chaucer's *TC* 3.1328: "at Loves reverence."

191–93   *O tendir youth . . . (Wommen I mene).* The narrator's evident desire to defend all women from the charges brought against them by Jealousy seems antithetical to the frequent stereotypes of women in medieval literature as inconstant, willful, and manipulative. See, for example, Chaucer's Merchant's Tale, Miller's Tale, Wife of Bath's Prologue and Tale, etc. For a more consistently cynical view, see Dunbar's

The Tretis of the Tua Marriit Wemen and the Wedo (poem 3). Compare this stanza and the next (through line 208) to the narrator's declamation on William Wallace in *The Wallace* 2.207–15.

191 ff.   The nine-line decasyllabic stanza rhyming *aabaabbab* beginning here and employed through line 416 is used in Chaucer's *Anel.* and was popular among the Middle Scots poets; see, for example, Dunbar's *The Golden Targe* (poem 59), and sections of Henryson's *Testament of Cresseid* (lines 407–69); Douglas' *Palis of Honoure* (Prologue, Parts 1 and 2); and *The Wallace* (2.171–359).

200   *Under thraldome and mannis subjectioun.* This line echoes Chaucer's Man of Law's Tale, where Custance proclaims, "Wommen are born to thraldom and penance, / And to been under mannes governance" (II[B¹]286–87). See also the argument the Sultan's mother puts forth against converting to Christianity: "What sholde us tyden of this newe lawe / But thraldom to oure bodies and penance" (II[B¹]337–38). The word *thraldom* also recurs throughout The Parson's Tale; for example: "sith so is that synne was first cause of thraldom, thanne is it thus: that thilke tyme that al this world was in synne, thanne was al this world in thraldom and subjeccioun" (X[I]770). The narrator of *The Kingis Quair* uses this same word to describe his imprisonment (line 191 [st. 28]).

202   *Allace, the wo! Allace, the sad grevance!* See also lines 107 and 227. Compare The Knight's Tale, *CT* I(A)2771: "Allas, the wo! Allas, the peynes stronge" and I(A) 2773–75.

203   *men of evill condicioun.* Compare the narrator's description of Jealousy in line 150 as "[o]fe evill condicioun evirmore."

209 ff.   *Loveris compleyne.* Compare the narrator's request in *The Wallace* that "sanctis," "lordys," and "yhe ladyis brycht" complain on behalf of William Wallace (2.216–33).

222   *All vertuouse womman Salamon holdith dere.* An allusion to Proverbs 31:10.

227   *Allace, the wo.* See explanatory note to line 202.

239   *thair varyit tyrannyis.* The narrator's portrayal of jealous men as tyrants is in keeping with what NS&P call "a growing mood of indignation and anger in the writer" which they characterize as "obsessional," adding "[n]o modest moral ur-

banity of Chaucer here" (p. 7). However, compare Chaucer's comment at the end of *The Legend of Lucrece* in *LGW*:

> For wel I wot that Crist himselve telleth
> That in Israel, as wyd as is the lond,
> That so gret feyth in al that he ne fond
> As in a woman; and this is no lye.
> And as of men, loke ye which tirannye
> They doon alday; assay hem whoso lyste,
> The trewest ys ful brotel for to triste. (lines 1879–85)

240–41   *the wikkitnes that lyis / In Jelousy.* Compare *TC*, where Criseyde exclaims: "O thou wikked serpent jalousie" (3.837); or when Troilus suspects Criseyde's unfaithfulness in Book 5 and "the wikked spirit . . . / Which that men clepeth woode jalousie, / Gan in hym crepe, in al this hevynesse" (5.1212–14).

245–53   *Quho schall me help, allace, for to endite . . . full nere ybrocht adoun.* Compare the narrator's appeal to Niobe for help in writing his complaint in *CLL*, lines 176–82.

267   *the anker in the stone.* A recluse in her cell. For a detailed discussion of anchoresses, see the introduction to *Ancrene Wisse*, ed. Robert Hasenfratz (Kalamazoo, MI: Medieval Institute Publications, 2000). NS&P (p. 67n267) suggest that this is "a partial memory of" *Romaunt*, line 6348: "Now lyk an anker in an hous," but in fact this must have been a common enough reference; in addition to the passage that L (p. 151n267) quotes from Charles d'Orleans' English *Balade* 97 ("O sely Ankir that in thi selle / Iclosed art with stoon and gost not out"), the same image occurs in *The Legend or Life of Saint Alexis* (Laud MS. 622) when Alexis' wife complains "I am boþe maiden & wijf, / I noot to whom telle my strijf, / I lyue as ankre in stone" (lines 418–20).

276   See explanatory notes to line 135 and 168–69.

297–98   *And thouch he speke . . . harmith hir allway.* In other words, there is a double standard operating, where men can speak to anyone they like, but if a woman even looks at another man, she is condemned.

303   *verreis.* L claims that "[t]he form of this word would indicate the meaning 'wars,' or 'makes war,' but the context seems to demand 'wearies'" (p. 151n303). I follow NS&P in glossing this word as "hesitates," which they suggest is a rare sense for the verb "vary" (p. 68n303).

304–06   *For Salamoun saith.* NS&P (p. 68n304 ff.) suggest that this is based on Ecclesiasticus 10:1, but if so, the relationship is obscure. Perhaps Proverbs 31:11 is the basis for the quotation.

311   *Thou Ecco, quhich of chiding is perfyte.* See Lenvoy de Chaucer at the end of The Clerk's Tale, which exhorts wives: "Folweth Ekko, that holdeth no silence, / But evere answereth at the countretaille" (*CT* IV[E]1189–90). See explanatory note to lines 87–88 of *CLL*, for the story of Echo and Narcissus.

313   *Thesiphone, thou lord of wo and care.* One of the three Furies. Compare Chaucer's *TC* 1.6–9, where the narrator asks Tisiphone for help in composing his story, and Lydgate's *Temple of Glass*, lines 958 ff.

317 ff.   The stanzas here through line 456 are in rhyme royal (seven-line stanzas rhyming *ababbcc*), so called because it is the stanza form used in *The Kingis Quair*, attributed in the MS to James I of Scotland. Henryson also uses it in *The Testament of Cresseid*, and Chaucer employs the stanza in *TC*, *PF*, portions of *Anel.*, and in a number of tales in *CT*.

317–18   *The passing clerk, the grete philosophoure / Sydrake.* A supposed philosopher in a thirteenth-century work, *Sidrac*, "an Old French prose book of knowledge, cast in question and answer form, enclosed within a framing adventure story" (*Sidrak and Bokkus*, p. xxi). Sidrac (Sidrak in the Middle English versions) answers a vast number of questions put to him by Boctus, the "Bokas King" of line 320. NS&P (p. 69n318) suggest that the poem reflects a knowledge of Gower's *CA* more than of the Old French text which recounts the dialogue between the title characters, but see explanatory note to lines 324–30. See also L's note (p. 151n318–23) for an extensive summary of the Middle English translation of the French narrative.

322   *Bokas King.* The heathen king converted by Sidrac (*Sidrak and Bokkus*, p. xxii). See explanatory notes to lines 317–18 and 324–30.

324–30   Although NS&P claim that "[n]early all of [the poet's] observations may be traced to his close reading of Gower's *Confessio Amantis*" (p. 8), in these lines the poet seems to be paraphrasing a portion of Sidrak's discussion in response to Bokkus' question on jealousy, here presented as question 87 in the Middle English *Sidrak and Bokkus*:

ȝit is þere a gelosye	ȝit þer is a ielousie
Þat comith of fowle herte and folye	Þat comeþ of foule herte and folie

And of wykked humours also	And of wicked humours also
That the herte geders vnto:	Þat the herte gadren to:
That gelosye is not of woman goode	Þat ielousie is of a womman þikke
For hit is full brennyng and wykked mode.	And þat is foule brenning and wicke.
The herte hit brenneth full of wykked þought;	Þe herte brenneþ so of wicked þoght
Rest in þe body may hit nought;	Þat in the body may it rest noght;
Mete and drynke he doþe forsake	Mete and drinke þei forgoon as tite
And all his ioye is from hym take.	And al ioye and al delite.
(Laud; lines 3397–3405)	(Lansdowne; lines 4299–4308)

As the EETS editors point out in their introduction to *Sidrak and Bokkus*, "in spite of the claim by Norton-Smith and Pravda that the author of *QJ* makes 'little use' of *Sidrac* (p. 69), a comparison . . . shows that in this instance at least there is a genuine debt" (p. xxxv).

330   *With this hote fevir that is cotidiane.* In Gower's *CA*, Genius describes jealousy as "[a] Fievere . . . cotidian, / Which every day wol come aboute" (ed. Macaulay, 5.464–65), an "unsely maladie" (5.459) and a "fieverous maladie" (5.589). Other medieval writers also characterize jealousy as a sickness; for example, in *The Kingis Quair*, the narrator asks the nightingale, "Or artow seke, or smyt with ielousye?" (line 401 [st. 58]).

334–35   *Of Herubus, the quhich that of Invye / The fader is.* L (p. 153n334–35) points out that this genealogy (of Envy from Erebus) ultimately comes from Cicero's *De Natura Deorum* (3.17).

337   *As Ethena, he birnyth in the fyre.* This is not a comparison Chaucer makes much use of, as it appears only in *Boece* (2.m.5 and elsewhere). The association is one inherited from classical tradition (see Ovid, *Metam.* 8.867 ff.), where the burning fires of Etna represent the Cyclops Polyphemus' jealous rage over Galatea's preference of Acis, a story also told in Gower's *CA* (2.97–200; see also 2.20 and 2.2837 ff.). See also Lydgate's *Reson and Sensuallyte*, where Diana warns against jealousy:

> Yif Venus Marke the [you] with hir bronde,
> Which that she holdeth in hir honde;
> The fire of whom, who kan take hede,
> Ys of perel more to drede
> Than is the fire, I dar wel seyn,
> Of smoky Ethna, the mounteyn. (lines 4117–22)

Mount Etna is identified by Claudian in his unfinished poem *De Raptu Proserpina* ("The Rape of Proserpina") as the place where Proserpina was abducted into the underworld by Pluto (see explanatory note to lines 73–76). Chaucer alludes to this version of the story in The Merchant's Tale (*CT* IV[E]2229 ff.), as do Gower (*CA*, 5.1277 ff.) and Osbern Bokenham (in the Life of Saint Anne from *Legendys of Hooly Wummen*, ed. Mary S. Serjeantson, EETS o.s. 206 [London: Oxford University Press, 1938], lines 1456–57). For further mention in Chaucer of Claudian as the source of the story, see also *HF*, lines 1507–12. Trevisa describes Etna in *De monte Ethna* (4.10).

351   *the prophete Daniele.* See Daniel 1:11–16.

355–56   *This tygir with his false ymagynyng / Lith as a devill into this erth lyving.* Compare *The Kingis Quare*: "There sawe I dresse him new[e] out of haunt / The fery tiger full of felonye" (lines 1086–87 [st. 156]; brackets in original). See also Chaucer's Squire's Tale, where the tiger is an image of deceit ("this tigre, ful of doublenesse" — V[F]543), and Dunbar's *Done is a battel on the dragon blak*, which describes Lucifer as a "deidly dragon," "crewall serpent with the mortall stang," and "[t]he auld kene tegir, with his teith on char, / Quhilk in a wait hes lyne for ws so lang, / Thinking to grip ws in his clowis strang" (poem 10, lines 9, 10, 11–13). Trevisa describes the tiger in *De tigride* (8.104), where he explains that it is possible to steal the tiger's cubs despite the fierceness of the beast, because the male does not care about the them, while the female can be tricked by a mirror, for when she sees her own reflection she thinks it is that of her offspring and delays long enough for the hunter to get away (see p. 1255/4–12).

359–60   *But cheritee . . . Quhich Crist of wedding clepith the habyte.* Matthew 22:1–14.

363–72   *Paule thus to the Corinthies doth writ . . . all it availit nocht.* Paraphrased from 1 Corinthians 13.

382–86   *And als that in this tyme present . . . for his wickit gelousy.* Apparently an allusion to a contemporary event. In his note to these lines, L states, "This fifteenth-century Scottish criminal is not named in any of the older histories" (p. 153n382–86).

394–96   Compare *CLL*: "And Male-Bouche gan first the tale telle / To sclaundre Trouthe of indignacion, / And Fals-Report so loude ronge the belle" (lines 260–62).

397–400   Paraphrased from Matthew 18:7–9.

404–06   Derived from Ecclesiasticus (Sirach) 25:23 (in Douay-Rheims; 25:16 in more recent translations): "And there is no anger above the anger of a woman. It will be more agreeable to abide with a lion and a dragon, than to dwell with a wicked woman." Note that the narrator has removed any mention of women in his paraphrase. See The Wife of Bath's Prologue (*CT* III[D]775 ff.).

422–23   *one emperoure . . . Henry.* Henry II, emperor of the Holy Roman Empire from 1002–24. See explanatory notes to lines 427 and 433, for details of the story.

427   *his lufe.* Cunegunda, Henry II's wife. According to Jacobus de Voragine's *Legenda Aurea*, the couple had a chaste marriage, but when Henry suspected Cunegunda of adultery with one of his knights he forced her to "walk barefoot a distance of fifteen feet over plowshares reddened in the fire," but, having prayed for God's help, Cunegunda was able to cross the obstacle safely (Jacobus de Voragine, trans. Ryan, 2.69). The Scottish version of the *Legenda* makes explicit Henry's jealousy:

þe feynd, þat ay wil besy be
to tempt, þat þame twa had Inwy,
& gert hyme fal In Ialusy,
venand his wyf had mysdone
vith a ȝunge knycht. (lines 696–700)

For the Scottish legend, see *Legends of the Saints in the Scottish Dialect of the Fourteenth Century*, ed. W. M. Metcalfe, 5 vols. STS first ser. 13, 18, 23, 35, 37 (Edinburgh: William Blackwood and Sons, 1896), vol. 1, lines 691–770 of XXII, the legend of "Laurentius."

433   *Laurence the blisfull marter.* The *Legenda Aurea* reports that Henry was saved from hell, despite his false suspicion, because of a chalice he had donated in honor of St. Laurence to a church in Eichstätt (Jacobus de Voragine, trans. Ryan, 2.69). See explanatory notes to lines 427 and 422–23.

437   *That of hote lufe ay cummith Jelousye.* The equivalency of jealousy with love occurs in Chaucer's *TC*, "al my wo is this, that folk now usen / To seyn right thus, 'Ye, jalousie is love!'" (3.1023–24), and elsewhere. Proverbial; see Whiting J22.

457 ff.   *Thir jelousyis full diverse ar of kynd.* Similarly, in Chaucer's *TC* 3.1030, Criseyde briefly discusses different types of jealousy, some more excusable than others.

467   *O cruell serpent aye lying in awayte!* Criseyde characterizes jealousy similarly in Chaucer's *TC*: "O thou wikked serpent, jalousye" (3.837).

468 *O sclanderouse tong.* Jealousy is commonly associated with lies and slander in medieval thought. Compare Gower's treatment of it in *CA* 5.429–746.

469–70 *Quhare that thou lovith thou feynyth . . . / gevith the wyte.* Compare Chaucer's *Anel.*, where Arcite pretends to love Anelida: "Withoute love he feyned jelousye" (line 126).

486 *That hath no suerd bot suffrance and pacience.* See explanatory note to line 548.

492 *Lesse settith of hir deth than hir gud name.* A theme the narrator expands on in lines 493–96 and reiterates in lines 525–26. For discussion of this subject in relation to Chaucer's *LGW*, see the Introduction, pp. 158–59. The idea is proverbial: "better to die with honor than live in shame"; see Whiting D239, for extensive citations. Compare also line 160 in *BC* and lines 546–48 in Roos' *BDSM*.

512–14 *And every othir lady . . . or thair ese.* At first glance, the passage seems to suggest that ladies "taking example" from this case would continue to risk their honor and pleasure under the hand of jealous, domineering men. The context seems to require reading *Ensample tak to adventure evirmo* (line 513) to mean something like "be warned against risking ever again."

516–17 *Quho schall thame mene of weping, eve and morowe, / Quhich seith tofore, syn rynnyth on thair sorowe?* A difficult passage, which L translates in his note: "Who shall bewail in their weeping, evening and morning, those who see beforehand, but who yet afterwards run to their own sorrow" (p. 154n516–17). Understanding *mene* as "pity" (see *MED, menen* v. [2], 4 [a]) makes more sense in the context, however, since it suggests that no one would feel sorry for someone who chooses suffering that could be avoided: "Who shall pity them in their weeping, evening and morning, / Those who see beforehand, yet afterwards hasten towards their sorrow." It is tempting to read *rynnyth on* with a second meaning of "impale [themselves] on," in line with other attested meanings in the *MED* (see *rennen* v., 25 [b]).

525–26 *A lady rather schuld hir deth ytak / Than suich a wrech till have onto hir mak.* This reiterates the theme of death before dishonor. See explanatory note to line 492, above, and the Introduction, pp. 158–59.

541 *Thy ladyis dangere.* For a discussion of the concept of *dangere*, see explanatory note to line 13 of *CLL*. Although in many cases *dangere* might mean simply

standoffishness, the context here suggests not only that the lady will forever be on her guard against him, but also that she will offer active resistance.

548   *suerd of cruell syte.* See also explanatory note to line 6. Compare Chaucer's *Anel.*, where the phrase "swerd of sorowe" occurs twice (lines 212, 270). Such metaphorical uses of "sword" were fairly common, as for example the "swerd of castigacioun" in Chaucer's *Lak of Stedfastnesse* (line 26). L (p. 155n548) also notes *Lancelot of the Laik*: "The dredful suerd of lovis [love's] hot dissire" (line 29). *Syte* (from Old Norse) is chiefly a northern word.

549–53   Compare line 176 and see explanatory note.

575–76   See explanatory note to line 135.

582 ff.   The address to lovers is a conventional envoy. Compare, for example, the apostrophes to lovers at the ends of *CLL*, lines 653 ff., and *BDSM*, 813–20; and to ladies in the latter, lines 821–28.

584 ff.   *Excusith it.* The narrator's request for understanding on the part of the reader for his simple and crudely executed poetry is conventional. See also the explanatory note to lines 160–62. Compare such disclaimers at the ends of *BDSM* (lines 829 ff.), *The Kingis Quair* (lines 1352 ff. [st.194–97]), and many of Chaucer's poems.

598–99   *Above the erth, the watir, or the aire, / Or on the fire.* A reference to the "four elements." In ancient and medieval thought all material bodies were thought to be comprised of earth, water, air, and fire, which were connected to the four humors that were thought to regulate temperament and health. Compare Chaucer's Knight's Tale: "ther nys erthe, water, fir, ne eir, / Ne creature that of hem maked is, / That may me helpe or doon confort in this" (*CT* I[A]1246–48). Genius explains the four elements at length to Amans in Book 7 of Gower's *CA*. See also Lydgate's *Secreta Secretorum*: "Al the wyse Philosofers in oone accorde sayne that iiije elementes bene in the worlde, Wherof euery corruptabill thynge is makyd; that Is to witte, Erthe, Watyr, Eeyre, and fyre: And euery of thes hath two Propyrteis; The Erthe is colde and dry; The watyr is colde and moiste; The eeire hote and moyste; The fyre hote and dry. In the body of euery man ben iiije humorus, answarynge to the iiije elementes: and like propyrteis therof they haue. Malencoly, colde and dry; Fleme, colde and moysty; Sangyne, hote and moyste; Colerike, hote and dry" (*Three Prose Versions of the Secreta Secretorum*, ed. Robert Steele, EETS e.s. 74 [London: Kegan Paul, Trench, Trübner and Co, 1898], pp. 236–37).

Textual Notes to *The Quare of Jelusy*

Abbreviations: **B** = J. T. T. Brown; **Ban** = the Bannatyne Club edition; **L** = Alexander Lawson; **MS** = Bodleian Library MS. Arch. Selden. B. 24 , fols. 138v–141v; **NS&P** = J. Norton-Smith and I. Pravda.

title	*Here beginnith the quare of Jelusy / Avise ye gudely folkis and see.* This rubric is a later insertion in an early sixteenth-century hand (NS&P, p. 62). (The rubric after line 316 is original.)
58	*voce.* MS: *woce.*
100	*ne.* MS: *he.*
116	*I.* Added above line in MS.
132	*think.* MS: *thing.*
137	*thoucht.* MS: *thouch.*
143	*be cummyn.* MS: *cummyn.* I follow Jeffrey's suggestion (p. 500) in adding *be* to emend the idiom to its standard construction. NS&P emend to *cummyn[g].*
146	*harme do to hir.* MS: *harme to do to hir*; in both cases *to* is inserted above the line; *to₁* has then been canceled.
194	*ibene.* MS: *I bene.* NS&P: *ibene.* L, B: *I bene.*
196	*benig.* The word in the MS could be read as either *benig* or *being*, since the minims render *ni* indistinguishable from *in*. I follow NS&P in reading *benig*. B reads *being*, which he emends to *bening*. L: *bening.*
220	*worldis.* MS: the *l* is written above the *r*. NS&P read *wordis* but emend to *wor[l]dis.* B: *warldis.* L: *wordis.*
350	*wele.* No longer legible in MS. I follow previous editors here.
398	*Wo.* The MS is damaged at this point, so only a small portion of the *W* is visible.
408	*is pes.* MS: *ha I . . . pes.* The *s* in *is* is now illegible. L: *In pes.* NS&P point out the presence of *ha* before *is*, noting that *ha* has been stricken; this seems likely, though the line through the word is so faint that it is difficult to tell for certain. Probably the scribe mistakenly began to copy "hath" from line 409 of his exemplar. NS&P say that the *p* in *pes* is illegible, but it is visible in the facsimile now that the MS has been restored.
413	*slepe.* MS: the middle letters *ep* are no longer legible. I follow previous editions.
441	*ground.* MS: only *grou* is legible. I follow previous editions.

446	*thair nede.* The final -*r* in *thair* and all of *nede* are now illegible. I follow previous editions.
467	*lying.* MS: *leving.* Emended for sense.
470	In the MS there is a stanza break after this line. I follow NS&P and L in moving the break to after line 472, as the poem moves at this point from seven- to nine-line stanzas. This is probably a scribal error, since the MS division yields a seven-line stanza followed by one of eleven lines instead of two stanzas of nine lines each. B resolves the problem by leaving the break after 470 and also adding one after 472, so that 471–72 stand alone as a couplet.
475 ff.	After this point in the MS, the edges of the pages along the binding have disintegrated to the point where many letters or words are missing at the beginnings of lines on the recto side of folios and at the end of lines on the verso side. There seems to be considerably more damage than when L edited the poem in 1910, as he does not note any lacunae before line 554. L relies on Ban for missing letters but tends to emend these readings heavily; I follow NS&P, who agree with Ban in most cases.
476	*Rather.* MS: only *th* legible here.
477	*Than.* MS: *T* illegible.
478	*That.* MS: *T* no longer legible.
479	*Or do.* MS: *Or* now illegible; the ascender is the only clear stroke left of *d*.
480	*For his.* MS: *or h* no longer legible.
481	*Hir.* No longer legible in MS.
482	*And.* MS: *A* illegible.
484	*Harmith.* MS: *ar* no longer legible.
490	*That.* MS: *T* no longer legible.
506	*wrocht.* MS: *r* illegible.
516	*morowe.* MS: *rowe* now illegible.
517	*sorowe.* MS: second *o* no longer legible.
519	*nevirmare.* MS: *a* and part of *m* illegible.
522	*contrare.* MS: *re* no longer legible.
523	*destitud.* There may have been a stroke indicating a final -*e* in MS, but if so it is no longer legible.
526	*mak.* So B. The MS is damaged here, so part of *m* is missing, but this looks like the best reading of the MS; NS&P emend to and L reads *make*.
532	*rewe.* Nearly illegible in MS.
544	*With.* MS: *i* and part of *W* no longer legible.
546	*Thou.* MS: *T . . . ou.* L: *Throuch*, with *uch* as an expanded abbreviation. I follow NS&P, B.
548	*rycht.* MS: only *ry* is visible, but I presume a missing superscript *t*.

554   *For.* Now missing from MS. L suggests *ʒit.* Fol. 228 has sustained the most damage, with the inside edge crumbled away on the bottom half of the folio. For this reason, lines 554–73 have lost initial words or portions of words.

555   *That.* Now missing from MS.

556   *So.* Now missing from MS.

557   *And.* Now missing from MS.

558   *Quho.* MS: only *ho* is visible.

559   *Bot in.* Now missing from MS. L: *And of.*

560   *Leving.* MS: only *ing* is visible.

561   *Thyne.* MS: only *yne* is visible.

562   *And both.* MS: only *h* is legible.

563   *Bot.* MS: only *t* is legible.

564   *That.* Now missing from MS.

565   *Ay to.* Now missing from MS, although NS&P could apparently read both the initial *A* and *to.* Laing (in Ban) conjectured *Still* instead of *Ay.*

566   *Eternaly.* MS: only *ly* is visible.

567   *And wele accordith.* MS: only *a cordith* is legible.

568   *Quho.* Now missing from MS.

569   *And quhens.* MS: only *uhens* is visible.

570   *Quhois love. Quhoi* now missing from MS. L reads *luve,* but the word, although very faint now, looks to be *love* in the post-conservation photograph in the facsimile volume. NS&P also reconstruct *luve.*

571   *For thi desert.* Now missing from MS.

572   *Thus may.* MS: only *ay* is legible.

573   *In Jelousy.* MS: only *sy* is legible.

604   *engrewe.* MS: *engrew* and part of a final letter legible, which I read as *e,* following previous editors.

605   *mischewe.* MS: only *mische* and part of *w* are legible. ·

colophon   *au* . . . Besides these two letters, only the top of a nearby ascender is still legible. Laing recorded the first six letters as *auchin,* and L, B read *auch,* which they interpreted as the beginning of the name Auchinleck, following Laing's conjecture. While agreeing that *au* is clearly visible, NS&P make a detailed argument against the *chin* reading, claiming that, the paper being "worn to a thin transparency," these letters are the reverse images of letters from the recto side of the folio (p. 15; for NS&P's full discussion, see pp. 15–16). As the leaf is now missing the edge in question, it is not possible to draw a firm conclusion.

and vocabulary, and we meet with but few really obsolete words or phrases."[5] When it has been discussed at all, critics have largely focused on the question of the poem's authorship.[6]

Another (very practical) reason for the poem's modern neglect has been that, despite the number of manuscript and printed copies that circulated over the years, the poem has not enjoyed a good critical edition in modern times. It has been printed several times, but the best known of these have reproduced a single manuscript and have not been readily available to modern readers.[7] I hope the present edition will make this charming if

───────────────

[5] Skeat (1897), p. lvi.

[6] Though even this discussion has not been abundant. For the argument for Roos' authorship, see especially Ethel Seaton, Sir Richard Roos, c. 1410–1482: Lancastrian Poet (London: Hart-Davis, 1961), pp. 80–90. Seaton goes on to attribute virtually all of the contents of the manuscript on which she focuses (London, British Library MS Harley 372) to Roos, an attribution that cannot be sustained on the scanty evidence she presents; her ascription of the Belle Dame sans Mercy is, however, widely accepted. See also Eleanor Prescott Hammond, "Chaucer and Lydgate," Modern Philology 1 (1903–04), 341–46, and James E. Blodgett, "Some Printer's Copy for William Thynne's 1532 Edition of Chaucer," The Library, 6th series, 1 (1979), 97–113.

[7] The poem was edited, from the Thynne print of 1532, in Walter W. Skeat, ed., Chaucerian and Other Pieces (Oxford: Clarendon Press, 1897), pp. 299–326. It was later edited from Harley 372 twice: see Seaton, pp. 960–62, and William A. Neilson and Kenneth G. T. Webster, eds., Chief British Poets of the Fourteenth and Fifteenth Centuries (Boston: Houghton Mifflin, 1916), pp. 303–09. The present edition is based on a different manuscript (see below).

and expression; we have only to alter the spelling, and there is nothing left to explain," adding, "It is a pity that the poem is somewhat dull, owing to its needless prolixity."[5]

The Middle English poem's effect on medieval readers is harder to gauge. On the one hand, the fact that two of the manuscripts misorder the lines so badly that the bulk of the poem is presented out of proper narrative sequence is suggestive; scribes were perhaps merely copying mechanically, but the lack of notation to correct this kind of error in either manuscript raises questions about whether medieval readers noticed or cared about inconsistencies in dialogue and plot.[6] On the other hand, the number of extant versions of Roos' translation in English manuscripts (seven) and early printed books (four) points to its popularity among medieval English readers. In addition to extant manuscripts, it is known that the Paston family in the fifteenth century owned two codices that included the poem,[7] and "John Howard, Duke of Norfolk, was to take copies of 'La belle d. s. mercy' and 'Les Acusacions de la d.' with him on an embassy to Scotland in 1481."[8] The fact that recent readers have not displayed the level of interest that the poem sustained among medieval audiences suggests that those early readers had access to some source of pleasure in this poem that twentieth- and twenty-first-century ones apparently overlook. The fact that we so clearly miss the point is the very reason it seems to me crucial to decipher what pleasures the poem might have offered its medieval audiences.

The French poem was clearly popular, generating a storm of protest amongst readers and writers, and its central debate was continued in a number of adaptations and responses in French, as well as Chartier's own responses to these reactions.[9] Like its French precursor, Richard Roos' Middle English *Belle Dame sans Mercy* contains at its core a love debate. This inner dispute between *l'amant* ("the lover") and *la dame* ("the lady") is flanked by an

---

[5] Skeat (1897), pp. lii and liii.

[6] Skeat gives the order of the lines: 1–428, 669–716, 525–572, 477–524, 621–668, 573–620, 429–476, 717–856, which, he explains, reflects the copying of this group of manuscripts from an exemplar in which "three leaves, each containing six stanzas, were misarranged" (1897, p. liv).

[7] This is clear from the pre-1480 inventory of their library, printed in *The Paston Letters and Papers of the Fifteenth Century*, ed. Norman Davis, 2 vols. (Oxford: Clarendon Press, 1971–76), 1.516–18 (see items 3 and 5). It is not possible to know for certain whether the Pastons owned French or English versions of the poem, since the two share the same title. Nevertheless, the fact that only one copy of the French poem survives in an English manuscript, while there are seven manuscripts that include at least a part of the translation, suggests that the English translation is more probable in the case of the Pastons as well.

The French poem that Roos translates itself enjoyed enormous popularity on the continent some fifteen or twenty years earlier, inspiring, amongst other things, a host of literary rebuttals.

[8] Boffey (1994), p. 120.

[9] Arthur Piaget gives a list of the French reworkings of and reactions to Chartier's poem, pp. xii–xiv.

"eyewitness" narrator, framed in turn in Roos' translation by a second narrator, whom I will call the "translator." The layered — or embedded — quality of the narrative, though entirely conventional, speaks to the debate's preoccupation with surface and depth, as it insistently calls into question the "true" meaning of the honeyed phrases of lovers. The translator begins by describing his half-sleeping state, which gives way to his sudden memory of an assignment to "translat . . . as part of [his] penaunce, / A boke called La Belle Dame sans Mercy" (lines 8–10). His conventional concern over whether or not he has the skill to execute this "commaundement" (line 18) confuses him momentarily, but finally he throws on his clothes and walks out into a vale of flowers; "bolded" (line 26) by this pleasant site, he determines to go ahead with the project.

The translator gives way at this point to the "eyewitness" narrator who ultimately relates the debate between lover and coveted lady. Much of the balance of the English poem follows Chartier. Like Chartier's narrator, this narrator appears at first to suffer from lovesickness, complaining that he is "[o]f al lovers the moost unfortunate" (line 32), but it quickly becomes clear that he takes no active interest in love because his own lady is dead, and his heart is "with hire undre hire tumbe igrave [buried]" (line 60). He declares that he should give up writing because he cannot understand or relate anything joyful. If forced to write something cheerful, his pen could never understand it, any more than his tongue could enjoy it. His mouth, laughing a little or a lot, would be belied by his eye, and his heart would resent such expressions of gladness (lines 47–52). In fact, his time as a lover has passed altogether.

These thoughts preoccupy the narrator as he rides looking for lodging. Arriving at a suitable spot he hears minstrels playing in a garden and at once determines to dodge the festivities. Instead he finds himself unexpectedly roped in by two friends. At the feast the narrator observes the lover (*l'amant*) serving at table with such a wretched expression that, if one were to judge by it, the main course would seem to be "a piteuous entremesse" ("a pathetic between-courses entertainment," line 156). After watching for a while the narrator escapes the feast for a seat alone in the arbor. Soon, however, *l'amant* and *la dame* conveniently approach the spot where the narrator is hiding so that he overhears their conversation.

The narrator sees the lover "As oon that hade ben ravisshed utterlye" (line 111), so that his "desire fer passed his reason" (line 114). The narrator's suggestion that women are responsible for excessive male desire parallels the lover's own subsequent declaration to the lady that "Fortune nat oon by his chaunce / Hath caused me to suffre al this payne, / But youre beauté" (lines 273–75). As in many medieval love debates, reason and will stand in opposition. *La dame*, having no desire "[t]o be rewled by manis goveraunce" (line 315), is characterized by a Boethian frame of mind in which reason is paramount, and she refuses to be swayed from "undreneth the standart of Daungere [Resistance]" (line 180) by any of *l'amant*'s feints or ploys. Not only does she repeatedly tell the lover he is wasting his time in pursuit of someone who remains indifferent to him, but she also distrusts his motives, at once expressing an utter lack of concern over the lover's antics and an anxiety about his potential to mask dishonorable intentions behind a seemingly straightforward countenance. Repeatedly she questions the depth of his "sickness" and suggests that his claims are unreliable, both because lovers often say more than they really mean with words said in jest ("wordis whiche said ben of the splene" [line 327]), and because love takes "gret plesaunce" (line 342) in lying while appearing to be sincere, adding that "Fayned Chere [Counterfeit Expression] right sone may . . . apeyse" the "currysshe [cur-like] hert [and] a mouthe that is curtese" (lines 391, 389).

L'amant, on the other hand, decries *la dame*'s restraint as that of a "marble hert, and yet more harde, perdé, / Whiche mercy may not perce for noo laboure" (lines 717–18). At the end of the long debate, the lady has the last word when she tells the lover, "Ye noye me sore in wasting al this winde" (line 795). This insult leaves the lover in tears to tear "his heere, for anguissh and for payne" (line 810) and causes him to plead for death. According to the narrator, who reports that "afterwarde oon tolde me this expresse" (line 809), the lover dies within a day or two of the debate (line 812). After cautionary statements to both lovers and ladies, the narrator ends his tale, and a few stanzas conclude the translator's frame.

In her summary of the criticism on Chartier's poem, Melissa L. Brown notes that in France it was "a literary sensation" and generated a great deal of response; women of the court supposedly took such strong exception to its depiction of a merciless lady that Chartier was expelled from the royal "Cour d'Amour."[10] Brown reads this turmoil as more in fun than in earnest protest, though many scholars have regarded the controversy as genuine.[11] Brown further suggests that scholarly readers of Chartier's poem frequently wonder whether or not the lady's "reasoning is meant to be taken seriously." At the same time, their disparaging remarks echo the lover's censure of her preternaturally cold heart, as her reasoned responses are taken to be representative of "emotional and sexual 'coldness,'" or as "camouflage for her sexual and emotional fears." Other discussions of Chartier's poem have assessed the lady as frigid, sophistic, deceitful, cynical, and hard. Brown argues in opposition to these views that "[t]o equate feminine strength and reason with a destructive cynicism that reveals a frigid and corrupt nature is to take a witty and clever poem far too puritanically."[12] In fact, to read the character in this way is more than puritanical: it is to understand her in twentieth-century terms, as a tease whose come-ons promise much but deliver nothing. In such a reading of her character, *la dame* is all about enjoying the game without paying up. Whether a consequence of fear or deceit, her refusal to give in to *l'amant* suggests in this schema a refusal to participate honestly in the game of love, as if she deliberately sets out to encourage the lover's parries and feints only for the enjoyment of refusing him. Stringing him along, she seduces the lover without any intention of ever letting him have his way with her — a regular "dame,"

---

[10] Brown, pp. 119–20.

[11] Brown, p. 119.

[12] Above citations and summary of the various arguments on Chartier's poem are from Brown, p. 120.

who, beneath her stunning exterior, suppresses heart-stopping manipulative skills and an empty shell of a heart in the best *noir* tradition.

What this suggests is that these critics have read the lady in much the same way that the character of the lover understood her. To them, as to him, she has a heart harder than marble. *L'amant*'s claim that *la dame* is somehow to blame for his desire for her, and that this in turn obligates her to take pity on him, is a stereotypical one that critics reproduce when they argue that her rejection should be read as frigid or hard. Usually in courtly laments it is the woman who dies, thereby creating a proper object for unrequited love/desire, because, after all, a dead woman cannot refuse the lover's advances and will never argue with him. This is the case, for example, in Chaucer's *Book of the Duchess* or Charles d'Orleans' fifteenth-century balade sequence, as well as for the narrator of this poem. But *la dame*'s response is similar to that of Shakespeare's Rosalind when she scorns the hyperbolic claims of sonnet writers in *As You Like It*: "men have died from time to time and worms have eaten them, but not for love."[13] *La dame* has her own version of this: "This sikenes is right easé to endure — / But [Only a] fewe people it causith for to dye" (lines 293–94). In fact, one of the problems the lover has with the lady in *La Belle Dame sans Mercy* is the lady's refusal to "play dead"; not only is she very much alive, but she also categorically declines to be a passive recipient of the lover's desire. Neither lover nor critics seem willing to take seriously her statement that she does not wish "[t]o be rewled by manis goveraunce" (line 315). She reminds *l'amant* that she has a will of her own, and that it may not agree with his:

As for pleasaunce, it is not alwey oon;	*pleasure; always the same*
That to you is swete me thinke a bitter payne.	*What; sweet*
Ye may not me constrayne (ner yet right noon)	*nor; anyone*
After youre list to love, that is but vayne.	*According [to]; desire; futile*
(lines 357–61)	

All of this points to her unequivocal resistance to being "remade" by the male gaze into a suitable object of desire: one passive and agreeable, lacking in agency, a vessel to be filled, without desires of her own.

In Brown's reading of Roos' translation, *la dame* is a "Dame" of another sort: a great lady, who distinguishes "charitable love" from "cupidinous love," rejects "courtly language" and its idolization of women, identifies "true courtesy" as stemming from character rather than class, and in general "exposes the follies of erotic courtly rhetoric in her debate with the Lover."[14] In this recovery operation, *la dame*'s "harmonizing of words and action would

---

[13] William Shakespeare, *As You Like It*, IV.i.101–03 (ed. Agnes Latham [London: Methuen, 1975]).

[14] Brown, pp. 128, 129, 130, and 139, respectively. Brown maintains that "[a]lthough the translation [of Chartier's poem] is inaccurate in a number of places, altogether it is accurate enough to justify using

inspire an active, virtuous response to both public and private temptation," and the lady is a realistic portrayal of a person who displays both individuality and depth of character and who understands "liberality as a personal value she has internalized as her own."[15] The lover, on the other hand, is "a static, unambiguous type" unable "to take responsibility for himself."[16] Displaying "a narcissism typical of the courtly lover," he suffers from "a case of 'arrested' development,"[17] for he is merely a conventional portrait wholly composed by courtly rhetoric and lacking any capacity for interiority. At some level Brown's interpretation simply inverts the arguments of critics who faulted *la dame* for her attachment to reason. Brown tries to recuperate the lady by suggesting that the lover's desire is fatuous, and that what other critics saw as the lady's coldness is really strength of character.

No matter how we read it, *la dame*'s studied indifference has spurred readers, both medieval and modern, to take sides. Such responses point to one of the pleasures of the poem: that is, its entertainment value *as* debate. So much critical response to debate poetry has spent itself in attempting to decide the winner of any given quarrel, and in this respect the response to *La Belle Dame sans Mercy* is no different. That scholars' engagement in the poem consists in either defending or attacking *la dame* therefore points to taking sides as one of the satisfactions common to debate poetry, evident from the relish with which readers reproduce in their own responses the debate of the principles. What critics of *la dame* and *l'amant* fail to notice is that the pleasure of the poem is dependent on the intractability of the characters — without it there would be no debate. Perhaps the point is not to choose the winner but to enjoy the battle.

If modern readers join in the fray as eagerly as their medieval counterparts once did because *la dame* provokes us so, there are nevertheless aspects of the poem that do not inspire such energetic reactions. Lewis' assessment of it as "an admirable exercise in poetical style" but "an essentially second-rate theme,"[18] along with Skeat's impression of it as "remarkably modern" but "somewhat dull" and needlessly prolix,[19] both suggest that modern readers still just don't get it. On the other hand, Brown's attempt to redeem the poem by recuperating it not only in

---

criticism of Chartier in discussing Roos" (p. 119). She also looks in Chartier's other writings for clues to the interpretation of both the French and English versions of the poem. Rossell Hope Robbins characterizes Roos' translation as differing from the French poem in that "the woman is to be praised for exposing the fatuity of *amor cortois*" (1973, 4.1094). In addition, Brown's own reading suggests that the two poems differ significantly enough to invite hesitation before relying mainly on criticism of Chartier's poem in reading Roos' translation.

[15] Brown, pp. 126, 130.

[16] Brown, p. 131.

[17] Brown, pp. 132, 134.

[18] Lewis, pp. 245, 246.

[19] Skeat (1897), pp. lii, liii.

feminist terms but also in aesthetic ones seems like wishful thinking. Her argument that the lady shows depth of character simply does not fit well with the sententious style *la dame* and *l'amant* both routinely employ. Many of their remarks to one another can be linked to proverbial expressions, and even when no specific proverb is invoked, much of what the lady and lover say has a proverbial quality — as if the two were continually speaking in the rhetoric of common sayings. This is to some extent true of any medieval debate poem, since the form reproduces this practice from "scholastic disputation, as well as pleading in a court of law."[20] But in *La Belle Dame sans Mercy*, the flooding of the narrative with proverbs has the effect of eliding individuality or uniqueness of voice. In comparison to the cuckoo and the nightingale's rhetoric in *The Boke of Cupide*, for example, where the two birds' responses seem as distinct and emphatic as their respective qualities of voice, the lady and the lover seem no more than mouthpieces for a conventionalized argument about love. Many of the sayings that the characters hurl at one another occur in both the French and the English versions. The fact that occasionally the English poem offers an entirely different proverb rather than translating the one that occurs in the French demonstrates Roos' awareness at some level of this proverbial quality, whether deliberately preserved or unconsciously imitated.

In some ways, *la dame* and *l'amant* seem to exist agonistically, through the necessity to come up with another saying to counter one proffered by the opponent. This imparts a quality of performance to the roles of *la dame* and *l'amant*. The poem does not so much invite exploration of what constitutes the identity of the two as the recognition of both the lady and the lover as verbal virtuoso performances. As with other medieval debates, part of the pleasure for contemporary audiences must have been to follow the pattern of argument and refutation; the fact that critics of Chartier's poem often wonder whether or not the lady's "reasoning is meant to be taken seriously" testifies to the power of this form to engage audiences interested in such linguistic pyrotechnics. At the same time, the heavy use of proverbs and proverbial rhetoric suggests that another aspect of the pleasure this poem might have provided includes the use of proverbial expressions as a kind of "spectacle"; for medieval audiences such riffs would resonate (both with everyday sayings as well as literary ones) in ways that we find hard to capture now — an extravaganza of the lover and lady "one-upping" each other not only through their use of the highly intricate rhetoric of debate, but also with everyday sayings complicated by their embeddedness within a literary form.

Differences between folk sayings and literary ones (or literary versions of the former) prove hard to capture,[21] but it is fair to say that a number of the proverbs used in this poem must have

---

[20] Stanley, p. 34. Compare, for example, the numerous proverbs used by the birds in *The Owl and the Nightingale*.

[21] For more discussion of this issue, see Archer Taylor, *The Proverb* (Cambridge, MA: Harvard University Press, 1931), especially pp. 4–5; Susan E. Deskis' introduction to *Beowulf and the Medieval*

been commonly known, as they survive today. Versions of "love at first sight" (Whiting L496), "love binds" (Whiting L497), "better bow than break" (Whiting B484), and "better said than done" (Whiting S73) punctuate the narrative alongside those more difficult to assess, such as "love puts reason away" (Whiting L533) or "who seeks sorrow, his be the receipt" (Whiting S523). At the same time, the way in which proverbs are situated and frequently recast suggests that even the most common of these have been fine-tuned to literary advantage. For example, when the lady advises the lover, "To overcome is good, and to refrayne / An hert whiche is deseyved folely" (lines 489–90), she adds to this, "For worse it is to breke than bowe, certayne — / Better bowe than falle to soudenly" (lines 491–92). Although there is only one identifiably proverbial saying here, "worse it is to breke than bowe" (Whiting B484), the other lines are constructed in such a way as to make them sound proverbial even if they are not. Such common sayings in the poem often cloak themselves in just this way within similarly worded formulations, and at the same time they often participate in a more literary kind of complication. For example, sandwiching the commonplace maxim between "[t]o overcome is good" and "[b]etter bowe than falle to soudenly" sets up a verbal play between "good," "worse," and "better." The effect of this rhetoric on the modern reader seems at best a kind of mind-numbed admiration. Lewis' and Skeat's reactions, cited earlier, suggest that the frequent use of proverbs makes the poem at once accessible and tedious. But for medieval audiences, this verbal play must have been at least part of the appeal of both English and French versions of the poem.

Perhaps in some measure because of its later date, and in part because of its two ventriloquized, lyric voices, Roos' poem finds itself in more diverse contexts than the other poetry in this volume. The earlier manuscripts, Oxford, Bodleian Library MS Fairfax 16; London, British Library MS Harley 372; and Longleat House MS 258, place it in the familiar Chaucerian context, while the later ones bring shorter lyric poetry to the fore. Cambridge, Trinity College MS R.3.19 offers poems by Chaucer and Lydgate alongside a number of unique lyrics,[22] much in the manner of the Findern manuscript (Cambridge University Library MS Ff.1.6), discussed in detail in the Introduction to *The Boke of Cupide*, above.[23] This pattern culminates in London, British Library MS Additional 17492, from the first half of the sixteenth century, where two lone stanzas from Roos' poem keep company with the lyrics of Sir

---

Proverb Tradition (Tempe, AZ: Medieval & Renaissance Texts & Studies, 1996), pp. 1–10; and Wendy Pfeffer's introduction, "The Definition of a Proverb," to *Proverbs in Medieval Occitan Literature* (Gainesville: University Press of Florida, 1997), pp. 1–11.

[22] See the description of the contents in Bradford Y. Fletcher's introduction to the facsimile volume.

[23] See p. 28.

Thomas Wyatt, Lord Surrey, and other early Renaissance poets.[24] Here, in its drastically shortened form, Roos' poem takes on a lyric identity in keeping with the poetry of the early sixteenth century that accompanies it.

One of the seven manuscripts containing copies of the English version of *La Belle Dame sans Mercy* attributes the poem to Sir Richard Roos.[25] Ethel Seaton has argued convincingly for a knight by this name favored by Humphrey, Duke of Gloucester, who in 1438 granted Roos an annuity of £20 and then enfeoffed him with a manor in Kent in the following year. Roos later served as a King's Knight under Henry VI (1442 until about 1460/61). Little is known of the last twenty years of his life, doubtless disrupted by the Wars of the Roses and especially the capture in 1460 of Henry VI and the declaration of Edward IV as king in 1461. Roos' nephew Thomas, Lord Roos, was executed in 1464, and Sir Richard Roos himself seems to have been at one point imprisoned, although his will shows that by the time of his death he had a position of some sort at the court of Edward IV.[26]

Roos may have encountered John Lydgate towards the end of Lydgate's life,[27] and he was a contemporary of poets such as Charles d'Orléans, George Ashby, John Metham, and Benedict (or Benet) Burgh.[28] Later poems such as *The Floure and the Leafe* and *The Assembly of*

---

[24] Interestingly, though the stanzas are taken from entirely different parts of the poem, they make a coherent complaint in the lover's voice against a heartless beloved.

[25] Harley 372, fols. 61r–69v.

[26] For the above details, see Ethel Seaton's biography of Roos, *Sir Richard Roos: Lancastrian Poet*, especially chapter 2, "Sir Richard Roos (c. 1410–81/2): Gloucester's Man and King's Knight," pp. 60, 63, 73 ff.

[27] Seaton notes that Roos was one of the retinue that came to witness the proxy marriage of Henry VI and Margaret of Anjou. The entourage then escorted her to England, and Lydgate wrote various compositions for the celebrations on her arrival in London on 28 May 1445 (pp. 65–67).

[28] It is unclear whether Roos would have known all of these poets, but they were moving in the same circles. Richard Roos' older brother Robert "escorted Charles d'Orléans to Burgundy on his liberation," and Seaton suggests that Richard may have accompanied them (pp. 45, 61). Seaton speculates that they probably knew each other in any case by the time Orléans accompanied Margaret of Anjou for part of her journey to England (p. 279). Seaton identifies Ashby, who was also in Queen Margaret's retinue during her journey to England in 1445, as "Writer to the Signet to Margaret of Anjou, known to us as a would-be poet" (p. 64). Metham's patron was Sir Miles Stapleton, married first to Elizabeth Felbrigg and then, when she died, to Katherine de la Pole (see Stephen F. Page, *Amoryus and Cleopes* [Kalamazoo, MI: Medieval Institute Publications, 1999], pp. 3–4); Richard Roos' wife was related by marriage to Elizabeth's Felbrigg's father, Sir Simon Felbrigg, who also had connections through marriage to the de la Pole family (Seaton, p. 39). Burgh (1413–83) supposedly dedicated two of his poems to William, Lord Bourchier (d. ?1472), and was at one point a tutor for the Bourchier family, which had connections

Ladies show that courtly love poetry continued to generate interest in the second half of the fifteenth century. In fact, *The Assembly of Ladies* appears in Longleat 258, one of the earlier manuscripts containing a copy of *La Belle Dame sans Mercy*, while *The Floure and the Leafe* may once have been included as well in pages now lost.[29] As Derek Pearsall notes, the debate around women's fidelity, popularized by the poetry of Chaucer and Gower, persisted in the fifteenth century through "the controversy provoked or supposedly provoked by Alain Chartier's portrayal of the cruel mistress in *La Belle Dame sans Merci*."[30]

It is difficult to assess which elements in a translation are not simply derivative of the original work. Both French and English versions take their part in the debate to which Pearsall alludes. Arthur Piaget, who edited the French poem, more specifically draws a parallel between Chartier's poem and Christine de Pisan's *Débat de deux amants*.[31] But it is also likely that Roos' English poem was not solely the product of French sources and influences. As Julia Boffey argues, the prologue to the translation "vaguely echoes the preludes to Chaucer's dreams"; at the same time, she suggests that the poem's French background provides a connection with other English poems that are also translations or adaptations of French works.[32] The presence in the latter half of the century of poems such as *The Assembly of Ladies* implies that Roos, whether directly or not, shared in contemporary poetic engagement with the themes of courtly love played out here. The grouping in manuscripts of *La Belle Dame sans Mercy* with dream visions, with other adaptations and translations of French works, or with poems containing similar themes suggests that the compilers of late-medieval codices at any rate saw the poem in a context of shared interests and generic similarities.[33] And, judging by

---

to Roos' family (William's mother, Isabel, was a cousin of Richard Roos [they shared the same paternal grandmother, Lady Beatrice Roos] and his grandfather was Sir William Bourchier, count of Eu, who married the widow of Edmund, earl of Stafford, a nephew of Lady Beatrice Roos); see Seaton (pp. 140, 487) and George Saintsbury's entry on Burgh from "The English Chaucerians," in *The Cambridge History of English Literature*, vol. 2, *The End of the Middle Ages*, ed. A. W. Ward, A. R. Waller, et al. (New York: Macmillan, 1933), pp. 238–39.

[29] See Derek Pearsall's introduction to *The Floure and the Leafe*, where he points out that the contemporary table of contents in Longleat 258 lists *The Floure and the Leafe*, although the poem is no longer in the manuscript (1990, p. 1).

[30] Pearsall (1990), p. 30.

[31] Piaget, p. ix.

[32] See Boffey (1994), pp. 114–15. Pearsall notes that "[d]eep into the century, French remains as a permanent backcloth to English as the language of a superior culture, frequently the basis for translation, as in poems like Sir Richard Roos's *La Belle Dame sans Merci* and the anonymous *Eye and the Heart*, and frequently invoked in courtly contexts" (2001, p. 22).

[33] See Boffey (1994), pp. 114–15.

the frequency with which they reproduced Roos' translation, they appear to have appreciated the poem.

Note on the text

Copies of *La Belle Dame sans Mercy* occur in seven manuscripts, listed in detail below. The poem also appears in several early printed editions, including Richard Pynson's *The Boke of Fame* (1526) and the editions of Chaucer printed by William Thynne, John Stow, and Thomas Speght. The text of the poem here is based on the copy in Longleat 258,[34] with emendations and some alternate readings from selected manuscripts recorded in the textual notes, according to the practices laid out in the General Introduction. The manuscripts can be divided into two groups: group A, comprised of Longleat 258, CUL Ff.1.6, Trinity R.3.19, and London, British Library MS Sloane 1710 (and the related prints by Pynson and Thynne); and group B, which includes Fairfax 16 and Harley 372.[35] Although Fairfax 16 is the earliest manuscript and seems marginally better metrically than some of the others, it must be discarded on the basis of its severe misordering of the lines: 1–428; 669–716; 525–572; 477–524; 621–668; 573–620; 429–476; 717–856.[36] The order is plainly unintelligible and represents a serious scribal error. Harley 372 shares this problem,[37] and these two manuscripts further contain some errors in comparison to the French.[38] Interestingly, a later hand has corrected Harley 372 in a number of such cases to the same readings as in Pynson and Thynne (which are themselves occasionally errors), though no correction of the misordered lines is evident.[39]

---

[34] Hammond (1905) gives a detailed description of Longleat 258 in "MS. Longleat 258 — A Chaucerian Codex"; see also J. Schick's brief description in his edition of *Lydgate's Temple of Glas* (pp. xxiv–xxv), and Julia Boffey and John J. Thompson's discussion (pp. 281–82).

[35] These groupings are from Boffey and Thompson, p. 283.

[36] It is also missing a stanza (lines 213–220). This is not a matter of leaves misordered and then misbound, since these jumps occur in the middle of pages, though, as Skeat points out, misordering of some past exemplar would account for this type of error (1897, p. liv).

[37] Frederick J. Furnivall, not realizing this, used it as the basis of his 1866 edition.

[38] For example, "eyen" ("eyes") instead of "pen" in line 47, where the French has "plume" ("pen").

[39] Boffey and Thompson note, "a sixteenth-century reader appears to have collated the copy in the B-group [i.e., Fairfax 16 and Harley 372] MS Harley 372 with one of the A-group texts (possibly a print) and to have made appropriate emendations in the manuscript" (p. 302n24).

Longleat 258, the Findern manuscript (CUL Ff.1.6), Trinity R.3.19, Sloane 1710, and Pynson's edition (and Thynne's, which is based on Pynson)[40] all avoid the problems in order of Fairfax 16 and Harley 372, and clearly represent a different lineage.[41] Of the manuscripts in this group, Longleat 258 and Findern are closest in their readings, while Trinity R.3.19 has many unique errors. Sloane 1710 is defective at both beginning and end (missing the first and final twelve stanzas), and is also missing lines 141–90, while BL Add. 17492 contains only lines 717–24, followed by lines 229–36, and appears to use the stanzas as a stand-alone lyric piece rather than as an excerpt from a larger work. The high level of unique errors in Trinity R.3.19, dated by Beadle and Owen at about 1478–83,[42] makes it unfeasible as a base text, despite its relatively early date.

Frederick J. Furnivall based his second EETS edition (1903) on Findern, which Skeat identified as "in some respects, the best MS," although he based his own edition on Thynne.[43] Skeat was unaware of the copy of the poem in Longleat 258. Longleat 258, according to the dates given by both Rossell Hope Robbins and J. Schick, is the earliest manuscript of these three (c. 1460–70).[44] The Findern manuscript (c. 1500) would seem to be about 30–40 years later than Longleat 258 and would make a good base manuscript. Findern's availability in facsimile and its later date,[45] however, have led me to select Longleat 258 instead, despite the fact that it is missing six stanzas due to a lost leaf. Ultimately my intention here is to provide a reasonable reading text based on a manuscript whose version of the poem is little known and would not otherwise be available. Though it is notoriously difficult to determine whether such strokes are meaningful, I have interpreted the L scribe's curls on final -r as final -e.[46] In cases where a horizontal stroke above a vowel might indicate a nasal consonant (*n*/*m*), I have expanded only in places where the stroke is more intensified in thickness and curvature than

---

[40] James E. Blodgett points out that Thynne relied on Longleat 258 for the final six stanzas, since Pynson had replaced these lines with his own *Lenvoy de limprimeur*.

[41] Boffey and Thompson discuss the relationships between Fairfax 16, Harley 372, Longleat 258, CUL Ff.1.6 (Findern), Trinity R.3.19, Sloane 1710, as well as the early prints of Pynson and Thynne, pp. 282–83.

[42] Beadle and Owen, p. xv.

[43] Skeat (1897), p. liv.

[44] Robbins (1973), p. 1301; Schick, p. xxiv.

[45] Findern appears to be a largely amateur production that involved more than 30 different hands (Beadle and Owen, p. xi) and contains a large number of scribal cancellations and revisions.

[46] Roger Dahood's discussion of this problem has proved extremely useful ("Abbreviations, Otiose Strokes and Editorial Practice: The Case of Southwell Minster MS 7," in *New Perspectives on Middle English Texts: A Festschrift for R. A. Waldron*, ed. Susan Powell and Jeremy J. Smith [Cambridge, UK: D. S. Brewer], pp. 141–49).

the scribe's usual hairline strokes, and this would seem to reflect the scribe's usage in spelled-out forms. Other strokes and flourishes are disregarded as otiose.

Alain Chartier's poem was written in 1424, and Ethel Seaton argues that Roos' translation probably dates to about 1441–42, just before Roos became a King's Knight; William P. Marvin, on the other hand, in his "Chronological Outline of Historical Events and Texts in Britain, 1050–1550," places it at 1450.[47] Skeat proposes 1450–60, while Frederick James Furnivall suggests simply 1460.[48] It is difficult to argue for one date over another on the basis of the poem's content, but one good reason for assigning an earlier rather than a later date is the presence of the poem in Fairfax 16, which is variously dated somewhere between the late 1430s and c. 1450.[49] Even if the latest date for Fairfax 16 is accepted, the fact that this copy of the poem has the lines misordered,[50] while a number of others have the correct order, shows that the Fairfax 16 version was itself copied from an imperfect exemplar, and thus the date of the poem's composition could be even earlier than Seaton suggested, but is probably not significantly later.

Indexed in

IMEV 1086.

Manuscripts

Oxford, Bodleian Library MS Fairfax 16 (*SC* 3896), fols. 50r–62v (1430–50). [Stanzas disarranged.]

London, British Library MS Harley 372, fols. 61r–69v (1450–75). [Stanzas disarranged.]

---

[47] In Wallace, 1999, pp. 852–80, at p. 874.

[48] Skeat (1897), p. lii; Furnivall, p. 51. Both Skeat and Furnivall identify the wrong Richard Roos, thus put-ting the translator's birth at 1429 rather than 1410. It is therefore not surprising that their dating of the poem would also be significantly later than Seaton's. See Seaton's introduction, pp. 15–16, for discussion of this error.

[49] John Norton-Smith (1979) puts the date at c. 1450 in his introduction to the facsimile volume, p. vii; Edwards (1996) dates it in the 1440s (p. 56); Boffey (1994) in the late 1430s or 1440s (p. 114); Robbins (1973) gives it a date range of 1425–50 (p. 1301).

[50] A fact which neither Hammond (1908) nor Robbins (1973) notes.

Longleat House MS 258, fols. 120r–136v (1460–70). [Base text for this edition.]

Cambridge University Library MS Ff.1.6 (Findern MS), fols. 117r–134v (c. 1500).

Cambridge, Trinity College MS R.3.19 (599), fols. 98r–108v (1500–25).

London, British Library MS Additional 17492, fols. 29v (lines 717–24) and 30r (lines 229–36) (1529–37).

London, British Library MS Sloane 1710, fols. 164r–176v (fifteenth century). [Bound with later materials, including seventeenth-century letters. Lines 93–140 and 191–764.]

Early printed editions

Pynson, Richard, ed. and printer. *[Chaucer's] The Boke of Fame*. London, 1526. [STC 5088. Includes *Lenvoy de limprimeur* of 6 rhyme royal stanzas replacing Roos' final 6 stanzas.]

Thynne, William, ed. *The Workes of Geffray Chaucer Newly Printed: With Dyuers Workes Whiche Were Neuer in Print Before*. London: T. Godfray, 1532. [STC 5068. Rpt. 1542, STC 5069; ?1550, STC 5071. Based on Pynson, with the final six stanzas from Longleat 258 (to replace Pynson's *Lenvoy de limprimeur*).][51]

Stow, John, ed. *The Workes of Geffrey Chaucer: Newly Printed, With Diuers Addicions, Whiche were Neuer in Printe Before: With the Siege and Destruccion of the Worthy Citee of Thebes, Compiled by Jhon Lidgate*. London: J. Wight, 1561. [STC 5075. Based on Thynne.]

Speght, Thomas, ed. *The Workes of our Antient and Lerned English Poet, Geffrey Chavcer, newly Printed*. London: G. Bishop, 1598. [STC 5077. Rpt. 1602, STC 5080; 1687. Based on Thynne.]

---

[51] See Blodgett.

La Belle Dame sans Mercy

	Half in a dreme, nat fully wele awaked,	*awakened*
	The golden slepe me wrapt undre his whynge;	*early morning sleep; wing*
	Yet not forthy I rose and, welny naked,	*Yet nevertheless; nearly*
	Alle soudenly myself remembringe	*suddenly*
5	Of a matere, levyng al other thinge,	*matter, giving up everything else*
	Whiche I shulde doo withouten more delaye,	*should do*
	For hem the whiche I durst not dissobaye.	*those whom; dared*
	My charge was this: to translat by and by	*translate*
	(Alle thing forgeve), as part of my penaunce,	*forgiven*
10	A boke called La Belle Dame sans Mercy,	*The Beautiful Lady without Pity*
	Whiche maister Alyn made of remembraunce,	*master Alain [Chartier] recorded*
	Cheif secretary with the kyng of Fraunce.	*Chief*
	And hereupon a while I stode musing,	*on this point; stood considering*
	And in myself gretly ymagenyng	*worrying over (pondering)*
15	What wise I shulde performe this said processe,	*How; complete; narrative*
	Considering by good avisement	*prudently*
	Myn unconnyng and my gret simplesse,	*My lack of skill; ignorance*
	And agaynwarde the streit commaundement	*in turn the direct commandment*
	Whiche that I hade; and thus in myn entent	*my mind*
20	I was vexed and turned up and down;	*down*
	Yet at the last, as in conclusion,	
	I cast my clothes on and went my way,	
	This forsaid charge havyng in remembraunce,	*keeping in mind*
	Tylle I came to a lusty grene valy	*Till; pleasant; valley*
25	Full of floures, to se a gret plesaunce.	*flowers; see; delight*
	And so bolded, with thaire benyng sufferaunce	*encouraged; kind tolerance*
	That rede this boke, touching this said matere,	*Who read; regarding*
	Thus I began, if it please you to here.	*hear*

Not long agoo, ryding an esy paas,   *riding [at] an easy (a moderate) pace*
30   I felle in thought, of joy ful desperate   *completely despondent*
     With gret disease and payn, so that I was   *discomfort (suffering)*
     Of al lovers the moost unfortunate,   *most unlucky*
     Sith by hire dart moost cruell, ful of hate,   *Since; her*
     The deth hath take my lady and maistres   *Death has taken; mistress*
35   And left me soul, thus discomfit and mate,[1]
     Sore languisshing and in wey of distresse.   *Greatly suffering*

     Than said I thus: "It falleth me to cesse   *Then; behooves me to cease*
     Either to ryme or dytees for to make,   *rhyme; works to compose*
     And I, surely, to make a ful promisse
40   To laughe noo more, but wepe in clothes blake.   *weep; black*
     My joyful tyme, alas, now is it slake,   *time; over*
     For in myself I fele noo manere ease;   *feel no kind [of] pleasure*
     Lete it be writen, suche fortune I take,   *fate; suffer*
     Whiche neither me nor deth noon other please.[2]

45   "If it were so, my will or myn entent
     Were constrained a joyful thing to writte,   *compelled*
     My penne cowde never have knowlech what it ment;   *pen could; knowledge*
     To speke thereof my tonge hath noo delite,   *tongue; no delight*
     And with my moueth if I laughe muche or lite,   *mouth; much or little*
50   Myn ey shulde make a countenaunce untrewe;   *eye should; duplicitous*
     Myn hert also wolde have thereof despite,   *heart; would feel resentful about it*
     The weping teres have so large issue.   *weeping tears; [an] outpouring [over it]*

     "These seke lovers, I leve that to heim longes,[3]
     Whiche lede there lif in hope of alegeaunce,   *Who lead their lives; relief*
55   That is to say, to make ballade or songes,
     Every of heim as they fynde here grevaunce.   *Each of them; suffer their pain*
     For she that was my joy and my pleasaunce,   *delight (desire)*
     Whos soule I pray God of His mercy save,

---

[1] *And left me alone (i.e., deprived of my beloved), thus overcome and dejected*

[2] *Which pleases neither me nor anyone else*

[3] *[To] these sick (i.e., lovesick) lovers, I leave that [which] is their prerogative*

	She hath my wille, myn hertis ordenaunce,	*heart's government*
60	Whiche bethe with hire undre hire tumbe igrave.	*is; tomb buried*
	"Fro this tyme forth, tyme is to holde my peas,	*From; [it] is; peace*
	It weryth me this matere for to trete;	*I find it tiresome; subject; expound*
	Lete other lovers put heimself in preas.	*Let; themselves into the crowd*
	There season is, my tyme is now forgete.	*[It] is their season; forgotten (past)*
65	Fortune by strenghe the forser hath unshete	*coffer has opened*
	Wherein was speryd al my worldly richesse,	*enclosed; riches (wealth)*
	And al the goodis whiche I have gete	*goods; I got*
	In my best tyme of youthe and lustynesse.	*happiness*
	"Love hath me kept undre his governaunce,	
70	If I mysdud, God graunt me forgevenesse;	*did wrong*
	Yef I dud well, yet felt I noo pleasaunce,	*If; did; nevertheless; satisfaction*
	It causid neither joye ner hevynesse.	*nor sorrow*
	For when she dide, that was al my maistresse,	*died, who; entirely my mistress*
	My good welfare than made the same purchasse;[1]	
75	The deth hath sete my boundes of witnesse,	*limits (boundaries); knowledge*
	Whiche for noothing myn hert shal never passe."	*cross*
	In this gret thought sore troubled in my mynde,	
	Alone thus rode I al the morowtide,	*morning*
	Tyll at the last it happed me to fynde	*I happened to find*
80	The place wherein I cast me to abide.	*where I decided to stay*
	When that I hade noo further for to ride,	
	And as I went my logging to purvey,	*room to get*
	Right sone I harde but litell me beside	*soon; heard only a short distance from me*
	In a gardyn, where mynstrellis gan to play.	*minstrels began*
85	With that anoon I went me bakkermore;	*right away; further away*
	Myself and I, me thought we were inowe;	*it seemed to me; enough*
	But twayne that were my frendis here-bifore	*two; friends previously*
	Hade me aspyed, and yet I wote not howe.	*spotted me; know; how*
	They came for me; awaywarde I me drowe,	*drew*
90	Summewhat by force, sumwhat by ther request,	*Somewhat; their*

---

[1] *My good fortune then had the same outcome*

That in noo wise I cowde myself rescowe,   *in no way could I excuse myself*
But nede I muste come in and see the fest.   *I must needs; feast*

At my commyng, the ladyes everychoon   *every one*
Bade me welcome, God wote, right gentilly,   *knows; courteously (graciously)*
95   And made me chere ever, oon by oon,   *entertained me constantly*
A gret delle better than I was worthy;   *A great deal; I deserved*
And of thaire grace sewed me gret curtesy   *their; showed*
With good disport, by cause I shulde not morne.   *entertainment, so that; grieve*
That day I bade still in thaire company,   *stayed*
100 Whiche was to me a gracious sojorne.

The bordes were sprede in right lityll space;   *tables; set up in [a] very short time*
The ladyes sate, eche as heim semyd beste.   *sat; it seemed best to them*
Were noon dud service within that place   *[There] were none [that] served*
But chosen men, right of the goodlyest: *Except*
105 And there were summe, paraventure moost fresshest,[1]
That sawe there juges, sitting ful demure,   *their judges; very grave*
Withoute semblant either to moost or lest,   *a sign of feeling; greatest or humblest*
Natwithstanding they hade hem undre cure.   *Although; them in their power*

Amongis al other oon I gan aspye,   *Amongst all [the] others one I did espy*
110 Whiche in gret thought ful often came and went,   *Who*
As oon that hade ben ravisshed utterlye,   *one who had been utterly transported*
In his langage nat gretly deligent;   *not very careful*
His countenaunce he kept with gret trament,   *he maintained his composure; torment*
But his desire fer passed his reason;   *far surpassed*
115 For ever his ey went after his entent,   *eye acted in accordance with; desire*
Ful many a time whan it was noo season.   *out of season (i.e., not appropriate)*

To make good chere right sore himself he payned,[2]
And outewardly he fayned gret gladnesse.   *simulated (feigned)*
To synge also by force he was constrayned,   *sing; perforce*
120 For noo pleasaunce, but verrey shamefastnesse,[3]

---

[1] *And there were some [men], perhaps the most recently arrived*

[2] *He was at great pains to assume a glad expression*

[3] *Not out of any desire, but [rather because of] proper modesty*

For the complaynte of his moost hevynesse	*lament; greatest*
Came to his voix alwey withoute request,	*voice; invitation*
Like as the sowne of briddis doith expresse	*sound of birds*
When they singe lowde in frith or in forest.	*loudly; park (woodland)*

125	Other there were that served in the halle,	*Others*
	But noon like, as after myn avyse,	*like [him], to my mind*
	For he was pale and sumwhat lene withalle;	*lean besides*
	His speche also trembled in ferful wise,	*fearfully*
	And ever alone but when he dud servise.	*[he was] always alone except; served*
130	Alle blake he ware and noo devise, but playne.	*black; wore; [heraldic] device*
	Me thought by him, as my witte cowde suffice,	*understanding could*
	His hert was noothing in his owne demayne.	*to no degree; control*

	To fest hem al he dud his diligence,	*entertain; exerted himself to the utmost*
	And wel he cowde, right as it semed me.	*could; seemed [to]*
135	But evermore when he was in presence,	
	His chere was done; it wolde noon other be.	*face; down*
	His scolemaister hade suche autorité,	*schoolmaster; authority*
	That al the while he bode stille in the place,	*stayed*
	Speke cowde he not, but upon hire beauté	
140	He loked stille with a right pituous face.	*piteous*

	With that, his hede he turned at the last,	
	For to beholde the ladies everychoon,	*every one*
	But ever in oon he sett his ey stefast —	*on one; set; eye steadfastly*
	On hire the whiche his thought was moost upon.	*her whom*
145	And of his eyn the shote I knewe anoon,	*eyes; arrow; recognized right away*
	Whiche fedred was with right humble requestis.	*winged (feathered); petitions*
	Then to myself I said, "By God aloon,	*alone*
	Suche oon was I, or that I sawe these gestis."	*[a] one; before; guests*

	Oute of the prese he went ful esely	*crowd; softly*
150	To make stable hevy countenaunce;	*To compose [his] dejected*
	And, witte ye well, he sighed tendirly	*know; sadly*
	For his sorowes and woful remembraunce.	*recollection*
	Then in himself he made his ordenaunce,	
	And forthwithal came to bringe in a messe;	*immediately; course [of the meal]*

| 155 | But, for to juge his moost rewful semblaunce, | *judging from; sorrowful expression* |
| | God wote it was a piteuous entremesse. | *pathetic between-courses entertainment* |

	After dyner anoon they heim avaunsed	*dinner right away they moved forward*
	To daunce aboute, these folkis everychoon,	*people*
	And forthwithal this hevy daunsed —	*at once; sorrowful [lover]*
160	Summetyme with twayne and sumtyme with oon —	*two; one*
	Unto hem al his chere was after oon;	*face was the same*
	Nowe here, now there, as fall by aventure,	*[it] happened by chance*
	But ever amonge, he drewe to hire aloon,	*all the while; alone*
	Whiche moost he dred of lyvyng creature.	*feared (i.e., stood in awe of); living*

165	To myn avise, good was his purveaunce	*my mind; foresight*
	When he hire chase to his maistres alone,	*chose her to [be] his mistress*
	If that hire hert were sette to his pleasaunce	*committed; pleasure*
	As muche as was hire beauteuous persone.	*body (appearance)*
	For who that ever sete his trust upon	
170	The report of thaire eyen, withouten more,	*their eyes*
	He might be deed and grave undre stone	*dead; buried*
	Or ever he shulde his hertis ease restore.	*Before*

	In hire failled noothing, as I cowde gesse,	*nothing was wanting; could perceive*
	Oon wise ner other, pryvé ner pert;	*[Neither] one way; another, covertly; overtly*
175	A garyson she was of al goodnesse	*stronghold (defense)*
	To make a frounter for a lovers hert;	*border fortress*
	Right yonge and fresshe, a woman ful covert;	*lively; reserved*
	Assured well hire port and eke chere,	*Her bearing very self-assured; also expression*
	Well at hire ease, withouten woo or smart,	*sorrow; hurt*
180	Alle undreneth the standart of Daungere.	*underneath; standard; Resistance*

	To se the fest it wered me ful sore,	*feast; exhausted; completely*
	For hevy joy doth sore the hert travayle.	*torture*
	Oute of the prese I me withdrewe therfor	*crowd*
	And sette me adowne alone behinde a trayle	*trellis*
185	Ful of leves, to see a gret mervaille,	*leaves; marvel*
	With grene wetheys ibounde wonderlye;	*pliant branches; skillfully*
	The leves were so thikke withouten faille	*thick*
	That thoroughoute might noo man me aspye.	*no one; notice*

La Belle Dame sans Mercy

	To this lady he came ful curtesly,	*courteously*
190	When he thought tyme to daunce with hire a trace.	*thought [it]; step*
	Sith in an erbere made ful pleasauntly	*Afterwards; pleasure garden*
	They rested heim fro thens but a litell space.	*themselves; thence only; time*
	Nigh heim were noon a certeyne of compace,[1]	
	But only they, as fer as I cowde see,	*Except; far; could*
195	And sauf the trayle there as I had chose my place,	*except the trellis where*
	There was noo more betwix hem twayn and me.	*the two of them*
	I harde the lover sighing wondre sore;	*heard; sighing*
	For ay the nere, the sorer it him sought.	*ever the nearer; afflicted him*
	His inwarde payne he cowde not kepe in store,	*suffering; keep in reserve*
200	Nor for to speke, so hardy was he nought.	*bold; not*
	His leche was nere, the greter was his thought;	*doctor (leech); nearer; greater*
	He mused sore to conquere his desire;	*strove greatly to subdue*
	For no man may to more penaunce be brought	*suffering (punishment)*
	Than in his hete to bringe him to the fire.	*heat*
205	The hert began to swell within his chest,	
	So sore strayned for anguisshe and for payne	*constrained; anguish*
	That al to peces almoost it tobrest	*pieces; shattered*
	When bothe at oonys so sore it dud constrayne;	*once did so severely pressure it*
	Desire was bolde but Shame it gan refrayne —	*curbed it (held it back)*
210	The toon was large, the other was ful close;	*The one was undisciplined; restrained*
	No litell charge was leyde on hym, certayne,	*No little; laid*
	To kepe suche warre and have so many foose.	*war; enemies (foes)*
	Ful often tyme to speke himself he payned,	
	But Shamefastnesse and Drede said ever "nay";	*Modesty; Fear*
215	Yet at the last so sore he was constrayned,	*utterly; compelled*
	When he hade longe put it in delay,	
	To his lady right thus then gan he say	*did*
	With dredful voix, weping, half in a rage:	*fearful voice, weeping, half insane*
	"For me was purveyd an unhappy day	*ordained*
220	When I first hade a sight of youre visage!	

---

[1] *None were near them [within] a certain range (distance)*

"I suffre payne, God wot, ful hote brennynge,   *suffer; burning hot*
To cause my deth al for my trewe servise,   *loyal (faithful)*
And I se well ye reke thereof noothinge,   *care*
Nor take noon hede of it in noo kynnys wise;   *heed; in any way (i.e., at all)*
225   But whan I speke after in best advise,   *judgment (thought)*
Ye sette it nought, but make therof a game;[1]
And though I sue so gret an enterprise,   *undertake*
It peyrith not youre worship ner youre fame.   *harms; honor*

"Alas, what shulde be to you prejudice   *injury*
230   If that a man doo love you fastfully,   *faithfully*
To youre worship, eschewing every vise?   *honor; vice*
So am I youres and wol be verreily;   *will; truly*
I chalang nought of right and reason why,   *dispute*
For I am hole submytted to youre servise;   *completely submitted*
235   Right as ye list it be, right so wol I   *desire; do I desire*
To binde myself where I was in fraunches.   *a free agent (lit., in freedom)*

"Though it be so that I cannot diserve
To half youre grace, but alwey lyve in drede,   *have*
Yet suffre me you for to love and serve   *allow me to love and serve you*
240   Withoute magré of youre moost goodlyhede;   *resentment; highest virtue*
Bothe faithe and trouthe I geve youre womanhede,   *loyalty; give your ladyship*
And my servise, withoute any callyng.   *demand/protest (lit., outcry)*
Love hath me bounde withoute wage or mede   *payment (reward)*
To be youre man and leve al other thyng."   *leave; thing*

245   When this lady had hard al his langage,   *heard; language*
She gave answere ful soft and demurely,
Withoute chanching of coloure or courage,   *changing; heart*
Nathing in hast but mesurably: *Not at all; haste; deliberately*
la dame   "Me thinketh, Sire, youre thought is gret foly.
250   Pourpose ye not youre laboure for to shese?   *Have you not made up your mind; cease*
For thinketh nat, whiles that ye lyve and I,   *do not think*
In this matere to sete youre hert in pese."   *matter; set; peace*

---

[1] *You consider it of no importance, but turn it into a joke*

La Belle Dame sans Mercy

l'amant "There may noon make the peas but only ye,   *peace*

       Whiche are the grounde and cause of al this warre,   *Who; war*

255   For with youre eyen the leters writen be,   *eyes; letters are written*

       Be whiche I am defyde and put afarre;   *By; challenged; further away*

       Youre pleasaunt loke, my verrey lodesterre,   *true lodestar (guide)*

       Was made heraude of thilke same defyaunce,   *herald; challenge (declaration of war)*

       Whiche utterly behight me for to berre   *urges me; hold up (bear)*

260   My faithful truste and al my affyaunce."   *allegiance (confidence)*

la dame "To lyve in woo he hath gret fantesye,   *misery; strong inclination*

       And of his hert also hath slepire holde,   *slippery (i.e., precarious)*

       That only for beholding of an eye

       Cannat abide in peas, as reason wolde.   *Cannot; wills*

265   Other or me if ye list to beholde,   *If you want to look at me or [some] other*

       Oure eyen are made to loke — why shulde we spare? —   *eyes*

       I take noo kepe neither of yonge ner olde;   *no heed; young nor*

       Who felyth smart, I counsaill him beware."   *feels pain*

l'amant "If it be so oon hurt another sore   *be the case that one*

270   In his defaute that felyth the grevaunce,   *Through his fault who feels*

       Of verrey right a man may doo no more,   *Legitimately*

       Yet Reason wolde it were in remembraunce;   *wishes; taken into consideration*

       And sith Fortune nat oon by his chaunce   *since; not only*

       Hath caused me to suffre al this payne,

275   But youre beauté, with al the circumstaunce,   *But [also]*

       Why list you have me in so gret disdayne?"   *does it please you [to] hold*

la dame "To youre persone ne have I noo disdayne,

       Ne never hade, truly, ner naught wil have;   *Nor*

       Ner right gret love, ner hatered, in certayne,   *Neither . . . nor*

280   Ner youre counsaille to knowe, so God me save.   *Nor; secret*

       If suche love be in youre mynde grave,   *mind fixed*

       That litell thing may doo you gret pleasaunce,   *[a] little; pleasure*

       You to begile, or make you for to rave,   *delude; become distraught [because of love]*

       I wil not cause noon suche encomberaunce."   *any such trouble*

l'amant "Whatever it be that me hath thus purchasid,   *has thus taken possession of me*

286   Wenyng hath not deceyved me, certayne,   *Presumption*

       But fervent love so sore me hath chasid   *afflicted*

	That I am unware casten in youre chayne;	*unexpectedly thrown; chain*
	And, sith so is as Fortune list ordeyne,	*since; chooses [to]*
290	Alle my welfare is in youre handis falle,	*your care*
	In eschewing of more mischevous payne,	*miserable suffering*
	Who sonnest deyeth, his care is lest of alle."	*soonest dies; least*

la dame	"This sikenes is right easé to endure —	*sickness; easy*
	But fewe people it causith for to dye —	*Only a few*
295	But what they mene, I knowe it verrey sure,	*grumble*
	Of more comfort to drawe the remedye;	
	Suche be there now, playnyng ful pituouslye,	*complaining*
	That fele God wote nat alther gretest payne,[1]	
	And yef so be love hurt so grevouslye,	*if*
300	Lesse harme it were oon sorowful then twayne."	*one; than two*

l'amant	"Alas madame, if that it might you please,	
	Muche better were, by way of gentilnesse,	
	Of oon sory to make twayn well at ease	*From one sorrowful (i.e., the lover); two*
	Than him to stroy that lyveth in distresse.	*destroy*
305	For my desire is neither more ne lasse	
	But my servise to doo for youre pleasaunce,[2]	
	In eschewing al manere of doublenesse	*duplicity*
	To make twoo joyes instede of oo grevaunce."	*one*

la dame	"Of love I seke neyther pleasaunce nor ease,	*seek neither*
310	Ner right gret love, ner gret affyaunce;	*Neither . . . nor; pledge of loyalty*
	Though ye be seke, it doith me noothing please —	*sick; does*
	Also I take noon hede to youre pleasaunce.	*no*
	Chese whoso woll there hertis to avaunce —	*Choose; will their hearts; thrust forward*
	Free am I nowe, and fre will I endure;	
315	To be rewled by manis goveraunce	*ruled by man's*
	For erthely good, nay — that I you ensure!"	

| l'amant | "Love, whiche that joy and sorowe doith depart, | *separate* |
| | Hath set the ladies oute of al servage | *bondage (servitude)* |

---

[1] *Who think that God does not know the most grievous suffering of all*

[2] Lines 305–06: *For my desire is only to labor for your gratification*

	And largely doith graunt hem for thaire part	*generously; their portion*
320	Lordship and rewle of every manere age.	*rule*
	The poure servaunt nought hath of avauntage	*poor servant (i.e., lover); nothing; gain*
	But what he may gete only of purchace;	*entreaty*
	And he that onys to love doith his homage,	*once; pays his*
	Ful often tyme dere bought is the rechace."	*dearly; ransom*

la dame	"Ladyes bith not so semple, thus I meane,	*are; simple*
326	So dulle of witte, so sotid of foly,	*deluded*
	That for wordis whiche said ben of the splene,	*are; in jest*
	In faire langage peynted ful pleasauntly,	*ornamented*
	Whiche ye and moo holde scoles of duly,	*others conduct schools; diligently*
330	To make hem al gret wondres to supoose,	*believe*
	But sone they can away thaire hede wry,	*swiftly; turn their heads away*
	And to faire speche lyghtly thaire eres close."	*quickly; ears close (refuse to listen)*

l'amant	"There is noo man that jangelyth besily,	*chatters busily*
	And sette his hert and al his mynde therfore,	
335	That by reason may playne so pituously,	*complain*
	As he that hath muche hevynes in store.	
	Whos hede is hole and saith that it is sore,	*is whole*
	His fayned chere is harde to kepe in mewe;[1]	
	But thought whiche is unfayned evermore	*unfeigned (true)*
340	The wordis preveth as the werkis sewe."	*prove genuine; works follow*

la dame	"Love is sotill and hath a gret awayte,	*subtle (clever); watchfulness/caution*
	Sharpe in worching, in gabbyng gret plesaunce,[2]	
	And him can venge of suche as, by deceyte,	*can avenge himself on those who*
	Wolde fele and knowe his secrete governaunce;	
345	And maketh hem to obey his ordenaunce	
	By chereful wayes, as in him is supposed;	*cheering; assumed (expected)*
	But when they fallen into repentaunce,	
	Then in a rage thaire counsaill is disclosed."	*secret; revealed*

---

[1] *His feigned expression is hard to keep under control (i.e., like a mewed hawk)*

[2] *Painful in deed, in lying great delight*

l'amant	"Sith for as muche as God and eke Nature	
350	Hath avaunsed Love to so high degré,	*promoted*
	Muche sharper is the poynt, this am I sure,	
	Yet greveth more the faute, wherever it be.	*hurts; lack (imperfection)*
	Who hath noo colde, of hete hath noo deynté	*heat; pleasure*
	The toone for tother axed is expresse;	*one; the other is expressly required*
355	And of pleasaunce knoweth noon the certaynté,	*happiness none knows; real nature*
	But it be wonne with thought and hevynesse."	*Unless; won*
la dame	"As for pleasaunce, it is not alwey oon;	*pleasure; always the same*
	That to you is swete me thinke a bitter payne.	*What; sweet*
	Ye may not me constrayne (ner yet right noon)	*nor; anyone*
360	After youre list to love, that is but vayne.	*According [to]; desire; futile*
	To chalange Love by right was never sayne,	*witnessed*
	But hert assent, bifore bonde and promese;	*Unless; marriage obligation (bond)*
	For strenghe ne force may not atayne, certayne,	*nor; encroach on (overpower)*
	A will that stont enfeffid in fraunchese."	*is enfeoffed in freedom*
l'amant	"Right faire lady, God mote I never please	*may God grant that I never please*
366	If I seke other right, as in this case,	*seek*
	But for to shewe you playnly my desease,	*show; anxiety*
	And youre mercy to abide, and eke youre grace.	
	If I purpose youre honoure to deface,	*reputation for purity to sully*
370	Or ever dide, God and fortune me schende	*punish me*
	And that I never unrightfully purchace	*[make sure] that*
	Oon only joye, unto my lyves ende."	*A single; life's*
la dame	"Ye and other that swere suche othes fast	*swear; oaths firmly*
	And so condempne and cursen too and fro,	*swear*
375	Full sycourly ye wene youre othes last	*surely you realize*
	Noo lenger than the wordis ben agoo.	*longer; have departed*
	And God and eke His seintis laugh also;	*saints*
	In suche sweryng there is noo stedfastnesse,	
	And these wrecches, that have ful trist thereto —	*trust*
380	After, they wepe and waylen in distresse."	*weep and wail*
l'amant	"He hath noo courage of a man, truly,	*heart*
	That sechith pleasaunce, worship to dispise;	*seeks pleasure (gratification), honor*
	Ner, to be called forth, is not worthy,	*Nor*

226

	The erthe to touche, the ayre in noo-kynde wise;	*earth; air; in no way (not at all)*
385	A trusty hert, a mouthe withoute fayntise:	*guile*
	These ben the strenghe of every man of name;	*strength*
	And who that leyth his faith for litell prise,	*expends; little value*
	He lesith bothe his worship and his fame."	*loses*

la dame	"A currysshe hert, a mouthe that is curtese,	*cur-like (mean); courteous*
390	Full well ye wote, they ben not according;	*compatible*
	Yet Fayned Chere right sone may theim apeyse,	*Counterfeit Expression; reconcile*
	Where of malice is sete al here worching;	*in; placed; their working*
	Ful Fals Semblant they bere, and Trewsemyng;	
	Thaire name, thaire fame, thaire tongis be bot fayned;[1]	
395	Worship in hem is put in forgeting,	*Honor; forgotten about*
	Nought repented, ner in noo wise complayned."	*Not at all regretted; lamented*

l'amant	"Who thinketh ill, no good may him befalle;	
	God of His grace graunt eche man his desert.	*[just] deserts*
	But, for His love, amonge youre thoughtis alle	
400	As thinke upon my woofull sorowes smert;	
	For, of my payne, whether youre tendre hert	*is it the case that your*
	Of swete pité be not therewith agreved?	*sad (distressed)*
	And if youre grace to me were discovert,	*shown*
	Then, by youre meane, sone shulde I be releved."	*favor*

la dame	"A lightsum hert, a foly of pleasaunce,	*merry; desire*
406	Ar muche better the lesse whille they abide.	*Are; less time*
	They make you thinke and bringe you in a traunce,	
	But that sekenesse wol sone be remedide.	*sickness will at once; cured*
	Respite youre thought and put al this aside;	*Give up; set*
410	Full good disportis weryth men al day.	*amusements tire*
	To helpe ner hurt my will is not aplide —	*nor; directed (applied)*
	Who troweth me not, I late him pas away."	*believes; let; pass (i.e., ignore him)*

l'amant	"Who hath a bride, a fawcon, or an hounde	*bird; falcon*
	That folowith him for love in every place,	*out of*

---

[1] Lines 393–94: *Entirely False Seeming (Pretense) they bear, and True seeming (outward appearance of truth); / Their names, their reputations, their tongues are only feigned (insincere)*

415	He cheryssheth him and kepith him ful sounde;	*takes good care of; keeps; safe*
	Oute of his sight he wol not him enchace.	*will; drive*
	And I, that set my wittes in this cace	*case*
	On you alone, withoute any chaunge,	
	Am put undre, muche forther oute of grace,	*further*
420	And lesse sette by than other that be straunge."	*less valued; others who are unknown*

la dame	"Though I make chere to every man aboute	*welcome*
	For my worship and of myn owne fraunchese,	*honor; generosity*
	To you I nell doo so, withouten doute,	*will not do*
	In eschewinge al manere prejudice.	*[For the sake of] avoiding; injury*
425	For, wote ye well, Love is so lityll wise,	
	And in beleve so lightly wol be brought,	*belief; will*
	That he takith al at his owne devise	*as he likes*
	Of thing, God wote, that servyth him of nought."	*not at all*

l'amant	"Iffe I, by love and by my trew servyse,	*by; true*
430	Lese the good chere that straungers have alway,	*Lose; welcome*
	Wherof schuld serve my trouth in any wyse	*Why should my loyalty serve in any way*
	Les then to heme that come and go al day,	*Less than to those who*
	Which hold of you nothyng, that is no nay?	
	Also in you is loste, to my semynge,	*is; in my opinion*
435	All courtesy, which of resoun will say	
	That love by love were lawfull deservynge."	*for; reward*

la dame	"Courtesye is allied wondir nere	*wonderfully close*
	To worschip, which hyme lovyth tendurly,	*honor*
	And he will not be bound for no prayere,	*entreaty*
440	Nor for no gifte, I say you verely,	*tell; truly*
	But his good chere depart ful largely	*spreads very generously*
	Wher hyme lyketh, as his conseit wil falle;	*it pleases him; fancy*
	Guerdoun constraynt, a gifte done thankefully —	*Reward compelled; given gladly*
	Thes twayn may not acord, nor never schale."	*two*

l'amant	"As for guerdoun, I seche none in this case,	*reward; ask none*
446	For that desert, to me it is to hye;	*too high (exalted)*
	Wherfor I asche your pardoun and your grace,	*ask*
	Sith me byhovyth deth, or your mercy.	*Since death or your mercy is necessary to me*
	To give the god wher hit wanteth, treulye,	*it is lacking*

450	That wer resoun and a courteys manere;
	And to your awn myche bettyr were worthy,
	Then to straungers, to schew heme lovely chere."[1]

right (reasonable)
much better would be

la dame	"What call ye good? Fayn wold I that I wyste!
	That plesith on, another smertyth sore;
455	But of his awn to large is he that liste
	Gyve myche, and lese all his goode fame therfore.
	On schuld not make a graunt, lytele nor more,
	But the request were ryght wele acordynge;
	Yif worschip be not kept and set byfore,
460	All that is lefte is but a lytell thynge."

I really wish I knew
What; causes another severe emotional distress
too open-handed; desires [to]
much; loses; reputation
One; gift, little
Unless; appropriate to it
honor
merely

l'amant	"Into this world was never formyd non,
	Nor undur heven creature ibore,
	Nor never schall, saffe only your parson,
	To whom your worschip touchith half so sore
465	But me, which have no sesoun, les ne more,
	Of youth nor age, but styll in your servyse;
	I have non yne, no wyt, nor mouth in store,
	But all beth given to the same offyse."

anyone
born
shall [be], except your person (i.e., yourself)
season, less
no eyes; in reserve
all are given; duty

la dame	"A full gret charge hath he, withouten fayle,
470	That his worschip kepyth in sykernesse;
	But in daunger he settyth his travayle
	That feffith hit with othyrs bysynesse.
	To hym that longeth honneur and noblesse,
	Upon non othir schuld not he awayte,
475	For of his awn so mych hathe the lesse
	That of othir mych folouth the conseit."[2]

responsibility
Who keeps his honor; secure possession
places (expends) his effort
Who joins; others' work (effort)
who possesses

l'amant	"Youre eyen have sette the prynte which that I fele
	Within myn hert, that, wheresoever I goo,
	If I doo thing that sowneth unto wele,
480	Nede must it come fro you, and fro no moo.

eyes; imprint
[so] that
expresses (indicates) happiness
It must necessarily; other

---

[1] *Than to strangers, show them [a] friendly face (i.e., treat them in a friendly manner)*

[2] *Who follows the opinions (whims) of others a great deal*

229

	Fortune will thus: that I, for well or woo,	*weal or woe (i.e., for good or ill)*
	My lif endure, youre mercy abiding;	*life; awaiting*
	And verrey right will that I thinke also	*true*
	Of youre worship, above al other thing."	*honor*
la dame	"To youre worship se wele, for that is nede,	*pay full attention*
486	That ye spende not youre season al in vayne;	*vain*
	As touching myn, I rede you take noon hede,	*advise; no heed*
	By youre foly to put youreself in payne.	
	To overcome is good, and to refrayne	*hold back*
490	An hert whiche is deseyved folely;	*deceived foolishly*
	For worse it is to breke than bowe, certayne —	*break; bend*
	Better bowe than falle to soudenly."	*[to] bend; too suddenly*
l'amant	"Nowe, faire lady, thinke, sith it first began,	*since*
	That love had sete myn hert undre his cure.	*power*
495	I never might (ner trewly I ne can)	
	Noon other serve whiles I shal here endure.	*None*
	In moost fre wise thereof I make you suere,	*promise*
	Whiche may not be withdrawe — this is no nay —	
	I must abide al manere aventure,	*fortune*
500	For I may not put to, ner take away."	
la dame	"I holde it for noo geft, in sothfastnesse,	*gift, certainly*
	That oon offrith when that it is forsake,	*offers; repudiated*
	For suche geft is abandonnyng expresse,	*[a] gift; [an] explicit surrender*
	That with worship agein may not be take.	*Which with honor may not be taken back*
505	He hath hertis ful fele that list to make	
	A geft lightly that put is in refuse;[1]	
	But he is wise that such conncept wol slake,	*[an] idea will let go*
	So that him nede nother stodye ner muse."	*he need neither meditate anxiously*
l'amant	"He shulde not muse that hath his service spent	
510	On hire whiche is a lady honourable,	
	And yef I spende my tyme to that entent,	*if; end*
	Yet at the last I am not reprevable	*at least; blameworthy*

---

[1] Lines 505–06: *He has too many hearts who wishes to give / A gift eagerly that is rejected (see note)*

	Of fayled hert, to thinke I am unable,	*deficient*
	Or me mistake when I made this request,	*did wrong*
515	By whiche Love hath, of enterprise notable,	*enterprising spirit*
	So many hertis geten by conquest."	*acquired*

la dame	"If that ye list to doo after my counsaille,	*wish; i.e., follow my advice*
	Sechith fairer and of more higher fame,	*Seek*
	Whiche, in service of Love, wol you prefaylle	*will benefit you*
520	After youre thought, according to the same.	*conforming (agreeable)*
	He hurtith bothe his worship and his name	*honor*
	That folely for twayne himself wol trouble;	*foolishly; two*
	And he also lesith his after game,	*loses; second game*
	That surely cannot sette his poyntis double."[1]	

l'amant	"This youre counsaile, by ought that I can se,	*as far as*
526	Is better said than doon, to myn avise;	*done; my mind*
	Though I beleve it not, forgyf it me	*forgive*
	Myn hert is suche, so hole, withoute fantise,	*so honest; deceit (guile)*
	That it may not geve grede in noo wise	*give credence; way*
530	To thing whiche is not sownnyng unto trouth;	*indicating loyalty*
	Other counsaille — it are but fantasise,	*they are; lies*
	Sauf of youre grace to shewe pité and routh."	*Except; show pity; compassion*

la dame	"I holde him wise that worchith folely,	*who works foolishly*
	And whan him list can leve and part therfroo,	*Yet when he desires; leave*
535	But in connyng he is to lerne, trewly,	*understanding; must learn*
	That wolde himself condit and cannot soo.	*control*
	And he that wol not after counsaille doo,	*i.e., follow advice*
	His sowte puttith he in desperaunce;	*legal suit; at risk*
	And alle the good that shulde falle him too	*fall to him*
540	Is lost and dede — clene oute of remembraunce."	*dead — completely forgotten*

l'amant	"Yet wol I sewe this matere faithfullye	*follow through with*
	Whils I may lyve, whatever be my chaunce,	
	And if it happe that in my trouth I dye,	*happens; loyalty; die*
	That dethe shall doo me not noo displeasaunce.	*displeasure*

---

[1] *Who cannot with certainty double his odds (see note)*

545	But when that I, by youre ful herd sufferaunce,	*callous permission*
	Shal dye so trewly and with so gret a payne,	
	Yet shal it do me muche the lesse grevaunce	
	Then for to lyve a fals lover, certayne."	*Than to live [as]*

la dame	"Of me gete ye right naught — this is noo fable —	*nothing at all*
550	I nell to you be neither herde ne streite;	*will not; harsh nor stern*
	And right wol not, nor maner custumable,	*neither law nor custom grants*
	To thinke ye shulde be sure of my conceyte.	*frame of mind*
	Who sechith sorowe, his be the resceyte!	*receiving [of it]*
	Other counsaille can I not fele ner see,	*understand (feel)*
555	Nor for to lerne I cast not to awayte;	*learn; plan; wait*
	Who wol therto, lete him assay, for me."	*Whoever wants to do that; try, for all I care*

l'amant	"Onys it must be assayed, that is noo nay,	*Some day; attempted*
	With suche as bethe of reputacion,	*are respected*
	And, of trewe love, the right devoure to pay	*feudal tax*
560	Of fre hertis, geten by deue raunson;	*noble; gotten; customary tribute*
	For fre wule holdith this opynyon:	*will believes this*
	That it is gret duresse and discomfort	
	To kepe a hert in so streite a prison,	*secure*
	That hath but o body for his disport."	*only one amusement*

la dame	"I knowe so many cases mervelous	*astonishing situations*
566	That I must nedis of reason thynke, certayn,	
	That suche entré is wonder perlous,	*entrance; perilous*
	And yet wel more, the commyng bake agayn;	*coming back (i.e., return)*
	Good or worship thereof is selden sayn;	*seldom witnessed*
570	Wherfore I wol not make suche aray	*preparations*
	As for to fynde a pleasaunce but barayn	*discover; barren*
	Whan it shal cost so dere, the first asay."	*dearly; attempt*

l'amant	"Ye have noo cause to doubte of this matere,	
	Nor you to meve with noo suche fantesyes	*to trouble yourself; false suspicions*
575	To put me fer al oute, as a straungere;	*far*
	For youre goodnesse can thinke and wel avise	*consider (think on)*
	That I have made a pref in every wise	*offered confirmatory evidence*
	By whiche my trouth shewith opyn evydence;	*faithfulness shows clear proof*

	My long abiding and my trewe service	
580	May well be knowe be playne experience."	*known by simple*

la dame	"Of verrey right he may be called trewe,	*faithful*
	And so must he be take in every place,	*understood*
	That can deserve and let as he ne knewe,[1]	
	And kepe the good, if he it may purchace;	*acquire*
585	For who that prayeth and sueth in any cace,[2]	
	Right ye wote well in that no trouth is preved;	*demonstrated*
	Suche hath there ben, and are, that gete grace	
	And lese it soon when they have it acheved."	*lose it right away; gained*

l'amant	"If trouth me cause, by vertu souverayne,	*the highest power*
590	To shewe good love and alway finde the contraye,	*show; yet; contrary*
	And cherith that that sleith me with the payne,	*cherish that which destroys*
	This is to me a lovely adversarye.	*lovable*
	Whan that Pité, whiche long aslepe doith tarye,	*does tarry*
	Hath sette the fyne of al my hevynesse,	*conclusion*
595	Yet hire comfort, to me moost nessarye,	
	Shal sette my will more surer in stablenesse."	*steadfastness*

la dame	"The woful wight, what may he thinke or saye?	*person*
	The contrary of al joy and gladnesse.	
	A seke body, his thought is al awaye	
600	From hem that felen noo sore ner sekenesse.	*those who feel*
	Thus hertis ben of divers besynesse,	*endeavors (concerns)*
	Whiche Love hath put to gret hinderaunce,	*harm*
	And trouth also put in forgetfulnesse,	
	When they so sore begyn to sighe askawunce."	*insincerely*

l'amant	"Now God defende, but he be haveles	*forbid; devoid*
606	Of al worship or good that may befalle	*honor*
	That to the worst turneth, by his lewdenes,	*wickedness*
	A geft of grace, or anything at alle,	*gift*
	That his lady vouchesauf upon him calle,	*condescend*

---

[1] *Who can merit [the name "faithful"] and pretend he did not know [i.e., that he deserved it]*

[2] *For whoever petitions and sues (chases) in any case (i.e., indiscriminately)*

610	Or cherisshe him in hounourable wise;	*treat; honorable*
	In that defaute, whatever he be that falle,	*[case of] failure, whoever*
	Deserveth more than deth to suffre twise."	*than to suffer death twice*

la dame	"There is noo juge isett of suche trespace,	
	By whiche of right oon may recoverd be.[1]	
615	Oon cursith fast, another doith manace,	*One curses; threatens*
	Yet dyeth noon, as for as I can se;	*none dies; far*
	But kepith thaire course alway in oo degré,	*the same*
	And evermore thaire laboure doith increse	*increases*
	To bringe ladyes be thaire gret sotilbté,	*ladies by; guile*
620	For others gilt in sorowe and desease."	*others' sins*

l'amant	"Alle be it so that oon doith so gret offence	*Although; someone does*
	And be not dede, nor put to juyse,	*dead; punished (brought to justice)*
	Right well I wote, him gayneth noo defence,	*it gains him*
	But he must ende in full mischevesse wise.	*miserable (unfortunate)*
625	And all that ever is good wille him dispice,	*all who; despise*
	For falshode is so ful of cursydnesse	*falsehood (deceitfulness); wickedness*
	That high worship may never have entirpryse	*honor; control*
	Where it reyneth and hath the wilfulnesse."	*it (i.e., falsehood) reigns; determination*

la dame	"Of that have they noo gret fere nowadayes,	*fear*
630	Suche as wille say, and mayteyne it thereto,	*maintain*
	That stedfaste trouthe is noothing for to prayes	*loyalty; unworthy of praise*
	In hem that kepe it long for wele or woo.	*those who*
	Thaire besy hertis passyn to and froo,	*Their eager; go*
	They ben so well reclaymed to the lure,	*brought under control (see note)*
635	So welle lerned hem to withholde also,	*trained to hold themselves back*
	And al to chaunge when love shuld best endure."	

l'amant	"Whan oon hath sette his hert in stable wise,	
	In suche a place whiche is both good and trewe,	
	He shuld not flitt, but doo forth his servise —	*flee (fly away)*
640	Alwey withouten chaunge of any newe.	*Always*

---

[1] Lines 613–14: *For such an injury (a crime), there is no judge seated [in court] / By which one may rightfully be restored*

	As soon as love begynnyth to remewe,	*begins; vary (undergo change)*
	Alle pleasaunce goith anoon in litel space;	*goes right away in a short time*
	As for my party, that shal I eschewe,	*part*
	Whilis that the soule abidith in his place."	*For as long as; remains*

la dame	"To love trewly thereas ye ought of right,	*in those cases when you*
646	Ye may not be mistaken, doutelesse;	*certainly*
	But ye be foule deceyved in youre sight	*deceived*
	By lyghtly understanding, as I gesse;	*carelessly; think*
	Yet may ye wel repele youre besynesse,	*disavow; endeavor*
650	And to reason sumwhat have attendaunce,	
	Muche better than to abide, by foule symplenesse,	*ignorance*
	The feble socoure of desesperaunce."	*weak ministrations; despair*

l'amant	"Rason, Counsaille, Wisdam, and Good Advise	*Reason; Judgment*
	Ben undre Love arested every oon,	*restrained*
655	To whiche I can accorde in every wise,	*agree*
	For they ben nat rebelle, but stille as stoon;	*defiant; at peace*
	Thaire wille and myn ben meduled al in oon,	*mingled all*
	And therewith bounden with so stronge a chayne,	
	That as in heim departing shal be noon	*them there shall be no separating*
660	But Pité breke the mighty bounde atwayne."	*Unless Pity breaks; to pieces*

la dame	"Who loveth not himself, whatever he be,	
	In love he stante forgete in every place;	*stands forgotten*
	And of youre woo yf ye have noo pité,	*your [own]*
	Others pité belove nat to purchace;	*expect not*
665	But bethe fully assured in this cace,	*be*
	I am alwey undre oon ordenaunce;	*the same rule*
	To have better trusteth not after grace,	
	And al that levyth take to youre pleasaunce."	*remains be pleased with*

l'amant	"I have myn hope so sure and so stedfast	
670	That suche a lady shulde not faille pité,	*lack*
	But now, alas, it is shit up so fast	*shut*
	That Daungere sheweth on me his cruelté,	*Resistance exercises; cruelty*
	And yef she se the vertu faille on me,	*if; strength (virtue) fail in*
	Of trewe service, then she to fayle also	*fail*

675	Noo wondre were; but this is the shorté:	*wonder; sure thing*
	I must suffre whiche way that ever it goo."	*suffer*
la dame	"Leve this purpose, I rede you for youre best;	*advise*
	For lenger that ye kepe it thus in vayne,	
	The lesse ye gete, as for youre hertis rest,	
680	And to rejoise it shal ye never attayne.	*attain; achieve*
	When ye abide good Hope to make you fayne,	*expect; happy*
	Ye shal be founde asoted in dotage,	*besotted (made a fool of); infatuation*
	And in th'ende ye shal knowe for certayne	
	That Hope shal pay the wrecchis for thaire wage."	*wretches*
l'amant	"Ye say as fallith moost for youre plesaunce,	*speak; falls (agrees)*
686	And youre power is gret — al this I see,	
	But Hope shal never oute of my remembraunce,	*be forgotten*
	By whiche I felt so gret adversité.	*adversity (difficulty)*
	For when Nature hath sett in you plenté	*placed*
690	Of al goodnesse, by vertu and by grace,	
	He never assembled hem, as semyth me,	*as [it] seems [to] me*
	To put Pité oute of his dwelling place."	
la dame	"Pité, of right, ought to be resonable	*reasonable*
	And to noo wight of gret disavantage;	*person; harm*
695	There as is nede, it shulde be profitable,	*Where there is need*
	And to the pitous shewing noo damage;	*pitiful causing*
	If a lady wol doo so gret outrage	*harm*
	To shewe pité and cause hire owne debate,	*degradation*
	Of suche pité cometh dispitous rage,	*spiteful*
700	And of the love also right dedly hate."	*deadly*
l'amant	"To comfort him that lyve al comforlesse,	*entirely without hope*
	That is noon harme, but worship to youre name;	
	But ye, that have an hert of suche duresse,	*disposition; hard-heartedness*
	A faire body iformed to the same,	*formed*
705	If I durst say, ye wyn al this defame	*dare; dishonor*
	By cruelté, whiche sitteth you full yll,	*suits; ill*
	But yef Pité, whiche may al this tame,	*Unless*
	In youre high hert may rest and tary styll."	*continue to tarry*

la dame	"Whatever he be that saith that he loveth me,	
710	And peraventure I leve that it be soo,	*believe*
	Ought he be wrothe, or shuld I blamed be,	*angry*
	Though I dydd not as he wol have me doo?	*Because; would*
	If I medelyd with suche or other moo,	*had sexual intercourse; more*
	It might be called 'pité manerlesse,'	*unmannerly (ungracious)*
715	And afterwarde, if I shuld lyve in woo,	
	Then to repent, it were to late, I gesse."	

l'amant	"O marble hert, and yet more harde, perdé,	*pardee (by God)*
	Whiche mercy may not perce for noo laboure,	*pierce*
	More stronge to bowe than is a mighty tre,	*tree*
720	What vayleth you to shewe so gret rigoure?	*good does it do you; hardness of heart*
	Please it you more to se me dye this houre	*Does it please*
	Before youre eyen, for youre disport and play,	*eyes; entertainment (sport)*
	Then for to shewe summe comfort or socoure	*some; relief*
	To respite dethe, whiche chacith me alwey?"	*put a stop to; pursues*

la dame	"Of youre desease ye may have allegeaunce;	*disease (discomfort); relief*
726	And, as for myn, I lete it overshake.	*let; pass away*
	Also, ye shal not dye for my pleasaunce,	
	Ner for youre heille I can noo sureté make.	*recovery; guarantee*
	I nyll not hate myn hert for others sake,	*will not*
730	Wepe thay, laugh they, or singe, this I warent,[1]	
	For this matere so wol I undretake	
	That noon of you shal make thereof avaunt."	*none; boast*

l'amant	"I can noo skille of songe, by God alone,	*know*
	I have more cause to wepe in youre presence;	
735	And wel I wote avaunter am I noone,	*boaster; none*
	For certaynly I love better silence.	
	Oon shulde not love by his hertis credence	*authority*
	But he were sure to kepe it secretly,	*Unless*
	For avaunter is of noo reverence	*[a] boaster; i.e., not deserving of respect*
740	When that his tonge is his moost enemy."	*greatest*

---

[1] *Whether they should weep, laugh, or sing, this I assure you*

la dame	"Malabouche in court hath gret commaundement:	*Slander; control (sway)*
	Eche man studith to say the worst he may.	*endeavors*
	These fals lovers in this tyme now present,	
	They serve to bost, to jangle as a jay.	*boast; chatter*
745	The moost secret wil well that sum man say[1]	
	Howe he mystersted is on summe partyse;	*distrusted; in some respects*
	Wherfore to ladies, what men speke or pray,	
	It shuld not be belovyd in noo wise."	*believed; way*
l'amant	"Of good and ille shal be and is alwey;	
750	The worlde is suche, the erthe it is not playne.	*even surfaced (i.e., uniform)*
	They that bith good, the pref shewith every day,	*are; evidence shows*
	And otherwise, gret velany, certayne.	*villainy [shows]*
	Is it reason, though oon his tonge distayne	*reasonable; speaks vilely*
	With coursed speche to doo himself a shame,	*cursed speech*
755	That suche refuse shuld wrongfully remayne	*rejection; devolve (remain)*
	Upon the good, renomyd in thaire fame?"	*known for their reputation*
la dame	"Suche as be nought, when they here tidingis new	*unworthy; hear tidings*
	That eche trespace shal lightly have perdon,	*transgression; easily (swiftly); pardon*
	They that purposith to be good and trew,	*intend*
760	(Welle sette by noble disposission	*prepared; disposition*
	To continue in good condicion),	*character*
	They are the first that fallith in damage,	*fall into trouble*
	And ful frely thaire hartis habundon	*freely; hearts abandon*
	To litill faith with soft and faire langage."	*little*
l'amant	"Now knowe I well, of verrey certaynté,	
766	If oon doo trewly, yet shal he be shent,	*destroyed*
	Sith al manere of justise and pité	*Since*
	Is banished oute of a ladis entent.	
	I cannot se but al is at o stent:	*one rate (i.e., of equal value)*
770	The good, the ill, the vise, and eke the vertu.	*vice*
	Suche as be goode, suche have the punisment	
	For the trespis of heim that bith untrew."	*those who are untrue (unfaithful)*

---

[1] *[Even] the most discreet (taciturn) [of them] much desires that some man will say*

La Belle Dame sans Mercy

la dame "I have noo power you to doo no grevaunce,
Nor to doo ponysshe noon other creature;   *punish*
775   But to eschewe the more encombraunce —   *avoid; encumbrance*
To kepe us from you al — I hold it sure.   *safe (prudent)*
Fals Semblant hath a visage ful demure,   *False Seeming; face*
Lightly to cacche the ladyes in awayte,   *catch; ambush*
Wherfore we moost, if that we will endure,   *must*
780   Make right good wacche; loo, this is my conceyte!"   *watch; lo; opinion*

l'amant "Sith that of grace o goodly worde aloone   *one*
May not be had, but alwey kept in store,
I pele to God, for He may here my moone   *appeal; hear; complaint*
Of the duresse whiche greveth me so sore.   *hardness*
785   And of pité I playne me furthermore,
Whiche He forgate in al His ordenaunce,
Or ellis my lif to have endid bifore,
Whiche He so soon put oute of remembraunce."   *forgot*

la dame "Myn hert, ner I, have doon you noo forfet   *nor; done; injury*
790   By whiche ye shuld complayn in any kinde.
There hurtith you nothing but youre owne conceyt;   *thought*
Be jugge youreself, for so ye shal it finde.   *judge*
Ons for alwey lete this synke in youre mynde —   *sink into*
That the desire shal never rejoysed be.   *attained*
795   Ye noye me sore in wasting al this winde,   *annoy; wind (i.e., breath)*
For I have said inought, as semeth me."   *enough*

This wooful man rose up in al his payne
And so deperted, with wepyng countenaunce —   *departed*
His woful hert, almoost it brast atwayne —   *broke in pieces*
800   Ful like to dye, walking forth in a traunce,   *trance (state of mental distraction)*
And said, "Now deth come forth, thyself avaunce,
Or that myn hert forget his properté,   *Before; propriety*
And make shorter al this woful penaunce   *distress (love-longing)*
Of my pore lif, ful of adversité."   *poor*

805   Fro thens he went, but whethire wist I nought,   *where (whither) knew I nothing*
Ner to what part he drowyth, in sothfastnesse.   *withdrew, truly*
But he noo more was in his ladys thought,

	For to the daunse anoon she gan hire dresse.	*right away; did direct herself*
	And afterwarde oon tolde me this expresse:	*explicitly*
810	He rent his heere, for anguissh and for payne,	*hair*
	And in hymself toke so gret hevynesse	
	That he was deed within a day or twayne.	*dead*

	Ye trewe lovers, thus I beseche you alle:	
	Suche aventours, fle heim in every wise,	*boasters, flee them*
815	And as people defamed ye heim calle;	*dishonored*
	For they, trewly, doo you gret prejudise.	*injury*
	Refuse hath mad, for al sich flateryse,	*Rejection; flatteries*
	His castellis stronge, stuffed with ordenaunce,	*castles; equipped; cannons*
	For they have hade longe tyme, by thaire office,	*[for a] long time*
820	The hole countré of Love in obeissaunce.	*whole; under [their] authority*

	And ye, ladies, or what astate ye be,	*whatever estate (rank)*
	Of whom worship hath chose his dwelling place,	
	For Goddis love, doo no suche cruelté,	
	Namly to hem that have deservyd grace.	
825	Nor in noo wise ne folow not the trace	*follow; path*
	Of hire, that here is named rightwisly,	*fittingly*
	Whiche, by reason, me semeth in this cace,	
	May be called la belle dame sanz mercy.	*the beautiful lady without pity*

L'envoy

	Goo litel boke, God sende thee good passage;	*poem*
830	Chese well thy way, be simple of manere,	*choose*
	Loke thy clothing be like thy pilgrymage,	*See [that]*
	And, specially, lete this be thy praiere	*prayer*
	Unto heim al that thee wil rede or here,	*those; will read or hear you*
	Where thou art wronge, after thaire help to calle,	*their help*
835	Thee to corecte in any part or alle.	*correct*

	Pray hem also, with thyn humble service,	
	Thy boldnesse to perdon in this cace;	
	For ellis thou art not hable in noo wise	*otherwise; able*
	To make thyself appere in any place.	*present yourself*
840	And, furthermore, beseche heim of thaire grace,	*beseech*

By thaire favoure and supportacion,   *sufferance*
To take in gre this rude translacion.   *receive with favor; unsophisticated*

The whiche, God wote, standith ful deceytute   *completely devoid*
Of eloquence, of meter, and colours;   *rhetorical elaboration*
845   Like as a best, naked, withoute refute,   *beast; shelter*
Upon a playne to abide al manere showres.   *plain; showers*
I can noo more but aske of heim socoures,   *assistance*
At whos request thou were made in this wise,   *you (i.e., the poem)*
Commaunding me with body and servise.

850   Right thus I make an ende of this prosses,   *narrative*
Beseching Him that al hath in balaunce,   *i.e., God*
That noo trewe man be vexed, causeles,   *without cause*
As this man was, whiche is of remembraunce;   *worthy to be remembered*
And alle that doon thaire faitheful observaunce   *do their*
855   And in thaire trouth purpose heim to endure,   *commit themselves*
I pray God sende heim better aventure.

Here endith la Bell Dame sanz Mercy.

Explanatory Notes to La Belle Dame sans Mercy

Abbreviations: see Textual Notes.

1–28   These first four stanzas have no parallel in the French original. They are in rhyme royal (seven-line stanzas rhyming *ababbcc*), so called because it is the stanza form of *The Kingis Quair*, attributed to James I of Scotland. Chaucer makes use of the stanza in *TC*, *PF*, portions of *Anel.*, and a number of the *CT*.

1–2   *Half in a dreme . . . undre his whynge.* The frame narrator's description of himself as half asleep describes a state not unusual in dream visions; compare Gower's *CA*, where Amans falls into a swoon near the beginning and end, but is not definitively asleep.

9   *as part of my penaunce.* As Brown points out (p. 121), the translator's *penaunce* resembles that of the narrator in Chaucer's Prologue to *LGW*.

11   *maister Alyn.* Alain Chartier, the author of the original French poem, dated 1424 (Piaget, p. vii), that forms the basis of Roos' translation.

12   *Cheif secretary with the kyng of Fraunce.* According to Sk, Chartier acted as secretary to both Charles VI and Charles VII (p. 517n11).

17 ff.   *Myn unconnyng and my gret simplesse.* The narrator's modesty is a standard disclaimer. See Lydgate's *CLL*, explanatory note to lines 190 ff., for further discussion of the convention.

22–25   *I cast my clothes on . . . a gret plesaunce.* Compare the opening lines of *RR*. Narrators of dream visions and love complaints often go to the woods, the fields, or a garden to wrestle with their problems. For more on the *locus amoenus* tradition, see the explanatory note to Clanvowe's *BC*, lines 58–60; compare also *QJ*, lines 19 ff.; and *CLL*, lines 15 ff.

29 ff.   The translation is in 8-line stanzas rhyming *ababbcbc*, following the French. Piaget notes that this was a common form in fifteenth-century French poetry (p. viii).

39–40   Compare the French: *il fault . . . que j'abandonne et delesse / Le rire pour le lermoyer*, "it is necessary . . . that I abandon and forsake / Laughter for the shedding of tears" (lines 9–12). Here, as elsewhere, the longer length of the English lines allows for added details, such as the *ful promisse* (line 39) or *clothes blake* (line 40).

41–44   In these lines the narrator of the French poem refers back to his need to quit writing verse (lines 13–16):

La me fault le temps employer,	To that end it is necessary for me to use my time,
Car plus n'ay sentement ne aise,	For I no longer have feeling or pleasure,
Soit d'escrire, soit d'envoyer	Either to write, or to address
Chose que a moy n'a autre plaise.	A work that is pleasing neither to me nor to another.

In the English there is no further reference to the "ryme or dytees for to make" (line 38); instead the narrator complains that his happy time is finished, and now his fate should be recorded: *Lete it be writen* (line 43).

47–48   Compare the French, which emphasizes the cause and effect between what the pen writes and the tongue speaks: *Ma plume n'y saroit attaindre, / Non feroit ma langue a les dire*, "My pen would not have the capacity (know how) to reach those (i.e., joyful things), / Nor would it cause my tongue to speak them" (lines 19–20).

49–52   In the French (lines 21–24), the eye contradicts the mouth through the outwards signs of the heart's feeling, its tears:

Je n'ay bouche qui puisse rire	I do not have a mouth that might laugh
Que les yeulx ne l'en desmentissent,	Without the eyes belying it,
Car le cuer l'envoyroit desdire	For the heart would attempt to contradict it
Par les larmes qui des yeulx yssent.	By the tears that would pour from the eyes.

53   *These seke lovers*. Lovers are often depicted as suffering from illness (i.e., lovesickness). See explanatory note to lines 31–35 of *BC*. Compare the French: *amoureux malades*, "enamored patients" (line 25).

55–56   *to make ballade or songes, / Every of heim as they fynde here grevaunce*. Where the English suggests that the choice of poetic form corresponds to the lovers' pain, the French represents it as a matter of taste: *Faire chançons, dis et balades, / Chascun a son entendement*, "To make songs, poems and ballades / Each according to his preference" (lines 27–28).

57–76   *For she that was my joy . . . hire tumbe igrave . . . myn hert shal never passe.* The narrator explains the reason that he is no longer able to suffer from lovesickness: the lady he loves is dead. He therefore differs from other lovers in that his "sickness" is grief, which can now never be alleviated by granting of the lady's favor. In the French, it is simply the narrator's *sentement*, "feeling/love" (line 31), that accompanies her to the grave, rather than his *wille* and *hertis ordenaunce* (line 59), and he refers to her as *la tresbonne*, "the very good" (line 45), rather than she *that was al my maistresse* (line 73).

75–76   Compare the French: *La mort m'assist illec la bonne / Qu'onques puis mon cuer ne passa*, "Death placed for me there the limit (boundary) / That afterwards my heart never surpassed" (lines 47–48).

77–84   For discussion of the setting, see explanatory note to lines 58–60 of *BC*.

103–04   *Were noon dud service within that place / But chosen men, right of the goodlyest.* The French reads simply: *Les plus gracieux les servirent*, "The most gracious served them" (line 76).

106   *there juges.* I.e., the ladies whom they desire as lovers; the word is the same in the French (line 79).

111   *As oon that hade ben ravisshed utterlye.* The French is *comme homme ravy*, "like a man enraptured" (line 83).

114   *his desire fer passed his reason.* The French reads the same: *desir passoit la raison* (line 86). Desire was associated with will. For more on the opposition between will (desire) and reason, see explanatory note to line 197 of *BC*. The proverbial version of this is "love puts reason away" (Whiting L533). Here, the lover's inability to curb himself is made evident in the following two lines, where "For ever his ey went after his entent, / Ful many a time whan it was noo season" (lines 115–16, "Always his eye acted in accordance with his desire / Full many a time when it was out of season [i.e., inappropriate]).

120   *For noo pleasaunce, but verrey shamefastnesse.* Compare the French: *Non pas pour plaisir, mais pour crainte*, "Not for pleasure, but for fear (awe)" (line 92).

127–28   *he was pale . . . in ferful wise.* Some of the typical signs of lovesickness; see *BC*, explanatory note to lines 31–35, for details. In the French, the lover is *Ennuyé*, *mesgre, blesve et palle*, "Exhausted, thin, ghastly and wan" (line 99), and, as in the English, his voice trembles (line 100).

130   *Alle blake he ware and noo devise, but playne*. The lover's clothes are unmarked by any heraldic device that would reveal his identity. The knight encountered by the narrator of Chaucer's *BD* wears black to symbolize his grief, as does the knight in *CLL* (who more precisely wears "blake and white" [line 131]). The image comes from the French: *Le noir portoit et sans devise*, "He was wearing black and without emblem" (line 102).

132   *His hert was noothing in his owne demayne*. Compare the French: *Et trop bien homme resembloit / Qui n'a pas son cuer en franchise*, "And seemed very much like a man / Who did not have his heart free" (lines 103–04).

137   *His scolemaister*. I.e., the lady he desires; presumably she "teaches" him about love. Compare Chaucer's *Complaint of Mars*, where Mars "hath wonne Venus his love, / And she hath take him in subjeccioun, / And as a maistresse taught him his lessoun" (lines 31–33). In the French poem, the lady is his *maistresse* (line 109), and it is love that constrains him: *Mais, a la fois, le contraignoit / Amours qui son cuer hardeoit / Pour sa maistresse qu'il veoit*, "But, at the same time, Love, who assailed his heart, constrained him / On account of his mistress, whom he noticed" (lines 107–09).

145–46   *of his eyn the shote . . . right humble requestis*. The trope is that of the lover who, when gazing at the desired love-object, is shot through the eye with Love's arrow, which then lodges in the heart. See *RR*, lines 1679–2008 (*Romaunt*, lines 1715–2100). Chaucer uses the image in *TC* 2.535 and 3.1086–88; and The Knight's Tale, where Palamoun "cast his eye upon Emelya, / And therwithal he bleynte and cride, 'A!' / As though he stongen were unto the herte" (*CT* I[A]1077–79; see also 1096–97). The French poem uses the same imagery (lines 117–18).

150 ff.   More signs of lovesickness; see explanatory note to lines 31–35 of *BC*.

153   *he made his ordenaunce*. According to the *MED* definitions, *ordinaunce* n. frequently occurs in contexts which refer to war or law. In the present case, the expression could be interpreted in a number of different ways, including "he marshaled his troops," "he prepared for war," "he decreed," "he organized himself." Though the phrase refers to the lover's attempt to control his expression, it could also suggest figuratively his preparation for battle (in the sense of trying to

win his lady's favor). The French reads: *Puis reprenoit son ordonnance*, "Then regained his composure." For more discussion of military imagery, see explanatory note to lines 175–80.

164   *Whiche moost he dred of lyvyng creature.* The French makes no mention of the lover's awe or fear of his lady: *Dont sur toutes plus lui chaloit*, "Which above all others was most necessary to him" (line 135–36).

174   *Oon wise ner other, pryvé ner pert.* The French uses a different opposition: *Ne plus avant ne plus arriere*, "Neither further before nor further behind" (line 146).

175–80 *A garyson . . . a frounter for a lovers hert . . . the standart of Daungere.* The narrator continues the terminology of military conquest from line 153, suggesting here that the lover will acquire a new fortress by defeating the garrison defending it beneath her *standart of Daungere* (line 180). The *standart of Daungere* might be said to represent the lady's proclaimed desire to keep herself aloof. *RR* similarly uses the language of war to describe the conquering lover (see explanatory note to line 13 in *CLL* for discussion of *Dangier*, "Resistence" in *RR*); compare to *CLL*, lines 250–59. The French poem uses these same terms (lines 147–52).

183–88 *Oute of the prese . . . noo man me aspye.* The narrator's vantage point enables him to see without being seen, establishing his credibility in reporting the dialogue between the lover and his lady which follows. Such setups are commonplace in medieval poetry. See, for example, *QJ* and *CLL*, where the narrators similarly eavesdrop. Spearing (1993) takes an extensive look at this trope.

201   *His leche.* The beloved as the doctor or source of the cure for lovesickness is a common trope; compare line 473 of *CLL*. The French poem uses the same term (line 173).

204   *in his hete to bringe him to the fire.* Love is often portrayed as hot, with the beloved as the source of heat. See, for example, *Romaunt*, lines 3707–09, where Venus carries a burning brand "Wherof the flawme and hoote fir / Hath many a lady in desir / Of love brought, and sore het"; Chaucer's *TC* 1.977–78, "Was nevere man or womman yet bigete / That was unapt to suffren loves hete." Compare also descriptions of love as a fever (in this case both hot and cold) in *BC*, line 39, and *CLL*, lines 229–45. The association is also quite common in religious contexts; see, for example, Nicholas Love's *Mirror of the Blessed Life*

of Jesus Christ: "as þe self prophete seiþ, *My herte verreyly hetede, with þe fir of cristes loue*" (ed. Michael G. Sargent [New York: Garland Publishing, 1992], p. 204/19–20; italics in original). Compare the French poem, where the image is one of self-immolation: *Car qui art ne se peut plus nuire / Qu'approchier le feu du tyson*, "For whoever burns cannot do more harm to himself / Than to approach the fire of embers" (lines 175–76).

205–07   *The hert . . . tobrest.* Compare Chaucer's *TC* 2.607–09: "For man may love, of possibilite, / A womman so, his herte may tobreste, / And she naught love ayein [i.e., return his love], but if hire leste." In the French, the heart similarly threatens to break because of these dual constraints (line 179).

209   *Desire was bolde but Shame it gan refrayne.* In *RR* Shame (*Honte*), along with Foul Mouth and Fear, is one of the three companions of Resistance (*Dangier*); the four guard the roses from lovers' attempts to steal them. See explanatory note to lines 175–80. In the French poem, it is *crainte*, "fear/awe" that restrains the lover (line 181).

211–12   Compare the French, where the image is of one *Qui porte en son cuer telle guerre*, "Who carries in his heart such war (strife)" (lines 183–84).

214   *But Shamefastnesse and Drede said ever "nay."* The French poem has simply *Se crainte ne l'eust destorné*, "If fear (awe) had not deterred him" (line 186). In *RR*, Fear is one of four companions who guard the rosebushes from the attentions of lovers. See explanatory notes to lines 175–80 and line 209.

215   *so sore he was constrayned.* The French specifies that *son cuer forsa*, "his heart compelled [him]" (line 187).

218   *With dredful voix, weping, half in a rage.* The English poem has embellished the French considerably: *Et dist bas en plorant adonques*, "And said quietly while crying (lamenting) thus" (line 190).

220   *I first hade a sight of youre visage.* "Love at first sight" is proverbial (see Whiting L496); the same trope is used in the French (line 192). Compare the passage in Chaucer's *TC* where the narrator discusses how Criseyde first came to love Troilus:

Now myghte som envious jangle thus:
"This was a sodeyn love; how myght it be
That she so lightly loved Troilus
Right for the firste syghte, ye, parde?" (2.666–69)

222   In the French, the lover accuses the lady more directly by saying *je muir pour vous bien vouloir*, "I die because you very much wish it" (line 194).

227–28   Compare the French: *Et si n'en povez pis valoir, / N'avoir mains honneur ne plus honte*, "And so you could not value it any worse, / To have neither less honor nor more shame" (lines 199–200).

230   *If that a man doo love you fastfully.* Compare the French, where there is no mention of faithfulness: *S'ung franc cuer d'homme vous veult bien*, "If the free heart of a man desires you very much" (line 202).

236   *To binde myself.* I.e., because of his love for her. See explanatory note to line 243 for more on the idea that love binds. The French reads: *Pour plus asservir ma franchise*, "In order to subjugate my freedom further" (line 208).

241–42   *Bothe faithe . . . withoute any callyng.* "Both faith and loyalty I give your ladyship, / And my service, without any demand/protest." The other MSS have *ayein callyng* for *any callyng* (see textual note), which would mean "revoking." The French reads somewhat differently: *Je serviray sans desservir / En ma loyauté observant*, "I will serve without profiting (or, recompense) / In my faithfulness compliant" (lines 213–14).

243   *Love hath me bounde.* "Love binds" is proverbial. Compare Gower's description of Venus in *CA* as "sche which mai the hertes bynde / In loves cause and ek unbinde" (ed. Peck, 8.2811–12); and *BC*, where the God of Love "can bynde and unbynde eke, / What he wole have bounde and unbounde" (lines 9–10). See Whiting L497 for further citations. The French poem does not use this metaphor: *me fist asservir / Amours d'estre vostre servant*, "Love makes me submit to being your servant" (lines 215–16).

247   *Withoute chanching of coloure or courage.* In other words, the lady does not fall in love with him, changing color being one of the signs of lovesickness (for more on this, see explanatory note to lines 31–35 of *BC*). This is one of the many signs

that she is restrained by reason rather than under the sway of emotion. The French uses the same imagery: *Sans muer couleur ne courage* (line 219).

253 ff.   In both the French and English versions, the lover continues to use the vocabulary of war, alluding also to the relationship between vassal and lord in words such as *faithful truste* and *affyaunce* (line 260). Describing the relationship between a lover and his lady in terms of vassal and lord is conventional, though the French poem does not use such language here (see the explanatory note to lines 257–60 for a detailed comparison to the French). *CLL* uses such language in line 551.

256   *Be whiche I am defyde and put afarre.* The *MED* cites this line under *defien* v. (1), 1 (b), "to despise (sth.), treat (sb.) with contempt, scorn; denounce (sth.)," and *afere* adv., meaning "in fear," which would render the line, "By which I am despised and put in fear." But *defien* v. (1), 2 (a), "to challenge (sb.) to fight, defy; declare war on (sb.)" and *afer* adv., (a) "at a distance, far off, afar" seem to fit the context better. The line then reads "By which I am challenged and put at a distance," which seems to be better supported by the French: *Par quoy deffier me feistes*, "By which you make me provoke a challenge." See explanatory note to lines 157–60, for further discussion of the *MED*'s reading of this stanza.

257   *my verrey lodesterre.* A phrase that has no parallel in the French (see explanatory note to lines 257–60). Compare Troilus's apostrophe to the absent Criseyde in Chaucer's *TC*: "Who seth yow now, my righte lode-sterre?" (5.232). The phrase is often used in religious contexts. See, for example, Lydgate's *Life of Our Lady* 5.700: "To lyfe eterne be thou our lode sterre."

257–60   Rather than simply encouraging him to keep his own faith, in the French the lover claims that in her look the lady offers both a challenge and a promise of faith on her part (lines 229–32):

Et que Doubz Regart transmeistes,	And that you would send Sweet Regard,
Herault de celle deffiance,	Herald of this challenge,
Par lequel vous me promeistes	By which you would promise me
En deffiant bonne fiance.	In challenging good faith (trust).

The *MED* suggests that *defyaunce* (line 258) should be translated as "rejection" (see *defiaunce* n., [a]), but this line from *BDSM* is the only example cited for this meaning. In addition, the context in the English (with *heraude*, line 258) and evidence of the French original would seem to support the *MED*'s meaning (b) "a challenge to combat; a declaration of war," which is how I have glossed it.

249

263   *only for beholding of an eye*. For discussion of "Love at first sight," see explanatory note to line 220.

269–72   These lines are difficult and differ somewhat from the French; the sense of the English is probably something like:

> If it be the case that one hurts another sorely
> Through the fault of the one who feels the grievance,
> Legitimately a man may do no more,
> Even though reason wishes it to be taken into consideration.

Compare the French (lines 241–44):

S'aucun blesce autry d'aventure	If one by chance wounds the other
Par coulpe de cellui qu'il blesse,	Through the fault of the one he wounds,
Quoy qu'il n'en puet mais par droitture,	While he cannot rightfully do any more about it,
Si en a il dueil et tristesce.	Yet he has pain and sorrow of it.

273–75   The lover claims that Fortune alone cannot be blamed for his lovesickness, for the lady's beauty is also at fault. Because of a few minor changes, the reading in P and Th suggests Fortune is entirely to blame: "And sithe fortune onely by her chaunce / Hath caused me to suffre all this payne / By your beaute" (H has been corrected to follow this reading by a later hand). Compare the French: *Et puis que fortune ou rudesce / Ne m'ont mie fait ce mehaing, / Mais vostre tresbelle jeunesce*, "And since fortune or unkindness (ignorance) / Has not at all caused this wound (unhappiness) / But your very attractive youthfulness" (lines 245–47).

      See explanatory note to line 80 of *QJ* for more on Fortune. The lady repeatedly makes the Boethian argument that one must rely on philosophy for stability, not Fortune. For discussion of the lady's use of Boethian themes, see Brown.

288   *That I am unware casten in youre chayne*. The metaphor differs slightly from the French, where the lover falls rather than being thrown into the lady's power: *Que je suy en voz las cheu*, "That I have fallen into your shackles (chains)" (line 260). The *MED* cites similar uses of *chaine*, 4 (b) to signify "a bond or force that constrains or dominates." For other uses of "chain" to refer to the bonds of love, see explanatory note to *CLL*, line 290.

300   *Lesse harme it were oon sorowful then twayne*. The *MED* identifies this as proverbial (see *twein* num., 2 [e]).

303–04   *Of oon sory . . . lyveth in distresse*. The French makes clear that the *oon sory* refers to the lover not the lady, saying it is better *D'un dolent faire deux joyeux*

/ *Que le dolent du tout desfaire*, "From one sufferer to make two happy people / Than to demolish utterly the one who suffers" (lines 275–76). The lover is therefore appealing to the lady to transform the single sad person (himself) into two joyful ones (himself and her) by returning his affection.

308   *In eschewing al manere of doublenesse / To make twoo joyes instede of oo grevaunce.* The French makes no mention of *doublenesse*, but focuses solely on the exchange: *Pour eschangier, sans riens mesfaire, / .Ij. plaisirs en lieux d'un mesaise*, "In order to exchange, without destroying anything, / Two pleasures in place of one constraint" (lines 279–80). Compare Theseus' advice to Palamoun and Emelye in The Knight's Tale, where, conversely, he tells the lovers: "er that we departen from this place / I rede that we make of sorwes two / O parfit joye, lastynge everemo" (*CT* I[A] 3070–72).

315   *To be rewled by manis goveraunce.* In Chaucer's Man of Law's Tale Custance proclaims, "Wommen are born to thraldom and penance, / And to been under mannes governance" (II[B¹]286–87); similarly the narrator of *QJ* describes women "lyving / Under thraldome and mannis subjectioun" (lines 199–200). But compare the French: *Je suy franche et franche vueil estre, / Sans moy de mon cuer dessaisir / Pour en faire .j. autre le maistre*, "I am free and free would like to remain so, / Without relinquishing my heart / In order to make another master of it" (lines 287–88).

324   *dere bought is the rechace.* The *MED* cites only this line for *rechace* n., "ransom, repurchase," suggesting the word is a calque on the French *les rachas* (line 296). Many of the English scribes evidently could not make sense of the line and transformed *rechace* into *richesse*, "wealth" (see textual note). The idea behind *rechace* seems to be that once a lover has declared his allegiance to Love, it costs him dearly to ransom himself from (or, buy himself out of) that bond. Compare the French: *Bien chier en coustent les rachas*, "The repurchases/ransoms of them (i.e., *Les servans* of line 293) are very expensive" (line 296).

325–32   *Ladyes bith not so semple . . . thaire eres close.* The lady suggests that women are too smart to be taken in by the insincere words of men who merely wish to seduce them. The falseness of the lover's words was a common concern of love poetry; see Benson's discussion, pp. 248–49, of courtly love and its scoundrels. The English poem corresponds closely to the French here.

329   The *MED* cites this line as an example of *holden scole*, "dispute" (see *scole* n., 2 [c]), but the context and comparison to the French would seem to require "conduct schools" (*scole* n., 1 [a]). The French reads: *Confites en belles parolles, / Don't vous autres tenez escolles / Pour leur faire croire merveilles*, "Concealed in pretty (i.e., deceitful) words, / Of which you others hold schools / To make them (i.e., the ladies) believe marvels" (lines 300–02).

338   *His fayned chere is harde to kepe in mewe.* The *fayned chere*, "feigned expression," is a common image in discussions of love. Compare *CLL*, where the knight complains that Lies use their "feyned port" to "hynder Truthe" (lines 429, 434). The idea of the expression being kept *in mewe* like a hawk does not come from the French, which reads *A peine sa faintise queuvre*, "Through effort conceals his pretense" (line 310).

345–48   In the French (lines 317–20) Love reveals his cruelty (or, wrath) in the final line of the stanza, while in the English his rage exposes the lovers' own secrets, seemingly as a consequence for their interest in Love's "secrete governaunce" (line 344):

Il les fait a soy consentir	He makes them be in agreement with him
Par une entree de chierté,	By an entry of affection,
Mais quant vient jusqu'au repentir	But when he comes upon repentance
Alors desqueuvre sa fierté,	Then he reveals his cruelty (wrath).

353   *Who hath noo colde, of hete hath noo deynté.* Whiting lists as proverbial based on this passage (C366); compare also W231, "white seems more by black." The French uses the same proverb (line 325).

364   *A will that stont enfeffid in fraunchese.* To enfeoff is to "to grant (land, an estate, an office, rights, revenue, etc.) under the feudal system" (see *MED enfeffen* v.). Lines 364–65 would translate something like: "Neither strength nor force can encroach on (overpower) / A will that is granted the right of freedom."

389–94   *A currysshe hert . . . tongis be bot fayned.* Line 394 in particular seems to have confused the scribes, since the manuscripts offer a number of different readings, none of which makes complete sense without emendation (see textual note to line 394 for details). Lines 389–92 seem fairly clear, with the sense that the cur-like (mean) heart and courteous mouth, normally incompatible, are quickly reconciled by a false outward display and placed in the power of *malice* ("hostility, ill will, wickedness, sin, malignancy, power to injure/destroy," line 392). Compare the French rendering of this idea (lines 361–64):

Villain cuer et bouche courtoise	The base heart and noble mouth
Ne sont mie bien d'une sorte.	Are not at all of one kind.
Mais faintise tost les racoise	But pretense quickly reconciles them,
Qui par malice les assorte.	Which through wickedness binds them together.

Though the *MED* cites only this line from *BDSM* for *currish* adj., the general idea may be proverbial, as Whiting lists a number of sayings that similarly point to a pleasant exterior hiding something unpleasant or poisonous (see C177, G12, H433, P289, and V19), including several illustrating the capacity for the face to hide what is in the heart. In *Of Content* Dunbar makes a similar comment: "Defy the warld, feyn3eit and fals, / Withe gall in hart and hwnyt hals [honeyed throat]" (poem 53, lines 16–17). For details, see explanatory note to *CLL*, line 426.

393–96   In these lines the French poem reiterates from the first half of the stanza the idea of the false tongue at odds with what is hidden in the heart (lines 365–68):

La mesnie Faulz Semblant s'aporte	The household of False Seeming carries
Son honneur en sa langue fainte.	Its honor in its false tongue.
Mais honneur est en leur cuer morte	But honor is dead in their heart
Sans estre plouree ne plainte.	Without being mourned or regretted.

In contrast, the English poem focuses on the comprehensive nature of the pretense (*Thaire name, thaire fame, thaire tongis be bot fayned* — line 394), and describes honor as forgotten rather than dead (line 395).

401–04   In these lines the English differs considerably from the French (lines 373–76):

Car de ma mort ne de ma perte	For my death or my loss
N'a pas vostre doulceur envie,	Your kindness does not desire,
Et, se vo grace m'est ouverte,	And, if your grace is revealed to me,
Vous estes garant de ma vie.	You are the surety for my life.

408   *that sekenesse*. The word in the French is *mal*, which can also mean "sickness" or "suffering" (line 380). The lady refers here not to love, but to the "lightsum hert" and "foly of pleasaunce" of line 405.

414   *That folowith him for love in every place*. The French reads: *Qui le suit, aime, craint et doubte*, "Who follows, loves, fears and dreads him" (line 386).

418   *withoute any chaunge*. Compare the French: *sans faintise et sans change*, "without pretense and without fraud" (line 390).

421–24   Where in the English poem the lady states that she wants to avoid injury without specifying whether she means to herself or the lover, in the French she argues that her lack of welcome is an attempt to spare the lover pain (lines 393–96):

Se je fais bonne chiere a tous	Though I give everyone a warm welcome
Par honneur et de franc courage,	In honor and out of a noble heart,
Je ne le vueil pas fair a vous	I would not wish to do so to you
Pour eschiver vostre dommage.	In order to avoid your pain (injury).

436   *That love by love were lawfull deservynge*. Proverbial; see Whiting L506, "Love for love is skillful guerdoning." See also L273 and L543. Compare Chaucer's *TC* 2.392. The French reads similarly: *Qu'amour soit par amour merie*, "That love be by love earned/rewarded" (line 408).

443–44   *Guerdoun constraynt . . . may not acord*. The French reads: *Guerredon, contrainte et renchiere / Et elle, ne vont point ensemble*, "Recompense, coercion and bidding / And her (i.e., courtesy/benevolence), do not at all go together" (lines 415–16).

447   *pardoun*. In the French this is *pur don*, "sheer gift," i.e., one that requires no exchange (line 419).

454   *That plesith on, another smertyth sore*. The *MED* identifies this as proverbial (see *plesen* v., 4; *on* pron., 3 [e]; *other* pron., 8).

467   *I have non yne, no wyt, nor mouth in store*. The list in the French also includes *cuer*, "heart" (line 439).

491   *worse it is to breke than bowe*. Proverbial: "better bow than break" (see Whiting B484 for examples). See especially *TC* 1.257–58: "The yerde is bet that bowen wole and wynde / Than that that brest." The expression is the same in the French poem: *rompre vault pis que ployer* (line 464).

502–04   Where in the English *la dame* argues that one cannot honorably take back a gift that has been given, in the French she simply says she thinks nothing of a gift *Ce qu'on offre a qui ne le prent, / Car le don est abandonné / Se le donneur ne le reprent*, "That one offers to someone who does not accept it, / For the gift is left to one side / If the giver does not take it back" (lines 474–76).

505–06   *He hath hertis ful fele that list to make / A geft lightly that put is in refuse.* This
difficult passage has given rise to a number of variants amongst manuscripts and
editors (see textual note to line 505). A literal translation of the emended lines
would read: "He has too many hearts who wishes to give / A gift eagerly that is
rejected." Perhaps having too many hearts suggests a kind of foolishness that is
meant to contrast with "he is wise" in line 507. Some readings, such as Th's,
which Sk also follows, make sense of the lines by placing *hert* in the singular and
revising *fele* to *fell*, meaning "treacherous" or "base": "He has a very treacherous
[base] heart who wishes to give / A gift lightly, which is rejected." Brown, using
Sk's edition, glosses "ful fel" as "very rash" (p. 122), another possible reading.

    The corresponding lines in the French poem offer their own difficulties and help
explain the confusion in the English: *Trop a de cuers qui entreprent / D'en donner
a qui les refuse*, "He has too many hearts (too much courage/generosity) who
ventures / To commit them to one who refuses them" (lines 477–78). The phrase
Trop a de cuers would seem to be a kind of pun, with *avoir de coeurs* used both
metaphorically, as a version of the idiom "to have courage/generosity," and literally,
"to have too many hearts," since the plural anaphor, *les*, in the next line requires a
plural referent, *cuers*. The phrase thus means both "he has too much courage/
generosity" and "he has too many hearts," an ambiguity that does not quite work in
English, where scribes had to chose between *fele*, "many," and *fel*, "rash" or
"cruel." In the following stanza the French offers a response by *l'amant* that plays
on *la dame*'s words through its reuse of use of *entreprendre* and *cuers*: *Par qui
Amours a entrepris / De tant de bons cuers la conqueste*, "By which Love under-
took / The conquest of so many good hearts" (lines 487–88).

524   *That surely cannot sette his poyntis double.* "Who cannot with certainty double
his odds." A difficult line, which Sk translates as "who cannot thoroughly afford
to double his stakes," adding "To *set* often means to stake" (p. 519n523–24). This
reading is supported by the *MED*, which cites this line from *BDSM* as one of two
examples of *setten* v., 14 (g): "to wager (sth.), stake; ~ ayenes." The line seems
to use a gaming metaphor that no longer makes sense to modern readers, but the
French has been helpful here: *Et cellui pert le jeu d'attente / Qui ne scet faire son
point double*, "And he loses the next game / Who does not know how to double
his winnings/advantage/odds" (lines 495–96). The lover who wants to woo two
women would have to double himself (or divide himself in two) and do twice as
much, as well as be duplicitous, since he would be wooing two different women
at the same time. Compare Chaucer's *Legend of Hypsipyle and Medea*, where the
narrator accuses Jason of double treachery: "There othere falsen oon, thow falsest
two!" (*LGW*, line 1377).

526   *better said than doon.* Proverbial; see Whiting S73. The French reads similarly: *mieulz dire qu'esploittier*, "better to say than to do" (line 498).

540   *Is lost and dede — clene oute of remembraunce.* Compare the French: *C'est de mourir en la poursuite*, "It is to die in the pursuit" (line 512).

546–48   *Shal dye so trewly . . . a fals lover.* This is akin to the proverbial notion that it is "better to die with honor than live in shame" (see Whiting D239), an idea that Chaucer takes up in detail in *LGW*. Compare lines 160 in *BC* and 492–96 and 525–26 in *QJ*. The French conveys the same idea (lines 518–20).

553   *Who sechith sorowe, his be the resceyte.* Proverbial; see Whiting S523. The French reads: *Qui se quiert le mal, si l'endure*, "Whoever seeks unhappiness, thus he suffers it" (line 525).

559–60   *devoure . . . deue raunson.* Not uncommonly, the lover speaks of love in terms of feudal taxes and the tribute due a lord by his vassals. Compare lines 253 ff. In the French the lover similarly asserts that *le devoir d'amours*, "the tribute (tax) of love" must be paid, since love has *prise et droit*, "the right to levy taxes and a just claim," over free hearts (lines 531–32).

565–72   *cases mervelous . . . entré is wonder perlous . . . the first asay.* The lady describes the lover's venture as if it were a knight's perilous quest from which he might not safely return. In his discussion of courtly love, Benson shows that knights were undertaking actual feats of arms and other trials to prove their love (pp. 249–51). The French similarly uses the language of quest, detailing *tant de cas merveilleux*, "so many marvelous situations" (line 537), *l'entrer en est perilleux*, "the entering of [which] is perilous" (line 539), and *l'essay*, "the risk/ordeal," that costs so much (line 544).

585   *who that prayeth and sueth in any cace.* The lady here charges the lover with wooing indiscriminately. There are legal overtones in the English terms *sueth* and *case* (underscored by the phrase "no trouth is preved" in line 586) that do not occur in the French: *Qui encor poursuit et requiert*, "Whoever persistently chases and entreats" (line 557).

608–12   These corresponding lines in the French (lines 580–84) convey a stronger sense both of the lady's effect on the lover and of the lover's guilt in the hypothetical case presented:

> Le don de grace et le bien fait   The gift of grace and the good accomplished
> De sa dame qui l'a refait   By his lady who has revived him
> Et ramené de mort a vie.   And brought him back from death to life.
> Qui se souille de tel meffait   Who tarnishes himself with such wrong
> A plus d'une mort deservie.   Has deserved more than one death.

613–16   In the French (lines 585–88) the judge and court curse and condemn the lover:

> Sur telz meffais n'a court ne juge   Against such crimes there is neither court nor judge
> A qui on puisse recourir.   To which one might appeal.
> L'un les maldit, l'autre les juge,   The one curses them, the other condemns them,
> Mais je n'en ay veu nul mourir.   But I have not seen anyone die of it.

In contrast, the English suggests that lovers curse and threaten when they do not get their way in love: *Oon cursith fast, another doith manace, / Yet dyeth noon, as for as I can se* (lines 615–16).

634–35   *reclaymed to the lure . . . hem to withholde.* The *MED* cites this line and translates "brought under control" (see *reclamen* v., 2 [d]) Sk translates as "taught to come back; a term in falconry" and sees the phrase in opposition to "*hem to withholde* [line 635], i.e. to keep themselves from coming back" (p. 520n634), but *welle lerned hem to withholde* would seem to mean "well trained to hold themselves back" — in other words, hearts do not come and go as they please (see line 633), but are taught to return when called and trained to remain at Love's behest, though they change just when love should be strongest. The French differs slightly: *Car ilz les ont bien reclamez / Et si bien apris qu'ilz retiennent / A changier desqu'ilz sont amez*, "For they have well called them back / And [they are] so well taught that they stay / To become changed as soon as they are loved" (lines 606–08).

656   *stille as stoon.* This proverbial phrase does not occur in the French: *Car nul d'eulx ne s'est rebellez*, "For none of them is disobedient (rebellious)" (line 628). For extensive citations of the proverb in English, see Whiting S772 and the related "Stone-still," S772a.

657   *Thaire wille and myn ben meduled al in oon.* Compare the French: *Ilz sont parmy desir meslez*, "They are in the midst of desire mingled" (line 629).

666–68   *I am alwey . . . to youre pleasaunce.* Compare the French: *Que je sui celle que je fus. / D'avoir mieulx ne vous affiez / Et prenez en gré le reffus*, "That I am that which I was. / Do not expect (trust) to have better, / And take in good part the refusal" (lines 638–40).

671–72   *But now, alas, it is shit up so fast / That Daungere sheweth on me his cruelté.* In the English poem *it* presumably refers back to the lady's "pité" (line 670); compare the French, where it is the lady herself that is closed up in her fortress: *mais elle est enfermee / Et lesse Dangier m'assaillir,* "but she is fortified / And allows Resistance to attack me" (lines 643–44). For more on *Daungere,* see explanatory note to lines 175–80.

673–76   Compare the French (lines 645–48):

Et s'el voit ma vertu faillir	And if she sees my virtue fail
Pour bien amer, el s'en saudra.	For loving well, she will go out from there.
Lors sa demeure et tart saillir	In that case her delay and late departure
Et mon bien souffrir me vaudra.	And my much-endured pain will be profitable to me.

     The English emphasizes the lover's suffering no matter what happens, whereas the French implies that the lover's pain is worthwhile if his failing virtue causes the lady to leave the metaphorical fortress where she is defended by Resistance, as presumably he then can get access to her (see explanatory note to lines 671–72).

697–98   *If a lady wol doo so gret outrage / To shewe pité and cause hire owne debate.* The *MED* cites line 698 as its only example of *debate* n., "lowering, degradation." Compare the French: *Se dame est a autrey piteuse / Pour estre a soy mesme cruelle,* "If a woman shows pity to another / In order to be merciless to herself."

714   *pité manerlesse.* This idea comes from the French: *pitié sans maniere* (line 686); the *MED* cites only this line under *manerles* adj.

717–24   *O marble hert . . . chacith me alwey.* The marble heart is proverbial and is listed in Whiting M370 under "as hard as marble (stone)"; compare the French: *cuer plus dur que le noir marbre,* "heart harder than black marble" (line 689). For the lover's suggestion that he will die if the lady does not comfort him, compare Troilus' speech in Book 5 of *TC*: "O lady myn, that I love and na mo, / To whom for evermo myn herte I dowe, / Se how I dye, ye nyl me nat rescowe!" (5.229–31). See also explanatory note to line 812. Lovers often claim hyperbolically that they will die for love, so it is not unusual for the lady to take this with a grain of salt. For more on this trope, see explanatory note to *CLL,* lines 512 ff.

741   *Malabouche.* "Foul Mouth" or "Slander." See explanatory note to lines 260–68 in *CLL,* for discussion of this allegorical figure. Though Foul Mouth's role is usually to spread tales about the lover to discredit him with his lady, the lady here

uses *Malabouche* to refer to the lovers themselves as tale-bearers who cannot be trusted in what they say to the ladies they attempt to win.

750   *playne*. The phrase in the French is *toute unie*, "completely uniform" (line 722).

777   *Fals Semblant*. "False Seeming," i.e., a hypocrite. In *RR* (lines 12361–540) False Seeming tricks Foul Mouth into confessing to him, strangles him, cuts out his tongue with a razor, and tosses him into a moat. This allows the lover passage into the rose garden.

799–800   *His woful hert, almoost it brast atwayne — / Ful like to dye*. A conventional expression of sorrow. See line 576 in *CLL* (and explanatory note). Although the lover seems utterly vanquished by the lady's refusal, the narrator's use of words such as *almoost* and *Ful like* suggests that the situation may be exaggerated. Compare the French: *A poy que son cuer ne creva / Comme a homme qui va mourant*, "His heart was just a little short of breaking / Like to a man who is going to die" (lines 771–72).

809   *oon tolde me this expresse*. Unlike the witnessed conversation between the two potential lovers, the narrator reports news of the lover's death at second hand. See explanatory note to lines 799–800. (The French reads the same, line 781).

812   *he was deed within a day or twayne*. Compare Troilus' death in Book 5 of *TC*. See explanatory note to *CLL*, lines 512 ff., for discussion of lovers' claims that they will die for love. In the French, the lover gets so upset he dies *de courroux*, "of rage" (line 784).

813 ff.   Addressing lovers and/or ladies (as at the beginning of line 821) at the end of the poem is typical of love complaints. Compare, for example, the apostrophes to lovers at the ends of *CLL*, lines 653 ff., and *QJ*, lines 582 ff.

829 ff.   The narrator's expressions of poetic inadequacy, as at the beginning of the poem, are conventional. Compare such disclaimers at the ends of *QJ* (lines 584 ff.) and many of Chaucer's poems. See also the explanatory note to lines 17 ff. The final four stanzas, like the initial four, have no parallel in the French original. These lines are an envoy addressed to the poem, a practice, borrowed ultimately from classical poets, that is used by Chaucer at the end of *TC*: "Go, litel bok, go, litel myn tragedye" (5.1786). See explanatory note to lines 674 ff. of *CLL*, for further discussion.

Textual Notes to La Belle Dame sans Mercy

Abbreviations: **F** = Bodleian Library MS Fairfax 16, fols. 50r–62v; **Ff** = Cambridge University Library MS Ff.1.6 (Findern MS), fols. 117r–134v; **FJF** = Frederick J. Furnivall; **H** = British Library MS Harley 372, fols. 61r–69v; **L** = Longleat House MS 258, fols. 120r–136v [base text]; **P** = Richard Pynson; **Sk** = Walter W. Skeat; **T** = Cambridge, Trinity College MS R. 3. 19, fols. 98r–108v; **Th** = William Thynne (1532).

title	L: *La bell dame sauns mercy* (in later hand). F: *Balade de La bele Dame sanȝ mercy*. Ff: *Chaucer's La belle dame sans mercy* (in later hand; note that this contradicts the colophon). H: *La belle dame sanȝ mercy translatid out of ffrenche by Sir Richard Ros* (in upper right corner in scribe's hand). T: *la bell dame saunce mercy* and *by Chaucer* (added in two different, later hands). P: *This boke called la bele Dame Sauns mercy was translate out of Frenche in to Englysshe by Geffray Chaucer flour of peotes in our mother tong.* Th: *La belle dame sans mercy.*
	In Ff, line 1 is preceded by *Prologe*. In P, the whole poem is preceded by *the prologue* followed by a plate at the top of the page.
1	*nat.* H: omits.
6	*more.* L: *any more.*
7	*hem.* L: *him.* F, Ff, H, P, Th: *hem.* T: *hyr.*
	the whiche. H: *to wham.* Th: *whiche.*
	dissobaye. H: *sey nay.*
8	*this.* Ff, T: *þus.*
9	*as.* L: *was.*
13	*I.* T: omits.
19	*thus.* L: *this.*
20	*vexed.* L: *wexed.*
26	*bolded.* T: *voldyd.* P, Th: *boldly.*
27	*rede.* T: *to rede.*
33	*hire.* F, Ff, H, T, P, Th: *his.*
34	*The deth hath.* T: *Dethe hath fro me.*
35	*thus.* T: *thys.*
36	*in.* L: omits.
39	*And I, surely.* T: *And yet therwith.*

41   *is it.* P, Th: *dothe it.*

42   *fele.* T: *fynde.*

43   *I take.* P, Th: *(as I take).*

47   *My penne cowde never have knowlech.* F: *Myn eyn cowth haue no knowlych.* H: *Myn eyen coude haue knowlege*, corrected by later hand in margin to *My penn could neuer know.* T: *My pen cowde haue no knowlege.* P, Th: *My pen coude neuer knowe.* "Eyes" is a mistake, since the French has *plume*, "pen" (line 19).

53   *heim.* This is a common spelling by the scribe for *hem*, as noted by Hammond (1905), p. 78.

           longes. L: *longed.*

56   *fynde.* F, Ff, H, T, P, Th: *fele.*

60   *bethe.* F, H, T, P, Th: *lyth.*

           with hire undre hire. P, Th: *here within this.*

           igrave. F, H: *in grave.*

64   *now.* T: *nygh.*

66   *was speryd.* F: *were sprad.* H: *was spradde*, with *spradde* corrected by later hand in margin to *sparede.*

72   *causid neither joye ner.* T: *causeth no ioy but.*

73   *al my.* F: *my good.* H, T, P, Th: *my.*

74   *My good.* F, H, T: *Al my.* P, Th: *My.*

75   *sete.* H: *sette*, corrected by later hand in margin to *shette.* P, Th: *shette.*

80   *cast.* H: *purposid.*

81   *for to.* H: *forth to.*

88   *yet.* F, Ff, H, T: omit.

           I. F: omits.

95   *ever, oon by oon.* F, Ff, H: *euereche be on and one.* T: *euery by oon and oone.* P, Th: *euery one by one.*

96–97   T transposes these lines.

97   *gret.* T: *theyr.*

98   *morne.* T: *mone.*

103   *Were.* L: *Where.* T, P, Th: *There were.*

           noon dud service within that. F, H: *none that serued in that.* Ff, T: *non þat dide seruyse within þat.* P, Th: *no deedly seruauntes in the.*

105   *there were summe.* F, H: *some they were.* Ff, T, P, Th: *sum þer were.*

106   *sitting.* P, Th: omit.

117   *good.* P, Th: omit.

           right. P, Th: omit.

           he. Ff: omits.

           payned. T: *feynyd.*

123   *expresse.* T: *doutles.*
124   *forest.* L: *fforest.*
126   *noon.* F, H: *not.*
          like. F, H, T, P, Th: *lyke hym.*
          as after. T: *for soth to.*
128   *His speche also trembled.* T: *He spake also tremblyng.*
132   *noothing.* T: *then nat.*
134   *And.* T: *As*
135   *But.* T: *And.*
136   *done.* L, F, Ff, H: *doo.*
          noon other. T: *no bettyr.*
144   *moost.* T: *euer.*
145   *And.* P, Th: *For.*
          shote. H: *sight*, corrected by later hand to *shott* in margin.
          knewe. L: *kewe.*
146   *fedred.* P, Th: *fearfull.*
148   *I, or that.* F, H: *ther that* (H: corrected by later hand in margin to *I or þat*). Ff: *or y that.*
          gestis. P, Th: *iestes.*
150   *hevy.* F: *his heuy.*
151   *tendirly.* H: *tendirly*, corrected by later hand in margin to *wondersly.* P, Th: *wonderly.*
155   *for to juge his.* T: *to beholde with.*
          moost. F: omits.
          rewful semblaunce. H: *iuful semblance.* P, Th: *wofull penaunce.*
156   *it.* F: *is.*
158   *aboute.* Th: *aboue.*
159   *hevy.* F, H, T: *heuy louer.* P, Th: *heuy man he.*
160   *sumtyme.* L: *sutyme.* There may be a suspension mark over the *u* to indicate an *m.*
          with₂. F, Ff, H, T: *but with.*
161   *after.* T: *euer.*
163   *amonge.* Ff: *anone.*
164   *dred.* T: *louyd.*
165   *good.* H: *god*, corrected by later hand above line to *good.*
170   *thaire eyen, withouten.* T: *suche oon then without.*
172   *he.* Ff: *she.*
173   *as.* Ff, T, P, Th: *that.*
174   *wise.* L, F, H: *vise* (H: corrected by later hand in margin to *wise*).
175   *garyson.* F, Ff, H: *garnison.* T: *grainyson.*

176	*frounter*. L: *frente*.
178	*well*. T: *well with*.
	hire port. P, Th: *of porte*.
	eke. F, Ff, H, T: *eke hir*. P, Th: *eke of*.
179	*Well*. T: *Went*.
184	*alone*. F, H: omit.
186	*wetheys*. P, Th: *wrethes*.
	wonderlye. T: *full wondyrly*.
188	*me*. T: omits.
189	*this*. F, Ff, H, T, P: *his*.
190	*he thought tyme*. T: *he hym thought*.
191	*Sith*. H: *Sithe*, corrected by later hand in margin to *Sett*. P, Th: *Set*.
193	*a certeyne of compace*. T: *a certayn space*. P, Th: *of a certayne compase*.
198	*nere*. L, Th: *more*. The word in the French is *prez*, "near" (line 170).
	sought. T: *thought*.
199	*His*. T: *Whos*.
204	*hete*. F, H: *hert* (H: corrected by later hand in margin to *heat*).
211	*on*. L: added by another hand in large gap between *leyde* and *hym*.
213	*payned*. T: *feynyd*.
213–20	Missing in F.
216	*hade longe*. Ff, H, T, P, Th: *full longe hadde*.
219	*unhappy*. T: *happy*.
221	*hote*. T: *sore*.
224	*noon hede of it*. T: *therof hede*.
	kynnys. T: *maner*.
225	*in*. F, Ff, T: *my*.
	advise. T: *deuyse*.
227	*sue*. L: *suffre*. T: *shew*.
228	*youre*. I have expanded the superscript abbreviation here and in lines 241, 668, 702, 734, 791, 793 with a final *-e* to reflect the scribe's spelling elsewhere.
230	*fastfully*. F, Ff, H, T, P, Th: *faythfully*.
231	*youre*. T: *euery*.
	eschewing. F, H: *escusyng* (H: corrected by later hand in margin to *eschewing*).
233	*chalang nought*. T: *shall nat*. H: *chalenge not*, with *not* corrected by later hand in margin to *nought*.
235	*right$_2$*. F, H: *even*. T: omits.
236	*To*. T: *Do*.
237	*be so that I cannot*. T: *so be I can hit nat*.
241	*geve*. Ff: *ȝe*.

263

242   *any*. F, Ff, H, T: *ayein.*

245   *his.* F, H, P, Th: *this.*

249   *la dame.* Based on F, Ff, and H, which include speech markers, I have added *la dame* here and throughout to indicate when the lady is speaking. I have also added *l'amant* where appropriate to mark the lover's speech, starting at line 253.

      youre thought is. F, H: *ye do full.* T: *your hert ys.*

251   *and.* Ff: *an.*

252   *this.* T: *your.*

      pese. T: *ese.*

256   *defyde.* T: *deferryd.*

      afarre. Ff, H, T: *a fer.* The *MED* cites H as an example of *afere* adv., meaning "in fear," but *afer* adv., (a) "at a distance, far off, afar" seems to fit the context better. See explanatory note for discussion of the French.

258   *thilke same.* T: *thys saunce.*

259   *for to berre.* F, Ff, H, T: *to forbarre.*

262   *hath.* P, Th: omit.

265   *to beholde.* P, Th: *ye may beholde.*

267   *noo.* T: *in.*

268   *felyth smart.* T: *seketh harme.*

270   *the.* Ff: *no.*

273   *nat.* H: marked for deletion. P, Th: omit.

      his. H: *his*, corrected by later hand in margin to *hir.* P, Th: *her.*

275   *But.* H: *But*, corrected by later hand in margin to *By.* P, Th: *By.*

278   *naught.* F, H, T: *neuer.*

281   *love.* F, Ff, H: *beleue* (H: corrected by later hand in margin to *loue*). T: *conseyte.*

282   *gret.* F, H, P, Th: omit.

      pleasaunce. P, Th: *displesaunce.*

283   *make.* T: *mok.*

285   *thus.* F, Ff, H: *this.*

286   *me.* T: omits.

287   *chasid.* T: *enbrasyd.*

297   *now.* H: *nought.* T: *few.*

301   *it.* F, H: *I* (H: corrected by later hand in margin to *it*).

302   *Muche better were.* T: *Hyt were bettyr.*

303   *sory.* F, H: *sorow* (H: corrected by later hand in margin to *sory*).

      well. L: omits.

306   *to.* T: *I.*

310   *Ner right gret love, ner gret affyaunce.* F, H, T: *Nor grete desire nor ryght grete affiaunce.* P, Th: *Nor haue therin no great affyaunce.* The French reads: *Ne grant espoir ne grant desir,* "Neither great hope nor great desire."

311   *doith.* F: omits.

316   *that.* H: written in margin by later hand and marked for insertion.

318   *al.* F, H: omit.

319   *hem.* T: *yow.*

       thaire. T: *yowre.*

321   *nought hath of.* H: *not hath of,* with *not* corrected by later hand in margin to *nought.* T: *hath noon.*

324   *bought is the rechace.* F: *bought ys rychesse.* H: *his richesse bought has.* P, Th: *bought is the richesse.* The French is *les rachas* (line 296), indicating the English should be *rechace,* not *richesse;* the explanatory note gives a more detailed comparison with the French.

329   *moo.* T: *me.*

       holde scoles of. H: *scoolys holden.*

       duly. H: *dieulye,* corrected by later hand in margin to *daily.* P, Th: *dayly.*

330   *al.* H: omits.

       wondres. L: *wondre is.*

337   *hole.* T: *nat sore.*

       sore. T: *nat sore.*

340   *preveth.* T: *present.*

       sewe. H: *sewe,* corrected by later hand in margin to *shew.* T, P, Th: *shew.*

341   *awayte.* F, H: *abayte* (H: corrected by later hand in margin to *awayte*).

342   *in gabbyng.* L: *and gabbyng.*

345   *hem.* L: *him.*

346   *him.* Ff, T, P, Th: *hem.*

350   *to.* L: omits.

351   *this.* L, T, P, Th: *thus.*

352   *Yet.* F, H: *It.*

       greveth. L: *grveth.*

354   *axed.* L: *axex.*

355   *noon.* T: *nat.*

       the. P, Th: omit.

       certaynté. Th: *certeyne.*

356   *be wonne.* Ff: *wone.* H: *be wonnen,* with *wonnen* corrected by later hand in margin to *one.* T: *wonen be.* P, Th: *one.*

357   *As.* L: *And as.*

358	*to you is*. L: *thought is*. F, Ff, H: *yow is* (H: *is* corrected by later hand in margin to *thinke*). P, Th: *yow thinke*.
360	*love*. T: *lyve*.
	vayne. L: *wayne*.
361	*chalange*. T: *shall*.
	never. T: *men*.
362	*and*. Ff, T: *or*.
363	*ne*. P, Th: *and*.
	certayne. P, Th: omit.
366	*as*. P, Th: omit.
371	*unrightfully*. F, Ff, H, T: *ryght wysly*.
372	*Oon*. L: omits.
377	*laugh*. T: *dysplesyn*.
386	*man of*. P, Th: *maner*.
387	*leyth*. H: *latith*. T: *lesyth*.
389	*currysshe*. P, Th: *cursed*.
393	*and*. F, H: *a*.
	Trewsemyng. H: *trewe menyng*, which Sk follows.
394	*be bot fayned*. L: *be unfayned*. F, H: *be not feyned* (H: *not* corrected by later hand in margin to *but*). P, Th: *but fayned*. Sk's emendation.
396	*Nought*. F: *Not*.
399	*youre*. T: *hys*.
401	*whether*. F, H: *wher*.
403	*if*. P, Th: *of*.
404	*Then*. P, Th: *That*.
	sone. T: omits.
410	*men*. P, Th: *me*.
411	*not*. T: omits.
412	*I*. Ff: omits.
	him. F, Ff, H: *yt*. P, Th: *them*.
413	*bride*. H: *bridde*, corrected by later hand in margin to *bird*.
415	*him$_2$*. H: omits.
416	*Oute*. T: *But*.
	him. H: omits.
	enchace. L: final *-e* unreadable.
419	*Am*. H: *And*, corrected by later hand in margin to *Am*.
422	*of*. P, Th: *for*.
425	*so*. T: omits.

429–76   L: a lost folio means these lines are missing; the missing lines are supplied by Ff, whose readings are closest to L. Beginning here, F and H misorder the lines: 669–716, 325–72, 477–524, 621–68, 573–620, 429–476, 717–856.

432   *heme.* P, Th: *hym.*

433   *is.* T: *ys to.*

436   *deservynge.* P, Th: *desyring.*

438   *tendurly.* F, H: *best and tendyrly.*

444   *may not.* P, Th: *can neuer.*

445   *case.* T: *place.*

448   *deth.* Ff: omits.

450   *a courteys.* F, H: *curteysy.*

452   *lovely.* T: *lowly.*

454   *another.* T: *and other.*

456   *all.* P, Th: omit.

461   *never formyd.* P, Th: *founded neuer.*

468   *But.* H: *That ne.*

475   *his.* F, H: omit.

477   L resumes at this point.

       eyen. L: *owne eyen.*

       the prynte. T: *theym present.*

481   *thus.* P, Th: *this.*

485   *se.* L: *so.*

486   *ye spende not youre season.* F, H: *your seson spend not.*

489   *refrayne.* F, H: *restreyn.*

492   *Better.* F, H, T: *And bettir.*

       falle to. P, Th: *to fall.*

494   *his.* F, H: *your.*

495   I_1. T, P, Th: *Hit.*

502   *it is.* L: *it* written above line.

505   *hertis ful fele.* L: *hertis ful fell.* F, H: *hert ful fele.* T: *hertis full fele.* P, Th: *an hert full fell.* See explanatory note for further discussion.

505   *list.* L: *list not.*

506   *in.* L: omits. P, Th: *to.*

508   *nother.* F, H: *neuer.*

509   *He.* F: *Who.*

511   *spende.* L: *spede.*

514   *Or.* L: *On.*

517   *counsaille.* L: *counsalle.*

518   *Sechith fairer.* T: *Secheth ferther.*

523	*lesith.* H: *hofithe* or *hosithe*, though the letter in question looks more like the scribe's *f* than his *s*. Sk reads *hosithe* as a scribal error for *leseth*, but *MED hoven* v. (1), 2 (a), "wait in readiness or expectation," makes *hofithe* a possibility too.
527	*Though.* L: *Thought.*
529	*it may not.* F: omits *not.* P, Th: *I ne may.*
530	*thing whiche.* T: *thynke that.*
531	*it are.* H: *it ar*, with *it* corrected by later hand in margin to *I see.* P, Th: *I se be.*
	fantasise. L: *fantese.*
532	*of.* Ff: omits.
533	*folely.* L: *not folely.* P, Th: *no foly.*
534	*And whan him list.* T: *When he.*
	part therfroo. L: *the part froo.*
537–38	Ff: these lines are transposed and marked *b* and *a* in margin for reversal.
538	*sowte.* F, H: *suerte* (H: corrected by later hand in margin to *sute*).
	desperaunce. T: *esperaunce.*
539	*And alle.* L: *Alle.*
	good. T: *goodys.*
540	*lost and dede.* F: *left as dethe.* Ff, H: *lefte as dede.* T: *left all deede.*
542	*may.* P, Th: omit.
	whatever be. T: *what oon by.*
544	*That dethe shal doo me not noo.* L: *They shal doo me not noo.* F: *That deth shal do me no.* H: *That deth shal not doo me noo*, with *That* corrected by later hand in margin to *Than*, and *not* marked for deletion. P, Th: *Than dethe shall do me no.*
545	*ful.* P, Th: omit.
551	*nor maner.* P, Th: *no man.*
553	*his be.* T: *by.* H: *is by*, corrected by later hand in margin to *his be.*
556	*therto.* H: *þer to*, with *to* corrected by later hand in margin to *of.* P, Th: *therof.*
557	*assayed.* H: *saied*, corrected by later hand to *assaied* by adding *as* above line.
559	*devour.* F, H: *dewtis.* P, Th: *honour.*
567	*entré.* P, Th: *auenture.*
568	*commyng.* L: *connyng.*
	agayn. L: *certayn.*
571	*barayn.* P, Th: *a barayne.*
575	*oute.* H: *ought*, corrected by later hand in margin to *out.*
577	*pref.* P, Th: *prise.*
582	*And so.* L: *so* written above line.
583	*deserve.* P, Th: *discerne.*
585	*sueth.* P, Th: *swereth.*
	cace. T: *place.*

586	*no.* F: omits.
	trouth. L: *th* written before *trouth* and canceled.
587	*grace.* L: omits.
590	*the contraye.* F, Ff, H, T, P, Th: *contrary.*
591	*that₂.* L: *al.*
592	*lovely.* T: *lothely.*
595	*hire.* H: *here,* corrected by later hand in margin to *hir.*
597	*he.* Ff, T: *ye.*
599	*body, his thought.* T: *bodyes thought.* F: *body thoughty.*
	al awaye. T: *alwey.*
600	*From.* F: *For.*
	hem. L: *him.*
	sore. F, Ff, H, T: *sorowe.*
602	*Love.* T: omits.
	gret. F, Ff, H, T: *ryght grete.*
604	*so.* F: omits. P, Th: *full.*
605	*haveles.* P, Th: *harmlesse.*
608	*anything.* L: *any othing.*
	at. F: omits.
609	*his lady.* T: *ys.*
614	*oon.* H: *one,* corrected by later hand in margin to *love.* P, Th: *loue.*
617	*thaire.* L: *hire.*
	oo degré. Ff: *ordre.*
618	*evermore.* F, H: *euere newe.*
619	*gret.* F, H: omit.
622	*juyse.* H: *juyse,* corrected by later hand in margin to *justice.* P, Th: *no iustyce.*
625	*that ever is good.* T: omits *ever.* P, Th: *euer said god.*
626	*so.* P, Th: omit.
627	*high.* F, H: *her.* T: *theyr.* P, Th: *his.*
629	*Of.* T: *Yef.*
	gret. F, H: omit. (H: added by later hand above line — *great*).
632	*for.* P, Th: *in.*
641	*remewe.* T: *renew.*
643	*As.* F, H: omit.
	that. F, H: *al that.*
645	*ye.* P, Th: *it.*
647	*deceyved.* F: *deceyved that.*
648	*lyghtly.* P, Th: *light.*
649	*youre.* F, H: *this.*

650	*sumwhat have.* P, Th: *haue some.*
651	*better.* F, H: *sunner.*
	foule symplenesse. F, H: *foly symplesse.*
652	*desesperaunce.* L: *deseperaunce.* T: *esperaunce.*
654	*oon.* L: *oooon.*
656	*stille.* T: *fall.*
657	*myn ben.* Ff: *mynd as.*
659	*as.* F, H: *is.*
661	*Who loveth not himself, whatever he be.* P, Th: *Ye loue nat your selfe what euer ye be.*
	loveth. T: *leuyth.*
662	*In.* P, Th: *That in.*
	he. P, Th: omit.
665	*in.* P, Th: *as in.*
668	*levyth.* T: *loueth.*
670	*faille.* P, Th: *lacke.*
674	*then she to.* L: *though she to.* P, Th: *though she do.*
675	*the.* P, Th: *my.*
676	*it.* T: *I.*
677	*Leve.* T: *Loue.*
	youre. F, H, P, Th: *the.*
678	*thus.* P, Th: *is.*
681	*fayne.* L: *gayne.*
682	*founde asoted.* T: *bounde assured.*
	dotage. Ff: *dotaye.*
684	*That.* P, Th: omit.
	Hope. L: omits.
	thaire wage. Ff: *your waye.*
690	*by.* T: *hygh.*
694	*of.* P, Th: *do no.*
697	*wol.* F, H: omit.
700	*dedly.* T: *dewly.*
701	*him.* T, P, Th: *theym.*
	lyve. T: *byn.*
702	*worship.* P, Th: *conforte.*
703	*have.* F, Ff, H, T: *bere.*
704	*A faire body iformed to the same.* P, Th: *And a fayre lady I must affyrme the same.*
705	*defame.* L: *fame.*
707	*may al this.* Ff: *may not þis.*

710   *that.* P, Th: *well.*

711   *Ought.* L: *Ough.*

            wrothe, or. T: *wrother.*

712   *as he.* L: *and.*

714   marginalia. H: *manerles pyte* written in margin.

            might. L: *night.*

            manerlesse. P, Th: *mercylesse.*

717   *yet more harde.* T: *more hardyr.*

718   *perce.* T: *parte.*

724   *chacith.* T: *calleth.*

725   *desease.* L: *dease.*

726   *overshake.* T, P, Th: *ouerslake.*

727   *ye.* L: *I.*

728   *heille.* T: *lyfe.*

729   *nyll not hate myn hert.* H: corrected by later hand in margin to *I will not hurt my selfe.* P, Th: *I wyll nat hurt my selfe.*

730   *laugh they.* T: *or lawgh.*

            singe. P, Th: *syng they.*

            this. T: *thus.* P, Th: omit.

731   *wol I.* L: *well to.* Ff: *wele I.* I emend for sense, based on T, P, Th: *wyll I.* The French helps clarify: *Mais, se je puis, j'y pourverray / Que vous ne autre ne s'en vante,* "But, if I can, I will ensure / That you nor another can boast about it" (lines 703–04).

732   *you.* P, Th: *them.*

733   *songe.* P, Th: *loue.*

735   *I₁.* P, Th: *ye.*

744   *to bost.* H: *to boste,* corrected by later hand in margin to *best.* P, Th: *best.*

            to₂. T: *and.*

745   *well that.* H: corrected by later hand in margin to *ywis yet.* P, Th: *ywis yet.*

746   *partyse.* H: *party,* corrected to *partyes* with addition of *es* by later hand.

747   *to ladies, what men speke or pray.* T: *these louers whatsoeuer they say.* P, Th: *whan so men speke or say.*

            men. L omits.

748   *noo.* L: *n* unreadable.

750   *erthe it is not playne.* L *erthe is playne.* F, H: *deth yt is not playn* (H: corrected by later hand in margin to *earth is not all*). P, Th: *therth is nat all playn.*

753   *distayne.* H: *disteryne,* corrected by later hand in margin to *distaine.* The *er* combination looks as if it has been written over with *a.*

756   *renomyd in thaire fame.* T: *renewyd in hys name.*

760	*Welle.* L: *Wolle.* T: *Wyll.* P, Th: *Wyll not.*
	noble. P, Th: *none yll.*
761	*continue.* L: *conceyve.*
	good. P, Th: *euery good.*
763	*thaire hartis.* F: *ther.* H: *theym.* P, Th: *the hertes.*
768	*banished.* L: *bannshed.*
770	*the ill.* F, H, T: *and ylle.*
	the vertu. Ff, T: *vertu.*
771	*suche₂.* F, Ff, H, T: *shal.*
772	*bith.* P, Th: *lyue.*
774	*doo ponysshe.* T: *promyse.*
776	*from.* L: *frendis.*
777	*visage.* P, Th: *face.*
779	*that we will.* P, Th: *we wyll here.*
781	*aloone.* P, Th: *nat one.*
782	*not.* P, Th: *nowe.*
783	*pele.* T: *speke.*
784	*so.* T: omits.
788	*He so soon.* H: *he* corrected by later hand in margin to *am.* P, Th: *so soone am.*
789	*noo.* T: omits.
791	*you.* T: *then.*
	owne. F, Ff, H, T: omit.
793	*Ons for.* L: *Thus for.* P, Th: *Thus.*
794	*the.* L: *ye.* T, P, Th: *your.*
	rejoysed. P, Th: *recouered.*
795	*al this.* T: *of your.*
798	*wepyng.* T: *heuy.*
	Marginalia in F: *Verba auctoris* ("words of the author").
800	*a.* L: written above line.
801	*Now.* T, P, Th: omit.
	thyself. T: *and thysylf.*
803	*shorter.* F: *short.*
807	*his.* T: omits.
809	*oon.* T: *and.*
	this. F: omits. H: *it.* T, P, Th: *thus.*
813	*Ye.* L, Th: *The.*
	thus. F, H: *this.*
813 ff.	P replaces the final six stanzas with his own, heading the section with *Lenuoy de limprimeur* ("envoy of the printer"). Thynne uses L from this point on.

814   *Suche.* T: *All.*

               aventours. F, Th: *aventures.* H: *aventure.*

               every. T: *any.*

817   L, Th: omit this line; supplied by Ff. There is a mark between lines 816 and 818 in the MS that seems intended to note the omission.

824   L, Th: omit this line; supplied by Ff. There is a mark between lines 823 and 825 in the MS that seems intended to note the omission.

               have. H: omits.

825   *folow.* L: *foule.* F, H: *folowe ye.*

828–29   *L'envoy.* L: *Lenvoy* (written between stanzas). F: *Explicit la bele dame san3 mercy.* Ff: *Explicit* in margin next to a line drawn to separate lines 828–29. H: *Explicit* in margin between stanzas and *Verba translatoris* ("words of the translator") next to line 829.

830   Marginalia in F: *Verba translatoris.*

832   *thy.* T: *in.*

833   *al.* F, H: omit.

842   *take.* F: *make.*

845   *Like.* F, H: *Wilde.*

854   *faitheful.* Ff: *faithfull of.*

colophon F, Ff: omit. H ends the poem with *Amen*, below which is written *Qui legit emendat scriptorem non reprehendat* ("Let the reader emend, not reprehend, the writer") at the bottom of the page. Th: *Explicit.*

Glossary

aforne *before*
after *after; afterwards*
agayn, agayne *toward; back; against;*
  away from; again
agaynis, agens, agenst *against; toward*
allace *alas*
als *as; also*
anon *right away; as soon as*
annoy *oppress*
ar *are*
avaunce *advance, thrust forward;*
  promote
axe *ask*
ay, aye *always, ever, forever*

bene *is, are*
blede *bleed*
bot *but, except; only*
bowes *boughs*
bren(ne) *burn;* **brent** *burned*
bye *by*

can, gan *do(es); did*
chere *face, expression*
clere *bright; light*
compleyn, complayn *lament, complain;*
  compleynyng *lamenting; lamentation*
condicioun *character*
consate *fancy, imagination, thought,*
  mind, opinion, judgment
cursit *cursed*

dedely *deathly*
deth *death*
dey *die*
discrecioun *discretion; judgment*
disese *suffering, discomfort*
doublenes(se) *duplicity; faithlessness*
dred(e) *fear; awe*

eke *also*
ensample *example*
entent *purpose, mind, intent, intention*
eny *any*
er *before*
erth(e) *earth*
ese, ease *pleasure, delight; comfort*
evill *wicked*

fals *false;* **falshed(e)** *falsehood*
fame *reputation*
feire *fair, attractive*
fo(o) *enemy, foe;* **foon** *enemies, foes*
fresh, fressh, fresch *fresh, new, recent;*
  young, youthful
fro *from*

gif *if*
grete *great*
grene *green; leafy; recent, fresh; young*
ground *ground; foundation*
gud(e) *good*

hem *them; themselves*
her *her; their; here*

hert *heart;* **hertis, hertys** *hearts; heart's; hearts'*
hevin, hevyn *heaven*
hevy *sorrowful, dejected*
hevynes(se) *sorrow, grief; misfortune*
hie, hye, high *high, exalted; great*
hire *her*
hit, hyt *it*
holsom(m)e *wholesome*
hote *warm, hot*

ife, yfe *if*

kynd *nature; race; category*

lak *lack*
levis, leves *leaves*
lewde, leude *ill-mannered, crude; ignorant*
lif, lyf *life*
lightly, lyghtly *lightly; easily; quickly*
list *like(s), want(s)*
litill *little*
loke, luke *look*
lufe, lufar(e) *love, lover*
lustyhede *beauty; joyfulness*
lych *like*
lyve *life, lives; live;* **lyves** *life's; soul's*

makith *makes*
menyng *intention*
mercie, mercy *pity, compassion, mercy*
mischance *trouble, misfortune*
mon *must*
mony *many*
mote *may*
mycht, myght *might* (modal)*; power, might; virtue*

nevir *never;* **nevirmore** *nevermore, never again*
nocht, noght *not; nothing; not at all*

ony *any*
oon *one*
othir *other*

penaunce, pennance *punishment, penance; hardship, suffering*
persaunt *piercing*
pitee *pity*
pitous(e), pytous(e) *compassionate; wretched, piteous;* **pitously** *piteously, wretchedly*
plesa(u)nce *delight, pleasure*
pleyn(e), playn(e) *field; flat; complete, full; honest, true; unembellished, plain; complain*
pleynly, playnly *fully, completely, unreservedly;*
port *deportment*

quhat *what*
quhen *when*
quhich *which*
quhilk *the which*
quhilom *once, once upon a time*
quho *who;* **quhom** *whom*
quhy *why; reason*
quod, quoth *said*

rage *insanity; rashness; passion; anger*
reherse *discuss; give an account of*
reule, rewle *conduct; control; rule*
reuth *pity, compassion*
routhe *pity, compassion*
rycht, ryght *right; very*

safe *save*
schall *shall*
sche *she*
schewe *show, reveal*
sclander(e), sclaundre *slander*
sclanderouse *offensive; slanderous*
se *see;* **sen(e)** *see; seen*
set(e) *set, placed; established*
sle *slay*
sleuch *killed*
sobir *quiet;* **sobirly** *quietly*
sonne *sun*
sore *painful; sorely, grievously, keenly,*
  seriously, greatly; completely, utterly
spere *sphere*
sterre *star*
suich *such*
suld *should*

teris, teres *tears*
thai *they*
thaire *their*
thame *them*
thare *there*
thir *these*
thocht, thoght *thought;* **me thoght** *it*
  seemed to me

thouch *though*
throuch *through*
tong *tongue*
treuth, trouth(e) *truth; faithfulness,*
  fidelity, loyalty; devotion
trewe, trwe *true; faithful, loyal; pure*
turment *torment; tormented*
tweyn(e) *two*
tyme *time*

veritee *truth*

walkit *walked*
wel(e) *well; very*
wel, well *spring*
wicht, wyght *person*
withoutyn *without*
wo *sorrow, misery, anguish;* **wofull**
  sorrowful, miserable
wol *will;* **wolde** *would; would like, wish*
womanhede *womanhood; womanliness;*
  womankind
wote *know(s)*

ye *you; yea* (interj.)
yit *yet*
ymagynyng *imagination*

Bibliography

Previous Editions

Boke of Cupide, God of Love

Conlee, John W., ed. *The Cuckoo and the Nightingale*. In *Middle English Debate Poetry: A Critical Anthology*. East Lansing, MI: Colleagues Press, 1991. Pp. 249–65. [Based on Tanner 346.]

Ellis, Frederick Startridge, ed. *The Floure and the Leafe, & The Boke of Cupide, God of Love, or The Cuckow and the Nightingale*. Hammersmith: Kelmscott Press, 1896. [Based on Tanner 346.]

Garbáty, Thomas J., ed. *The Cuckoo and the Nightingale, or The Book of Cupid, God of Love*. In *Medieval English Literature*. Lexington, MA: D. C. Heath, 1984. Pp. 620–29. [?Based on Thynne; see above, p. 40n77.]

Scattergood, V. J., ed. *The Boke of Cupide*. In *The Works of Sir John Clanvowe*. Cambridge, UK: D. S. Brewer, 1975. Pp. 9–18 (introduction), 33–53 (text), and 81–86 (notes). [Based on Fairfax 16.]

Skeat, Walter W., ed. *The Cuckoo and the Nightingale*. In *Chaucerian and Other Pieces*. Pp. lvii–lxi (introduction), 347–360 (text), and 526–29 (notes). [Based on Thynne.]

Vollmer, Erich, ed. *Das mittelenglische Gedicht The Boke of Cupide (The Cuckow and the Nyghtyngale), Clanvowe zugeschrieben*. Berliner Beiträge zur germanischen und romanischen Philologie 17. Berlin: E. Ebering, 1898. [Based on Fairfax 16.]

A Complaynte of a Lovers Lyfe

Krausser, E. "The Complaint of the Black Knight." *Anglia* 19 (1896), 211–90. [Based on Fairfax 16.]

MacCracken, Henry Noble, ed. *The Complaint of the Black Knight.* In *The Minor Poems of John Lydgate.* EETS e.s. 107; o.s. 192. 2 vols. London: Oxford University Press, 1961–62. 2.382–410. [Rpt. of 1911–34 ed. Based on Fairfax 16.]

Norton-Smith, John, ed. *A Complaynt of a Loveres Lyfe.* In John Lydgate, *Poems.* Oxford: Clarendon Press, 1966. Pp. 47–66 (text) and 160–76 (notes). [Based on Fairfax 16.]

Skeat, Walter W., ed. *The Complaint of the Black Knight.* In *Chaucerian and Other Pieces.* 1897. Pp. xliii–xlv (introduction), 245–65 (text), and 504–08 (notes). [Based on Thynne.]

The Quare of Jelusy

The Bannatyne Miscellany. Ed. W. Scott, T. Thompson, and D. Laing. Vol. 2. Edinburgh: Bannatyne Club, 1836. Pp. 159–84.

Brown, J. T. T., ed. *The Quare of Jelusy.* In *Miscellany Volume.* Scottish Text Society, third ser. 4. Edinburgh: W. Blackwood and Sons, 1933. Pp. 191–94 (introductory note) and pp. 195–212 (text). [No notes are included.]

Lawson, Alexander, ed. *The Kingis Quair and The Quare of Jelusy.* London: A. and C. Black, 1910. Pp. 104–23 (text) and pp. 149–55 (notes). [No separate introduction for *QJ*.]

Norton-Smith, J., and I. Pravda, eds. *The Quare of Jelusy.* Middle English Texts 3. Heidelberg: Carl Winter, 1976.

La Belle Dame sans Mercy

Furnivall, Frederick J[ames], ed. *La Belle Dame Sanz Mercy.* In *Political, Religious, and Love Poems.* EETS o.s. 15. London: N. Trübner and Co., 1866. Pp. 51 (introductory note) and 52–80 (text). [Based on Harley 372.]

————, ed. *La Belle Dame sans Merci.* In *Political, Religious, and Love Poems.* EETS o.s. 15. London: Kegan Paul, Trench, Trübner and Co., 1866; rev. ed. 1903. Pp. 79 (introductory note) and 80–111 (text). [Based on Findern.]

Gröhler, Hermann. *Über Richard Ros' mittelenglische Übersetzung des Gedichtes von Alain Chartier "La belle dame sans mercy."* Breslau: Lindner, 1886. [Based on Harley 372.]

Bibliography

Skeat, Walter W., ed. *La Belle Dame sans Mercy*. In *Chaucerian and Other Pieces*. 1897. Pp. li–lv (introduction); 299–326 (text); and 517–20 (notes). [Based on Thynne.]

Sources and Analogues

Albertus Magnus. *On Animals: A Medieval Summa Zoologica*. Trans. and annotated by Kenneth F. Kitchell, Jr., and Irven Michael Resnick. 2 vols. Baltimore: Johns Hopkins University Press, 1999.

Bartholomaeus Anglicus. *On the Properties of Things*. See Trevisa, John.

Benoît de Sainte-Maure. *Le roman de Troie*. Ed. Léopold Constans. 6 vols. Paris: Firmin-Didot, 1904–12.

Boccaccio, Giovanni. *Genealogie deorum gentilium libri*. Ed. Vincenzo Romano. Bari: G. Laterza, 1951.

Chartier, Alain. *La belle dame sans mercy, et les poésies lyriques*. Ed. Arthur Piaget. Second ed. Lille: Librairie Giard, 1949.

———. *The Poetical Works of Alain Chartier*. Ed. J. C. Laidlaw. London: Cambridge University Press, 1974.

Chaucer, Geoffrey. *The Riverside Chaucer*. Gen. ed. Larry D. Benson. Third ed. Boston: Houghton Mifflin Company, 1987.

Deschamps, Eustache. *Oeuvres complètes de Eustache Deschamps*. Ed. Auguste Henry Édouard and Gaston Raynaud. 11 vols. Société des anciens textes français 9. Paris: Firmin-Didot, 1878–1903. Rpt. New York: Johnson Reprint Corp., 1966.

Douglas, Gavin. *The Palis of Honoure*. Ed. David J. Parkinson. Kalamazoo, MI: Medieval Institute Publications, 1992.

Dunbar, William. *The Poems of William Dunbar*. Ed. Priscilla Bawcutt. 2 vols. Glasgow: Association for Scottish Literary Studies, 1998.

Ginsberg, Warren. *Wynnere and Wastoure and The Parlement of the Thre Ages*. Kalamazoo, MI: Medieval Institute Publications, 1992.

Gower, John. *The Complete Works of John Gower*. Ed. G. C. Macaulay. 4 vols. Oxford: Clarendon Press, 1899–1902. Vols. 2 and 3 rpt. as *The English Works of John Gower*. EETS e.s. 81–82. London: Paul Trench, Trübner, and Co., 1900–01; rpt. London: Oxford University Press, 1957. [Vol. 1: the French works; vol. 4: the Latin works. The standard edition of Gower's works for nearly a century.]

———. *Confessio Amantis*. 3 vols. Ed. Russell A. Peck. Kalamazoo, MI: Medieval Institute Publications, 2000–. [Vol. 1: Prologue, Books 1 and 8; vol. 2: Books 2–4; vol. 3: Books 5–7.]

Guido delle Colonne. *Historia destructionis Troiae*. Ed. Nathaniel Edward Griffin. Cambridge, MA: The Mediaeval Academy of America, 1936.

———. *The "Gest Hystoriale" of the Destruction of Troy: An Alliterative Romance Translated from Guido de Colonna's "Hystoria Troiana."* Ed. G. A. Panton and D. Donaldson. EETS o.s. 39, 56. London: Oxford University Press, 1968. [Rpt. of 1869–74 ed., as one vol.]

———. *Historia destructionis Troiae*. Trans., intro., and notes Mary Elizabeth Meek. Bloomington: Indiana University Press, 1974.

Guillaume de Lorris and Jean de Meun. *Le roman de la rose [The Romance of the Rose]*. Ed. Félix Lecoy. Les Classiques Français du Moyen Age 92, 95, 98. 3 vols. Paris: H. Champion, 1970–74.

Hasenfratz, Robert. *Ancrene Wisse*. Kalamazoo, MI: Medieval Institute Publications, 2000.

Henryson, Robert. *The Poems of Robert Henryson*. Ed. Denton Fox. Oxford: Clarendon Press, 1981.

Hyginus. *The Myths of Hyginus*. Ed. and trans. Mary Grant. University of Kansas Publications, Humanistic Studies 34. Lawrence: University of Kansas Press, 1960.

———. *Hygini Fabulae*. Ed. Peter K. Marshall. 2 vols. Stuttgart: Teubner, 1993.

Bibliography

Jacobus de Voragine. *The Golden Legend: Readings on the Saints*. Trans. William Granger Ryan. 2 vols. Princeton: Princeton University Press, 1993.

The Kingis Quair. Ed. John Norton-Smith. Oxford: Clarendon Press, 1971; rpt. Leiden: E. J. Brill, 1981.

Kulcsár, Péter, ed. *Mythographi Vaticani I et II*. Corpus Christianorum, Series Latina 91c. Turnhout: Brepols, 1987.

Lancelot of the Laik and Sir Tristrem. Ed. Alan Lupack. Kalamazoo, MI: Medieval Institute Publications, 1994.

Lydgate, John. *The Fall of Princes*. Ed. Henry Bergen. *Lydgate's Fall of Princes*. 4 vols. Washington, DC: The Carnegie Institution of Washington, 1923–27.

———. *King Henry IV's Triumphal Entry into London*. Ed. Henry Noble MacCracken. In *The Minor Poems of John Lydgate*. EETS e.s. 107; o.s. 192. 2 vols. London: Oxford University Press, 1961–62. 2.630–48. [Rpt. of 1911–34 ed.]

———. *The Life of Our Lady*. Ed. Joseph A. Lauritis, Ralph A. Klinefelter, and Vernon F. Gallagher. *A Critical Edition of John Lydgate's Life of Our Lady*. Pittsburgh: Duquesne University, 1961.

———. *The Pilgrimage of the Life of Man*. Ed. F. J. Furnivall. Intro., notes, glossary, and indexes by Katharine B. Locock. EETS e.s. 77, 83, 92. London: K. Paul, Trench, Trübner and Co., 1899–1904. [Lydgate's translation of Guillaume de Deguileville.]

———. *Reson and Sensuallyte*. Ed. Ernst Sieper. *Lydgate's Reson and Sensuallyte*. EETS e.s. 84 and 89. 2 vols. London: K. Paul, Trench, Trübner, and Co., 1901–03.

———. *The Siege of Thebes*. Ed. Robert R. Edwards. Kalamazoo, MI: Medieval Institute Publications, 2001.

———. *The Temple of Glass*. Ed. John Norton-Smith. In *Poems*. Oxford: Clarendon Press, 1966. Pp. 67–112 (text) and 176–91 (notes).

———. *Troy Book*. Ed. Henry Bergen. *Lydgate's Troy Book, A. D. 1412–20*. EETS e.s. 97, 103, 106, and 126. 4 vols. London: K. Paul, Trench, Trübner and Co., 1906–35; rpt. as 2 vols. Millwood, NY: Kraus Reprint Co., 1973.

Machaut, Guillaume de. *The Judgment of the King of Bohemia (Le jugement dou Roy de Behaingne)*. Ed. and trans. R. Barton Palmer. The Garland Library of Medieval Literature 9, ser. A. New York: Garland Publishing, 1984.

Ovid. *Metamorphoses*. Trans. Frank Justus Miller; rev. G. P. Goold. Loeb Classical Library. 2 vols. Cambridge, MA: Harvard University Press, 1984. ["Ovid in six volumes," vols. 3–4: vol. 3 contains Books 1–8, vol. 4, Books 9–15.]

Parthenius. *Erotika pathemata: The Love Stories of Parthenius*. Trans. Jacob Stern. New York: Garland Publishing, 1992.

Pausanias. *Description of Greece: With an English Translation*. Ed. and trans. W. H. S. Jones. 5 vols. London: W. Heinemann, 1918–35. Rpt. Cambridge, MA: Harvard University Press, 1966–75.

Pearsall, Derek, ed. *The Floure and the Leafe, The Assembly of Ladies, and The Isle of Ladies*. Kalamazoo, MI: Medieval Institute Publications, 1990.

Sidrak and Bokkus: A Parallel-text edition from Bodleian Library, MS Laud Misc. 559 and British Library, MS Lansdowne 793. Ed. T. L. Burton with the assistance of Frank Schaer et al. 2 vols. EETS o.s. 311–12. Oxford: Oxford University Press, 1998–99.

Trevisa, John. *On the Properties of Things: John Trevisa's Translation of Bartholomaeus Anglicus De proprietatibus rerum: A Critical Text*. Gen. ed. M. C. Seymour. 3 vols. Oxford: Clarendon Press, 1975–88.

The Wallace: Selections. Ed. Anne McKim. Kalamazoo, MI: Medieval Institute Publications, 2003.

Bibliography

Facsimile Volumes

Beadle, Richard, and A. E. B. Owen, intro. *The Findern Manuscript (Cambridge University Library MS. Ff.1.6)*. London: Scolar Press, 1978.

Beattie, William, bib. note. *The Chepman and Myllar Prints: Nine Tracts from the First Scottish Press, Edinburgh, 1508, Followed by the Two Other Tracts in the Same Volume in the National Library of Scotland*. [Edinburgh]: Edinburgh Bibliographical Society, 1950.

Boffey, Julia, and A. S. G. Edwards, intro. *The Works of Geoffrey Chaucer and The Kingis Quair: A Facsimile of Bodleian Library, Oxford, MS Arch. Selden. B. 24*. Cambridge, UK: D. S. Brewer, 1997.

Brewer, D. S., intro. *Geoffrey Chaucer, The Works, 1532; with Supplementary Material from the Editions of 1542, 1561, 1598 and 1602*. Menston: Scolar Press, 1969.

Brewer, D. S., and A. E. B. Owen, intro. *The Thornton Manuscript (Lincoln Cathedral MS. 91)*. London: Scolar Press, 1975.

Edwards, A. S. G., intro. *Manuscript Pepys 2006: A Facsimile: Magdalene College, Cambridge*. Norman, OK: Pilgrim Books, 1985.

Fletcher, Bradford Y., intro. *Manuscript Trinity R. 3. 19, Trinity College, Cambridge University: A Facsimile*. Norman, OK: Pilgrim Books, 1987.

Fox, Denton, and William A. Ringler, intro. *The Bannatyne Manuscript: National Library of Scotland, Advocates' MS. 1.1.6*. London: Scolar Press in association with the National Library of Scotland, 1980.

Norton-Smith, John, intro. *Bodleian Library MS Fairfax 16*. London: Scolar Press, 1979.

Robinson, Pamela, intro. *Manuscript Tanner 346: A Facsimile: Bodleian Library, Oxford University*. Norman, OK: Pilgrim Books, 1980.

———, intro. *Manuscript Bodley 638: A Facsimile: Bodleian Library, Oxford University*. Norman, OK: Pilgrim Books, 1982.

Skeat, Walter W., intro. *The Works of Geoffrey Chaucer and Others: Being a Reproduction in Facsimile of the First Collected Edition 1532, from the Copy in the British Museum.* London: Alexander Moring, De La More Press; Henry Frowde, Oxford University Press, [1905].

Criticism and Reference Works

Bennett, H. S. *Chaucer and the Fifteenth Century.* Oxford: Clarendon Press, 1947; rpt. 1961.

Benson, Larry D. "Courtly Love and Chivalry in the Later Middle Ages." In *Fifteenth-Century Studies: Recent Essays.* Ed. Robert F. Yeager. Hamden, CT: Archon Books, 1984. Pp. 237–57.

Bianco, Su[san]. "A Black Monk in the Rose Garden: Lydgate and the *Dit Amoureux* Tradition." *The Chaucer Review* 34 (1999), 60–68.

———. "New Perspectives on Lydgate's Courtly Verse." In Cooney, 2001. Pp. 95–115.

Blodgett, James E. "Some Printer's Copy for William Thynne's 1532 Edition of Chaucer." *The Library* sixth ser. 1 (1979), 97–113.

Boffey, Julia. "The Reputation and Circulation of Chaucer's Lyrics in the Fifteenth Century." *Chaucer Review* 28 (1993), 23–40.

———. "English Dream Poems of the Fifteenth Century and Their French Connections." In *Literary Aspects of Courtly Culture: Selected Papers from the Seventh Triennial Congress of the International Courtly Literature Society.* Ed. Donald Maddox and Sara Sturm-Maddox. Cambridge, UK: D. S. Brewer, 1994. Pp. 113–21.

———. "Proverbial Chaucer and the Chaucer Canon." In *Reading from the Margins: Textual Studies, Chaucer, and Medieval Literature.* Ed. Seth Lerer. San Marino: Huntingdon Library, 1996. Pp. 37–47. [Concurrently published as *Huntingdon Library Quarterly* 58.1 (1996).]

———. "Bodleian Library, MS Arch. Selden. B. 24 and Definitions of the 'Household Book.'" In *The English Medieval Book: Studies in Memory of Jeremy Griffiths.* Ed. A. S. G. Edwards, Vincent Gillespie, and Ralph Hanna. London: British Library, 2000. Pp. 125–34.

Bibliography

Boffey, Julia. "'Forto Compleyne She Had Gret Desire': The Grievances Expressed in Two Fif-teenth-Century Dream-Visions." In Cooney, 2001. Pp. 116–28.

Boffey, Julia, and A. S. G. Edwards. "'Chaucer's Chronicle,' John Shirley, and the Canon of Chaucer's Shorter Poems." *Studies in the Age of Chaucer* 20 (1998), 201–18.

———. "Bodleian MS Arch. Selden. B. 24 and the 'Scotticization' of Middle English Verse." In *Rewriting Chaucer: Culture, Authority, and the Idea of the Authentic Text, 1400–1602.* Ed. Thomas A. Prendergast and Barbara Kline. Columbus, OH: Ohio State University Press, 1999. Pp. 166–85.

Boffey, Julia, and John J. Thompson. "Anthologies and Miscellanies: Production and Choice of Texts." In *Book Production and Publishing in Britain, 1375–1475.* Ed. Jeremy Griffiths and Derek Pearsall. Cambridge, UK: Cambridge University Press, 1989. Pp. 279–315.

Brown, Carleton, and Rossell Hope Robbins, eds. *The Index of Middle English Verse.* New York: Columbia University Press, 1943.

Brown, Melissa L. "The Hope for 'plesaunce': Richard Roos' Translation of Alain Chartier's *La Belle Dame sans Mercy.*" In *New Readings of Late Medieval Love Poems.* Ed. David Chamberlain. Lanham, MD: University Press of America, 1993. Pp. 119–43.

Chamberlain, David. "Clanvowe's Cuckoo." In *New Readings of Late Medieval Love Poems.* Ed. Chamberlain. Lanham, MD: University Press of America, 1993. Pp. 41–65.

Conlee, John W., ed. *Middle English Debate Poetry: A Critical Anthology.* East Lansing, MI: Colleagues Press, 1991.

Connolly, Margaret. *John Shirley: Book Production and the Noble Household in Fifteenth-Century England.* Aldershot, UK: Ashgate Publishing, 1998.

Cooney, Helen, ed. and intro. *Nation, Court and Culture: New Essays on Fifteenth-Century English Poetry.* Dublin: Four Courts Press, 2001.

Costomiris, Robert. "Bodleian MS Tanner 346 and William Thynne's Edition of Clanvowe's 'Cuckoo and the Nightingale.'" *Library* 20.2 (1998), 99–117.

Curtius, Ernst Robert. *European Literature and the Latin Middle Ages.* Trans. Willard R. Trask. Princeton: Princeton University Press, 1990.

Cutler, John L., and Rossell Hope Robbins, eds. *Supplement to the Index of Middle English Verse.* Lexington: University of Kentucky Press, 1965.

Duffell, Martin J. "Lydgate's Metrical Inventiveness and His Debt to Chaucer." *Parergon* 18 (2000), 227–49.

Edwards, A. S. G. "Bodleian Library MS Arch. Selden B.24: A 'Transitional' Collection." In *The Whole Book: Cultural Perspectives on the Medieval Miscellany.* Ed. Stephen G. Nichols and Siegfried Wenzel. Ann Arbor: University of Michigan Press, 1996. Pp. 53–67.

Elbin, Lois A. *John Lydgate.* Boston: Twayne, 1985.

Forni, Kathleen. *The Chaucerian Apocrypha: A Counterfeit Canon.* Gainesville: University Press of Florida, 2001.

Frost, William, ed. *Selected Works of John Dryden.* New York: Holt, Rinehart and Winston, 1966.

Ginsberg, Warren. See under "Sources and Analogues," above.

Hahn, Thomas. "Early Middle English." In Wallace, 1999. Pp. 61–91.

Hammond, Eleanor Prescott. *Chaucer: A Bibliographical Manual.* New York: Peter Smith, 1908; rpt. 1933.

———. "MS. Longleat 258 — A Chaucerian Codex." *Modern Language Notes* 20.3 (1905), 77–79.

Holsinger, Bruce. "Vernacular Legality: The English Jurisdictions of *The Owl and the Nightingale.*" In *The Letter of the Law: Legal Practice and Literary Production in Medieval England.* Ed. Emily Steiner and Candace Barrington. Ithaca: Cornell University Press, 2002. Pp. 154–84.

Bibliography

Howes, Laura L. *Chaucer's Gardens and the Language of Convention*. Gainesville: University Press of Florida, 1997.

Hunt, Richard William, Falconer Madon, et al. *A Summary Catalogue of Western Manuscripts in the Bodleian Library at Oxford*. 7 vols. Oxford: Clarendon Press, 1895–1953.

Jack, R. D. S., ed. and intro. *The History of Scottish Literature*. Vol. 1: *Origins to 1660*. Gen. ed. Cairns Craig. Aberdeen: Aberdeen University Press, 1988.

Jacobs, Nicolas. "Clanvowe." *Notes and Queries* 25 (1978), 292–95.

Jeffery, C. D. "*The Quare of Jelusy*, Lines 141–6." *Notes and Queries* 27 (1980), 500–01.

Justice, Stephen. "Lollardy." In Wallace, 1999. Pp. 662–89.

Kellog, Alfred L. *Chaucer, Langland, Arthur: Essays in Middle English Literature*. New Brunswick, NJ: Rutgers University Press, 1972.

Lampe, David. "Tradition and Meaning in *The Cuckoo and the Nightingale*." *Papers on Language and Literature* 3 (1967), 49–62.

Lerer, Seth. *Chaucer and His Readers: Imagining the Author in Late-Medieval England*. Princeton: Princeton University Press, 1993.

Lewis, C. S. *The Allegory of Love: A Study in Medieval Tradition*. London: Oxford University Press, 1936; rpt. 1959.

MacQueen, John. "Poetry: James I to Henryson." In Jack, 1988. Pp. 55–72.

McColly, William. "*The Book of Cupid* as an Imitation of Chaucer: A Stylo-Statistical View." *The Chaucer Review* 18 (1984), 239–49.

McFarlane, K. B. *Lancastrian Kings and Lollard Knights*. Oxford: Clarendon Press, 1972.

McKim, Anne M. "'Makand hir mone': Masculine Constructions of the Feminine Voice in Middle Scots Complaints." *Scotlands* 2 (1994), 32–46.

289

McNamer, Sarah. "Female Authors, Provincial Setting: The Re-Versing of Courtly Love in the Findern Manuscript." *Viator* 22 (1991), 279–310.

Otey, Kirsten Johnson. "'Þe law of God in here modyr tonge': The Vernacular Theology of Sir John Clanvowe." Ph. D. Diss. University of Colorado, 1999. *DAI* 60.12 (2000), p. 4443A.

The Oxford Classical Dictionary. Ed. Simon Hornblower and Antony Spawforth. Third ed., rev. Oxford: Oxford University Press, 2003.

Palmer, R. Barton. See Machaut, Guillaume de, under "Sources and Analogues," above.

Patterson, Lee. "Court Politics and the Invention of Literature: The Case of Sir John Clanvowe." In *Culture and History, 1350–1600: Essays on English Communities, Identities, and Writing*. Ed. David Aers. Detroit: Wayne State University Press, 1992. Pp. 7–41.

———. "Writing Amorous Wrongs: Chaucer and the Order of Complaint." In *The Idea of Medieval Literature: New Essays on Chaucer and Medieval Culture in Honor of Donald R. Howard*. Ed. James M. Dean and Christian K. Zacher. Newark, NJ: University of Delaware Press, 1992. Pp. 55–71.

Pearsall, Derek. *John Lydgate*. London: Routledge and Kegan Paul, 1970.

———. "Chaucer and Lydgate." *Chaucer Traditions: Studies in Honour of Derek Brewer*. Ed. Ruth Morse and Barry Windeatt. Cambridge, UK: Cambridge University Press, 1990. Pp. 39–53.

———. "Lydgate as Innovator." *Modern Language Quarterly* 53.1 (1992), 5–22.

———. *John Lydgate (1371–1499): A Bio-Bibliography*. Victoria, BC: University of Victoria, 1997.

———. "The Idea of Englishness in the Fifteenth Century." In Cooney, 2001. Pp. 15–27.

Pearsall, Derek, and Elizabeth Salter. *Landscapes and Seasons of the Medieval World*. Toronto: University of Toronto Press, 1973.

Piaget, Arthur. See entry under Chartier, Alain, in "Sources and Analogues," above.

Potkay, Monica Brzezinski. "Natural Law in *The Owl and the Nightingale.*" *Chaucer Review* 28 (1994), 368–83.

Renoir, Alain, and C. David Benson. "John Lydgate." In Severs and Hartung, vol. 6. 1980. Pp. 1809–1920 and 2071–2175.

Riach, Mary. "A Study of Three Late Medieval Love Poems: *The Cuckoo and the Nightingale, The Court of Love,* and *La Belle Dame sans Mercy.*" Oxford: University of Oxford, 1967. [Thesis (Bachelor of Phil.).]

Robbins, Rossell Hope. "The Findern Anthology." *PMLA* 69 (1954), 610–42.

———. "The Chaucerian Apocrypha." In Severs and Hartung, vol. 4. 1973. Pp. 1061–1101 and 1285–1306.

Roscow, Gregory. "Clanvowe's *Boke of Cupide,* Lines 185–6." *Notes and Queries* 45.2 (1998), 183–84.

Russell, J. Stephen. *The English Dream Vision: Anatomy of a Form.* Columbus: Ohio State University Press, 1988.

Rutherford, Charles S. "The *Boke of Cupide* Reopened." *Neuphilologische Mitteilungen* 78 (1977), 350–58.

Sandison, Helen Estabrook. *The "Chanson d'Aventure" in Middle English.* Bryn Mawr, PA: Bryn Mawr College, 1913.

Scattergood, V. J. "The Authorship of *The Boke of Cupide.*" *Anglia* 82 (1964), 137–49.

Schick, J. *Lydgate's Temple of Glas.* EETS e.s. 60. London: Kegan Paul, Trench, Trübner, and Co., 1891.

Schirmer, Walter F. *John Lydgate: A Study in the Culture of the XVth Century.* Trans. Ann E. Keep. London: Methuen, 1961.

Seaton, Ethel. *Sir Richard Roos, c. 1410–1482, Lancastrian Poet*. London: Rupert Hart-Davies, 1961. [Somewhat bizarre detective work but rich in historical information surrounding Roos' poem.]

Severs, J. Burke, and Albert E. Hartung, gen. eds. *A Manual of the Writings in Middle English, 1050–1500*. 10 vols. to date. New Haven: Connecticut Academy of Arts and Sciences, 1967–. [Severs is gen. ed. for vols. 1–2; Hartung is gen. ed. for vols. 3–.]

Skeat, Walter W., ed. *Chaucerian and Other Pieces*. Oxford: Clarendon Press, 1897; rpt. London: Oxford University, 1935, 1959. [Supplemental vol. (7) to *The Complete Works of Geoffrey Chaucer*. 6 vols. Oxford: Clarendon Press, 1894.]

Spearing, A. C. *Medieval Dream-Poetry*. Cambridge, UK: Cambridge University Press, 1976.

———. *Medieval to Renaissance in English Poetry*. Cambridge, UK: Cambridge University Press, 1985.

———. *The Medieval Poet as Voyeur: Looking and Listening in Medieval Love-Narratives*. Cambridge, UK: Cambridge University Press, 1993.

Stanley, Eric Gerald, ed. *The Owl and the Nightingale*. London: Nelson, 1960.

Strohm, Paul. "Hoccleve, Lydgate and the Lancastrian Court." In Wallace, 1999. Pp. 640–61.

Utley, Francis Lee. "Dialogues, Debates, and Catechisms." In Severs and Hartung, vol. 3. 1972. Pp. 669–745 and 829–902.

Wack, Mary Frances. *Lovesickness in the Middle Ages: The Viaticum and Its Commentaries*. Philadelphia: University of Pennsylvania Press, 1989.

Wallace, David, ed. *The Cambridge History of Medieval English Literature*. Cambridge, UK: Cambridge University Press, 1999.

Whiting, Bartlett Jere, with the collaboration of Helen Wescott Whiting. *Proverbs, Sentences, and Proverbial Phrases from English Writings Mainly before 1500*. Cambridge, MA: The Belknap Press of Harvard University Press, 1968.

Abbreviations

Wimsatt, James. *Chaucer and the French Love Poets: The Literary Background of the Book of the Duchess*. Chapel Hill: University of North Carolina Press, 1968.

Witt, Michael A. "The *Owl and the Nightingale* and English Law Court Procedure of the Twelfth and Thirteenth Centuries." *Chaucer Review* 16 (1982), 282–92.

Yeager, R. F. "Literary Theory at the Close of the Middle Ages: William Caxton and William Thynne." *Studies in the Age of Chaucer* 6 (1984), 135–64.

Volumes in the Middle English Texts Series

The Floure and the Leafe, The Assembly of Ladies, and *The Isle of Ladies*, ed. Derek Pearsall (1990)

Three Middle English Charlemagne Romances, ed. Alan Lupack (1990)

Six Ecclesiastical Satires, ed. James M. Dean (1991)

Heroic Women from the Old Testament in Middle English Verse, ed. Russell A. Peck (1991)

The Canterbury Tales: Fifteenth-Century Continuations and Additions, ed. John M. Bowers (1992)

Gavin Douglas, *The Palis of Honoure*, ed. David Parkinson (1992)

Wynnere and Wastoure and The Parlement of the Thre Ages, ed. Warren Ginsberg (1992)

The Shewings of Julian of Norwich, ed. Georgia Ronan Crampton (1993)

King Arthur's Death: The Middle English Stanzaic Morte Arthur and Alliterative Morte Arthure, ed. Larry D. Benson and Edward E. Foster (1994)

Lancelot of the Laik and Sir Tristrem, ed. Alan Lupack (1994)

Sir Gawain: Eleven Romances and Tales, ed. Thomas Hahn (1995)

The Middle English Breton Lays, ed. Anne Laskaya and Eve Salisbury (1995)

Sir Perceval of Galles and Ywain and Gawain, ed. Mary Flowers Braswell (1995)

Four Middle English Romances: Sir Isumbras, Octavian, Sir Eglamour of Artois, Sir Tryamour, ed. Harriet Hudson (1996)

The Poems of Laurence Minot (1333–1352), ed. Richard H. Osberg (1996)

Medieval English Political Writings, ed. James M. Dean (1996)

The Book of Margery Kempe, ed. Lynn Staley (1996)

Amis and Amiloun, Robert of Cisyle, and Sir Amadace, ed. Edward E. Foster (1997)

The Cloud of Unknowing, ed. Patrick J. Gallacher (1997)

Robin Hood and Other Outlaw Tales, ed. Stephen Knight and Thomas Ohlgren (1997)

The Poems of Robert Henryson, ed. Robert L. Kindrick (1997)

Moral Love Songs and Laments, ed. Susanna Greer Fein (1998)

John Lydgate, *Troy Book: Selections*, ed. Robert R. Edwards (1998)

Thomas Usk, *The Testament of Love*, ed. R. Allen Shoaf (1998)

Prose Merlin, ed. John Conlee (1998)

Middle English Marian Lyrics, ed. Karen Saupe (1998)

John Metham, *Amoryus and Cleopes*, ed. Stephen F. Page (1999)

Four Romances of England: King Horn, Havelok the Dane, Bevis of Hampton, Athelston, ed. Ronald B. Herzman, Graham Drake, and Eve Salisbury (1999)

The Assembly of Gods: Le Assemble de Dyeus, or Banquet of Gods and Goddesses, with the Discourse of Reason and Sensuality, ed. Jane Chance (1999)

Thomas Hoccleve, *The Regiment of Princes*, ed. Charles R. Blyth (1999)

John Capgrave, *The Life of St. Katherine*, ed. Karen Winstead (1999)

John Gower, *Confessio Amantis*, Vol. 1, ed. Russell A. Peck (2000); Vol. 2 (2003)

Richard the Redeless and *Mum and the Sothsegger*, ed. James Dean (2000)

Ancrene Wisse, ed. Robert Hasenfratz (2000)

Walter Hilton, *The Scale of Perfection*, ed. Thomas Bestul (2000)

John Lydgate, *The Siege of Thebes*, ed. Robert Edwards (2001)

Pearl, ed. Sarah Stanbury (2001)

The Trials and Joys of Marriage, ed. Eve Salisbury (2002)

Middle English Legends of Women Saints, ed. Sherry L. Reames (2003)

The Wallace: Selections, ed. Anne McKim (2003)

Three Purgatory Poems (The Gast of Gy, Sir Owain, The Vision of Tundale), ed. Edward E. Foster (2004)

William Dunbar, *The Complete Works*, ed. John Conlee (2004)

Other TEAMS Publications

Documents of Practice Series:

Love and Marriage in Late Medieval London, selected, translated, and introduced by Shannon McSheffrey (1995)

Sources for the History of Medicine in Late Medieval England, selected, introduced, and translated by Carole Rawcliffe (1995)

A Slice of Life: Selected Documents of Medieval English Peasant Experience, edited, translated, and with an introduction by Edwin Brezette DeWindt (1996)

Regular Life: Monastic, Canonical, and Mendicant Rules, selected with an introduction by Douglas J. McMillan and Kathryn Smith Fladenmuller (1997); second edition, selected and introduced by Daniel Marcel La Corte and Douglas J. McMillan (2004)

Women and Monasticism in Medieval Europe: Sisters and Patrons of the Cistercian Reform, selected, translated, and with an introduction by Constance H. Berman (2002)

Medieval Notaries and Their Acts: The 1327–1328 Register of Jean Holanie, introduced, edited, and translated by Kathryn L. Reyerson and Debra A. Salata (2004)

Commentary Series:

Commentary on the Book of Jonah, Haimo of Auxerre, translated with an introduction by Deborah Everhart (1993)

Medieval Exegesis in Translation: Commentaries on the Book of Ruth, translated with an introduction by Lesley Smith (1996)

Nicholas of Lyra's Apocalypse Commentary, translated with an introduction and notes by Philip D. W. Krey (1997)

Rabbi Ezra Ben Solomon of Gerona: Commentary on the Song of Songs and Other Kabbalistic Commentaries, selected, translated, and annotated by Seth Brody (1999)

John Wyclif: On the Truth of Holy Scripture, translated with an introduction and notes by Ian Christopher Levy (2001)

Second Thessalonians: Two Early Medieval Apocalyptic Commentaries, translated with an introduction by Steven R. Cartwright and Kevin L. Hughes (2001)

The Glossa Ordinaria *on the Song of Songs*, translated with an introduction and notes by Mary Dove (2004)

Medieval German Texts in Bilingual Editions Series:

Sovereignty and Salvation in the Vernacular, 1050–1150, introduction, translation, and notes by James A. Schultz (2000)

Ava's New Testament Narratives: "When the Old Law Passed Away," introduction, translations, and notes by James A. Rushing, Jr. (2003)

History as Literature: German World Chronicles of the Thirteenth Century in Verse, introduction, translations, and notes by R. Graeme Dunphy (2003)

To order please contact: MEDIEVAL INSTITUTE PUBLICATIONS
Western Michigan University
Kalamazoo, MI 49008–5432
Phone (269) 387–8755
FAX (269) 387–8750

http://www.wmich.edu/medieval/mip/index.html

Medieval Institute Publications is a program
of The Medieval Institute, College of Arts
and Sciences, Western Michigan University

Typeset in 10.5 pt. Times New Roman
with Times New Roman display
Manufactured by Edwards Brothers, Inc.—Ann Arbor, Michigan

Medieval Institute Publications
College of Arts and Sciences
Western Michigan University
1903 W. Michigan Avenue
Kalamazoo, Michigan 49008-5432
www.wmich.edu/medieval/mip/

 WESTERN MICHIGAN UNIVERSITY